HITLER'S
ARISTOCRATS

ALSO BY SUSAN RONALD

HITLER'S ARISTOCRATS

The Secret Power Players in
Britain and America Who
Supported the Nazis, 1923–1941

SUSAN RONALD

ST. MARTIN'S PRESS
NEW YORK

Library of Congress Cataloging-in-Publication Data

Names: Ronald, Susan, author.
Title: Hitler's aristocrats : the secret power players in Britain and America who
    supported the Nazis, 1923–1941 / Susan Ronald.
Description: First edition. | New York : St. Martin's Press, 2023. | Includes bibliographical
    references and index.
Identifiers: LCCN 2022051604 | ISBN 9781250276551 (hardcover) |
    ISBN 9781250276568 (ebook)
Subjects: LCSH: Germany—Foreign relations—1933–1945. | Fascists—
    Great Britain—Biography. | Fascists—United States—Biography. | Elite (Social sciences)—
    Political activity—History—20th century. | Aristocracy (Political science)—History—20th
    century. | World War, 1939–1945—Collaborationists—Great Britain. | World War,
    1939–1945—Collaborationists—United States. | Propaganda, German.
Classification: LCC DD256.8 .R663 2023 | DDC 940.53/108621—dc23/eng/20221101
LC record available at https://lccn.loc.gov/2022051604

First Edition: 2023

10 9 8 7 6 5 4 3 2 1

For
Auntie Baba
and
in memory of
Uncle Larry
truly great, greatly loved

CONTENTS

DRAMATIS PERSONAE

(Main characters only, in alphabetical order.)

Astor, Viscountess Nancy Witcher Langhorne, American-born British politician and first woman to take her seat in the House of Commons (Conservative-Plymouth). Always outspoken, she was anti-Semitic and anti-Catholic and looked sympathetically on Hitler's Nazi Party until the invasion of Czechoslovakia in March 1939. She was not a fascist.

Astor, Waldorf, 2nd Viscount Astor, American-born British politician and husband of Viscountess Astor who was compelled to give up his seat in the Commons on inheriting his title. He sat in the House of Lords and made sympathetic statements about Hitler hoping appeasement would work. He was not a fascist. In May 1940 he urged Chamberlain to resign and backed Winston Churchill as prime minister.

Baldwin, Stanley, served as prime minister three times in the interwar period (May 1923–January 1924, November 1924–June 1929, June 1935–May 1937). He must bear some burden for Britain's lack of preparedness in dealing with the dictators.

Bedaux, Charles, French-born American efficiency engineer and millionaire who developed close relationships with the Nazis and the Windsors. He was arrested and charged with treason in the United States and committed suicide before standing trial.

Bohle, Ernst, British-born German chief of the Auslands Organization (AO). He surrendered in May 1945 and was tried and convicted at the Ministries Trial at Nuremberg, serving four years of his five-year sentence before receiving a full American pardon.

Carl Edouard, Duke of Saxe-Coburg and Gotha, English-born royal who took up his grandfather's German titles at the behest of his grandmother Queen Victoria. Stripped of his British titles after the Great War, he became an early and ardent Nazi and head of the German Red Cross. He is the grandfather of King Carl of Sweden, its current monarch.

Chamberlain, Neville, British prime minister from 1937 to 1939 and main proponent of appeasement.

Channon, Henry "Chips," Chicago-born British diarist, socialite, and Conservative member of Parliament whose diaries give a stunning portrait of his own and others' Nazi sympathies. When Hitler invaded Czechoslovakia, like many, he changed his viewpoint.

Churchill, Winston, British prime minister, 1940–45 and 1951–55. In the "wilderness" for ten years prior to the outbreak of war.

Ciano, Galeazzo, son-in-law of Benito Mussolini and Italian foreign minister from 1936 to 1943. After the fall of Mussolini, he was tried and convicted of treason and executed in 1944.

Cooper, Alfred Duff, 1st Viscount Norwich, Conservative politician, diplomat, political and military historian, and writer. He was a supporter of Churchill and against appeasement. After the war, he became ambassador to France.

Cooper, Lady Diana, 1st Viscountess Norwich, English aristocrat, actress, socialite, and wife of Duff Cooper.

Coughlin, Father Charles E., Canadian-born American-Catholic radio priest whose base was in Detroit. Initially a supporter of Roosevelt and the New Deal, he became an implacable enemy, anti-Semite, and supporter of Hitler. He also accepted money from Hitler's bankers.

Cunard, Lady Maud "Emerald," San Francisco–born socialite and aristocrat who championed Joachim von Ribbentrop and Wallis Simpson in her social set.

Dirksen, Herbert von, aristocratic German diplomat who served in Warsaw, Moscow, and Tokyo before becoming the German ambassador to the Court of St. James's from 1938 to 1939. He pretended to be ambassador Joseph P. Kennedy's friend to keep America out of the war.

Dodd, William E., U.S. ambassador to Berlin, 1933–37. Dodd was an historian and author. He tried to accurately portray the excesses of the Nazi regime to the State Department and the president.

Dodd, Martha, journalist daughter of Ambassador Dodd and a Soviet sympathizer and spy.

Eden, Anthony, foreign secretary under Chamberlain and again under Churchill. Eden later became prime minister during the Suez Crisis in 1956. He was pro-American and anti-appeasement.

Ford, Henry, inventor of the assembly line in automobile manufacturing, Ford was wildly anti-Semitic in the 1920s and '30s and wrote pamphlets against the Jews. (He recanted, too late.) He was the man Hitler most admired in America.

Freeman-Mitford, Edward, 2nd Baron Redesdale, English aristocrat and landowner who was the father of the six Mitford girls (Nancy, Diana, Pamela, Jessica, Unity, and Deborah). He was a Nazi sympathizer who saw his error in 1939 and turned against Hitler.

Freeman-Mitford, Unity Valkyrie, English aristocrat known for her extremism as a fascist and anti-Semite. She inserted herself into Hitler's inner circle in the forlorn hope of marrying him and shot herself when Britain declared war on Germany. She died of her wounds in 1948.

Gienanth, Ulrich von, German cultural attaché to the United States who oversaw all print propaganda for the Nazis in the United States. He worked in conjunction with I.G. Farben's New York subsidiary Chemnyco and was asked to leave the country with the German consuls in 1941. He did not serve time as a war criminal.

Goebbels, Dr. Paul Joseph, Hitler's head of propaganda who masterminded changing public sentiment within Germany to make the population believe Hitler's lies.

Göring, Hermann, head of the Luftwaffe, Göring was the only top Nazi with a significant military background. He was behind much of the looting and vied against Goebbels and Hess to become Hitler's number two.

Grandi, Count Dino, Italian aristocrat and fascist diplomat who served as minister of justice, minister of foreign affairs, and president of the Italian parliament. He escaped to Spain in 1943 and then to Portugal and several places in South America before returning to Italy in the 1960s.

Hanfstaengl, Ernst "Putzi" Sedgwick von, outspoken German-American businessman and head of the Nazi English-speaking foreign press service.

Harmsworth, Harold, 1st Lord Rothermere, press baron and monarchist who believed in restoring the European monarchies after the Great War and was an early supporter of Hitler in the hope he would restore the Hohenzollerns.

Hesse, Prince Christoph of, nephew of Kaiser Wilhelm II and brother-in-law of Prince Philip, Duke of Edinburgh. He was killed in a plane crash in October 1943.

Hesse, Prince and Landgrave Philipp of, head of the electoral house of Hesse from 1940 to 1980. Prince Philip, Duke of Edinburgh, was named after him. He was married to Princess Mafalda, the daughter of King Victor Emmanuel II of Italy, and acted as the intermediary between Hitler, Mussolini, and the Italian king.

Hitler, Adolf, chancellor and dictator of the Third Reich from January 30, 1933, to May 8, 1945.

Hohenlohe-Waldenburg-Schillingsfürst, Princess Stephanie zu (née Stephanie Richter), Viennese-born Christian of Jewish origin who sold information to maintain her luxurious lifestyle and became a spy for Hitler. She was interned in the United States during the war, but completely rehabilitated afterward.

Hohenzollern, Prince August Wilhelm "Auwi" von, fourth son of Kaiser William II and ardent Nazi who was a close friend of Princess Stephanie.

Ilgner, Max, I.G. Farben man who set up the American secret operations and its American subsidiary and "research center" called Chemnyco and masterminded I.G. propaganda campaigns internationally.

Ilgner, Rudolf, younger brother of Max Ilgner who took over the operations of Chemnyco. Ilgner gathered and disseminated intelligence on behalf of I.G. Farben in the United States and utilized the German consuls and Princess Stephanie to that end.

Kennedy, Joseph P., father of president John F. Kennedy, became the American ambassador to the Court of St. James's from March 1938 to October 1940. He was a fascist sympathizer and an arch anti-interventionist.

Kerr, Philip, 11th Marquess of Lothian, was an early advocate of a closer relationship with Germany and Hitler. As British ambassador to the United States in 1939–40, he worked tirelessly to help Roosevelt push through the Lend-Lease Act before his sudden death.

Krupp, Gustav von Bohlen und Halbach, headed the Krupp armaments empire and was initially reticent to involve himself with the Nazis but became a major supporter long before war broke out. He was the head of the German industrial association and led other industrialists into the Nazi orbit.

Lamont, Thomas W., partner and investment banker with the House of Morgan. Lamont had been a major financial adviser regarding reparations in the Treaty of Versailles.

Lindbergh, Anne, author, aviatrix, and daughter of Dwight Morrow, a partner at Morgan Bank. She was the wife of Charles A. Lindbergh.

Lindbergh, Charles A., aviator and first man to fly solo across the Atlantic. He and his wife Anne were the first to map transatlantic airline routes. He was an admirer of the Nazis and the Luftwaffe and became an outspoken and dangerous proponent of noninterventionism in America.

Londonderry, Edith, aristocrat and political hostess who dedicated her life to her husband's career in politics and created the fabulous garden at Mount Stewart in Northern Ireland.

Mooney, James, president of General Motors Overseas. He was awarded the German Order of the Eagle in 1938 for the Aryanization of General Motors in Germany and engaged in informal diplomacy on behalf of Roosevelt and Germany.

Morgan, Jack, chairman of the House of Morgan. He was both anti-German and anti-Semitic but backed loans to rebuild Germany after the Great War.

Mosley, Diana (née Freeman-Mitford), English aristocrat, writer, and socialite noted for her beauty and Nazi sympathizing.

Mosley, Sir Oswald "Tom," English aristocrat and politician who was a member of Parliament as a Conservative, Labour, and Independent politician. He was also a notorious womanizer and second husband of Diana Mitford.

Mussolini, Benito, Italian fascist dictator from October 31, 1922, to July 25, 1943. He was replaced by King Victor Emmanuel when Italy's military position became untenable.

Norman, Montagu, 1st Baron Norman, pro-fascist, anti-Semitic governor of the Bank of England from 1922 to 1944.

Preussen, Friedrich Wilhelm von Crown Prince, last heir to the Hohenzollern throne and avid Nazi supporter.

Price, George Ward, *Daily Mail* journalist and author and Nazi sympathizer.

Ramsay, Captain Archibald Maule, rabidly anti-Semitic Scottish Unionist member of Parliament who formed the Right Club. He is the only MP to have been interned under Defence Regulation 18(b), suspected of espionage.

Ribbentrop, Joachim von, German ambassador to the Court of St. James's, 1936–38, then German foreign minister. He was tried and found guilty at Nuremberg and executed.

Ritter, Nikolaus Adolf Fritz von, German aristocrat who spoke flawless American English and set up spy rings in both the United States and Great Britain.

Roosevelt, Franklin Delano, thirty-second president of the United States who served from 1933 to 1945. He was the only president to be elected to four terms in office.

Schacht, Hjalmar Horace Greeley, German economist and head of the Reichsbank as well as Hitler's economics minister. He was tried at Nuremberg for crimes against humanity and found not guilty.

Schmitz, Hermann, chief executive officer of I.G. Farben from 1935 to 1945. He became a convicted war criminal after the Nuremberg trials and served four years in prison.

Shirer, William L., American journalist and broadcaster who wrote the seminal book *The Rise and Fall of the Third Reich*. He was a reliable eyewitness to what was happening in Germany during Hitler's rise.

Tennant, Ernest, British businessman and investment banker who tried to see the good in the Nazi regime, hoping that Germany's economy would be rebuilt under Hitler.

Thompson, Dorothy, journalist and radio broadcaster who spoke fluent German. She was the first journalist to be deported from Nazi Germany.

Thyssen, Fritz, Nazi enabler and industrialist who fled the Nazis in 1938. After the war, he admitted "spoliation" and gave 15 percent of his assets to his victims before dying a year later.

Vane-Tempest-Stewart, Charles, 7th Marquess of Londonderry, aristocrat and British Secretary of State for Air (1931–35) who became an admirer of Hitler and spoke out in favor of the Nazis. He sat in the House of Lords.

Wenner-Gren, Axel, Swedish engineer and industrialist and one of the wealthiest men in the world. He had several financial dealings with supporters of Hitler (including Göring) and the Duke of Windsor.

Wiedemann, Fritz, Hitler's commanding officer during the Great War. Beginning in 1933, he was one of Hitler's three adjutants specializing in secret agreements and foreign espionage. He and Princess Stephanie were lovers. He was also head of the U.S. West Coast German-Japanese spy ring.

Windsor, Edward, Duke of, former prince of Wales and king of Great Britain, Edward was a Nazi sympathizer with an overbearing sense of entitlement who never wanted to become king.

Windsor, Wallis, Duchess of, born in Baltimore as Bessie Wallis Warfield, Wallis was the wife of businessman Ernest Simpson when she met and began her affair with Edward, Prince of Wales.

Wohlthat, Hermann, Hermann Göring's main economic adviser for the Four-Year Plan who engaged in diplomatic and industrial espionage on behalf of the Third Reich.

Wood, Edward, 1st Earl Halifax, former viceroy to India and foreign secretary who implemented Chamberlain's appeasement policy.

AUTHOR'S NOTE

The world of the 1930s is an unrecognizable "other country" to us to-day. The Great Depression, caused by the 1929 Wall Street stock market crash, wreaked economic, social, and political devastation. It was felt around the world, save (annoyingly to capitalists) in the Soviet Union, then called USSR—the Union of Soviet Socialist Republics—now called the Russian Federation. Then, too, the crash was a decade *after* the end of the carnage of the Great War. (It could hardly be called the First World War until the sequel had begun, could it?) The "Spanish flu"—bred in the trenches of Flanders fields—became the 1918–20 pandemic, killing another estimated fifty million people. Hitting as it did when the world's populations were already deeply scarred by the trench warfare of 1914–18, during which millions of young men died, it was seen as an interminable plague. The cry of *never again!* among the Allied nations was sung as a magnificent obsession before becoming a propaganda tool to be wielded by Adolf Hitler and his Nazi Party. But how? That is the first point of this book.

Writing in 1953, the novelist L. P. Hartley began his seminal work *The Go-Between* with: "The past is another country: they do things differently there." Agreed, all our modern conveniences that we consider essential, from cars to electricity and refrigeration, were rare. Of course there was no internet and all the joys and problems it brings either. But as far as the use and purpose of propaganda is concerned, things were remarkably similar, only the means of communication was different.

Hadn't Nobel laureate Sinclair Lewis eerily foretold, in his devastating political novel *It Can't Happen Here* in 1935, the story of a presidential insurrection against democracy? Haven't we all seen what accomplices, enablers, and influencers can do today? Haven't we seen those in power, or people aiming to grab power, do as they wish with the aid of "spin," or as I prefer to call it by its original name, propaganda? Power and propaganda. Two mighty forces.

And that is the second point of this book. Hitler's sales pitch to the German people was to *vote* for his dictatorship. Just imagine—*voting* to lose your rights. And because the chaos was so extreme in Germany, they did—never realizing that Hitler's plan to annihilate and conquer would soon wreak a more deadly havoc. Hitler laid the blame for all Germany's ills on his political enemies, the church, and especially the Jews. It is one thing for a leader—any leader—to declare himself above the rule of law. However, for demagoguery to succeed, the very first step requires garnering a following through indoctrination, not only of the masses but also of the politically motivated, business leaders, and money men (and today, women). Any rise to power is foreshadowed by persuasive voices whispering, then chattering loudly behind the scenes. As the movement gathers pace, metaphoric microphones are put under the enablers' noses, and their words bleat out at us through megaphones of one ilk or another, before their messages are finally transformed into print or broadcast media and—more readily today—across social media. There are many analogues in history.

As a biographer and historian, I believe that the past matters. History matters. Facts matter. But above all else, *context matters*. Changing history and facts—canceling them as if they did not exist or changing them to suit some twenty-first-century weaponized truism is another form of propaganda and lie. Just as in the days of Hitler's rise to power, when the powerful preyed on others' hopes and fears, propaganda and lies can still work their magic on the minds of individuals and nations today. That is why, in my opinion, it is so important to understand those murky puppeteers behind the scenes. That is also why I am a firm believer in democracy, freedom of the press, and freedom of speech—for all its tremendous messiness and contradictions. If we lose the power of informed debate, we become unable to avoid unfairness in society and to value differing viewpoints. Worse, we lose democracy. We must learn from our past mistakes and triumphs, not color them with a false paintbrush of bias or opinion or reinvent definitions for existing words calling the "truth" a "lie," or we shall never learn to become better people and leave a healthier, happier, safer planet behind us for our children and grandchildren.

HITLER'S MASTERY WAS not "the big lie" but rather in getting millions to believe it. The Treaty of Versailles, combined with the rhetoric and position of his powerful enablers within a bankrupt Germany, made his rise possible. Once his revised history took hold to "make Germany great again," he dragged those who feared another war toward the halfway house of appeasement. The elite appeasers mistakenly believed they could contain the criminal megalomaniac who was Hitler, while failing to rearm their own countries.

Some of these elite appeasers often became the "Hitler's aristocrats" referred to in the title of the book. To capture the essence of how people thought, acted, and accepted the new isms (communism, socialism, fascism, Nazism) in their own rapidly changing "foreign country," I put Hitler's aristocrats' actions within the historical context of their times. The key to understanding their world—and ensuring crimes against humanity never happen again—means that we need to understand *why* things happened, *who* facilitated the outcomes, and *why* they succeeded or failed. In the main, this is a book about the influencers and enablers who actively worked toward blinding Germany, Great Britain, and the United States to what Hitler and his fellow criminals were doing. Women (who have been previously written out of the history simply because they were women) will take their rightful place alongside the men, for good or ill. I specifically do not study the French point of view because the French experience was vastly different from the Anglo-American alliance that grew and flourished in the period. Where appropriate, however, I do mention what was happening in France.

I have had to be selective in writing about these people—there were literally hundreds. So, to qualify as one of my "aristocrats," the main prerequisite was that they strode on an international stage that particularly affected Germany, Britain, and America, exerting their power on world events. They were active propagandists, political hostesses, bankers, members of parliaments or Congress, the nobility, diplomats, spies, industrialists, and, as a group, multinational corporations.

THERE ARE A few housekeeping points I would like to make here, too. Aside from most archive closures due to COVID-19, and the lack of documents online, the greatest challenge in writing this book has been using memoirs, postwar testimonies, and diaries intended for publication as my references. Some of the secret service files in the United Kingdom and United States contain inaccurate information. Unpicking the reality and truth from the supposition or fiction about these aristocrats—including how they would prefer to be remembered—has been thought-provoking, constantly reminding me that *history* becomes the real arbiter of greatness or defeat. As the reader, you need to know that many of the people quoted in this book were on trial for their lives, attempting to avoid trial, imprisoned without trial, or that they simply lied about any complicity with the Nazi regime during the Cold War, when many of their memoirs were written. I also highlight others who were incredibly courageous in their fight against the spread of the Nazi ideology throughout Germany, the Americas, and the United Kingdom.

Many cities and countries have changed names in the period. I use the original names and, where required, insert today's name in parentheses or in a footnote on the same page. So, for example, the Great War of 1914–18 is *not* called the First World War. I believe it helps to bring the reader back in time to use the original expressions. The only exception is in the case of the United Kingdom of Great Britain and Northern Ireland. Many people, including Hitler, simply called the four home nations (England, Wales, Scotland, and Northern Ireland) "England." To be more accurate (my sincere apologies to Northern Ireland), I opt to call my home Great Britain or simply "Britain." All English sources are spelled as written in the country of English-speaking origin. All foreign language sources are translated into English.

Above all, I do hope that you will find much unknown history in the book, that you will find it thought-provoking, and above all that you enjoy reading it.

Susan Ronald
Oxfordshire,
England

By the clever and continuous use of propaganda, a people can even be made to mistake heaven for hell, and vice versa.

—Adolf Hitler

Prologue

London, May 13, 1937

The German embassy's celebrations for the coronation of King George VI had been six months in meticulous preparation. Even so, their plans had gone awry through an anti-German conspiracy brewed by Jews and Freemasons, Joachim von Ribbentrop asserted. As the tall, slender, fair-haired German ambassador to the Court of St. James's, Ribbentrop repeatedly bemoaned that it should have been Edward VIII's coronation, and he would never forgive Germany's enemies for making them celebrate the coronation of the wrong king. Germany had lost its most valuable ally, Ribbentrop told his aides. "Don't you know what expectations the Führer has placed on the King's [Edward's] support in the coming negotiations?" an imperious Ribbentrop lamented to his secretary, Fritz Hesse, shortly after Edward's abdication in December 1936. Everything Hitler had worked for depended on an agreement with Great Britain. Ribbentrop also wrote to Hitler: "Seldom in history has greater baseness been shown than by the circles around Edward VIII whose work finally led to his being deprived of the English throne."[1]

Ribbentrop had been dubbed "Ambassador Brickendrop" by the British press for giving the Nazi salute when he presented his credentials to Edward on October 30, 1936. Then, within two months of arriving in London, having assured Hitler that he was *the* Anglo-Saxon expert in the Nazi hierarchy, Edward abdicated. Ribbentrop repeated his *Hitlergrüsse* (Nazi salute) to George VI when presenting his credentials again, but this time, all the other ambassadors were present, too. Oh, how they tittered. . . . Ribbentrop resented the stain on his reputation, claiming that he had fallen backward and not given the Hitler salute.

Ribbentrop had advised Hitler that Edward VIII was a "strong man intent on bringing his country into line with Germany." When the king announced he was giving up his throne for the woman he loved, Ribbentrop felt duty bound to dispel the "lie." His December 10, 1936, dispatch regarding the abdication stressed "a systematic agitation has been fomented in Britain against the King . . . his friendly attitude towards Germany had undoubtedly gained the King very powerful enemies in this country." As soon as Ribbentrop returned to Berlin for Christmas, he repeated the allegations that Edward had been deposed by "an anti-German conspiracy of Jews, Freemasons and diverse reactionaries."[2]

The führer's other eyes and ears in London, Princess Stephanie zu Hohenlohe-Waldenburg-Schillingsfürst, Hitler's *liebe Prinzessin*, had warned the führer that Ribbentrop had misunderstood the king's situation. Consequently, the German ambassador's rancor toward the princess knew no bounds. And now Hitler's *liebe Prinzessin*, that diabolical Hohenlohe woman, was causing Ribbentrop undue agitation. True, Princess Stephanie was no more of royal Hohenlohe blood than Ribbentrop's "von" was genuine, though the ambassador would hardly make such a disagreeable comparison. But she was under the protection of Hitler's personal adjutant and former company commander from the Great War, Captain Fritz Wiedemann. The unanswered question for Ribbentrop was whether Wiedemann protected Princess Stephanie for his own reasons, Hitler's, or Dr. Goebbels's, whom Wiedemann had served at the 1933 Chicago World's Fair.[3]

Ribbentrop fumed whenever he thought about the ersatz princess. Was *he* not the German ambassador? Was *he* not Hitler's trusted eyes and ears in all matters relating to the British and other Anglo-Saxon nations? Could *he* not determine who should or should not be invited to the official celebrations? Ribbentrop had challenged his führer's insistence on Stephanie's attendance, stating categorically that the British aristocrats would decline their invitations if she were present. Representatives of the British government thought she was an adventuress, and they would boycott the reception, too. Would it not be a faux pas, he asked Hitler, to court social disaster when the previous king—who played golf with Princess Stephanie—had so divided the country? Alas, for Ribbentrop, it seemed not. He had crossed her name off the guest list once. Wiedemann, on Hitler's orders, sent a telegram reinstating her. Ribbentrop ignored the order. When Stephanie advised Wiedemann that her invitation had not arrived, Wiedemann ensured that the führer himself sent a cable ordering his dear princess's attendance.[4] Ribbentrop, ever petty and vindictive, had only one recourse left open to him: she would be invited, but Stephanie's name would be expunged from the Court Circular in *The Times*.[5]

And so, on the evening of May 13, Stephanie, looking every inch the born-and-bred princess—Titian-haired, voluptuous, radiant, bejeweled, and wearing the designer Molyneux's most sumptuously beaded gown—entered the crowded German embassy ballroom on the arm of the rather tall and good-looking Captain Fritz Wiedemann. The San Francisco–born hostess Lady Maud "Emerald" Cunard rushed over to embrace her dear friend and Ribbentrop's "nemesis princess." Stephanie made her way through the aristocratic throng and political power brokers, bowing her head regally in response to the welcoming gazes of her fellow foreign nobility. She acknowledged Lady Nancy Astor's wave with smiling eyes. Lord and Lady Londonderry shook her hand warmly. Of course, Lord Rothermere—Stephanie's employer of many years—motioned for her to join him and the other press barons. She saw Churchill, hunched over with a cigar in his mouth and whisky glass in his hand, glaring at her. She pretended to ignore his penetrating gaze.

"I could see that she was greeted wholeheartedly from all sides and accepted everywhere as belonging to 'high society,'" Wiedemann wrote later. "Cleverly she knew, before the eyes of all those present, to approach the Duke of Kent, who politely rose from his chair and chatted with her animatedly for some minutes."[6] Prince George, Duke of Kent, was the youngest son of George V, and youngest brother of "Bertie," the new King George VI. Later, Stephanie enthused to Wiedemann, "Did you see, Fritz, twice he jumped up from his chair when I addressed him."[7]

Stephanie Hohenlohe was no one's fool. She may have married into the Continental aristocracy by stealth, but in greeting her old friend—and the reception's guest of honor—she had stabbed Ribbentrop in the back. General Werner von Blomberg—an unimpeachable source seated next to the Duke of Kent—told Hitler that Princess Stephanie was indeed an old friend of the British royal family. She was sure, too, that Blomberg witnessed the warmth with which Prince Otto von Bismarck (grandson of the great unifier of Germany in 1871) and his wife embraced her. At a stroke, Ribbentrop was defeated, and Stephanie had asserted her place once again as Hitler's "Dear Princess."

PART I

THE MAGIC WEAVERS

———

Charming is in as great request as physic, and charmers
more sought unto than physicians in time of need.

—William Perkins,
A Discourse of the Damned Art of Witchcraft,
Cambridge, 1608

1

Chaos

In all chaos there is a cosmos, in all disorder a secret order.

—Carl Jung

Princess Stephanie's admiration for Adolf Hitler began long before he came to power in 1933. She, and other propagandists—irrespective of nationality—reacted positively to the rise of the Nazis given the massive geopolitical, economic, and social displacement in Europe during the 1920s. In fact, Stephanie was a mere thread woven into the intricate tapestry of "new" international aristocrats who helped make Hitler's rise to the lofty position of German chancellor possible in January 1933. The Great War had changed everything. Indeed, life after 1918 for all of Europe's and America's aristocrats was transformed—in some cases beyond recognition.

"Everything, apparently, had been cut loose from its moorings," American journalist Dorothy Thompson wrote in 1920. "Democracy, socialism, nationalism, were all assuming new, strange forms. All traditions were disintegrating."[1] For a woman who wrote about the woes of Central Europe in a rather impertinent and thoroughly American way, she succinctly described in three sentences the utter chaos that reigned. A legendary journalist before the age of thirty, Thompson knew you had to watch the faces of those interviewed, understand their posture, and consider the cadence and tone of their voices. Described more than once as absentminded—"a lady who would forget her pajamas"—she knew it was her duty to report the news accurately. She saw the story behind the news story where other, more experienced journalists already felt they had plumbed the depths and moved on.

Arriving in Vienna in the spring of 1921 for the *Public Ledger* on a "no publish, no fee" basis, Thompson wrote "flavorful pieces about Viennese life" concentrating on the cult of its magnificent coffee (palaces with silk brocade walls had been built for it) and its tart wine. She called Vienna a beautiful city of "Germanic cleanliness and Latin ease," picking out the soft Austrian accents, the "easygoingness, carelessness, laziness and easy tolerance" of the Viennese. Above all else, she observed the deadened atmosphere of bygone grandeur and high culture hovering just above the heads of those in the starving city.[2]

For Thompson, the inhabitants of the former Austro-Hungarian Empire had become constricted in their new identities on a very personal level, just as its multicultural people and nobility had become disenfranchised. On October 17, 1918, the Hungarian parliament decreed an end to the union with Austria and declared itself an independent country, in what became known as the Aster, or Chrysanthemum, Revolution. Ten days later Czechoslovakia was born. November 3 dawned with the formation of the West Ukrainian People's Republic. Three days after that, Poland proclaimed its independence in Krakow. A further eight republics were declared before the cease-fire came into effect on November 11. In less than a month, the old Austro-Hungarian Empire's aristocratic titles and traditions had become meaningless.

Austria, after the war, was overrun by *Raffkes*—war profiteers—"lolling in lilac velvet and plate-glass limousines," Thompson wrote. "They swarmed from Poland, or wriggled up from the debris left in Austria by the war, and through their special abilities managed to keep on top of the slime." The black marketeers centered around Vienna's coffee houses, mainly at the fabled Café Atlantis opposite the Imperial Hotel.[3] It was impossible to replace clothing or shoes. Seat covers from trains were often removed by stealth as leather to resole or refurbish tattered clothing. Cobblers could only repair shoes with wood, and each loud step on Vienna's cobbled streets became a reminder of the sheer poverty engulfing its population. There was no coal for warmth, no flour, no oil, no meat except at extortionate black-market prices. New trousers were often made from old potato sacks.[4]

. . .

As DIFFICULT AS life was in Austria, Hungary was worse. "The Magyars are a strange, mystic people," Thompson wrote, "a people in 1921 seething with resentment. . . . Nowhere are capital and labor farther apart; nowhere is the Jewish question more strained. Here is the center of the monarchist fight. Here is the most vigorous irredentism. Here is a nation whose social structure has been more violently assailed than that of any European country except Russia."[5]

In the Hungarian capital Budapest, rising like poisonous methane gas from the slime heap emerged Béla Kun, the son of a lapsed Jewish notary and a Jewish-born Protestant mother. His 133-day Hungarian Soviet Republic established in March 1919 nationalized most of the country's private property, including its private industry. Initially, his communist-inspired propaganda hit home with those who were starving, homeless, unemployed, and defeated by life. Kun failed, however, to redistribute the wealth stolen from the aristocracy to the peasant classes. Within weeks, Kun's regime became loathed by peasants, workers, industrialists, and aristocrats alike.

His indiscriminate terror and bloodthirsty treatment of Hungarians came under the microscope of the Allies during the peace talks in Paris. In response to international criticism, Kun absurdly demanded that Hungary's old borders be restored, especially in Upper Hungary. By the end of his first month in power, an ill-equipped and poorly trained Hungarian "Red Army" was at war with the Kingdom of Romania and the newly established Czechoslovakia, both aided militarily by France. Kun was obliged to accept a French-backed ultimatum and fled the country on August 1, 1919.[6]

Briefly—for twenty-three days—Archduke Joseph August of Austria declared himself regent, appointing his own prime minister. But the Allies would not countenance a Habsburg at the head of any government. Emperor Charles IV of Hungary, who had briefly ascended the Austro-Hungarian throne on Franz Joseph's death in November 1916, attempted to keep the empire together as a federal union, but failed. Eventually, Admiral Miklós Horthy was asked by parliament to become regent for the vacant throne. The Hungarian White Terror followed for two years, during which many Jews were slaughtered. Eventually, Horthy would become Hitler's puppet.

These monumental changes occurred in less than a year. "On the outskirts of Budapest," Dorothy Thompson wrote, "one cannot find many people who are worrying about St. Stephen's crown."[7] Hungary was a truncated nation strangled by bedlam. Soon enough, Horthy would enlist Princess Stephanie to right the wrongs done to their country.

CENTRAL EUROPE REELED from the political, economic, and social changes. The crop failures and the war forced many well-to-do Austrians to sell part or all of their estates to make ends meet. New jobs and purposes in life needed to be found. Austrians were almost as dazed by the loss of their right to have a Habsburg emperor as they were by uncertainty over how they might possibly rebuild their past lives. The diplomatic corps had always provided a haven for many aristocrats, where a plethora of ambassadors and consuls proudly displayed their *von* or *zu* before their double- or triple-barreled family names. Nobles still cherished their defunct titles of *Erzherzogl* (Archduke), *Herzog* (Duke), *Graf* (Count), *Freiherr* (Baron), *Ritter* (Knight), or *Edel* (Elder). They clung to a life that no longer existed, in a country that was unrecognizable as their own.

The population had to opt for one of the myriad nationalities on offer so they could henceforth be called Italian, Czechoslovak, Yugoslav, Hungarian, Austrian, or Romanian. (Even these new nationalities hid other national identities such as German, Moravian, Slovakian, and Bohemian.) It was the dizzying world changing apace.

PRINCESS STEPHANIE WAS one of Adolf Hitler's most avid "aristocratic" propagandists. She was born as the lowly Stephanie Julianne Richter in September 1891. The Vienna of her childhood was envied as Europe's most splendid capital of high culture. As if vying to match Vienna's grandness, Stephanie constantly reinvented her youth, when she was, in fact, only the love child of Ludmilla Richter and a moneylender called Max Wiener.

Years earlier, Ludmilla (née Kuranda) had converted from Judaism to Catholicism when she married the lawyer Dr. Johann Richter. Yet throughout his wife's pregnancy with Stephanie, Richter languished in a Viennese prison, convicted of embezzling money from an underage client.[8] With her husband in jail, Ludmilla reputedly sold her favors to Wiener to make ends meet. Biographers have assumed that when Richter was released, he was all too happy to accept a lump sum from Wiener in exchange for giving the baby girl his last name.[9] Though Stephanie was fully Jewish biologically, she never saw the inside of any synagogue, and never celebrated any Jewish festivals. Nor would she ever say that she was Jewish. Until the advent of Adolf Hitler's Third Reich, no one else would have considered her Jewish either.

Stephanie claimed to have led a sheltered childhood and was brought into Vienna's high society by the childless Princess Franziska "Fanny" von Metternich. It was a bald lie. In fact, her uncle Robert Kuranda was her benefactor. Aged sixteen, Robert upped sticks and made his way to South Africa to fight as a mercenary in the Anglo-Zulu War of 1879 with the cavalry regiment Seventeenth Lancers, also known as the Duke of Cambridge's Own.* When the regiment returned to India, Kuranda switched sides and fought for the Boers, until the British were in the ascendant, and he switched sides again. In 1884, as the land agent for Alois Hugh Nelmapius (one of the first men to mine gold successfully in the Transvaal), Kuranda was shown some "quartz" on a farm. And so, he bought the farm—more than likely in his own name. It became the first diamond mine at Doornfontein (modern-day Johannesburg).[10] Kuranda was a diamond millionaire overnight, along with his great friends Solomon "Solly" Joel and Solly's uncle, Barney Barnato, who had recently merged his company with that of Cecil Rhodes to form De Beers Consolidated Mines.[11]

When Ludmilla told her brother about her love child, and that her husband had not returned home after his release from prison, Robert ensured their futures. As that new breed of diamond millionaire, he could also facilitate their entry into high society. More than likely, it was

---

* The Seventeenth Lancers are most famous for their part in the Crimean War and the Charge of the Light Brigade.

Robert who arranged for Princess Fanny to teach Stephanie the ways ladies adopted in Viennese society. Other virginal young women bred to become aristocratic wives of forlorn kings and pauper princes made a fine art of gossip, usually telling tales of cuckolded husbands at their *contessen soirées*. Yet Stephanie was never invited to these evenings. Even by the age of fifteen, there was nothing virginal about Stephanie. But as she was determined to marry a prince, she concentrated on meeting him instead by mastering country pursuits such as horseback riding, hunting, fishing, and shooting. By sixteen, Stephanie had already had affairs with Count Rudolfo Collerado-Mansfeld and the Polish count Josef "Gizy" Gizycki, a tall, dark, athletic man with jet-black hair, black eyes, and a "long nose and cruel nostrils," Stephanie recalled. At the time, however, Gizycki was married to the future American publisher Eleanor Medill "Cissy" Patterson.*

By 1911 Stephanie had become the mistress of Archduke Franz Salvator of Austria-Tuscany. Franz Salvator, however, was married to Archduchess Marie Valerie, the third daughter and fourth child of Emperor Franz Joseph of Austria and his empress Elisabeth. There was, of course, never any question of Franz Salvator marrying Stephanie, nor leaving the imperial archduchess.

That said, Stephanie became pregnant in the spring of 1914, and something had to be done. It was Emperor Franz Joseph himself who arranged her "shotgun wedding" to Prince Friedrich Franz von Hohenlohe-Waldenburg-Schillingsfürst. The prince had met Stephanie several times at court but little more. He was chosen as the sacrificial

---

* Cissy was dubbed one of the "Three Graces" in Washington society alongside Alice Roosevelt (daughter of Theodore), and Marguerite Cassini (daughter of the Russian ambassador). She married Gizy against her parents' wishes and had a daughter with him. It was a violent marriage, and she absconded in the dead of night with their daughter Felicia to England. Gizy lied to the nursemaid that the couple had reconciled, and took Felicia to Paris, then on to his castle stronghold in the Ukraine. Cissy's family, being newspaper people, publicized the kidnap and prevailed on President Taft to intervene on Cissy's behalf with Czar Nicholas II. Gizy was forced—as only the czar could do with real threats—to give up possession of his daughter. Felicia would marry American newspaperman Drew Pearson. Cissy was one of the first women to head a national newspaper, *The Washington Times-Herald*.

husband because he had a title, little money, and was an inveterate gambler. Naturally, he was compelled by his emperor to agree to the sham marriage. Stephanie, so the legend goes, paid off his debts (probably with money from Archduke Franz Salvator) in return for a "good show" to Viennese society.

Royal consent was required, which the Austrian emperor gave; but the Hohenlohe-Waldenburg-Schillingsfürst clan were much aggrieved. Stephanie was unsuitable. To spare the Hohenlohe blushes, the couple were quietly married in London on May 12, 1914, at the Roman Catholic cathedral in Westminster. Only Stephanie's mother was present as a witness, with the other required witness hired (as was the custom) at short notice. The newlyweds adjourned to separate hotels after the ceremony. Stephanie was twenty-three, and finally married to her prince. Her son, Franzi, was born that December.

AFTER THE GREAT War, Princess Stephanie found herself a Hungarian national—a choice made for her in 1919 by her princely husband, since his family's main estate was within Hungary's borders. She spoke no Hungarian and had never lived in the country. By July 1920, Friedrich Franz had met someone else, and having done his duty to Stephanie, demanded a divorce. This time, there was no Franz Salvator to rescue her, even though the archduke had survived the war. As with all the Austro-Hungarian nobility, his "right to rule" had been rescinded. Stephanie was left no option but to agree. Ten days after the divorce was granted, Friedrich Franz married Countess Emanuela Batthyány, who had left her husband and three children to become the prince's second wife.[12]*

Princess Stephanie zu Hohenlohe-Waldenburg-Schillingsfürst was a single, divorced mother, marginalized as a citizen of a country where

---

* After 1918, Friedrich Franz served at the Hungarian embassy in Bern, Switzerland, and was expelled as a spy. During the Hitler era, he was the Chief of German Propaganda and Director of Nazi Espionage in Switzerland. As the Allies closed in at the end of World War II, Friedrich Franz and his second wife escaped to Brazil, eluding interrogation and possible punishment.

she did not speak the language. Nonetheless, Stephanie would prove to be resourceful in maintaining the style to which she wished to become accustomed, as so many "upper-class" and former aristocratic Europeans were forced to do.

2

The "Big Lie"

I have resolved to be the destroyer of Marxism.
— Adolf Hitler at his trial for treason, 1924

Many believe the rise of fascism was a direct response to the October 1917 Bolshevik revolution and subsequent Russian civil wars. When Czar Nicholas II was deposed in the February 1917 revolution, the Allies hoped that the new Soviet government under Alexander Kerensky and the Russian Duma (parliament), would be more democratic than the Romanov totalitarian state.* Within six months, Vladimir Lenin's 1917 October revolution toppled Kerensky's provisional Soviet government, making hopes for democracy futile.

During these critical six months in 1917, the war raged on in the east. The Treaty of Brest-Litovsk in March 1918, which removed Russia (now called the Soviet Union) from the war, had been hailed as a victory for the kaiser's imperial army.† Once Lenin successfully secured power for communism, a human wave of aristocratic White Russian émigrés flooded into Europe's capitals, bringing with them their notions of superiority and opulence, knowledge of how to reach accommodation within a totalitarian state, and unremitting anti-Semitism. Many White Russian émigrés would become key propagandists for Hitler.

---

* Such hopes were entirely misguided. The czarist regime was medieval. Democracy cannot be successfully grafted onto a feudal society.
† Leon Trotsky as Lenin's foreign minister had failed to persuade the Germans to stop fighting Russia initially, resulting in temporary territorial gains for Germany.

They instilled their visceral hatred for the communists into the Nazi creed, believing that "the myth of a mysterious Jewish-Masonic-Bolshevik plot" was behind the toppling of the Russian, German, and Austro-Hungarian empires. This was the first big lie. It was the White émigrés who exported their revulsion of Jews and the fake pamphlet *The Protocols of the Elders of Zion*.[1] What is easily forgotten today is that many of these White émigrés were Russian by nationality, but Baltic German, Lithuanian, Latvian, or Ukrainian by heritage and culture. Among the White émigré adventurers who most influenced Hitler in those early days were Alfred Rosenberg (later the ideologue of the Nazi Party) and Max Erwin von Scheubner-Richter (who championed Hitler's drive toward the east and other foreign policy decisions) through their *völkisch* organization, the Aufbau Vereinigung. Other members of the Aufbau included General Erich Ludendorff and Hitler's friend and publisher, Max Amann.

In truth, most Germans felt cheated by the peace, with many aristocrats and frontline soldiers alike hoping for a resurgence of pan-Germanism. As early as 1920, outlawed underground paramilitary organizations were formed throughout Germany from the enormous remnant of the imperial army.[2] Those who were attracted to bolshevism were labeled the enemies of German reconstruction. A speaker at a paramilitary rally in Regensburg encapsulated the right's position: "Friend and foe shall know that in future one must take a position and show his colors, whether left—Bolshevism—or right Reconstruction. There is no middle position."[3] Reconstruction soon equated Nazism. It was the Allied inability to understand the German viewpoint that led to the immediate failure of the peace. Given this history, it is no wonder that, without effective leadership throughout the Weimar era and the Gothic mindset that refused to be vanquished, a Hitler would rise into the vacuum at the top.

The communist-inspired Spartacist uprising of 1919 predictably led to armed outrages by Freikorps* groups aimed at defending Germany against communism. Wildcat strikes and bloodthirsty atrocities became

---

* Irregular German paramilitary groups from the former disbanded imperial German army.

a common feature of life throughout Germany in the ensuing months. The murders and reprisals continued until May 1919.[4] And yet the Freikorps violence was often mistaken by many Germans as the intervention of their disbanded imperial army acting to protect the nation from bolshevism. Few recognized they were simply dangerous vigilantes.

So WHERE WERE the German aristocracy and diplomats who might have found a middle way? For most, the new Weimar Republic made them wonder if they still had a place in this alien country. Their royal, princely, and noble properties had been "restructured." The Wittelsbachs in Bavaria and the Von Hesses at Kassel (also related to the British royal family) were forced to cede vast swathes of their lands to the German state. What lands remained for their benefit had to be administered at arms' length through independent foundations. Their German bank accounts were frozen, and only their art, jewels, and internationally convertible investments could be relied on to rebuild their fortunes.[5] Since property had always been the hallmark of royalty and nobility, the German aristocrats, just like their Austrian and Hungarian counterparts, suffered a nosedive in their wealth, social standing, political power, and economic future. Most stared helplessly at a bleak horizon.

In fact, Weimar had been foisted onto the vanquished nation. It represented a new Germany with a dead imperial past, dead traditions, and no road map toward democracy. The German nobility had been devastated by the war of 1914–18, and like the Hungarians and Austrians, they were deeply aggrieved by the transformations they had been made to endure.[6*] Many German officers on the Western Front (most of noble birth) and the majority of common frontline soldiers—like Corporal Adolf Hitler—believed Germany had *not* lost in the West. With just short of six million men demobilized, and an approved German

---

* With 1,773,700 war dead and an additional 4,216,058 soldiers wounded and 1,152,788 taken captive, there were 7,142,546 German casualties, or 54.6 percent of the 13 million people mobilized for war. Compare this with British war dead, 700,000 approximately, or 11.5 percent of the mobilized 6 million men. France's statistics were worse, with 52 percent of mobilized men killed (source: bbc.co.uk).

standing army of only one hundred thousand soldiers, the mind bog-
gles that the Allies believed these men would not take up arms to rectify
what they saw as an unjust peace.

The "peace" festered and infected German thinking. To paraphrase
the psychoanalyst Carl Jung, from the "disorder a secret order" was
born. In *Mein Kampf*, first published in July 1925, Hitler blamed the
Jews for spreading the lie that General Erich Ludendorff lost the war in
the West. In retaliation, he advocated that only "the big lie" could work
against Germany's enemies since "in the big lie there is always a certain force of credibility" that would prove irresistible to the masses, who
more readily "fall victims to the big lie than the small lie."[7] It became a
compelling argument to a defeated nation.

Yet France remained vengeful, with some good reason. Not only had
it been invaded in 1871 by Bismarck's newly unified Germany and lost
Alsace-Lorraine but also most of the war of 1914–18 had been fought
on French soil. From the British and American viewpoints, Germany
had begun the war using the excuse of Archduke Franz Ferdinand's assassination in Sarajevo to promote pan-Germanism to dominate Europe. They also continued to fight in the East long after Russia had quit
the field of battle. And so the Allies compelled the leaders of Weimar to
sign the Versailles peace treaty giving Germans the "sole fault" or *Alleinschulde* for the hostilities. Any future "military freedom" (*Wehrfreiheit*)
or self-determination for Germany was out of the question.

AND WHAT ABOUT Germany's powerful industrialists? The mightiest of
them all, Gustav Krupp von Bohlen und Halbach, only saw the devastation of smashed and idle equipment on his factory floors in 1920.
He proclaimed, "If Germany should ever be reborn, it should shake off
the chains of Versailles." Krupp loathed the Allies. They had made sure
his company, known as "the anvil of the Reich," would be prohibited
from making any more armaments and cannons. "The machines were
destroyed, the tools were smashed, but the men remained. . . . Their skill
had to be maintained at all costs," Krupp said. "Although for the time being all indications were against it—one day a change would come."[8]

As Germany's premier armaments manufacturer, Krupp said, "Everything within me revolted against the idea . . . that the German people would be enslaved forever."[9] Krupp refused to accept the peace, and, contrary to popular myth, was instrumental in rearming Germany almost immediately after the Versailles diktat was signed. The Krupp empire, Weimar's Chancellor Karl Joseph Wirth,* and General Hans von Seeckt, the genius commander of the Reichswehr nicknamed "The Sphinx," were the triumvirate that made Krupp's vision for an armed future possible.

Krupp's German resurrection, however, required deception on a massive scale. Allied "snoopers" checked Krupp's every move, just as military experts monitored the size of the Reichswehr to one hundred thousand soldiers. And yet Krupp successfully undertook his mission for rearmament within a year of the Versailles Treaty's signature. After World War II it became apparent that, as General Telford Taylor said, "Truly, there was a deep continuity from the Weimar Republic to the Third Reich, as the Krupps and the Generals knew."[10†]

Had Krupp forged weapons in secret? Not exactly. American intelligence officers reported that Krupp had filed "twenty-six patents for artillery control devices, eighteen for electrical fire control apparatus, nine for fuses and shells, seventeen for field guns, and fourteen for heavy cannon which could only be moved by rail." The American secretary of war even told the press. The problem was that by May 1921 America, like Britain, had revised its thinking. The terms imposed on Germany were overly harsh. So the British and American governments turned a blind eye, as did their press.

It was simple for Krupp to take advantage of the chaos that reigned on the Continent. In 1921 he acquired a controlling stake in the Swedish steel firm Aktiebolaget Bofors, which became his primary weapons-manufacturing unit for the next fourteen years. Krupp hedged his bets on the outcome of the war, too, with his most extensive foreign holdings

---

* Wirth was chancellor between May 1921 and November 1922.

† General Telford Taylor is best remembered for his role as a lawyer for the prosecution at the Nuremberg trials following the war.

located in the Netherlands, shrouded by his wholly owned enterprise Blessing and Company. Literally, as the kaiser was forced to abdicate, Blessing bought Krupp's stockpiles from Essen, Magdeburg, and Düsseldorf, saving all manner of military weaponry for another day. Then Krupp began to shuffle corporate names and ownerships like playing cards and placed his best engineers outside Germany. All Krupp needed was a new powerful leader to change everything . . . so things could stay as they once had been.[11] Even so, Krupp was slow to join the Nazi Party.

INDUSTRIALIST FRITZ THYSSEN was quick to take an active role in nominating the "Austrian corporal" (a favorite term of President Paul von Hindenburg for Hitler) as Germany's leader. In October 1923, he went to Munich to meet with the man he felt was a great patriot, General Erich Ludendorff, to help stop the occupation of the Ruhr by the Allies. "There is but one hope," Ludendorff told Thyssen, "and this hope is embodied in the national groups which desire our recovery." Ludendorff recommended that Thyssen meet Adolf Hitler.[12]

Hitler had joined the fledgling German Workers' Party (Deutsche Arbeiterpartei, or DAP) in September 1919. He soon took control, concentrating on his speechifying and propaganda, and became its leader by February 1920, when it was renamed the National Socialist German Workers' Party (NSDAP), more commonly called the Nazi Party.

So Thyssen went along to several public meetings where Hitler spoke. He was mesmerized by Hitler's oratory and the military discipline of his followers. Several days later, Thyssen asked to be introduced to Hitler. The meeting was arranged at the home of Dr. Max Erwin von Scheubner-Richter, the young Baltic German–Latvian nobleman who was the Aufbau Vereinigung's guiding light and pivotal liaison between Hitler and General Ludendorff leading up to the failed putsch of November 1923. What's more, Scheubner-Richter was also an adviser to Hitler's ideologue, Alfred Rosenberg, who was a member of both the Aufbau and the NSDAP. As a nearly forgotten player on the Nazi stage, it had been Scheubner-Richter who "coordinated their activities and brought the two far rightists [the NSDAP and the Aufbau Vereinigung] ever closer politically."

Nearly a year earlier, in October 1922, Scheubner-Richter had arranged a secret conference between Hitler, Ludendorff, and Walter Nicolai, who headed up the pro–Kirill Romanov intelligence service to put Kirill on the murdered czar's throne. The purpose of their meeting was to agree on a joint strategy and philosophy for the future.[13]* Naturally, Hitler's cherished Lebensraum (translated as living space) toward the East flew in the face of such an alliance if Grand Duke Kirill Vladimirovich came to the throne, the czarists warned. Scheubner-Richter stressed that "the national Germany and the national Russia must find a common path for the future" and that the *völkisch* champions of each should work toward a common goal. Whether Hitler agreed on that day remains a mystery.

Taking a leaf out of Mussolini's book with his "March on Rome" that same month, Hitler had begun to believe in a planned "military expedition" against the Bavarian government. By the time he met with Thyssen, he realized he would need a great deal of money. If Thyssen knew, or even cared, about Hitler's links to the pro-czarist ambitions of Scheubner-Richter, it did not matter. Thyssen had been converted to Hitler's creed, and it had been agreed between the groups in October 1922 that Hitler would lead the way for them all. Enlisting the support of several other industrialists, Thyssen handed over one hundred thousand gold marks to Hitler for his "beerhall putsch" on November 9, 1923.[14]

Sixteen Nazi members, including the charming and dangerous Max Erwin von Scheubner-Richter and four policemen, were killed that day. Scheubner-Richter had been walking arm in arm with Hitler when he was shot in the lung, dying instantly. As he fell, he dislocated Hitler's shoulder. Other familiar names who marched that day among the two thousand Nazis were Erich Ludendorff, Hermann Göring, the rabid

---

* After the murder of Czar Nicholas and his immediate family, there was a scramble to claim legitimacy as his rightful heir among the exiled Romanovs, primarily Grand Duke Nicholas (grandson of Czar Nicholas I) and Grand Duke Kirill Vladimirovich (grandson of Czar Alexander II). For more on the Aufbau Vereinigung and the White émigrés assisting Hitler's rise to power, read Michael Kellogg's stunning book *The Russian Roots of Nazism: White Émigrés and the Making of National Socialism, 1917–1945*, Cambridge University Press, 2006.

anti-Semite newspaper publisher Julius Streicher, and Alfred Rosenberg. Hitler managed to escape temporarily by hiding at the home of
his German American friend, Ernst "Putzi" Sedgwick von Hanfstaengl.

HANFSTAENGL'S INVOLVEMENT WITH Hitler began in 1922 with a telephone call from his Harvard classmate, Warren Robbins, the new chargé
d'affaires at the American embassy in Berlin. Back in 1908, the tremen-
dously tall, lantern-jawed, and leonine Putzi had performed with Robbins during their Harvard days in one of the more uproarious Hasty
Pudding shows, where Putzi—all six foot four inches of him resembling
Lurch of *The Addams Family*—played the starring role as Gretchen
Spootspfeifer in *The Fake Fakirs*. Robbins played one of "Gretchen's"
devotees.[15] Since graduation, Putzi had lived in New York, working at
the family art gallery. He had returned to Munich earlier in 1922 with
his wife, Helene, and son, Egon, out of nostalgia, perhaps in the hope he
could make a difference to Germany's fortunes.

Robbins's "official call" asked Putzi for a favor: the embassy wanted to
understand firsthand what was going on in Bavaria and planned to send
Captain Truman Smith, the handsome six-foot-four assistant military
attaché, to explore the area and meet as many mood makers as possible.
"Admittedly, he's a Yale man," Robbins lamented, "but in spite of that he
is a nice, bright chap."[16] It was up to Putzi to introduce Smith to as many
people as possible. Putzi reminded Robbins that he had only recently
resettled in Munich, promising nonetheless that he would do what he
could. His introductions for Smith amounted to a few paltry society
connections and his newspaper publisher, Paul Nikolaus Cossmann, of
the *Münchner Neueste Nachrichten*. As it turned out, Cossmann was extremely helpful, pointing Smith in the direction of General Ludendorff
and some industrialists. Smith heard Hitler speak and chatted with the
Wittelsbach crown prince Rupprecht.

"I'm telling you, he's got such a way with words and says exactly what
the hungry Germans want to hear today," Smith enthused to Putzi about
Hitler. "Nationalistic but with a socialist side—and anti-Jew. He'll probably tone things down over time, as others before him have done, but this
guy has a concept and a talent for speaking that takes people along with

him." Since Smith had been recalled to Berlin, he asked Putzi to please take over for him by meeting Hitler that same evening after his speech.[17]

Accompanied by Alfred Rosenberg (to whom he had taken an instant dislike), Putzi asked himself repeatedly why he, the grandson of the American Civil War general William Heine (a pallbearer at the funeral of Abraham Lincoln), was listening to some nobody in a beer cellar in Munich. His mother's Sedgwick family was one of New England's most respected names. He had supped with the Teddy Roosevelts of Oyster Bay and slept with Djuna Barnes. It all seemed surreal.

Putzi had heard Teddy Roosevelt speak, and considered him a great orator. His Harvard classmates, too, would go on to powerful positions in the United States. He had played piano at the Harvard Club in New York early each morning, receiving appreciative nods from Franklin Delano Roosevelt, who was an ever-present member at breakfast time. But nothing had prepared him for this Hitler nonentity.

Hitler's rhetoric was compelling. He preached a new doctrine as if he were enlightening his audience to an evangelical faith. First, Hitler established the historical context of Germany's world since 1918; then he described how their woes were brought down upon their country by foreigners and Jewish bankers. (All part of the "big lie.") Once he saw that his audience was with him, Hitler's tone became more aggressive, more impassioned, and slyly malicious. He ridiculed the kaiser and his advisers, the left-wing politicians who made the country lie prostrate before the victors, the Bavarian separatists, and the communists. He made fun of Catholics, who sought deliverance in the confessional rather than through action as a community. Hanfstaengl felt he was watching a master in the making. Here was a man who could turn the dull seething masses into a deeply motivated community.

After the meeting, Rosenberg introduced Hanfstaengl to Hitler, as he still wiped the sweat from his brow. Hitler was anxious to know what Hanfstaengl would report back to Captain Smith. Hanfstaengl replied that he was impressed and "agreed with ninety-five percent" of what Hitler said. Hitler promised that they would discuss the other five percent at an appropriate moment.[18] Hitler had never been to America and had met no Americans until Captain Smith and Hanfstaengl. It was a connection he was anxious to cultivate.

Shortly after their first meeting, Hitler invited Putzi as his "plus one" to the home of the fabulously wealthy Bechsteins, of piano fame, in Berlin. Aside from discussing Frau Bechstein's rock-like jewels, and her selling them to raise money for the NSDAP, Hitler told Putzi how much he had admired the British and American war propaganda. Of course, Putzi replied that the American methods of public relations made popular by the publicity expert Ivy Lee could readily be applied to Germany.* So, too, could American press methods, mass marketing, and direct mail. Hitler was intrigued.

The two men became close in the year that followed. Putzi taught Hitler what rhetoric was acceptable for which audiences, grooming Hitler in the niceties of polite society. Hitler had not yet become a fully fledged serial killer drunk on genocide. So Putzi took credit for making Hitler *salonfähig* ("housetrained," or more politely, presentable in a salon). Perhaps that was one reason why his proximity to Hitler in these early days was frowned upon by other Nazis. Party members despised Putzi as a clown and a dangerous influence on their leader. Their jealousy grew when they heard that Hitler had fled Munich for the safety of the Hanfstaengl country home at Uffing after the failed putsch, some seventy kilometers from the city. Two days later, Hitler gave himself up. He was tried and sentenced to five years in Landsberg prison, but only served 264 days of his sentence.

BEFORE 1923, FEW knew that in the murky recesses of Adolf Hitler's mind, he saw a secret order amid the disorder. The date of the founding of the Weimar Republic—November 9—was a humiliating cloak of dishonor that weighed Hitler down. He vowed to make that November day into *"der Tag"* or "the day" when *he* would transform disgrace into victory and lead the next German Reich. That is why he chose November 9 as the day for his beer hall putsch in Munich. It is why November 9 became the Nazi Party holiday during the years of the Third Reich. It is why Kristallnacht took place on November 9. But it would be another

---

* Hitler would later engage the services of Ivy Lee to help him create his international image as "a man of peace."

decade before Hitler would become chancellor of the Third Reich, coming to power on January 31, 1933. His message was simple: he would build prosperity, peace, and make Germany great again. All the people had to do was adhere to the *Führerprinzip*: one folk, one Reich, and one leader. And the leader must be obeyed, always.

The Alchemists

The Universe is full of magical things patiently waiting for our
wits to grow sharper.

— Eden Phillpotts, English author and
inspiration for Agatha Christie

To succeed in world domination, Hitler needed his alchemists, who
could magically create synthetic fuels to set Germany on the road to
economic self-sufficiency, also known as autarky. The international
chemical giant I.G. Farben (Interessen Gemeinschaft Farbenindustrie
Aktiengesellschaft)—creator of Zyklon-B, used in the Holocaust to murder millions—would become his scientific magician that made World
War II possible.

The foundations of I.G. Farben can be traced back to experiments for
the development of synthetic colors for textiles in the mid-nineteenth
century. By 1876, Germany had seventeen chemical factories set close to
the Rhine and its tributaries, surpassing Britain's six synthetic dyeworks
and France's five manufacturing plants. That same year, the whole of the
United States had a mere eleven graduate students in the field of organic
chemistry and no original discoveries.[1]

By 1914, the German chemical giants began competing with one another for the same markets and products. Friedrich Bayer and Company,
Kalle and Company, and Leopold and Cassella had been manufacturing organic chemicals in the northern Rhine town of Barmen. Another
company, then known as Messrs Meister, Lucius and Bruning, at the
nearby town Hoechst, was trading in pharmaceuticals. It soon adopted

the town's name for their company instead. The Aktiengesellschaft für Anilinfabrikation, or Company for Aniline Production, founded by Carl Martius and Paul Mendelssohn-Bartholdy (son of the Jewish composer), operated from Berlin in 1867. Today, it is known as Agfa. The company Badische Anilin & Soda Fabrik, which had been producing bottled coal gas for gas-lighting works, expanded its operations into a broader range of aniline products. It was more commonly known as BASF. It produced the colors madder red and alizarin red, making it wildly successful.[2]

By the outset of the Great War, Carl Bosch, a chemist and engineer, and Fritz Haber at BASF made the commercial breakthrough in synthesizing ammonia. Haber, a converted Jew, put on the airs of a German Junker, down to the shaved head and cheek marred by a dueling scar. He had risen through the ranks by his genius and problem-solving acumen to become a director at BASF but remained ashamed of his Jewish origins. Even before Hitler, being a Jew was rarely a passport to success.

But why was ammonia so important? Originally intended as a fertilizer, Bosch and Haber thought it was the solution to feed the world's growing population. In fact, both Haber and Bosch would receive the Nobel Prize for chemistry for their synthesizing Haber-Bosch process in 1918. It seems that the Nobel Prize panel forgot that on April 22, 1915, Haber and his gas troop, known as the Pionierkommando 36, were the first to unleash deadly chlorine gas (some 5,730 cylinders, each weighing 200 pounds) along the mile-long frontline at Ypres against French territorials and an Algerian division of the French army. The gas drifted into the Allied trenches, first blinding, then asphyxiating the French soldiers.[3*]

To SAY THAT the sciences had become politicized is an understatement, especially in the rhetoric between French and German scientists. France was still in the throes of the disruptive social divisions caused by the Dreyfus affair—known as *L'affaire* within France—which, for twelve long years, gave rise to virulent anti-Semitism as well as renewed

---

* Chlorine attacks the mucous membranes of the nose, mouth, and throat.

anti-German feeling.[4]* French physicist Pierre Dunhem famously denounced "Jewish physics" and especially the discoveries of Albert Einstein. "For a supporter of the principle of relativity to speak of a velocity greater than that of light," Dunhem wrote, "is to pronounce words bereft of sense."[5] Dunhem held to his beliefs and sank into oblivion.

Once the United States entered the war in 1917, all German companies had their American assets confiscated by the Office of the Alien Property Custodian. Versailles ensured that the German chemical industry would suffer major setbacks for unleashing biological warfare. Bayer's state-of-the-art manufacturing unit at Rensselaer, New York, was auctioned off to an American company. Manufacturing bases in France were forfeited. BASF found that some of its most valuable dye patents had been sold to France. Hoechst and Agfa had to hand over significant assets in dyes, medicines, and photographic technology. But a vengeful France wanted more.

The German companies had worked together during the war in the national interest, and so they turned collectively to Carl Bosch to find a solution. At the treaty negotiations, Bosch scaled the wall of the German delegation's quarters to meet secretly with his French counterpart. He proposed if the French dropped their demand that all of the major chemical plants in Germany be destroyed, the companies that had cooperated together, meaning the *Interessen Gemeinschaft* (community of interests), would share the technology behind the Haber-Bosch process *and* how to synthesize nitrates with the French.[6] The French almost bit off his hand to accept, and the German factories were saved.

FIVE YEARS LATER, on the afternoon of November 13, 1924, the leaders of these same chemical companies met to discuss a possible merger. Bosch put the case forward for a single unified corporation as the best foundation for their collective success. He persuaded others that a network

---

* In 1894, the Jewish French army captain Alfred Dreyfus had been accused and convicted of treason for selling French military secrets to the German embassy in Paris. The real culprit was a French army major called Ferdinand Walsin Esterházy, who was of Hungarian descent.

of local manufacturing units in other countries would overcome many problems and biases against German manufacture. Besides, he had a new product—a synthetic fuel—that he would be willing to share with those who joined in the merger. Bosch's finance director at BASF, Hermann Schmitz, who rose from poverty by virtue of his huge intellect, gave the assembled directors compelling statistics to take away with them about their collective influence and cost savings. It took just over a year for BASF, Bayer, Hoechst, Agfa, Weiler-ter-Meer, and Griesheim to sign the deal. The smaller firms of Kalle and Cassella remained legally separate but wholly owned subsidiaries of their new company: Interessen Gemeinschaft Farbenindustrie Aktiengesellschaft, or I.G. Farben.

Within the year, Bosch contacted Standard Oil of New Jersey, sending a deputation of executives to Standard's New York refineries. They hinted that I.G. Farben's Bergius process for refining residue-heavy oils and tars into premium liquid fuel products could make for an interesting cooperation between the two companies. In March 1926, Frank A. Howard, chief of the Standard Oil Development Company, came to Ludwigshafen to check out the claims for himself. He was stunned at what he saw and immediately sent a cable to Standard's president, Walter C. Teagle: "This matter is the most important which has ever faced the company. . . . [I.G. Farben] can make high-grade motor fuel from lignite and other low-quality coals in amounts up to half the weight of the coal. This means absolutely the independence of Europe in the matter of gasoline supply. Straight price competition is all that is left." Teagle, who was in Paris, rushed to Ludwigshafen. A cautious agreement was finally reached between the two giants in August 1927 that would allow Standard Oil access to the Bergius process for the United States. In addition, the two companies agreed to a joint research and development program, building a plant for this purpose in Louisiana.[7] It was the beginning of a dark business relationship.

By 1931, responding to the new challenges of world economic conditions, Bosch divided the conglomerate into three product divisions. Carl Krauch was responsible for all high-pressure hydrogenation chemistry in the Hitler era, meaning all products from synthetic nitrogen to coal mines and oil. Fritz ter Meer was responsible for the traditional pharmaceuticals, solvents, dyes, and other organic and inorganic chemicals.

Fritz Gajewski was responsible for explosives, specialized paper products, photographic equipment, artificial fibers, and cellophane.[8] Eventually, Hermann Schmitz would take over as head of I.G. Farben. Krauch,
ter Meer, Gajewski, and Schmitz all faced charges at Nuremberg after
World War II.

I.G. Farben became one of the largest corporations in the world before the Nazi era. It was Germany's largest contributor to foreign exchange, a crucial element to any thriving economy. Not only did I.G.
Farben become critical to the development of synthetic chemicals, but
it made Hitler's dreams of world domination possible. But before that,
it created close affiliations with American corporations and became a
quasi-governmental department under Hitler.

"Brideshead"

Where can we hide in fair weather, we orphans of the storm?
—Evelyn Waugh, *Brideshead Revisited*

Fascism was on the rise in Britain, too. Rotha Lintorn-Orman, a twenty-eight-year-old lesbian who had served as an ambulance driver during the Great War, returned to England decorated for bravery and unable to comprehend the world she found. She was shocked by repeated strikes in the workplace and was certain that the rise of the labor movement made Britain ripe for a socialist revolution. She, like so many others, felt her world had imploded. Would the British Empire go the way of the German, Austro-Hungarian, Ottoman, and Russian empires, she wondered?

In May 1923, Rotha's mother gave her fifty thousand pounds (approximately £2 million pounds or $2.44 million today) to defend Britain from the "Red Menace." Inspired by Mussolini, she set up the new British Fascisti Party in London and began recruiting like-minded souls. There was nothing treasonous about her move. After all, the Conservative press—*The Times*, *The Morning Post*, and *The Observer*—had all hailed Mussolini as a "Roman genius." Rotha's British fascistis were dedicated to the monarchy, the defeat of communism, and a love of uniforms.[1] Unusually, there were many more women than men on its Grand Council, too.

Indeed, Prime Minister Ramsay MacDonald, on the left of the political spectrum, wrote friendly letters to Mussolini; Austen Chamberlain (half-brother of the future prime minister Neville) exchanged photographs with Il Duce and joined him on family holidays; and Winston Churchill extolled Mussolini's virtues in his newspaper articles.[2] Italian fascism did not alarm or delight. Instead, it was greeted as an efficacious means to a higher standard of living, free from civil strife like the ten-day general strike experienced in Britain in 1926.

And so, from 1922, Britain watched agog as Mussolini's fascism empowered a willing Italian aristocracy, stopped industrial action, and gave his country back its pride of place among great nations. The regeneration of "Italian self-respect" made the British take notice of what was essentially an Italian phenomenon.[3] Some of those in power wondered aloud if the same could be done in Britain.

Nonetheless, British admiration for Mussolini's fascism was seen from afar. The repression of opposition parties, the assassination of the socialist politician Giacomo Matteotti, and the invasion of Corfu were known and commented upon, but not properly digested in public debate. Right-wing governments sprouting like mushrooms across the Continent were seen as bulwarks against the hated communism—the one ism that assuredly would dissolve private ownership and wealth.*

TAWDRY LEADERSHIP FAILED to address the economic, political, and class woes throughout the empire, too. That led to "democracy fatigue" for many powerful aristocrats, bankers, and industrialists. Some intellectuals were alarmed by the shift to the extremes of communism and fascism, but nothing, seemingly, could stop the polarization of the population.

The public was fed up with repeated scandals over the "sale of honours," the governing coalition's Irish and Indian policies, and the reluctance to allow new blood into the cabinet. Excluded from the inner circle, one of the young and foremost members of Parliament decided to fight the next election as an independent. His name was Sir Oswald "Tom" Mosley. Handsome, intelligent, financially independent, an inveterate and unrepentant womanizer, and a gifted orator, Mosley was married to Lady Cynthia "Cimmie" Mosley, the daughter of Lord Curzon and his

---

* Dictatorial governments proliferated in Hungary (1921), Italy (1922), Yugoslavia (1929), and Romania (1931). Salazar's 1932 dictatorship in Portugal (Britain's longest continuous ally) would be highly praised in Britain.

first wife, Mary Leiter—she of the Marshall Field's of Chicago fortune. In the November 1922 election, Mosley ran as an Independent to retain his seat at Harrow and won 66 percent of the vote. The following November, when Britain's first Labour prime minister was elected, Mosley still won 60 percent. Understanding he could only change things if he were prime minister, in March 1924 Mosley joined the Labour Party.[4] Eight years later, Mosley would form the British Union of Fascists with backing from the great British maverick press baron, Harold Harmsworth, 1st Lord Rothermere.

Like Mosley, many thought that Labour's James Ramsay MacDonald was "a wind-filled figurehead" and that the succession of national governments was "a morass of compromise." The Conservative leader Stanley Baldwin was portrayed as lazy, allowing government to "slummock along anyhow" and cultivating the uniquely "English complaint, an underworked brain."[5]

Lord Rothermere wholeheartedly endorsed Adolf Hitler before 1933 as a man of peace, waving away notions of Nazi violence as an exaggeration, a momentary aberration, or an internal German matter. By then, Princess Stephanie had become Rothermere's main conduit to Hitler. Other British aristocrats acted as Hitler's mouthpieces, hoping to stave off "the red terror" and another war, which many felt was a direct result of the overly harsh Treaty of Versailles.

Some went to plantations in Africa—most famously to the "White Highlands" of Kenya, like Lord William Scott (son of the Duke of Buccleuch) and Lord Erroll, the Marquis of Graham (later the 7th Duke of Montrose, portrayed by Charles Dance in the movie *White Mischief*). Others remained in Britain, like the deeply anti-Semitic Viscount Lymington (later the Earl of Portsmouth) and the Welsh 2nd Viscount Tredegar, who became infatuated with Princess Stephanie. The vast majority were essentially Conservative (Tory) voters and had been described in the *News Chronicle* as "Boiled-Shirt" fascists—or "fascist sympathisers who maintained a footing within conventional politics, even though they despised it." Above all, they hoped to "rejuvenate Conservatism, but kept open the extra-parliamentary alternative."[6]

David Freeman-Mitford, 2nd Baron Redesdale, made famous as "Uncle Matthew" in his daughter Nancy's books *Pursuit of Love* and

Love in a Cold Climate, was disillusioned, too. He became one of Hitler's outspoken aristocrats, promoting the führer in the House of Lords. That said, his was a slow and painful conversion; just as his seeing the light of day was sudden and shameful. He is also remembered as plain David Mitford—father of six of the most beautiful and independently minded girls of diverse opinion to grow up under one roof: Nancy, Diana, Pamela, Unity, Jessica, and Deborah. There was a son, too, named Tom. Only Diana (once she married her second husband, Sir Oswald "Tom" Mosley, leader of the British Union of Fascists) and Unity became propagandists for Hitler, though neither would ever see it that way in their lifetimes. In their eyes, Adolf Hitler was prevented from being a man of peace by wrongheaded leaders of France, Britain, and the United States.

UNTIL THE GREAT War, the relationship between the British aristocracy and the German nobility was strong. German princes and princesses and other high German nobility had long been sought as spouses of kings and queens in Britain; in the main because they, too, were Protestant. Queen Victoria's husband was the German Prince Albert, Duke of Saxe-Coburg and Gotha. The couple spoke German at home and taught their children the language alongside English.[7]

Late in her reign, Victoria masterminded the departure to Germany of her Eton-educated fifteen-year-old grandson, Charles, Duke of Albany, to assume her beloved Albert's German titles as part of her master plan to ensure European peace through "cousinhood" marriages. Charles became Carl Edouard, a good German. He fought in the Great War and was afterward stripped of his British titles and citizenship. Worse still for Carl, after 1918 the title of Duke of Saxe-Coburg and Gotha was no longer recognized in the Weimar Republic. It was hardly surprising that the ex-duke became embittered and an active aristocrat for Hitler. Understandably, the trials and tribulations of their German cousins were keenly felt by the British monarchy.

"All the princely families of Europe knew each other," HRH Prince Philip, Duke of Edinburgh, wrote to the historian Jonathan Petropoulos. "There is even a saying that if you were not descended from Queen Victoria or Christian IX of Denmark, you were not of 'Royal Blood.'" Prince

Philip was a descendant of both. The youngest of Prince Philip's four sisters, Princess Sophie of Greece and Denmark (at age sixteen), married the great-grandson of Queen Victoria, Prince Christoph of Hesse.

Philip attended Sophie's wedding at Kronberg on December 15, 1930.[8]* By March 1933, Prince Christoph von Hessen was an important cog in Hitler's Nazi research center (Forschungsamt), which gathered information on Nazi Germany's enemies. Christoph's older brother, Prince Philip, was "one of the few followers whom Hitler had always treated with deference and respect." He was married to Princess Mafalda, daughter of Victor Emmanuel III, king of Italy, who backed the fascist dictator Benito Mussolini.[9]

But the relationship between the royal houses of Germany and Britain was severed by the Great War. In 1917, King George V of Great Britain gave in to pressure to change the family name to Windsor from Saxe-Coburg-Gotha, disowning his grandfather Prince Albert's German roots. The English Battenburg branch was rechristened, too, as Mountbatten. Still more monumental changes were afoot. In 1918, through the League of Nations, the British Empire undertook the mandate burdens in Palestine, Africa, and Asia, replacing the Ottoman and German empires as temporary overlords. That said, much of the power and puff of the days of empire were gone.

THE WRETCHED SLAUGHTER of so many young aristocratic men irretrievably changed their postwar world.[†] With some two million men wounded, scarred for life, or suffering from post-traumatic stress disorder, tragic stories abounded. Eton College, where it is still reputed that future British government policy is made on its playing fields, posted its bronze plaque in memory of one thousand former students, all dead.

---

* It is worth noting, too, that Philip's mother was from the House of Battenburg: Princess Alice of Battenburg, who married Prince Andrea of Greece and Denmark.

† Six million men were mobilized from Great Britain alone. (Within the empire, some 8.9 million men were mobilized.) Around 11.5 percent of the British non-officer classes were killed, compared to 17 percent of officers. An additional two million men were wounded with over 150,000 missing in action (sources: Britannica.com and bbc .com/news/magazine-25776836).

The backbone of the British forces—privates, corporals, and sergeants—had suffered heavily, too. Survivors had changed their mindset. "Going into service" as manservants or housemaids fell out of fashion. Many tried their hand at running their own businesses, but most flocked to the cities. Finding gardeners, butlers, maids, cooks, and other servants for patrician homes became challenging.

Traditionalists, like the fictional hero Charles Ryder in Evelyn Waugh's *Brideshead Revisited*, felt that this modern world was built upon shifting sands, devoid of beauty and values that mattered. Ryder, speaking for Waugh, thought Britain's youth were "collaborationists who had given up the unequal struggle, all doubts resolved, all duty done, the undisputed heirs-at-law of a century of progress, enjoying the heritage at their ease."[10] Those who came of age in the 1920s became Waugh's "vile bodies," the "bright young things" enjoying a superficial modern life, decadent, unaware of the dangers in the shadows.

FEW EPITOMIZED THE superficial, modern, and decadent better than the heir to the throne. Born Edward Albert Christian George Andrew Patrick, of Saxe-Coburg and Gotha, on June 23, 1894, in Richmond, but known as David to family and friends, he was potentially the most dangerous admirer of Hitler. Entitlement, boredom, a nonanalytic mind, and a craving for everything modern were Edward's key drivers. Hang tradition, duty, loyalty, and particularly the Crown. His father, King George V, told Edward in 1919, "You must always remember your position and who you are." But Edward's problem remained: he did not know who that was.[11] Above all else, Edward was weighed down by the nearly unbearable burden that succeeding to the British throne represented.

Edward's relationship with his parents was not a happy one. His mother, Mary, Duchess of York, was born Princess Mary of Teck (part of the Kingdom of Württemberg in Germany) at Kensington Palace.* Sadly,

---

* Mary of Teck had been the fiancée of Prince Albert Victor, George's elder brother. Shortly after the engagement announcement, Albert Victor died of unknown causes during an influenza pandemic. In the interests of not allowing the perfect bride to go

Mary lacked most motherly instincts and was aloof even for a royal mother of the times. She thought Edward was rambunctious and rather plain looking (like herself). Worse, she could not fathom his perfectly normal inclination to ask awkward questions. The answers she gave were invariably unsatisfactory. Both parents were rigid and often treated the children as if they were toy sailors.

Edward's father had a cruel streak: his retribution was fearful, brutish, frequently mocking the offending child, and producing sheer terror. George V's visceral rage—in the main for minor offenses like wearing the wrong kilt or being tardy—were possibly behind the stammer that afflicted Edward's younger brother Bertie. A royal librarian summed up their childhoods: "The House of Hanover, like ducks, produce bad parents. They trample on their young." As Edward grew into adulthood, he became quite self-deprecating, yet chafed at authority. Still, he was conscious that he would be king one day and do the ordering.[12]

Edward's patchy education was most deficient when it came to English literature—in part, because he never read a book for pleasure. His knowledge of literature was lamentable, once asking his private secretary, Sir Alan "Tommy" Lascelles, if he had ever heard of "an extraordinary little book" called *Jane Eyre*.[13] When he went up to Oxford, Edward took no interest in his studies and left without obtaining his degree. He was quite simply a lazy thinker. Worse, he was well aware of his inadequacies.

WHEN WAR CAME in August 1914, the closeness between the British and German royal families remained one of the most searing and painful divisions for George V, Queen Mary, and their children. Hadn't they all forgathered for Edward VII's funeral in 1910? Edward could hardly believe that cousins like "Charlie," the Duke of Saxe-Coburg and Gotha, who had grown up in England, were now enemies of Great Britain. Then, too, the traditional fishing grounds for prospective British brides among the German aristocracy were now closed to the Crown.

---

begging elsewhere, Mary was persuaded to marry Albert Victor's younger brother George.

Still, that hardly mattered given Edward's propensity for women of American heritage who were already married. With the outbreak of war, special dispensation was made for Edward to serve in the Grenadier Guards (he was only five foot seven inches tall when the minimum requirement was six feet). Age twenty-two, his equerries decided it was high time that "the little man" lost his virginity and arranged for Edward's first sexual encounter with a prostitute called Paulette. Then came Marguerite Alibert, whose working name was Maggie Meller. Maggie was a courtesan in the best Parisian tradition, most noted for her flair as a dominatrix. As with all his women, Edward became besotted with Maggie, but the war intervened. So he wrote her letters instead. Indiscreet letters. Letters that openly criticized the conduct of the war. Letters that would have caused real damage to the Allies if they fell into German hands. He mocked his father in them to Maggie, a courtesan whom he had known for a mere three days.

With the war's end, Maggie became geographically and socially undesirable, and Edward began his first long-term love affair with Freda Dudley Ward,* the wife of a Liberal politician. Maggie, not one bit amused at being dumped, reminded him that she still had his love letters with "all those foolish, indiscreet comments about the conduct of the war, insulting abuse about his father" and intimated he would have to pay dearly for their return. He called Maggie's letter "a real stinker."

The official story claims Edward asked for his letters back and Maggie complied. The truth is rather different. In despair, he wrote to his equerry, "How I curse myself now, tho' if only I can square this case it will be the last one, as she's the <u>only</u> pol I've really written to. . . . I'm afraid she's the £100,000 or nothing type, tho' I must say I'm disappointed and didn't think she'd turn nasty."[14] It hadn't dawned on him that Maggie was no lady. She held onto the letters and used them to blackmail Edward should she ever need to. That need arose when she shot and murdered her Egyptian husband in their Savoy Hotel suite in

---

* Born Winifred May Birkin, her mother was the American Claire Lloyd Birkin (née Howe). Freda's husband divorced her on the grounds of adultery in 1931, two years after her affair with Edward had ended. Naturally, Edward was not mentioned as the corespondent.

London in 1923. Edward was whisked out of the country by his household when Maggie's case came up in court. Apparently, she blackmailed Edward for help. Despite the overwhelming evidence against her, an acquittal was duly awarded, and the prince's letters were returned and burned.[15]

The former viceroy of India and foreign secretary George Marquess Curzon of Kedleston wrote to his wife just before Maggie's trial in September 1923: "The French girl who shot her so-called Egyptian prince in London and is going to be tried for murder, is the fancy woman who was in the Prince's 'keep' in Paris during the war. . . . It is fortunate that he is off to Canada and his name is to be kept out."[16]

Nonetheless, Edward's sex life (and love life) remained a concern. As "the cuckoo in the nest" of other households for years to come as well as heir to the throne, he was hardly the royal to lead a nation in political, economic, and moral decline by example.

Duplicitous Émigrés

Gott schütze Deutschland. (God protect Germany.)
—Joachim von Ribbentrop's last words,
October 16, 1946

The repayment of Germany's war debt in foreign currency and the country's civil unrest gave rise to its terrible 1923 hyperinflation. Many former soldiers of aristocratic pretentions fled to Switzerland, which remained reasonably unaffected by the war. Others were more adventurous, seeking their fortunes in America. Such was the case with Heinz Spanknoebel, who settled in Detroit and became the *Landesgruppen leiter* of the Auslands Organization (AO) of the Nazi Party.* Spanknoebel's choice of Detroit was no accident. He wanted to be near Henry Ford and his *Dearborn Independent*, soaking up the right-wing anti-Semitic rhetoric so dear to Mr. Ford's heart.

In 1923, Ford was waging a long-running war against a Jewish lawyer who had created the National Council of Farmer's Cooperative Marketing Associations. The *Dearborn Independent*'s series of articles titled "How the 'Jewish Question' Touches the Farm" claimed that the "Jew is not an agriculturalist" and is only interested in "land that produces gold from the mine, and land that produces rent." Ford's newspaper printed

---

* The AO was the foreign ministry of the Nazi Party, as opposed to the government's foreign ministry and its network of consulates and embassies. It was only one of many Nazi Party organs that shadowed government departments, adding to the confusion in the chain of command.

his articles prophesizing the invasion of the Jews as quoted from *The Protocols of the Learned Elders of Zion*'s sixth protocol: "We shall soon begin to establish huge monopolies, colossal reservoirs of wealth, upon which even the big Gentile properties will be dependent. . . . [W]e will mask it by a pretended effort to serve the working classes."[1] Ford knew the document was a fake but printed it anyway. The inflammatory words rang out as a battle cry to Spanknoebel's ears.

Spanknoebel returned to Germany to serve under Rudolf Hess. He coordinated all local German groups in America into a national movement "that could serve as an advertisement" for the Nazi regime's objectives. There were other immigrant "Spanknoebels" in America who had served in the Freikorps in the 1920s and backed Hitler's beer hall putsch. Most settled in the largest twenty cities across the United States. Ribbentrop's brother-in-law, Hans-Heinrich Dieckhoff, oversaw Spanknoebel's activities during the Nazi era while serving as the German ambassador to Washington between 1937 and 1938.[2]

New York's German American communities provided cover for another aristocratic German émigré in 1924: Nikolaus Adolf Fritz von Ritter. Ritter was born into a minor aristocratic family from Rheydt in North Rhine–Westphalia and had a superior air of entitlement about him. In 1923, when hyperinflation hit, Ritter was the superintendent of a textile firm in East Prussia and decided to immigrate to New York just as the exchange rate of one mark to the dollar was in the trillions. He had already become an ardent Nazi. By the time Ritter married Aurora Evans, a Titian-haired, Alabama-born schoolteacher, in 1926, Ritter was also addicted to New York's high life.

But it was Ritter's smile that most people remembered. "Even when angry he smiles," Ritter's self-confessed German spy, Vera Erickson, told the British secret service. He had irregular teeth, with one tooth on the upper left side of his mouth protruding to force his upper lip over the gum whenever he laughed or spoke emphatically.[3] At some point during Nazi rule, he had the offending tooth capped in gold. But by then no one knew him as Ritter any longer. He went under the pseudonyms of Dr. Rheinhardt, Dr. Rantzau, Dr. Renken, Mr. Richards, Dr. Hansen, or Mr. von Jorgensen. By then, too, he was running the Abwehr's spy networks in both Great Britain and the United States. Those who disliked

him called him Fatty, a nickname he shared with his friend Hermann
Göring.

As the Weimar years progressed, I.G. Farben spread its wings, too,
with its own duplicitous émigrés. It supported only those political parties friendly to capitalism and its business. A little-known offshoot of
I.G. Farben based in New York City was established as its "research
center." It was labeled in internal documents as a "Committee on Political Economics," gleaning intelligence on American businesses. By
1929, under the auspices of Max Ilgner, a main I.G. board signatory and
whose uncle was I.G.'s leader, Hermann Schmitz, the New York company began "to furnish information regarding financial and industrial
conditions in the United States."[4]

Back in Germany, Carl Bosch's pet project, the synthesizing of fuel
at the I.G. Leuna plant, was soaking up huge amounts of capital—some
161 million marks by 1929. Given the depression caused by the 1929
Wall Street crash and the fact that banks like Morgan were clamoring
for repayment of their loans (fruitlessly), Bosch was faced with the
threat that the Leuna plant might close or require a government subsidy.

Instead, that November, Schmitz made Standard Oil an incredible
offer. In exchange for 2 percent of Standard's stock, which had a cash
value of around $35 million, I.G. ceded all rights to its fuel hydrogena-
tion technology outside Germany. A joint venture company, Standard-
I.G., 80 percent of which was owned by the Americans, was set up to
exploit the patents and know-how of I.G. on an equal basis arising from
any future research and discoveries. Standard's Walter Teagle had a seat
on the board of I.G.'s new subsidiary, the American I.G. Chemical Company.[5] Using Standard's stock as collateral, it became simple for American I.G. to raise $30 million through bond issues, with the Morgan
investment bank as the lead issuer.

Bosch, ever wary of the global political situation, instituted safe-
guards for its overseas businesses—just in case. All of I.G.'s assets in the
United States would belong to a Swiss holding company, and I.G. Farben would never appear on any paperwork. Why? It made I.G. bomb-
proof in the event of another default on German reparations. It would

also be impossible to confiscate its assets (including its several thousand patents) in the event of another war.[6] Wall Street was aware of the subterfuge.

When Max Ilgner returned to Germany in 1929, he left his brother Rudolf in charge of the New York City research committee, which was incorporated less than a year later on October 23, 1930, as U. S. & Transatlantic Service Corporation.[7] With the new and solid links to both Standard Oil and the House of Morgan, I.G.'s main task, to engage in industrial espionage, was made easy. The winds of change were already blowing by 1930, with Germany facing a worldwide depression and its Center Party leaning ever closer to the right. German President Hindenburg would have to make difficult choices in the few years ahead.

America and the Finance Wizards

Life is essentially a cheat.

—F. Scott Fitzgerald

American "aristocrats" were fashioned from inherited wealth or political entitlement rather than noble birth. Since the rise of the American robber barons in the nineteenth century—Vanderbilt, Carnegie, Rockefeller, Astor, and Morgan to name a few—the term "aristocrat" had become the common currency for someone with oodles of money. By the 1920s, Europe, too, was compelled to accept "aristocrats" as those having power or money rather than a noble heritage. There remained, however, a certain hankering for an elevation of one's station in life, giving birth to the *Social Register*. Anyone whose name appeared in that bible of high society was an American blue blood. America's patrician immigrants were compelled to make way for the new generation of robber-baron railroad men, new industrialists, muckraking publishers, and Wall Street traders. What you *had* was more important than who you *were*.

Nonetheless, most Americans lived rural lives or were drawn together in small towns, as depicted by Sinclair Lewis in his satirical novels about the parochial small-mindedness of middle America, *Main Street* (1920) and *Babbitt* (1922).* His novel *Arrowsmith* (1925) showed how that same middle America misunderstood and mistaught the burgeoning world of

---

* Lewis was married to Dorothy Thompson between 1929 and 1942. He received the Nobel Prize for literature in 1930.

science; while his *Elmer Gantry* (1927) satirized the traveling medicine men who still haunted middle America by selling quack medicines for easy money using quotes from the Bible to fleece their unsuspecting clients. This majority was far removed from America's "aristocracy."

Captains of American industry and finance in the 1930s like the inventor of the assembly line, Henry Ford; Thomas J. Watson of IBM; Alfred P. Sloan, chief executive officer of General Motors; James Mooney, of General Motors Overseas; and Prescott Bush (father and grandfather of the Bush presidents), of Brown Brothers Harriman & Company, were all, in one form or another, paid-up members of the American "aristocrats" who supported Adolf Hitler. Unwittingly, other internationalists like Thomas Lamont of J.P. Morgan facilitated Hitler's rise. Patriotic Americans like Charles A. Lindbergh and Joseph P. Kennedy joined their ranks before Britain declared war against Germany in September 1939. Both Lindbergh and Kennedy would recant—too late—after the attack on Pearl Harbor.

America's aristocrats effectively ran the country's economy and were intimately tied to banking. Living in city mansions and country estates, they saw financial opportunity in the defeated nations of Europe. In the main, they were Yankee bankers and industry moguls.

American banking was largely unregulated, often engaging with their industrial clients in corporate subterfuge to attract unwitting investors and telling scandalous lies about perceived commercial enemies, particularly if they were Jewish or Catholic (in that order).

THEY PROVIDED KNOWLEDGE of foreign countries alongside American embassies, too. Where Europe feared another war in the 1920s, America was determined to reap the peace dividend by lending heavily to rebuild the continent. In addition, the United States held fast to the ideal of staying out of any future European conflict. No doughboys would die on foreign soil ever again. Paradoxically, the Versailles financial bailout and the Wall Street crash of 1929 would help Hitler to power.

American exports to the Allies during the Great War raised the U.S. economy out of the doldrums while providing "credits" for purchases of war materiel from the American arms companies Remington and

Winchester. By the war's end, the Allies recognized peace could endure only if they contributed heavily to Germany's reconstruction. However, the British pound was weak. France was hell-bent on revenge and in no position to contribute. Montagu Norman, the dapper, rule-bending, and secretive governor of the Bank of England, turned to the United States for a solution.

Norman had fond memories of his time in Germany studying music and was a former schoolmate of the equally secretive investment banker Edward "Teddy" Grenfell, of Morgan Grenfell in London.* Tall and slender, sporting a Van Dyck goatee, often wearing his wide-brimmed hat redolent of Rembrandt's *The Sampling Officials*, Norman looked more like a courtier of Stuart kings than a twentieth-century financial wizard. And like any wizard, he kept the secrets of his office behind an opaque veneer. Few suspected he would become one of Hitler's cherished aristocrats. By inveigling his friends at Morgan Grenfell to spearhead new German loans while also cozying up to Hjalmar Schacht of the Reichsbank, Norman believed he best served his sole mistress—that Old Lady of Threadneedle Street—the Bank of England. Through his magical sleight of hand, he wielded his power throughout the 1920s and 1930s, making London the main trading center for all foreign exchange.

IN EARLY 1924, Norman warned the Morgan Bank that the occupation of the Ruhr by the French had created a "black spot" that would "ignite another war" if the bank did not back the plan to halt German hyperinflation. But Jack Morgan was vehemently anti-German. Like Norman, he was also anti-Semitic. When Schacht issued the new *Rentenmark*† to stop hyperinflation in November 1923, Schacht persuaded the Allies that his plan would fail without the "prestige and moral endorsement of

---

* Norman began his career at the Anglo-American investment bank of Brown Shipley and Company. After Norman left, the bank was redubbed Brown Brothers Harriman & Company of New York.
† A mark backed by gross domestic product rather than gold.

the Morgan bank." Jack Morgan had to swallow hard to become a supporter of the country he so disliked.

Eventually, Morgan weighed in as the lead banker for the $110 million U.S. portion of the German loan, making Germany the largest sovereign borrower of American money for the entire decade. The public offering was backed by mighty American companies like Ford, General Motors, E.I. du Pont, General Electric, Standard Oil of New Jersey, and Dow Chemical. Through the genius of Schacht's economic management and additional foreign investments in new manufacturing plants, the German economy was revived.[1] Still, the underlying political weakness of Weimar became permanent. The financial wizards—Hjalmar Schacht, Jack Morgan, Tom Lamont, Montagu Norman, and the British chancellor of the exchequer, Philip Snowden—feared that, despite their best efforts, their plan for Germany was failing.[2]*

At the same time, Hitler raised his rallying cry that foreign economic aid came "from the Jewish bankers." Hitler ranted how these foreign "Jews" were making Germany subservient to their own cause. "International Jewish world finance needed these lures to enable it to carry out its long-desired plan for destroying Germany which thus far did not submit to its widespread super-state control of finance and economics," Hitler wrote.[3]

There was no basis whatsoever for Hitler's statement. American Jewish firms—led first and foremost by Jacob Schiff's Kuhn, Loeb and Goldman Sachs—were excluded from the fundraising due to Jack Morgan's anti-Semitic views. In fact, during the interwar period, Jewish banks were systematically discriminated against by Yankee bankers due to widespread anti-Semitism.[4] So much for Hitler's *Weltanschauung,* or "philosophy of life," about the Jews betraying Germany. Hitler's "*Wahnsystem,* or capacity for self-delusion," British ambassador to Germany, Sir Nevile Henderson, wrote in 1940, "was a regular part of his technique. It helped him to both work up his own passions and to make his people

---

* Philip Snowden was often lampooned in the press by Churchill as a "spiteful, vindictive Death's-head . . . [and] sworn tormentor who used the Rack, the Thumbscrew and the Little Ease of taxation with gusto."

believe anything that he might think good for them."[5] It was all part of
the big lie.

BY 1929, ANOTHER rescue plan had to be devised urgently for Germany
or the world banking community would collapse. Owen D. Young, the
former chairman of General Electric and founder of Radio Corporation
of America (RCA), led the second reparations conference in June 1929.
Tom Lamont of Morgan was his shadow. It was the end of the decade
of the "rugged individualist"—that Wild West show of greed and triumphalist economic trade without regulations and precious few laws to
protect the small investor from corporate lies. And yet this was the decade when the United States became *the* world economic powerhouse,
supplanting the British Empire.

Between the talks and the implementation of the Young Plan, the
1929 Wall Street crash occurred. Most hadn't recognized the causes,
even in its long aftermath. Rampant prosperity had gone to everyone's
head, some said. Philosophies abounded about the valuable lessons to
be learned as some stockbrokers threw themselves out of their office
windows to their deaths. The Christmas bonuses of all Morgan partners
had been $1 million at the end of 1928, so they could afford to be stoic
and philosophical, despite the company's losses. Each new expression
that prosperity was just around the corner had become monotonous
as the market continued to slide. By April 1930, the remorseless pain
and suffering became almost too great to bear. Only Adolf Hitler was
smiling.

Why? In May 1928 Hitler's NSDAP had only won 2.6 percent of the
vote, giving them a paltry twelve seats in the Reichstag. In the aftermath of the Wall Street crash, the Nazis held 107 seats, or 18.3 percent
of parliamentary members. Weimar's chancellor, Heinrich Bruening,
had to contend with a Nazi Party out for communist blood, both in the
Reichstag and on the streets, compelling him to convene the German
parliament as little as possible and to rule by emergency decree. Carl
Bosch of I.G. Farben had become highly influential and was behind one
such emergency decree, raising German duties on oil imports by 70
percent as well as blocking imports of nitrogenous fertilizers. By 1931,

Bosch dictated economic policy in the final six months of Bruening's cabinet. During the intensifying chaos caused by the crash of 1929—only five years after Germany's hyperinflation—Hitler's relentless propaganda finally paid off.

As HITLER ROSE inexorably to power, former New York governor Franklin D. Roosevelt ran for president in 1932, promising a "new deal for the American people" that included regulations for Wall Street. The New Deal made enemies of the Yankee bankers, whom Roosevelt had biblically labeled "the money changers." They should not be allowed back into the temple unless they mended their ways, he said. But President Hoover beat him to the punch and opened the Pecora hearings to investigate. Ferdinand Pecora, a swarthy, tough Sicilian immigrant lawyer with flashing black eyes, stupendous salt-and-pepper pompadour, and a mind like a steel trap, became the bankers' nemesis.

The House of Morgan's "preferred list" came under Pecora's scrutiny and was made public. The names on the list were a litany of "friends" to whom Morgan sold stocks at rates far below market prices. These "good, sound straight fellows," according to Jack Morgan, could buy shares at a discount of up to 30 percent of the current market prices and sell them sixty days later for huge profits.

Morgan's preferred list raised unthinkable questions. National heroes like General John J. Pershing and Charles A. Lindbergh caused consternation, as well as the names of Democrats Owen D. Young (of General Electric and the Young Plan to bail out Germany); former secretary of war Newton D. Baker; former chairman of the War Industries Board and financier Bernard Baruch; the son-in-law of President Wilson, Senator William G. McAdoo;* former President Calvin Coolidge; former solicitor general and ambassador to the Court of St. James's John W. Davis; Norman H. Davis, President Wilson's main financial adviser for the Treaty of Versailles. The list read like a who's who of national politics.

---

* Senator William McAdoo was embarrassed because he was also a former secretary of the treasury under President Wilson (March 6, 1913–December 15, 1918) and sat on the Pecora committee.

Among the industrial giants implicated were Myron Taylor, of U.S. Steel; Walter Teagle, of Standard Oil of New Jersey; Walter Gifford, of AT&T; Sosthenes Behn, of ITT; and last, but certainly not least, John J. Raskob, builder of the Empire State Building,* chairman of the 1928 Democratic National Committee, vice president of finance at U.S. industrial giants DuPont and General Motors until 1928, and then current board member of DuPont. Publicly shaming such powerful individuals who had *not* acted illegally but who were guilty of gross moral and ethical misconduct became the challenge.[6]

The Pecora hearings were an anathema to all the men on the Morgan list and almost all Wall Streeters (with the notable exception of Joseph P. Kennedy). The hearings shone a spotlight on the good names of Wall Street from Morgan's to National City Bank and on to Chase, and the view from the public's gallery showed them to be seedy. Pecora lifted the veil on practices that should have been illegal but were not. New laws needed to be passed, and Pecora would head the team to write the Securities Act of 1933, requiring investors to receive all significant financial and other information relevant to the sale of stocks and to prohibit "deceit, misrepresentations, and other fraud in the sale of securities."[7] Kennedy, against Pecora's wishes, became the first Securities and Exchange Commissioner.

Back when he had been assistant secretary of the Treasury, Morgan partner Russell C. Leffingwell had known Roosevelt, who was then the assistant secretary of the navy in the Great War. Since Leffingwell knew the president personally, he dashed off memos to other Morgan partners, citing how Roosevelt, having gone to Groton and Harvard, was cut from the same cloth as them, and he went into some detail about the pride the president felt in his old New York Dutch roots. "All that is the background of the man who is a peril to American institutions," Leffingwell had mockingly written, "according to Hoover the foreign mining engineer." Morgan Bank then privately campaigned to slip Leffingwell into the post of secretary of the Treasury, just to ensure Roosevelt would

---

* It was mocked during the Great Depression as the "Empty State Building" due to its few tenants.

remain financially sound from a Wall Street viewpoint.* But Roosevelt was against tying himself to the bankers, especially ones from Morgan.[8]

The squalid ethics of Wall Streeters had been laid bare by Ferdinand Pecora. One by one, the mighty lions of Wall Street were exposed for their corruption and manipulation of the markets. Unabashed, many of those from Morgan's "preferred list" joined the ranks of Hitler's aristocrats in one way or another.

---

* William H. Woodin was Roosevelt's first secretary of the Treasury, serving from March 4, 1933, to December 31, 1933, resigning on the grounds of ill health. Henry Morgenthau Jr. became secretary of the Treasury on January 1, 1934, and remained in his post until July 31, 1945, having been reappointed by President Truman after Roosevelt's death (source: home.treasury.gov/about/history/prior-secretaries).

The Gambler and Propagandist

They will make you their king.
—Princess Stephanie to Lord Rothermere

At some point in 1923, Princess Stephanie traded her apartment in Vienna for one at 45 Avenue George V, just off the Champs-Élysées in Paris. She had been making her way by the kindness of friends—like Solly Joel, the "Ace of Diamonds" and cohort of her uncle Robert—and aristocratic acquaintances from the Hungarian Esterhazys to equally impecunious Russian royals like Grand Duke Dmitri (once the lover of Coco Chanel). Stephanie "Riviera-ed" in the winter among maharajas, kings, queens, princesses, and American millionaires, oblivious to the old guard's sense of foreboding that its world was invaded by ungrammared men and their loud wives, whose only positive attribute was money.[1] No one knew yet that she was a paid propagandist for the highest bidder.

By the mid-1920s, she had perfected the art of selling inside information, be it through Solly Joel's investments or political patronage. What was gossip to most was a treasure trove of fairy dust in her hands. At the gaming tables, she was mad keen on chemin de fer and baccarat, winning spectacularly and losing in greater measure. And it was in the casino in 1927 that she targeted Britain's leading press baron, Harold Harmsworth, Lord Rothermere. He was "a fabulous plunger at the casino tables," Stephanie said, often choosing his bets on a whim.[2] Both were mavericks and opportunists and were destined to rub along together to mutual advantage for over ten years. Both denied any amorous liaison, but Rothermere did write telegrams to Stephanie with greetings like, "I miss your smile, girlie."[3]

In her unpublished memoir, Stephanie recounted how she found Rothermere rather depressed one day at the Monte Carlo Sporting Club. Apparently, he was dispirited because there was no good news story for him to sink his teeth into as an editorial for his newspapers.[4] Even so, the *Daily Mail* was not noted for its groundbreaking investigative journalism. It reveled in the realm of ultraconservative opinion and trusted *The Times* as a daily or *The Observer* as a Sunday paper to lead on insightful news.

Nonetheless, Stephanie claimed she had the cure. Rothermere's eyes lit up, and he invited Stephanie to lunch the next day at La Dragonnière, his villa perfumed by its two acres of orange groves overlooking the Mediterranean Sea at Cap Martin. There they could discuss the matter away from prying ears. Stephanie felt it was more of an interrogation and thought his questions bordered on rudeness. Rothermere, however, immediately understood that he had been gifted an angle to *the* story that may help restore the Hungarian monarchy. He saw a way for his pro-monarchist worldview to help defuse the powder keg that was brewing in Central and Eastern Europe.

What had happened to the once great Austro-Hungarian Empire that straddled so many countries, Rothermere asked Stephanie? She answered fully. Even before the days of Béla Kun and the White Terror, Hungary had been treated as a poor relation, she said. Why had it been broken up into some twelve little states that were new to democracy and powerless against a strong Germany? Essentially, because it suited France. And why was Hungary singled out to lose over 70 percent of its territory under the Treaty of Trianon that the Americans had insisted on signing separately?* She replied with one word: influence. Why were the Kingdom of Romania; the Kingdom of Serbs, Croats, and Slovenes (later Yugoslavia); and the First Austrian Republic the main

---

* The United States never ratified the Treaty of Versailles because the "French treaty," as the Senate called it, made the United States subject to the League of Nations. The Treaty of Trianon was signed directly between most of the Allies (including the United States) and the Kingdom of Hungary and was essential to obtaining reconstruction finance from the United States.

beneficiaries of the land grab from Hungary? Impatient, Rothermere bellowed for his secretary to get him a map of Hungary.[5]

Stephanie passionately urged Rothermere, a man with the power of the great British press behind him, to begin a campaign to right the wrongs done to her new homeland. She had targeted her man well. Rothermere had been listening to this man everyone was talking about—Adolf Hitler—who had called for a restoration of the Hohenzollern monarchy in Germany. Why not a return of the Habsburg kings in Austria and Hungary, too, Rothermere wondered?

Stephanie implored Rothermere to go to Hungary and speak to the people. She could arrange for him to meet whomever he wanted. And the Hungarians, she said, "will make you their king." The casual phrase, which Stephanie equated to giving him the keys to the city, was "misinterpreted" by Rothermere.[6]

THAT SPRING, ROTHERMERE spent a brief time in Hungary, meeting its power brokers as Stephanie had arranged. He never seemed to have considered that Stephanie was most likely working as an agent for the Hungarian regent admiral Miklós Horthy* or the Habsburg princes—all of whom would back Adolf Hitler. Rothermere was "erratic, a creature of rapidly changing moods, able to back his idlest impulses with his millions," she wrote, "and perfectly ruthless in carrying out any scheme that might bring him journalistic fame or personal prestige."[7]

Against this background, Rothermere undertook two Stephanie-inspired editorials in the *Daily Mail*, the first in June 1927, the second in August that same year. In the first article, entitled "Hungary's Place in the Sun?" Rothermere prophetically wrote: "Eastern Europe is strewn with Alsace-Lorraines. By severing from France the twin provinces . . . the Treaty of Frankfurt in 1871 made another European war inevitable." In fact, "the same blunder has been committed on a larger scale in the peace treaties which divided up the old Austro-Hungarian Empire

---

* As a kingdom without a king, Horthy's title was "regent," but like a king, it was he who appointed the prime minister to run the government. (See appendix III.)

[with] dissatisfied minorities in half a dozen parts of Central Europe, any one of which may be the starting point of another conflagration."[8]

The British government was aghast. British readers were enthralled and took up the cudgels of fair play for the Hungarian underdog. The French were apoplectic with rage. The Hungarians were jubilant. Rothermere was thrilled. In the weeks that followed, over two thousand letters of support arrived each day at the *Daily Mail*. In all, several hundred thousand letters were cataloged by staff specially hired to cope with the postal deluge. Several deputations arrived in London from the most remote parts of Hungary to thank the press baron.

Rothermere's second article appeared in August, to the dismay of the British government. That November, twenty-five bound volumes several inches thick and two feet in height were presented to Rothermere containing the signatures of 1.25 million Hungarians scrawled on parchment in thanks for his support. On his birthday in April 1928, truckloads of gifts—anything from wine or local produce to gilt swords studded with precious gems—arrived from a grateful Hungarian people. Then came the zinger. A Hungarian journalist suggested that perhaps the great British lord would be prepared to accept the vacant throne of his country?[9] Stephanie would always believe that Rothermere took the offer seriously.

When the Hungarian parliament passed a resolution in 1928 to express the thanks of its people, Rothermere decided to send his strikingly tall, dark, and handsome son Esmond to Hungary instead. Of course, the idea of a British king of Hungary—even an elected one by popular acclaim—was preposterous. Ever the dutiful son, Esmond left London on May 13, 1928, to receive the gratitude of the entire nation. Prime Minister Baldwin wrote with derision to his chancellor of the exchequer, Winston Churchill, "What a fool Rothermere is allowing his boy to make of himself in Hungary! They haven't a ray of humour between them."[10]

Baldwin viewed Esmond and Rothermere with derision. Had he seen the film of Esmond's visit in Hungary, he may have felt quite differently. Twenty-eight trains were needed to carry the officials who planned to watch Esmond receiving the honorary doctorate at Szeged University. The crowds welcoming him were tremendous. All talk of "kingship" ended in secret between Esmond and his father on his return. Stephanie's first mission to ensnare Rothermere proved a resounding success. For an arch-manipulator, gambler, and propagandist, there was nothing quite so delicious as having a press baron—who was also a gambler and propagandist—tucked neatly in her beaded handbag. Together they became a propaganda force to be reckoned with, promoting first the stability of the former Austria-Hungary and then Adolf Hitler's Third Reich.

PART II

A TAPESTRY OF LIES

In war-time, truth is so precious that she should
always be attended by a bodyguard of lies.

—Winston Churchill

Hope and Renewal

An oppressed nation will not be able to spend on its own welfare . . . but must sacrifice [its fruits] on the altar of exactions and
of tribute.

—Adolf Hitler to industrialists in Düsseldorf,
January 27, 1932

Adolf Hitler had always intended for there to be a war of annihilation.
How else could he eradicate the race problem that so consumed him?
How else could he be rid of the communist threat? How else could he
eliminate the alleged superiority of the British Empire, the French Empire, and the United States—the very Allied forces that had defeated
imperial Germany? To succeed, however, Hitler needed his lies to be
believed.

To be voted into power, Hitler had to dissemble. He had to claim he
was a man of peace who sought to reclaim Germany's rightful place on
the first rung of the world's nations. But what about the street violence,
some asked? That was the communists, Hitler replied. The Jews? Were
they all communists? Ah. Hitler had claimed, too, that the Jews ran Germany's culture and the economy. He ducked the issue, instead lowering
the tone to basic prejudice. It was a facile and brilliant subterfuge that
played well with his anti-Semitic and anticommunist following. As part
of the same master plan, Hitler also adopted policies he never intended
to enact, the most significant being restoration of the Hohenzollern
monarchy.

It was good business to pretend to reinstate the disgruntled *Edel,* or "elders," of Germany's imperial past. The lie was far more compelling than the truth. In fact, Hitler had a full bag of tricks to placate Germany's traditional elite. Paul von Hindenburg, Weimar's octogenarian president since 1925, was from a minor aristocratic landholding family. He was also the general who led the imperial army and represented Germany's old guard. Yet after the 1930 election, even Hindenburg was inclined to embrace Hitler for his stance on the Hohenzollerns. Surely, that was a good sign, many reflected. By then, too, most aristocrats had learned to ignore Hitler's jibes about the aristocracy's limited intelligence and indolence, as he had written in *Mein Kampf*. They believed Hitler would reinstate them to power.

The idea of embracing the old ruling families, however, was not solely Hitler's brainchild. "Many of the titled officers in the affiliated patriotic [right-wing] organizations professed dual loyalties," Putzi Hanfstaengl wrote later. "[Bavarian] Crown Prince Rupprecht used to be referred to quite frequently as 'His Majesty,' and a proportion of the *Kampfbund* [fighting league] membership was distinctly monarchist. So much so that for many years Hitler let it be understood that he intended to restore monarchical forms of government."[1] It was sweet music played for the benefit of an aristocracy that had been discarded. Hitler saw that their aristocratic international networks had remained intact, despite their power base within Germany having been destroyed. He was determined to use them to his advantage for propaganda and the creation of a "listening post" at the heart of foreign governments.

That said, Hitler "the revolutionary" would never have been able to penetrate the closed world of the *Edel* without the help of Hermann Göring. Raised in the castle of Göring's godfather, Hermann von Epenstein, who was a wealthy converted Jew, physician, and businessman, young Göring led what can only be described as a privileged but bizarre childhood. His mother was Epenstein's mistress for some fifteen years, and his father lived with them, albeit in an annex. Epenstein supported all five of the Göring children but had a special place in his heart for young Hermann. When Epenstein died, he left the castle to Hermann, leading many to believe that he was Epenstein's son.

Göring exerted his magnetic charm well and enjoyed his role as the Nazification leader of the German aristocracy. Prince August Wilhelm, or "Auwi," the ex-kaiser's fourth son and an ardent Nazi, introduced Göring to his cousin, Prince Philipp of Hesse, and Philipp's younger brother, Christoph.[2]* Prince Philipp was pleased to exchange views with Göring, the Great War flying ace, who was now a rising star at the Reichstag. Both fervently believed that the aristocracy had an active role to play in the wealth and health of the nation.

The Nazi Party was extremely well organized. With German precision, Hitler and his associates built up an intricate party structure that mimicked the government's. Intelligence was passed back to Hitler's leadership from the grassroots level by relatively few people. The party's political arm had a separate organization divided into two groups. The first undermined and attacked the government. It also tracked foreign affairs and the Reich press office. The second created a state within a state. It mainly concentrated on agriculture, justice, the national economy, and labor. It also disseminated the propaganda division's literature and arranged for speakers regarding race, culture, and advancement of technology.[3] Hitler was consciously forming a state framework to implement when he became chancellor.

UNDOUBTEDLY, THE 1929 Wall Street crash helped Hitler. International lenders were clamoring for repayments of their foreign loans, further destabilizing Germany. For businesses trading with Germany, the situation bordered again on disaster. Chancellor Bruening's deflationary economic policy had made the poorest in society angry. Hunger and privation had set in again.† Much of the discord and mayhem was fueled by the Nazis, of course. Hitler directed the Nazi violence at the political opposition through an increasingly uncontrollable SA. Their political assassins were

---

* Carl Edouard had been an early convert to Nazism, inviting Hitler to Coburg for "German Day" in October 1922. He was a generation older than the Hesse brothers and Göring.
† This policy was in the interest of protecting I.G. Farben's foreign exchange earnings, which were substantial and helpful to the Bruening government. Hermann Warmbold, the economy minister and I.G. employee assigned to the government, was solely interested in protecting I.G.

sent onto the streets to disrupt the smooth working of the government and society.[4]

A few days after the September 14, 1930, elections, Harvard-educated Putzi von Hanfstaengl received a telephone call from deputy führer Rudolf Hess asking to meet. Half an hour later, Hitler and Hess were seated in Putzi's library. "Hanfstaengl," Hitler interrupted as Putzi tried to congratulate him on the result, "I want you to take over the foreign press department. You know England and America." Putzi was to awaken the foreign press to "what we are trying to accomplish."[5] Naturally, Hanfstaengl was thrilled to be at the center of Nazi power, but then warned Hitler to temper his flair for sowing mayhem, affirming that street violence would not read well in the foreign press. Hitler merely shrugged and shook his head, denying any responsibility.

IN JANUARY 1931 the Nazi Party opened its headquarters at Palais Barlow on the Brienner Strasse in Munich, mainly with funds from Fritz Thyssen. It was renamed the Braun Haus; decorated with pseudoclassical pomposity, brown eagles, and neo-mythical Nazi heraldry; and draped with vast Nazi flags. There, Putzi had a small office on the third floor, adjacent to the former chicken farmer, Heinrich Himmler. The small, humorless Himmler was responsible for creating Hitler's special bodyguard unit, known as the Schutzstaffel, better known as the SS.[6] From the moment they donned their black uniforms, similar to—but more stylish than—Mussolini's *fascisti*, the SS swore an oath of loyalty to Hitler personally. Hitler did not care if they had been "pimps, murderers, homosexuals, alcoholics or blackmailers." Despite calls from Hitler's ideologues Alfred Rosenberg and General Ludendorff to throw the undesirables out of the party, Hitler refused. Such men would always be useful.[7]

Hanfstaengl's international network of friends was huge—and growing. He had become the boon companion to the English-speaking press corps in Berlin, too. Not only was he affable, but he also talked freely about Hitler's plans, making Hanfstaengl a sought-after commodity. "Big, dark, blessed with a cultured New England mother, subjected to American society at an early age," the Berlin correspondent for the *Chicago Daily News*,* Edgar Mowrer, wrote, Putzi "should have been Nazi-proof." Mowrer was unaware that Putzi held many Nazi views and was extremely anti-Semitic.

HANFSTAENGL SET UP Hitler's first foreign press conference, asking Louis P. Lochner, the diminutive, bespectacled, balding raconteur chief of the Associated Press in Berlin, to meet Hitler at the Kaiserhof Hotel later that same day. Lochner naturally agreed. But Lochner's tête-à-tête was in fact a news conference with a few dozen journalists eagerly waiting. Putzi had briefed Hitler thoroughly on topics of greatest interest to them and led the "impromptu" press conference with the first question. "A few hours later," Lochner recalled, "the world press was full of snappy, pithy, direct quotations from the man who had hitherto been regarded as a crack-brain and political amok-runner." At a stroke, Putzi had made Hitler an international leader of significance.

Next, Hanfstaengl approached William Randolph Hearst, who had been friends with his New England mother and done business with his German father.[8] Hearst was an isolationist who didn't like New York Governor Franklin D. Roosevelt and hoped *any* democratic candidate other than FDR would be selected for America's 1932 presidential election. Hearst reveled in politics and had already encouraged other foreign leaders to write their personal stories for his American papers. Benito Mussolini and his Jewish mistress, Margherita Sarfatti, were among the first.

Hanfstaengl did not have a hard sell. Hearst, too, believed Hitler would be the next German chancellor. So Hearst gave Hanfstaengl the go-ahead for a series of articles—the first to appear on September 28 in the United States, just two weeks after the German election—earning

---

* The editor of the *Chicago Daily News* was internationalist Frank Knox, who ran for vice president with Alf Landon in the presidential campaign of 1936 against Franklin Roosevelt. Knox had served under Theodore Roosevelt's command as a "Rough Rider" in Cuba at the Battle of San Juan Hill and would later become President Franklin D. Roosevelt's secretary of the navy from July 1940 to April 1944.

Hanfstaengl a juicy 30 percent of Hitler's fee. It was entitled ADOLF HIT-
LER'S OWN STORY: HE TELLS WHAT IS THE MATTER WITH GERMANY AND
HOW HE PROPOSES TO REMEDY IT.

Then Putzi's former lover Djuna Barnes contacted him, asking to
interview Hitler in October 1931. Hitler wanted to be paid two dollars
a word, and she couldn't find a publisher at that price. Still, there were
dozens of other newspaper owners and magazines prepared to pay Hitler's fee, often as much as three thousand dollars for a thousand-word
article.

Dorothy Thompson would succeed where Djuna Barnes failed. Of
course, Thompson had tried to interview Hitler immediately after the beer
hall putsch of 1923, then again after his release in early 1924, but Hitler had
remained "lofty and remote from all foreigners."[9] In the meantime, she
had done her research and plowed through *Mein Kampf*—calling it "eight
hundred pages of Gothic script, pathetic gestures, inaccurate German,
and unlimited self-satisfaction." Her grasp of German was excellent, and
she understood that Hitler was not only attacking "the dollar-chasers,
the money-grubbers, the profiteers" but, incredibly, that "Hitler's movement was going to *vote* dictatorship in! [. . .] Imagine a would-be dictator setting out *to persuade a sovereign people to vote away their rights.*"[10]

Thompson's article appeared in April 1932, three months before the
German elections would make the NSDAP the second largest political
party. She had been immediately struck by "the startling insignificance
of this man who has set the world agog. He is formless, almost faceless,
a man whose countenance is a caricature. . . . He is the very prototype
of the Little Man."[11] She was horrified by the xenophobia in Berlin, writing that "Unless things change radically, there will be a war in Europe
within the decade." Thompson believed that Adolf Hitler, that "awkward
Austrian," the "perverter of Nietzsche," and "the champion of the blond
beast" (that is, the mythical Aryan), would start it.[12] If only the world's
leaders had her insight.

HANFSTAENGL CONTINUED TO deal with all the big press barons in Britain and America. He remained aloof, yet part of Joseph Goebbels's circle.
Soon enough, he would learn it was a dangerous position to maintain.

Goebbels, Hitler's most devoted acolyte and master of propaganda, would later become Reichsminister for Propaganda and Enlightenment within Germany. He would not tolerate any competition.

Goebbels was attracted to Nazism in 1922 through his anti-internationalist and racist beliefs. In March 1924, Goebbels wrote in his diary that "The Jewish spirit of decay is most terribly effective in German art and science, in theatre, music, literature, in schools and in the press."[13] Goebbels, like Hitler, believed he was destined to change Jewish influence in Germany's culture forever.

Paul Joseph Goebbels was five feet four inches tall, swarthy, and thin and had a club foot, neurotic personality, and quick and dark intellect. He had been a loner before becoming enthused with cultural politics. Goebbels was an admirer of Henry Ford's polemic, *The International Jew*, based on *The Protocols of the Elders of Zion*, which proclaimed that there had been a conspiracy among Jewish "elders" in the late nineteenth century to achieve world domination. Although *The Protocols* had been published in Russia in the early twentieth century, it only appeared in German in 1920 and became an instant bestseller.

"I believe that The Protocols of the Elders of Zion are a forgery," Goebbels wrote in his diary in 1924, "not because of its worldview or the Jewish aspirations outlined therein as these are too fantastical. It lays out a systematic plan to destroy the world and leave nothing but ruins behind." He then added, "I do not believe that the Jews are so boundlessly idiotic that they would have not kept such important protocols a secret."[14]

Like Hitler, Goebbels had a well-polished oratory style. His every gesture was calculated to reach a crescendo at the right moment, whipping the crowd into a frenzy. His profound baritone voice was pleasing but shocking in a man of such a small stature. Often, his audience became enraptured by his alternating between a heartfelt tone and confrontational caricature of his opponents.[15]

IT WAS GOEBBELS who advocated a more radical course for Hitler at this juncture. He masterminded the Jewish New Year "demonstration"—billed as "direct action"—which took place September 12, 1931, on Berlin's main thoroughfare, Kurfürstendamm. Over a thousand SA men dressed up as civilians jostled, abused, and generally roughed up any passersby whom they deemed Jewish. Twenty-seven SA thugs were tried and sent to prison. Goebbels was outraged and telephoned Reich Chancellor Bruening to complain about the severity meted out to the agitators.

He threatened Bruening that the Center Party backed the Nazis in finding "the sentences intolerable." Moreover, the Center Party joined the Nazis in its strong "condemnation of the red terror," intimating that Jews walking to and from their synagogues were all communists plotting the government's demise. Bruening backed down, announcing that neither Goebbels's Berlin paper *Der Angriff* ("The Attack") should be banned nor that the leader of the Kurfürstendamm "demonstration," Count Wolf-Heinrich von Helldorf, should be punished. Helldorf only received a six-month suspended sentence and a hundred-mark fine.[16]

IN THE TWO years before seizing power, Hitler had moderated his tone, understanding Hanfstaengl's advice that he needed to appeal to the foreign press by toning down his racial policy. Hitler also had to placate Mussolini about the borders of South Tyrol, which had a large German population, too. Lebensraum was still advocated, but now directed toward the east. Any war or seizure of western territory was aimed solely at France: "If Satan were to come today and offer himself as an ally against France," Hitler said, "I would give him my hand."[17]

Privately, Hitler hadn't changed. He had written his second book in 1928, but it was decided by his friend and publisher, Max Amann, to "refrain from publication." *Mein Kampf*'s national sales had trickled to a mere 3,015 copies by 1929, and any new book would detract from future sales. More important, at a time when the Nazi Party needed funds from industrialists to fight on in the next national election—the very people Hitler lambasted in the second book—publication was impracticable.[18] Besides, with Göring's guidance, Hitler believed he could convert all the major industrialists to the Nazi cause.[19] The party needed their commitment and money to be elected.

· · ·

THIS WAS THE background to the meeting of industrialists attended in Düsseldorf by six hundred members of the German Industrieklub on January 27, 1932. An Englishman, Ernest Tennant—the only foreigner present—was a middle-aged investment banker by profession and an industrialist by inclination. His business interests in steel extended from Britain to Norway, Sweden, Germany, and the United States. By 1931, Tennant's German agent for his Swedish steel partner, Superfosfat, was Eugen Lehnkering—a former flying officer from the German imperial air force. Together, Tennant and Lehnkering traveled through the Ruhr, visiting steelworks in Lehnkering's shiny new car.

Of course, Tennant hadn't realized that those who displayed wealth were reviled until they were hounded by mobs "shaking their fists and shouting 'Schieber, Schieber!'" ("Profiteer, profiteer!"). On more than one occasion, they were shot at.[20] By September 1931, unemployment in Germany had risen by 400 percent, to 4,350,000, and would rise by another million souls by September 1932.[21]

Lehnkering, a Nazi supporter, led Tennant to believe that these demonstrations were all led by communists, for whom any self-respecting capitalist like Tennant had acquired a strong distaste. Tennant's experiences in Germany, however, were not isolated communist-inspired incidents. Just days after the September 14, 1930, elections, when the NSDAP polled 6.5 million votes and gained their 107 (of 577) seats in the Reichstag, Nazi mobs smashed windows on one of Berlin's fashionable main streets, Unter den Linden.[22]

Fritz Thyssen attended the fateful meeting at the German Industrieklub that January and, like Tennant, thought Hitler's speech was thought-provoking. "We will never forget that the German people waged wars of religion for 150 years with prodigious devotion, that hundreds of thousands of men once left their plot of land, their property, and their belongings simply for an ideal, simply for a conviction," Hitler asserted. "If the whole German nation today had the same faith in its vocation as these hundreds of thousands, if the whole nation possessed this idealism, Germany would stand in the eyes of the world otherwise than she stands now!"

At this point, the speech was punctuated by loud applause. Hitler waited for it to die down. "Our situation in the world . . . is but the result of our own underestimation of German strength," he said, gazing at the nodding heads and calls of "very true." He had won over the audience. "Only when we have once more changed this fatal undervaluation of ourselves can Germany take advantage of the political possibilities which, if we look far enough into the future, can place German life once more upon a natural and secure basis." Then he concluded, "and that means either new living space [Lebensraum] and the development of a great internal market or protection of German economic life against the outside world and utilization of all the concentrated strength of Germany."[23]

Although Gustav Krupp von Bohlen und Halbach was not present,* Hitler knew the Krupp representatives in the room, and believed they were swayed by his arguments. Hitler also knew that Krupp had been developing new armaments throughout the 1920s in secret and that his designers had returned to Essen in March 1926, when the Allied Control Commission left the city. There was no doubt that Hitler was appealing to Krupp's sense of *Wehrfreiheit* (freedom to make war), and the speech was intended to win Krupp over to the Nazi cause.[24]

"In order to realize this end, I founded the National Socialist movement thirteen years ago," Hitler said. It was the National Socialist aim to create a legacy of hope and renewal "intolerant of anyone who sins against the nation and its interests, intolerant of anyone who will not acknowledge its vital interests or who opposes them, intolerant of and pitiless towards anyone who shall attempt once more to destroy or undermine this body politic."[25] Tennant was carried away by the long, tumultuous applause and cheers. Afterward, Fritz Thyssen took Tennant to the club room for a drink. They discussed the speech, and Thyssen said, "Hitler would become Germany's Cromwell."

On his return to London, Tennant sent a recap of the conference to a friend in the Foreign Office. It was a detailed report, citing "thousands of spectators" in the streets hoping to see Hitler. Tennant was quite clear that Hitler, if in power, would repudiate the "War Debts or Reparation

---

* On marrying Bertha von Krupp, Kaiser Wilhelm changed Gustav von Bohlen und Halbach's last name to Krupp von Bohlen und Halbach.

Debts," which Hitler called "Tribute Debts," and refuse to recognize the limitations imposed on Germany by the Treaty of Versailles.[26]

But Tennant had missed the main point: Hitler had conveyed an air of hope and renewal through a future war—and another war was feared by Britain. Yet, foreign minister Joseph Austen Chamberlain believed that he had his hand firmly on the tiller of foreign policy and hoped France would gradually abandon its *cordon sanitaire* around Germany.[27]*

By the time Hitler made his Düsseldorf speech in 1932, Britain, like America, faced widespread unemployment, a financial depression, and old and tired leadership. The May 1929 general election saw Labour's James Ramsay MacDonald again as the prime minister of a minority government, with the uninspiring Philip Snowden as his chancellor of the exchequer. Snowden steadfastly refused to allow deficit spending, despite the growing Great Depression. Then, too, Snowden ignored Sir Oswald Mosley's plan to grapple with unemployment. Mosley was gifted and intelligent. Many thought he was the "coming man."

---

* The *cordon sanitaire* was the French way of isolating Germany after the war of 1914–18 through a network of alliances like the Little Entente and included the march into the Ruhr by French and Belgian troops in 1923.

Winds of Change

It is an appalling inheritance which we are taking over.
— Adolf Hitler, proclamation to the German people,
February 1, 1933

On February 25, 1932, Hitler became a German citizen automatically when he was selected as the minister of the interior of the state of Brunswick. Finally, he could run against Hindenburg for the presidency. Chancellor Bruening, of course, backed the octogenarian president, urging voters to cast their ballot for Hindenburg "So Germany May Live." On March 11, Goebbels wrote in his diary, "Deep uneasiness is rife everywhere. The word 'Putsch' haunts the air."[1]

The New York Times reported in its front-page headline: "GERMAN ELECTION IN DOUBT ON EVE OF THE VOTE TODAY; DISCONTENT AIDS RADICALS—REPUBLIC IS IN BALANCE—OPPONENTS OF HINDENBURG SEEK TO OVERTHROW DEMOCRATIC RULE—ALL OF EUROPE IS WORRIED." The article pointed out, "You have on the one hand, the inherent saneness, stolidity and patriotism of the German people; on the other you have an enormous discontent affecting literally every class in the community. Present conditions cannot continue; there must be a change."[2] After heavy polling on March 13, 1932, Hitler came second behind Hindenburg, with 30.1 percent of the vote. A runoff election was scheduled for April 10.

The British radical conservative newspaper *Truth* (secretly owned by the high-ranking civil servant Sir Joseph Ball) called all the candidates for the presidency in Germany—formerly thought to be "a nation of thinkers"—"stupid enough even to satisfy the English distrust of brains." Hitler was an iconoclast, and *Truth* ripped into every fiber of his campaign. "He is a National Socialist, but his Nationalism is the Nationalism of the Jingo, and his Socialism the Socialism of envy. As an anti-Semite he satisfies the resentment of the dispossessed, who depend on the old order and cannot find their level in the new, simply because he gives them a scapegoat for that resentment."[3]

"In Paris the consensus of opinion is that had Hitler been elected there would have been an end to a feeling of security in France and Europe," the *Nottingham Journal and Express* quoted. In the opinion of the French journalists, "the cure for Hitlerism cannot be found at the polls." Interjecting its own British bias, the articles added that Hitler has "taken advantage of circumstances. He has practiced upon the nerves of a people driven to distraction—almost to despair—by the terribly depressed condition of the country. . . . We all congratulate Germany today on the sound sense displayed by the people who voted against Hitler but we must offer more than congratulations."[4] Most British people were likeminded: Germany had been brought low in the 1920s by war reparations and could founder again in the worldwide depression precipitated by Wall Street.

Conversely, the former prime minister David Lloyd George spoke for most British aristocrats and parliamentarians when he said that "Hitler represented 'a bulwark against Bolshevism.'" J. L. Garvin, the editor of *The Observer*, owned by Waldorf Astor, was compelled to lean as far to the right as he possibly could as a result of his and Astor's distaste for the left.[5]

What few aristocrats realized was that Oswald Mosley's earlier visit to Italy accompanied by Harold Nicolson and the former MP Bill Allen (heir to the W. H. Allen publishing company) inspired Mosley's shutting down his New Party in April 1933 to become a fascist. Mosley's wife, Cimmie, was hostile to her husband's search for a fresh political strategy among Mussolini's fascists. "If he gets entangled with the boys' brigade," Nicolson warned her, "he will be edged gradually into becoming a revolutionary."[6] Politically, Nicolson would abandon his friend Mosley shortly afterward.

. . .

BEFORE THE GERMAN runoff election took place, the threat of Nazi violence was palpable. The NSDAP waved away blockades and street fighting as separate "maneuvers" to protect Berliners against insurgent communists. The rumors of an insurrection tied to the runoff enabled the Berlin and Prussian police to search offices where both the SA and SS units congregated. They were looking for—and found—documentary evidence of a putsch.

A bite-size article in *Le Matin* in Paris reported Hitler's manifesto was seized in the police raids on his Berlin and Prussian offices. If Hitler did not win the election, the Nazi document stated, "all shock chiefs are to order their men to remain quiet and avoid provoking members of the Opposition parties." At the time, Hitler's "shock troops" were estimated at 520,000 armed men (the German army was still limited to 100,000), who could be deployed anywhere in Germany within forty-eight hours. The Nazi document concluded, "In the course of 1932, Hitler would certainly assume power; if not legally, then methods of force will have to be employed."[7]

Neither Goebbels's innovative propaganda machine nor the leaked Nazi manifesto affected the runoffs significantly. Hindenburg had only been a few hundred thousand votes short of an outright win in the first election and comfortably sailed over the finishing line. Hitler had campaigned by air—a first for any presidential race in the world—reaching mass audiences in three or four far-off locations a day. It was hailed by the Nazis as "a triumphal progress, proof of Hitler's closeness to the people." The subliminal message was Hitler was modern, embracing new technologies. Hindenburg was a tired octogenarian.[8]

BY THE SPRING of 1932, some Americans of German descent felt the need to interpret their new hero, Adolf Hitler, to the American public. On March 27, in seven cities across the United States—Chicago, Detroit, New York, Rochester, Philadelphia, Cleveland, and Milwaukee—a campaign to "Teach America of Hitler" was declared by the "independent" Teutonia organization.* Their leader admitted that, like the Nazis, some of their monthly meetings had become "riotous affairs," but only because "Communists and anarchists tried to break them up."

There were a few in the United States, however, who knew better. On March 22, J. K. Jenny, a consultant to the foreign relations department of the chemical giant DuPont, reported to headquarters in Wilmington, Delaware, "It is a matter of common gossip in Germany that I.G. is financing Hitler. Other German firms who are supposed to be doing so are Krupp and Thyssen."[9] Jenny was right about I.G. Farben and Thyssen, although Gustav Krupp had not yet leapt into Hitler's arms. Bertha Krupp—who really owned the company and had the money—was against Hitler as long as he held to a socialist agenda.

As the German runoff elections slated for April 10 approached, nerves everywhere became jangled. Foreign exchanges were jittery, stock prices volatile, and "the German Reichsbank's weekly report—which is closely watched in this period of uncertainty—was negatively favorable."[10] Schacht knew what to report, and what to leave out. He had resigned as Reichsbank president in 1930 in protest of the Young Plan for the rescheduling of German debt and began talks with Göring that same year on how best to assume power. Certainly, he was in a privileged position regarding the long-term goals of the NSDAP. Mrs. Schacht duly donned a diamond-studded swastika pin when entertaining or at private gatherings, leaving no doubt about the Schachts' allegiance.

Dr. Schacht understood Hitler had little understanding of economics and threw all his efforts into extending Hitler's range of financial supporters. Schacht was instrumental in garnering funds for the Nazi Party and became the calm international banker's voice persuading his financial and industrialist friends to back Hitler. At the time of the 1932 elections, Schacht said to Hitler, "Your movement is carried internally by so strong a truth and necessity that victory cannot elude you long."[11]

---

* Founded in 1924 with a membership of thousands of German American U.S. citizens, Teutonia had one thousand members in Chicago alone, according to its leader, Fred Grissibl.

• • •

ONE OF HINDENBURG'S first moves after the April election was to sign
a decree (*Verbot*), tabled by General Groener, banning the SA.* Its
leader, Ernst Röhm, was furious, urging Hitler to act immediately. Instead, Hitler asked Göring to put out feelers among their aristocratic
supporters and was told "by a well-known lady who is a close friend
of General Kurt von Schleicher," the cabinet member and political rival of Hitler's, that Schleicher did not approve of the ban and wished
to resign. It had been known for some while that the general wanted
the SA militias to be attached to the German army, something that
Hitler vehemently opposed. In the circumstances, Hitler decided to
wait and see.

On April 28, Schleicher met Hitler to invite him into the cabinet.[12]
On May 8, Goebbels wrote in his diary, "Everything goes well, Bruening will fall in a few days. The President will withdraw his confidence
in him."[13] Goebbels was slightly optimistic. For over a year, Bruening
had ruled the country by presidential decree and without the consent of
parliament. With Schleicher whispering poison into Hindenburg's ear,
Goebbels hoped it was only a matter of time before Bruening would be
summoned. On Sunday, May 29, Bruening was sent for and asked to
resign after a presidential harangue.

Bruening "had relied too much upon his superiority over his opponents," French ambassador André François-Poncet wrote later. "He
had underestimated their tenacity, their boldness, their astuteness, their
lack of scruple. He had proved better able than any other Chancellor of
the Reich to find favor abroad, principally among Anglo-Saxons; yet he
remained a poor psychologist."[14]

Bruening's demise sounded the death knell for German democracy.
On that same Sunday, the Nazis won an absolute majority in the local
Berlin diet elections. The following day, Hindenburg met with Hitler,
offering to lift the ban on the SA, a presidential cabinet of Hindenburg's

---

* The SS were merely viewed as Hitler's bodyguard corps at the time, so they were
not banned.

own choosing, and dissolution of the Reichstag if Hitler would back the government. Hitler agreed.

HINDENBURG CHOSE FRANZ von Papen as his next chancellor on June 1—a man who was not even a member of the Reichstag. "Papen enjoyed the peculiarity of being taken seriously by neither his friends nor enemies," François-Poncet tittered in his memoir. Papen had been expelled from the United States in 1917 for spying while serving as the German military attaché. Although he sat in the Prussian state Landtag, he was never asked to speak on its behalf. A Center Party member, he leaned quite far to the right, but the right wing of the party viewed him with "aversion and mistrust. . . . He was reputed to be superficial, blundering, untrue, ambitious, vain, crafty, and an intriguer; his sole asset lay in a certain self-possession and in a winning, almost unconscious daring."[15]

Papen's supporter, General Schleicher, viewed democracy as a hindrance to military power and was determined to use Papen as his pawn to lever the politicization of the Reichswehr (German army). He dreamed of a sociomilitary state that would rob the Nazis of their fellow travelers.

The Papen cabinet was immediately nicknamed the "Barons' Cabinet," with Baron Constantin von Neurath as its minister of foreign affairs.* The German newspapers and public derided Papen's choices. In short order, Papen proved he was incapable of dealing with the international problems facing Germany, and foreign journalists dined out with descriptions of his incompetence. It was evident Papen had no idea how to stop the Nazi-dominated Prussian Landtag from revolt.

Then, three days after taking the job, Papen dissolved the Reichstag and slated new elections for July 31. On June 15, he idiotically lifted the ban on the SA, and a storm of violence broke out in the streets. "In Prussia alone," American journalist William L. Shirer wrote, "between June 1 and 20 there were 461 pitched battles in the streets which cost eighty-two lives and seriously wounded four hundred men."[16]

---

* Once Hitler came to power, Neurath and his fellow noblemen would linger on in the cabinet as useful pawns to help control the German aristocracy.

The Nazi Party won 230 seats, or 37 percent of the vote. The communists were reduced to a mere 11 seats, with foreign analysts equating the rise of Hitler with the death of communism in Germany. The Nazis were the largest party in the Reichstag but still lacked an overall majority, even when combined with the German nationalists. Goebbels, Göring, and of course Hitler opted for a policy of obstruction. On August 30, Hermann Göring was elected as president of the Reichstag by 367 votes, supported by the Catholic vote. Promising loyalty and thanking his fellow members, he was able to set in motion the Nazi end game. Göring obstructed any and all hindrances, thereby providing the chaos upon which the Nazis feasted. Dissolution of the Reichstag was imminent.

On November 6, voters went to the polls yet again to choose a new Reichstag. The country suffered from election fatigue and lack of action to help Germany's nearly seven million unemployed. The Nazis lost thirty-five seats and two million voters. The communists gained eleven new seats, and the German nationalists, fourteen. Hitler had to ask himself if he had already peaked as a potential leader. Nonetheless, within days he turned Papen's victory into defeat by steadfastly refusing to join a Papen government. To Goebbels, it seemed like brinksmanship.

The elections played havoc with the party's coffers, too. The SA thugs alone cost over two million marks a week. When Thyssen declared he would make no further contributions to the Nazis since they were losing ground, Goebbels despaired, writing on December 8, "We are all very discouraged, particularly in the face of the present danger that the entire party may collapse and all our work be in vain."[17]

GUSTAV KRUPP, SEEING the rise in Communist seats, decided at long last to join his fellow industrialists to support the Nazis. He, like all capitalists, was shaken to the core by the Communist Party's gains. The time had come to act. At the behest of the "tycoons," a draft letter was prepared, throwing weight behind Hitler "to combat Bolshevism." It became known as the *Industrielleingabe* (industrial petition), and was given to Baron Kurt von Schröder, the rabid Nazi banker friend of Dr. Schacht, to collect the bankers' and industrialists' signatures. With all the important business leaders backing it, the letter was sent to the president's secretary on November 28.

It categorically stated that exclusion from politics of "the Communist Party, whose attitude is negative to the state" must take place with immediate effect. "Entrusting the leader of the largest national group with the responsible leadership of a presidential cabinet . . . will eliminate the blemishes and mistakes with which any mass movement is perforce affected; it will incite millions of people, who today are still standing apart, to a positive attitude." In other words, hang democracy, and pick Hitler or else.[18]

Unknown to the tycoons, Hindenburg had offered Hitler the chancellorship, albeit with strings attached, four days before the letter was delivered. Hitler refused. General Schleicher, still believing he held the whip hand, went on national radio promising "a planned economy with price controls, an end to wage cuts, and the confiscation of Junker estates for the peasants."[19] It was unmitigated stupidity. Schleicher thought he could woo the unions, confiscate more aristocratic lands, and control money from the Ruhr industrialists. As a result, Schleicher was dismissed on January 28, and Adolf Hitler was sworn in two days later as Germany's chancellor.

Charade

On the surface an intelligible lie; underneath, the unintelligible truth.

—Milan Kundera,
The Unbearable Lightness of Being

On January 9, 1933, the French weekly *La revue hebdomadaire* and the daily *Aux écoutes* reported Princess Stephanie had been arrested at her Biarritz apartment for espionage. The article said she had inspired several pro-Hitler articles in France, and allegedly had been paid ninety million French francs. But Stephanie was never charged. According to her memoir, she was not in France at the time, having accepted an invitation to travel to New York "on an ocean liner" the previous December.[1]* The question is: Why were the French authorities unable or unwilling to prosecute? Had Stephanie been protected by powerful French Nazi sympathizers? In the following nine months, other articles would appear in the French press, calling Stephanie the "operetta princess," the princess "in the service of Hitler's Germany," or simply "undesirable."[2]

Although Stephanie would always deny the charges, there is a strong ring of truth to the French allegations.[3] She claimed she had given up her Biarritz apartment in 1932. Could it have been because her uncle Robert's associate and diamond millionaire Solly Joel had died in May 1931, and that it wasn't her flat to give up? Possibly. After all, her vast apartment on Avenue George V belonged to the British shipping and

---

* See appendix III.

insurance tycoon Sir William Garthwaite, but the princess called it her official home between 1923 and 1932.*

LORD ROTHERMERE HAD hired Stephanie as his "special correspondent" in July 1932, and he was certainly paying her. Later, Stephanie explained how Rothermere lectured her about politics then, recalling how "he was banging his right fist into his left palm, emphasizing again and again that *now* was the moment for action, that it was *now* that the restoration of the monarchies should be brought about, that it was now and only now that a powerful rampart against Bolshevism could be erected in Germany."[4]

In fact, the princess had undertaken three assignments that year for Rothermere. The first was in August, when Stephanie delivered Rothermere's "unconditional support" to the ex-kaiser. She told him that the British press baron wanted to place "all the Rothermere newspapers at his [the ex-kaiser's] disposal and convince him of the vital necessity of issuing a pronouncement without delay." The ex-kaiser did not take the bait, nor did he categorically refuse it.

Her second assignment was to visit Steenokkerzeel in Belgium, where the former empress Zita, widow of the last Habsburg emperor of Hungary, Charles IV, resided. There, Rothermere's message was couched as a question. "In view of the present happenings in Germany, which in my deliberate opinion, will have the result of reestablishing the Hohenzollerns on the throne of Germany," Rothermere began, "do you not think that now is the opportune time to put forward the suggestion that one of the Habsburg princes should succeed to the throne of Hungary?" Rothermere's apparent choice was Zita's son, Crown Prince Otto.[5] The empress's lady-in-waiting, Countess Victoria Mensdorff, met Stephanie, but it is unclear if Stephanie ever met Zita.[6]

And so Stephanie traveled on to Budapest to meet with Admiral Horthy and Prime Minister Gyula Gömbös at the end of October.

---

* I wrote several times (by email and letter) and telephoned the heirs of Sir William Garthwaite, but they declined to respond to my queries about Sir William's relationship with Stephanie.

Rothermere's reply to Gömbös's cryptic November letter of thanks provides the greatest insight into his meddling in European affairs.[7] "Do not worry too much about the claims of Hungary's foreign creditors, even to the extent of paying pengöes* [*sic*] to their credit into a 'blocked account,'" Rothermere advised. "In these days, when richer nations are obliged to suspend the service of their foreign debts, I see no reason why mutilated and impoverished Hungary should be '*plus royaliste que le roi*.'"[8]

CONVERSELY, IT IS highly unlikely that Rothermere was paying Stephanie to foment discontent or promote Hitler in France. He would not have wanted to stick his head above the parapet in a foreign country where he had his "getaway" home, La Dragonnière, at Cap Martin. That said, Stephanie had attracted the attention of both the British and French secret service bureaus when embroiling Rothermere in the restoration of the Hapsburg monarchy in 1927. The secret services knew about her missions to the kaiser, Empress Zita, and Gömbös and assumed that she was making trouble for the French-inspired Little Entente. If they had got some of their facts wrong, they were not wholly incorrect.

Apparently, too, Prince Ferdinand Lichtenstein, who lived in Vienna, had offered Stephanie 300,000 pounds payable in thirds—with one-third up front—if she could entice Rothermere to take up the cause for the revision of the Versailles Treaty's Polish corridor.[9] The French Deuxième Bureau unraveled the plot through a letter and other incriminating evidence left in Stephanie's safe in the Biarritz apartment. Nevertheless, the French delayed notifying the British secret services for five years.[10†]

If Rothermere hadn't been involved in Lichtenstein's plan, it is unclear how Stephanie had wheedled any money from the prince. However, someone was paying her to whisper sweet nothings about the restoration of the monarchies in France. If not Rothermere, then who? The most likely French candidates were Jean Luchaire, the right-wing journalist

---

* The Hungarian currency.
† See appendix III.

and publisher of *Notre temps*, or Otto Abetz, a German former drawing instructor and girls' school art teacher, or both. Either way, the cash payment would have come through Putzi Hanfstaengl as chief of the foreign press office.

Luchaire was already accepting money from the Nazis to infiltrate the highest social and political echelons of French society, making him a prime contact for Stephanie. As a survivor, she may have sought to re-create a French-style relationship with Luchaire *à la* Rothermere. For her, two paymasters were always better than one. But Luchaire, unlike Rothermere, needed money, and got it from the Nazis. He was also widely known as financially corrupt. Still, Luchaire was a leader in the "rejuvenation" of the right-wing movement in France and right-wing youth movements across Europe.[11] Her good friend and fourth son of the kaiser, the Prince Auwi, a Nazi, may have introduced them.

Abetz, a fluent French speaker, had met Luchaire in 1930 in Germany. Soon after their meeting, Abetz moved to Paris, and in 1932 he married Luchaire's secretary. The youthful, blond, and handsome Abetz was introduced into right-wing high society by Luchaire and led to believe he could establish cultural links between France and Germany.* In 1932, Abetz's specialty was cultivating "wealthy" and influential women like Stephanie among the literati in the salons of Paris. And so, the charade surrounding Stephanie's expulsion from France may never be known for certain.

THE FRENCH SERVICE de Renseignements ("Intelligence Services"), comprising the Deuxième Bureau (literally the "Second Office," the investigative intelligence service) and several military intelligence departments, were all too aware of the danger that these right-wing individuals placed on France's fragile democracy. In fact, as early as 1922, the chief of French military intelligence reported, "Humiliated by its defeat, Germany is obsessed with thoughts of revenge. . . . One single

---

* Which he did, but not until 1934. He was deported in 1936 and returned as German ambassador during the German occupation of France in 1940–44. Luchaire was appointed his head of the collaborationist press.

danger dominates all others at the moment, and that is the German danger."[12]

Although the French had blown Stephanie's cover and she was allegedly deported to Spain, her spying days were just beginning. Abandoned and broke across the border in Spain's leftist Basque country, Stephanie cabled her lawyer friend, Captain Donald Cranmore Malcolm, in London.* How long she languished in Spain (if at all) is unknown, but it was Malcolm who paid for her passage to England.

Of course, Stephanie's deportation paled compared with the news from Germany. On January 30, 1933, Hitler was appointed chancellor by President Hindenburg. Forty-eight hours later, on February 1, Hitler dissolved the Reichstag. Three days later, Hitler dissolved the provincial and municipal assemblies, with President Hindenburg authorizing the government to take whatever steps were required "for the protection of people and State." Officially, this meant forbidding strikes (a sop to the industrialists), public assemblies (except for Nazis), and suspension of the freedom of the press.

Still, Goebbels despaired. He had been passed over for a ministerial position and hadn't the money to print his own propaganda leaflets. Luckily for him, Frau von Schröder, wife of the Cologne banker, donated twenty thousand reichsmarks to Goebbels and his Berlin Gau election campaign within the fortnight.

I.G. FARBEN WAS too powerful to allow the economic downturn, politics, and street violence to adversely impact its factory floors—be it by actual violence or talk of revolution. The Nazis knew that I.G. had in its possession the key to self-sufficiency in synthetic petroleum products,

---

* Captain Donald Malcolm was an American citizen who resided at 20 Place Vendôme in Paris. He never reached the grade of "captain" in the Great War and was demobilized as a "lieutenant." His business address was British American Securities in Lombard Street in the City of London. On his U.S. passport application of 1920, he gave his job as "banker." He often gave his home address as the Yale Club at 50 Vanderbilt Avenue in New York City. According to MI5, together with Stephanie they made good money "assisting 'people' to get money out of Germany" (source: TNA, KV-2-1696-2, 37–44; ancestry.com; HO 382/250).

and autarky was a matter of great interest among those closest to Hitler advocating war, like Goebbels and Ribbentrop. The problem for I.G., however, was that by 1933 and after the investment of 300 million reichsmarks in its Leuna plant, synthetic oil cost approximately forty-five pfennigs per liter.* Refined petroleum cost seven pfennigs. After so many years in development, not only was synthetic fuel grotesquely un-economic to produce and sell, but it threatened the survival and inde-pendence of the giant chemical concern. Still, Carl Bosch resisted calls to abandon his synthetic fuel project, promoting the idea of expanding their capital base instead. With Hitler as chancellor, Bosch proposed a "joint venture" whereby the German state would finance development of products essential to Germany, forgetting the adage that when sup-ping with the devil, a long spoon is required.[13]

For some of Bosch's fellow I.G. bosses, however, their main preoccu-pation was with Hitler's extreme rhetoric about eliminating the "danger-ous influence of Jews at the top levels of the nation's leading industrial concerns." Many of the key men on the I.G. supervisory board (*Aufsichts-rat*) were of Jewish heritage: Otto von Mendelssohn-Bartholdy, Ernst von Simson, Alfred Merton, Arthur von Weinberg, and Kurt Oppenheim, as well as the inventor of chlorine gas as a chemical weapon, Fritz Haber. Both Goebbels's *Der Angriff* and the Nazi Party's newspaper, *Völkischer Beobachter,* had pointed to I.G.'s "disgraceful" behavior by accepting Jews in high places for years.[14]

AGAINST THIS BACKGROUND, twenty-five of the wealthiest men in Ger-many received an invitation to attend a "conference" at the official Ber-lin home of Hermann Göring, president of the Reichstag, "during which the Reich chancellor will explain his policies." The date set was February 20, 1933, at six P.M. It was Göring, not Hitler or Goebbels, who sent out the invitations. Gustav Krupp accepted his with alacrity, as did four of the I.G. Farben supervisory directors, including the I.G. big boss, Baron Georg von Schnitzler, the commercial chief and head of I.G.'s Dyes Committee. Also present were Friedrich Flick, a coal mine owner

---

* At the time, the reichsmark was worth about 4.2 to the dollar and 14.1 to the pound.

and director of the mighty Dresdner Bank; Hugo Stinnes, leader of the German coal industry; Otto Wolff and Ernst Poensgen, coal mine owners and steel magnates; and the influential financiers Kurt von Schröder and Walther Funk. Irrespective of their personal viewpoints about the Nazis, they came to hear what Hitler had to say about German industry now that he had secured the office of chancellor.

Gustav Krupp von Bohlen, as president of the Reichsverband (National Industry Association), sat closest to the low rostrum, just in front of the I.G. Farben directors. Göring, who knew many of these powerhouses of German industry personally, introduced Hitler.

"We are about to hold the last election," Hitler announced, pausing long enough to let that sink into the minds of the attendees. "Private enterprise cannot be maintained in a democracy," he continued.[15] Warming to his theme, and assiduously keeping away from his usual anti-Semitic rhetoric, Hitler assured his listeners that it was "the noblest task of leadership to find ideals which would bind the German people together," like nationalism and the strength and authority of leadership. He intended to eliminate the communist threat; eliminate trade unionism; and restore the German Wehrmacht to its former glory. "Regardless of the outcome," Hitler concluded, there would be "no retreat." Similarly, should he not be voted in as chancellor in the forthcoming March election, he would remain in office "by other means . . . with other weapons."[16]

Göring took the rostrum again after Hitler. He stated, "The sacrifice asked for will be so much easier to bear if industry realizes that the election of March 5 will be the last one for the next ten years, possibly for the next hundred years." Krupp then stood, thanking Hitler for sharing his thoughts, after which Dr. Schacht cried out, "and now gentlemen it is time to pay up!" Krupp rose first, while the others whispered between themselves. He pledged a million marks. Schacht received an additional million from all the others combined.[17]

THROUGHOUT THAT FEBRUARY, the Nazis ran roughshod over the opposition, since Göring was president of the Reichstag and Wilhelm Frick the new minister of the interior. Together they had the police forces of all Germany under their command. No opponent was left unbloodied. The SA (who fomented the street violence) was transformed overnight from a renegade, lawless organization into the guardian of order by Göring and Frick.[18]

With the SA "assisting" the police, the communists were harassed, their headquarters raided twice, and the use of hand grenades and machine guns liberally applied. Catholic centrists found their meetings, debates, and rallies obstructed, and some members were wounded and killed. Yet Bruening and others stood their ground with courage and determination, angering their increasingly nervous Nazi opposition. The SA were making martyrs of them all. Hitler decided to act secretly and changed tack.[19]

On the night of February 27, Hitler and Prince Auwi were dining at the Goebbels's Dahlem home when Putzi Hanfstaengl telephoned. The Reichstag was on fire, he said.[20] Vice Chancellor Papen was entertaining President Hindenburg at the exclusive Herrenklub at the time. "We noticed a red glow through the windows and heard sounds of shouting in the street," Papen later wrote. "One of the servants came hurrying up to me and whispered: 'The Reichstag is on fire!'"

At the French embassy, Ambassador André François-Poncet was called away from the official dinner he was hosting, where the Reich minister of finance, Schwerin von Krosigk, was present. From the windows overlooking his garden, he could see the huge glass dome of the Reichstag ablaze, "as scarlet as if through fireworks." When he returned to tell the others in the dining room, only Krosigk could not disguise his joy, exclaiming "Thank God!"[21]

Later, Goebbels claimed he hadn't believed Hanfstaengl, and he refused to tell Hitler about his message. If that were so, why had Hitler and Goebbels driven into Berlin? Papen and Göring were already on the scene. The fire had been set in thirty places according to firefighters. "Carried out by Communists," Goebbels recorded, "Göring is furious. Hitler in a rage."[22] Within hours, a hapless Dutch communist, Marinus van der Lubbe, was arrested.

A Prussian Ministry of the Interior official, Hans Gisevius, testified at the Nuremberg trials after World War II that "it was Goebbels who first thought of setting the Reichstag on fire." Rudolf Diels, the Gestapo chief, added, "Göring knew exactly how the fire was to be started and had ordered him 'to prepare, prior to the fire, a list of people who were to be arrested immediately after it.'" By 1942, Göring boasted to General Franz Halder, chief of the German General Staff, that he had masterminded events.[23]

On February 28, 1933, President Hindenburg decreed a suspension in constitutional protection throughout Germany. Despite setting fire to the Reichstag; muting the communist and Catholic centrist voices; and curtailing freedom of the press, freedom of speech, and the right to assemble, Hitler's Nazi Party only polled 17,277,180 votes, an increase of 5.5 percent but only 44 percent of the total. The communists lost about a million supporters, and the Catholic centrists increased their vote by just shy of two hundred thousand. Papen's nationalists were disappointed with their 8 percent of total votes cast; however, in pooling their votes with the Nazis, Hitler would have a majority of sixteen seats in the Reichstag. It was far short of the two-thirds majority needed to carry out his bold plan for a dictatorship.[24]

"The street gangs had seized control of the resources of a great modern State," historian Alan Bullock wrote, "the gutter had come to power."[25] The industrialists saw matters differently. For them, it was a choice between communism and Nazism. There was no middle road. Hitler never hid from them that basic freedoms would need to be curtailed. Like others before, and many afterward, the industrialists fooled themselves that the Nazis could be controlled. "Germans soon noticed the surprising fact that several news organs of big business, such as the *Deutsche Allgemeine Zeitung* and the *Rheinisch-Westfälische Zeitung*, abruptly switched from hostility to support for Hitler."[26]

FROM MARCH 6, the unintelligible truth was shrouded by the intelligible lie. Even so, most Germans were too bewildered to notice—ground down by years of political instability and economic despair. On March 9, on Hitler's orders, General Franz Ritter von Epp overthrew the government of Bavaria and set up a Nazi regime. Other politicians were threatened by Nazi brutality and the impossibility of obtaining funds from their usual backers. On March 23, Hitler announced his "law for removing the distress of the people and Reich,"* known as the Enabling Act. The Reichstag passed it without any changes by a vote of 441–84. Only the Social Democrats held firm against the new Third Reich. The Nazi deputies sprang to their feet and burst into the "Horst Wessel Song," the Nazi anthem, named after the pimp and Nazi martyr who was its lyricist.

In the first thirty days, laws were passed at a feverish pace. On March 22, Dachau concentration camp, for the detention of political prisoners, was established by the SS on Hitler's orders. On March 31, the provincial administrations were dissolved except in Prussia and ordered to be reconstituted based on the votes cast in the Reichstag election—minus any Communist seats that remained vacant. Hitler's power had surpassed the kaiser's, Bismarck's, and undoubtedly the Weimar Republic's in ordering something they had never dared. But it was only the beginning.

On April 1, Goebbels's highly publicized anti-Jewish boycott took place, as a carefully orchestrated and necessary act of revenge and reprisal against German and foreign Jews who were spreading "untrue atrocity stories" against Germany to undermine the fatherland. Storm troopers "discouraged" shoppers from using Jewish-owned establishments or visiting Jewish professionals, some holding signs reading "the Jews are our misfortune."[27] Then, on April 7, regional Reich governors were empowered to appoint and remove local governments, dissolve diets, and appoint or dismiss state official judges as they saw fit. Naturally, these Reich governors were all Nazis and were required to carry out "the general policy laid down by the Reich Chancellor."†

There were more aberrations to come. The "Law for the Restoration of the Professional Civil Service," outlawing political opponents and Jews; the "Limiting Law on Jews in Public Education" that extended through university level; and the infamous book burnings at universities.[28] The Geheim Staatspolizei, soon to be known as the Gestapo, came into being. Unofficially, there were secret orders, like the April 21 decree, with detailed instructions, for "coordinating" unions on May 2. The misuse of

---

* "Gesetz zur Behebung der Not von Volk und Reich."
† Reichstatthalter is the German term for "Reich governor."

everyday words became a Nazi trademark: "coordinating" meant "occu-pation" of German-wide trade union premises. Then, too, there was the "taking into protective custody" of all trade union leaders. The criminal inclination of the regime was also marked by the theft of all trade union funds.

In the first one hundred days, Hitler became master of all he sur-veyed. The defenders of the old ways found that they could do noth-ing to control him. Dr. Hans Luther, the conservative president of the Reichsbank, was "kicked upstairs" and became the German ambassador to Washington. Dr. Hjalmar Schacht, who advocated the "truth and ne-cessity" of Nazism, was destined to resume his position as Hitler's eco-nomic wizard and give international legitimacy to the immoral regime.

Germany had changed beyond recognition. Hitler's supporters—a large minority—were happy to surrender individual liberties to have political stability in what became known as *Gleichschaltung,* or the coor-dinated surrender of liberty to the Nazi totalitarian regime. "The no-tion that the German Government can possibly utter falsehoods," wrote French ambassador François-Poncet, "is [a] difficult conception by the German brain. Germans bear an innate respect for lawful authority; this makes them accept anything official with the utmost docility."[29]

The Wounded Giant

We must move as a trained and loyal army willing to sacrifice for
the good of a common discipline.
                        —Franklin D. Roosevelt, inauguration speech,
                                                    March 3, 1933

During these chaotic events, and two days after Germany's November
election, Franklin D. Roosevelt was elected the thirty-second president of
the United States. These momentous events unfolded in Germany as Roosevelt assembled his cabinet and team of advisers. He knew the German
situation was a lower priority than sorting out the American economy.

When the stock market finally hit rock bottom on July 8, 1932—
some two years and nine months after the original crash—President
Hoover's fate was in little doubt. Over two thousand investment houses
had failed despite Hoover's belated policy initiative, the Reconstruction
Finance Corporation, which aimed to help banks and worthy but struggling businesses recover.

Even the mighty House of Morgan had seen its net worth halve between 1928 and 1932. "Apple days" were common on Wall Street, where
the former masters of the financial universe hauled themselves onto the
sidewalks of New York to sell apples to supplement their suddenly mea-
ger income. New York's Central Park looked like a hobo's encampment.
Hoovervilles, shantytowns of homeless families, sprang up throughout
America just about anywhere. By 1930, it was not unusual to glance
at a newspaper to see another run on some bank somewhere. Then,
too, it was the heyday of celebrity bank robbers: Pretty Boy Floyd, John

Dillinger, Bonnie and Clyde, Baby Face Nelson, Ma Barker, and Machine Gun Kelly, to name a few. The businesses that boomed were those selling new bank vaults and bootleg liquor. Since 1920, Prohibition had gifted a lucrative black-market business to the big-city gangsters like Al "Scarface" Capone and George "Bugs" Moran. President Roosevelt, a "Yankee Wet," was determined to make the selling of alcohol legal again to wipe out organized crime.

Superstition, racism, and ignorance were rife. In the century following the Civil War, the Ku Klux Klan alone is estimated to have lynched some 3,500 Black people. In fact, dating from 1867, the Klan may be the "earliest phenomenon that can be functionally related to fascism in America," according to Robert O. Paxton in his *The Anatomy of Fascism*.[1] By the late 1920s, the murder of Catholics and Jews by Klansmen could still be counted on the fingers of one hand, despite the geographic spread of the Klan outside its traditional southern patch. From California to New York, the Klan disseminated anti-Catholic hate mail to its five million registered supporters across America. In Florida, Protestants were led to believe that their marriages would be dissolved and their children made illegitimate if the Catholic candidate, Al Smith, became president in 1928.[2]

JEWS, TOO, WERE in the racist frame. In 1931, when a *Detroit News* reporter interviewed Hitler in his Munich office, he seemed surprised that a large picture of Henry Ford hung over the future leader's desk. Hitler gazed reverently at the Ford portrait and said, "I regard Henry Ford as my inspiration."

Ford had used his *Dearborn Independent* for hundreds of articles, some of which were "repackaged into booklets and distributed around the world" to give Ford's message: "The Jew has no civilization to point to . . . no great achievement in any realm." Ford, the king of mass production and assembly line manufacturing of cars, also mass-produced anti-Semitism for American and world audiences.[3] Then, too, over thirty million Americans listened to the Catholic radio priest Charles E. Coughlin's anti-Semitic broadcasts, made from his Detroit pulpit.[4]

. . .

ECONOMICALLY, AMERICA SEEMED bankrupt. Around thirteen million people were out of work. Some hitched rides in boxcars and slept without shelter, hoping to find work somewhere—anywhere. Hoover had answered their plight with the refrain that "America needed a good laugh, a good song" and approached popular movie star and cowboy humorist Will Rogers to write a joke to stop panic hoarding.[5] New investors and experienced traders alike who had believed the stock market was a one-way bet papered the walls of their bathrooms with valueless stock certificates to help keep them warm. Barter became a way of life, and those who still had jobs had to become inventive.

Most Americans faced utter despair by the 1932 presidential election. It could be said that Roosevelt's magnetism and personality won him the White House as much as the idea—not dissimilar to the average German's idea—that something drastic had to be done. Most of Roosevelt's supporters felt that he was a friend whom they had invited into their home. His opponents would say that he was inconsistent, too much of a patrician and elitist to come to grips with the problems of the rural poor, and more comfortable in the Northeast and Europe than in middle America.

Joseph P. Kennedy, father of the future president and a major fundraiser on the Roosevelt bandwagon, had accused his candidate of inexperience and vacillation.[6] So why did he support Roosevelt? Aside from the fact that Republicans shunned Irish Catholics, Kennedy held "a deep-rooted fear that America's freewheeling capitalist system would be obliterated by a communist revolution."[7] Like many Europeans, Kennedy feared communism. Even at this stage, he secretly thought that fascism was the only way to put America back on its feet.

It is safe to say that Roosevelt's leadership style was akin to tossing a pebble in the water to see how the ripples flowed out. If he didn't get a clear signal from the first pebble, he'd toss another one in and see if he liked that result better. If two advisers gave him contrary advice, he would often tell both that they were right to their faces. Then he would decide his own course of action. Roosevelt's modus operandi allowed him to remain in control. He listened and changed his mind, often depending on the reaction of his cabinet. Still, Roosevelt never shilly-shallied on the burning need for action. That's what made the president's need to stand on the sidelines simply watching Hitler seize power so excruciating.

ROOSEVELT'S INAUGURATION TOOK place on March 4, 1933, one day before the German terror election. The new president not only faced the worst depression in American history and had to put the country back to work but also had the task of overseeing foreign policy. In time, he would assume far greater responsibilities than the secretary of state Cordell Hull or the assistant secretary of state Sumner Welles would like, but such was the presidency of Franklin Roosevelt. Since the night of February 27, Roosevelt had been asking his advisers if the destruction of the German Reichstag hadn't been some provocative machination of Herr Hitler.

On Roosevelt's first evening as president, the radio newscasts and late newspapers led the foreign reports with headlines like "HITLER WILL BE THE NEW CZAR WHATEVER THE VOTE" and "HITLER READY TO SEIZE SUPREME POWER."[8] The next morning's newspapers were even more upsetting for Roosevelt: "VICTORY BY HITLER EXPECTED TO DOOM GERMAN REICHSTAG" and "HITLER'S REGIME SCORES SWEEPING VICTORY AT POLLS."[9] Little did the president realize that the entirety of his four terms in office would be overshadowed by the German dictator.

Roosevelt's first "fireside chat," aimed at quelling America's economic chaos, took place eight days after his inauguration. In his inaugural address, he had said that the "[p]ractices of the unscrupulous money changers stand indicted in the court of public opinion." He urged the people of America on a new course, where "there must be an end to a conduct in banking and in business which too often has given to a sacred trust the likeness of callous and selfish wrongdoing."[10] A new law was speedily enacted that should reassure bank depositors.[11] The 1933 Securities Act, intended to end false speculation on the stock market, soon followed. A raft of other new legislation would put people back to work and provide additional safety through the social security, minimum wage, and workers' compensation legislation. For now, Hitler needed to remain a lower priority on his agenda.

WHILE THE NEW administration went to work for America, the news from Germany was ever more alarming. Not only were essential freedoms curtailed, but the violence never ceased against the press, political opponents, Catholics, and Jews. Roosevelt was well aware that political opponents were being silenced or killed, and that Germany had turned into a totalitarian state. "Almost from the very start of the New Deal," Irwin Gellman wrote, "Roosevelt spoke out forcefully against the German government's persecution of its Jewish population," drawing "attention to this emerging reign of terror in its infancy because it offended the sense of decency and fair play."[12]

Roosevelt believed that the president is the right person to be an "activist" in foreign affairs. He strengthened ties with the British and the French yet unilaterally declared that all world leaders should abandon offensive weaponry. He frequently omitted to tell his cabinet members concerned with foreign affairs precisely what he had said or done. "It has its advantages, but makes everybody jumpy," the debonair American career diplomat Jay Pierrepont Moffat said, "as to what the President has said to foreign representatives."[13] The situation was made worse by the fact that the president had been unable to appoint an ambassador to Germany.

Equally, there had been an air of extreme disquiet about Germany in the U.S. State Department. The Nazis' Jewish boycott of April 1—originally slated to last a month—was the object of disdain in the U.S. press. Colonel Robert R. McCormick, the owner of the *Chicago Tribune*, spoke for them all when he wrote, "High minded American, Christian journalists of international reputation and unquestioned integrity claimed to report only a tenth of the miserable spectacle of which they were eyewitnesses. Did Hitler expect the Jews to remain silent in the face of such reports?"

McCormick made no bones about the fact that Hitler's claims of Jewish defamation of Germany antedates any foreign or Jewish protests by at least a decade. The moral indignation of Jewish leaders around the world was more than justified. "To hold German Jewry responsible for these expressions of moral indignation is preposterous. The Hitler government knows full well that the Jews in Germany swallowed their pride, suppressed their emotions and docilely submitted to their fate."[14] The "big lie" was exposed, but its believers in America and elsewhere continued to trust in the Jewish "deep state" that Hitler advertised.

But who could represent the United States as its next ambassador to Germany? Roosevelt had asked former Ohio governor James M. Cox,* as well as former Cleveland mayor Newton D. Baker Jr. and Nicholas M. Butler, president of Columbia University. They all declined "for personal reasons." Despite Hanfstaengl's best efforts, the postelection seizure of power in Germany weighed heavily on everyone's minds.

Roosevelt's choice ultimately fell on Professor William E. Dodd, a professor of American history for twenty-five years in Chicago. "At 12 o'clock in my office at the University of Chicago," Dodd's diary begins on June 8, 1933, "the telephone rang. 'This is Franklin Roosevelt; I want to know if you will render the government a distinct service. I want you to go to Germany as Ambassador.'"[15] Dodd was given two hours to accept. After speaking to his employer and then his wife, Dodd accepted the most difficult ambassadorial post in Europe, perhaps in the world. But would he be up to the job?

---

* Cox had run as the unsuccessful 1920 Democratic presidential candidate. Roosevelt was his choice for vice president.

Saluting Hitler

My father would come home . . . depressed and alarmed at the
never-ending brutality of the Storm Troopers.
                              —Martha Dodd, *My Years in Germany*

William E. Dodd's first appointment as U.S. ambassador to Germany
was with the National City Bank in New York City on July 3, 1933. He
needed to review the "financial problems of German-American banks,"
which involved the payment of some $1.2 billion to American creditors
"who had been hoodwinked by bankers into making loans to German
Corporations." Dr. Schacht had declared a take-it-or-leave-it standstill
agreement, "whereby American obligations were being paid in cheap
marks rather than no marks at all."[1] With National City Bank and Chase
National Bank alone holding more than a hundred million dollars in
German bonds, the only thing the bankers could agree upon was that
Dodd must prevent the Germans publicly defaulting and upsetting the
financial markets, yet again.

Dodd understood, too, that these same bankers were undergoing
microscopic inspection for wrongdoing by the federal government that
spring. In early 1932, Thomas W. Lamont of Morgan expressed directly
to Hoover the bank's opposition to any investigation of their practices.
Lamont was ignored, due to the public hue and cry against the bankers.[2]
Dodd's meetings with the bankers and briefings from the State Department demonstrated to the former academic just how tricky it would be
to please everyone with power in the United States.

That same afternoon, Dodd met about "the Jewish question" with

Judge Julian W. Mack, investment banker Felix Warburg, Judge Irving Lehman (of the New York Court of Appeals and brother of Governor Lehman), Rabbi Stephen S. Wise, and Max Kohler (who was writing a biography of the Seligmans, a Jewish banking family from New York). For an hour and a half, Dodd was told about the systematic persecution of Jews and how all Jewish property was being confiscated. Dodd already knew he could not intervene on an "internal matter" but promised he would do all he could as a humane individual to protest the maltreatment of American Jews in Germany. Roosevelt hoped that with Dodd's ability to appeal to the "old" German culture in their native tongue as a learned history professor in the finest traditions, official White House intervention could be avoided.[3]

THE JEWISH BOYCOTT had taken place, laws restricting Jews from activity in the civil service or teaching had been enacted, and Jewish students were asked to leave state education (allegedly to relieve classroom overcrowding) in early April. On April 25, Gustav Krupp wrote to Hitler that he wished "to co-ordinate production in the interest of the whole nation . . . adopting the leadership concept [*Führerprinzip*] of the new German state." Free trade could only lead to an appalling lack of alignment with government policy going forward.

As William Manchester succinctly wrote, "The factories, like the nation, needed a dictator. Obviously, his name should be Krupp." On May 4, 1933, the newspapers reported that Krupp was the führer of German industry. His first act was to expel all Jews from the Reichsverband. Even so, Krupp retained a single twenty-year employee, electrical engineer Robert Waller. In the seemingly incongruous but wise words of the German Jewish political theorist Hannah Arendt, "Every Nazi had his favourite Jew."[4]

Culture, too, would be subject to "alignment." That May, books declared to be un-German were burned as part of the *Gleichschaltung* aligning German culture with the Nazi ideal. No books were allowed by leftist thinkers, Christian Scientists, Jehovah's Witnesses, or Jews, no matter their content. Some Catholic books were banned, too. On Dodd's first business day in Germany, a law forcing the sterilization of individuals with physical or mental disabilities was passed.

Two weeks after his arrival, Dodd received an ailing Dr. Fritz Haber, the man who had served the kaiser so well with his poison gas process in the Great War. I.G. Farben had fired Haber, a Nobel laureate, who, as a sixty-four-year-old chemist of undoubted international repute, felt compelled to resign his directorship of the Max Planck Institute, too. Haber was deeply aggrieved that Germany still classed him as a Jew, despite his early conversion to Christianity and lifelong admiration of the Junker type. He asked the ambassador if he might be able to immigrate to America, but Dodd had to turn him down since the German quota was full. Dodd promised nonetheless to write to the Department of Labor, just in case.[5] Haber left Germany shortly after their interview, bringing his wife and children to safety in England.

"I can conceive of your inner conflicts," Albert Einstein wrote to Haber from the United States. "It is somewhat like having to give up a theory on which one has worked one's whole life." Of course, Einstein had never believed in German superiority like Haber, who suddenly found the strictures of Nazism "odious in the extreme."[6] A broken man with a severe heart condition, Haber found a position at the University of Cambridge. However, working among the young men who had been the victims of the poison gas attacks during the 1914–1918 war proved too great a challenge. So Haber jumped at Chaim Weizmann's invitation to join the faculty of the Daniel Sieff Institute in Mandatory Palestine.* While en route to take up his position in January 1934, Haber died in Basel.[7]

Einstein and Haber were the human faces of the mass exodus of Jewish scientists to Britain and America. Shortly after the March terror election, Wilhelm Mann, a Nazi Party member and head of I.G.'s pharmaceutical division, wrote to the heads of all I.G. offices overseas warning, "We therefore *urgently request you* . . . to contribute to the *clarification of the actual facts* in a manner which you deem suitable and adaptable

---

* In November 1949, the institute was renamed the Weizmann Institute for Science with the approval of Daniel Sieff's parents.

to the special conditions of your country ... that states there is *not a true word* in all the lies and atrocity stories being disseminated abroad."[8] As Germany's largest company, this was I.G.'s official stance. It would only harden once its complete accommodation with the Nazi regime had been sealed.

DODD'S FIRST SIX months in Berlin were momentous. He instantly sensed it was dangerous to openly question the regime yet found it impossible to do nothing. He was bitter about the imprisonment or beatings American citizens received for not making the full Nazi salute, called the *Hitlergruss*. Temporarily, Dodd was placated.

But soon enough, the American journalist Edgar Mowrer, president of the Press Association, was blatantly harassed by the Nazis. Dodd realized all his endeavors were fruitless when the German government advised it could not be held responsible for "the behaviour of its unruly Storm Troopers." Mowrer was ordered to leave Germany within three days. The dark, gaunt, stoop-shouldered Mowrer turned to Dodd for help, but the ambassador urged him to go.[9]

Dodd could hardly advise otherwise, despite Mowrer's disbelief. Dodd urged Mowrer to tell the world what was happening but from a safer distance. The ambassador recognized that, while in Germany, he was reduced to frowning at the parades, the huge black, red, and white flags with their "*Hakenkreuz*"* unfurled along the city's broad avenues. Soon enough, Dodd learned to distinguish Hitler's followers by their colors: brown for the SA, black for the elite SS, and blue for the police.

At first, Dodd's twenty-three-year-old daughter, Martha, a fair-haired, effervescent beauty, enthused at the German order, pomp, and ceremony. On an August tour of Germany in a Chevy with the American correspondent Quentin Reynolds and her brother, Bill, Martha was

---

* The term "swastika" had not yet been popularized as part of the Nazi symbology. It was called the "*Hakenkreuz*" in German, or "broken cross" in English, since the left-facing swastika had been considered (until the rise of the Nazis) an ancient symbol of good luck in Hinduism, Buddhism, and Jainism. Hitler adopted a right-facing swastika, perverting its meaning in Western cultures while retaining the ancient Sanskrit meaning of "conducive to well-being."

wildly enthusiastic toward the people who *"heiled"* as they passed. To the dismay of her brother and Reynolds, she *"heiled"* back "as vigorously as any Nazi." That is, until they arrived at Nuremberg. Martha's exhilaration suddenly vanished when they stopped to see a young girl "brutally pushed and shoved." They saw the girl's "tragic and tortured face, the colour of diluted absinthe. She looked ghastly. Her head had been shaved clean of hair and she was wearing a placard across her breast," just as sinners in the Middle Ages had been obliged to do. "She was a Gentile who had been consorting with a Jew. The placard said: 'I have Offered Myself to a Jew.'" Bill and Quentin had to pull Martha away from the scene. Still, it would be some while before Martha concluded that Germans were suffering from a form of "mass-insanity."[10]

By October, Martha, whose love life was even more complicated than Princess Stephanie's, had conquered the hearts of Berlin's Gestapo chief, Rudolf Diels, and Hitler's foreign press chief, Putzi Hanfstaengl.* She had grown particularly fond of the blushing, handsome Crown Prince Friedrich, the youngest son of Wilhelm, the last crown prince of the German Empire and Kingdom of Prussia. Friedrich was a guest at Martha's birthday party that month, because she only wanted "attractive" people there. Also present was Princess Stephanie, "a notorious Princess—at least, she had become one through marriage—but I didn't know about her then," Martha wrote. "She was bored to death and the only thing that held her was the promise of Hanfstaengl's appearance."

Putzi duly "roared in" shortly after midnight and met Princess Stephanie at the door, just as she made to leave. He lured Stephanie off to one side, where they spoke in hushed tones. Then Stephanie left. Putzi had a drink and "tore out several exciting and flamboyant songs. He always left the piano crumpled and exhausted, not to mention himself and listeners." Then, as swiftly as he had arrived in his "splurge of not-entirely-real dynamic energy," Putzi departed, wishing "Papa" Dodd his best. The outsized Nazi court jester's visit was brief, but memorable.[11]

---

* Martha was a classic "bolter." She had married in secret the year before on a whim, after being engaged to two other men. She had lived with her husband as his wife only on brief occasions before she decided to abandon him to travel with her parents to Germany.

Martha Dodd thought nothing of the little tête-à-tête between Putzi and Princess Stephanie. Given that Martha was a young, desirable, and beautiful woman accustomed to holding the center of attention, why should she? But Stephanie and Putzi were already old acquaintances, working together toward the common goal of making Hitler palatable to the foreign press, especially to the British.

"His Lordship's Ambassadress"

It shall be my worthy task, Your Imperial Highness, to restore you
to the throne.
　　　—Lord Rothermere to Crown Prince Wilhelm, April 1933

Since Princess Stephanie's French debacle, she (and her dogs) called
London's Dorchester Hotel home. She could again afford the best, earning five thousand pounds annually and five thousand pounds in expenses, thanks to Lord Rothermere's generosity.[1*]

Of course, Princess Stephanie was in Berlin at the behest of Rothermere in October 1933. The princess had told him that the kaiser's
fourth son, the most ardent Nazi of them all, Prince Auwi, was a close
friend. Rothermere's assignment for Stephanie had begun in April
1933. She was to wave her wand to arrange a meeting between the kaiser's eldest son, Crown Prince Wilhelm, and his lordship. After all, if
Rothermere were to act on Wilhelm's behalf to bring about a restoration
of the Hohenzollern monarchy, it would pay to make friends with the
heir apparent.

For some considerable time, Crown Prince Wilhelm had made
his support for Hitler abundantly clear. The tall, slender Prince Friedrich Wilhelm von Preussen, known as Wilhelm, was the last heir to

---

* For an approximate value in today's sterling, £1 multiplied by £72.04 would be appropriate. That makes Stephanie's annual retainer £360,200 and her expenses payment worth another £360,200 or approximately $276,923 using an exchange rate of
$1.3 to one pound. Other biographers have not stated that she was paid £5,000 annu-
ally in expenses, but in one of her memoir drafts, she states this clearly.

the Hohenzollern throne. While he and his five brothers were dispar-
aged for their lack of intellect, their support for Hitler's policies was
significant in quelling any rebellion among the former German ruling
classes.* On Potsdam Day, March 21, 1933, Wilhelm was on hand to
applaud Hitler's speech at the Garrison Church. It was "a speech deeper
and more moving than I have ever heard from a German statesman,"
the silver-haired crown prince wrote to Rothermere nine months later.[2]
"The German divided within himself loses the power to act," *The New
York Times* reported Hitler saying on the day. "Only the nation's decay,
the general breakdown, compelled a feeble generation to bow . . . to the
claim that we were guilty of causing the war," Hitler proclaimed. "Crises
without end have since convulsed our nation."[3]

Crown Prince Wilhelm had done much to publicly support Hitler's
ascent to power. By his own reckoning, he "brought about two million
votes from [right-wing] Stahlhelm comrades and German Nationalists."
Before that, Wilhelm had tried to persuade Chancellor Bruening to
resign in favor of Hitler. When General von Schleicher took over as
chancellor, Wilhelm renewed his efforts to bring Hitler into the government. He supported rearmament and the Nazi Party to the full, convinced that after the thunderous round of meetings between Hermann
Göring and his father years earlier, Hitler would reinstall the monarchy
in some form.[4] And yet Hitler had done nothing.

ROTHERMERE FELT THAT he could tip the balance in favor of the Hohenzollerns and sent Stephanie out as his royal ambassadress. Since this
was not a Nazi Party matter, Stephanie was ordered to make contact
direct with the Hohenzollern royal family. Her friend Prince Auwi was
a "national speaker" (*Reichsredner*) under the control of Dr. Goebbels.
The stork-like Auwi had grown a moustache to hide his receding chin
and slicked back his hair to show his high forehead (a perceived sign of

---

* Friedrich Wilhelm (1882–1951), Eitel Friedrich (1883–1942), Adalbert (1884–1948),
Augustus Wilhelm "Auwi" (1887–1949), Oskar (1888–1958), and Joachim (1890–1920).
Joachim committed suicide at the family hunting lodge near Potsdam. The kaiser's last
child was a girl, Viktoria Luise (1892–1980).

intelligence). He declared in a June 1931 speech, "Where a Hitler leads, a Hohenzollern can follow." That shook the trees as much as any thunderstorm.

Auwi also told Putzi Hanfstaengl, "I shall make a point of keeping with Hitler. . . . After all I am the best horse in the Hohenzollern stable." Auwi had been elected to the Reichstag in 1933 and appointed to the Prussian Staatsrat that July. But had Stephanie also been aware that Auwi, as an SA major general (*Obergruppenführer*), would tell Putzi or even his putative boss, Goebbels, about her mission? Chances are she did, and hoped that Auwi—called "ceaselessly dense, horrifically superficial" by his father's *Hausminister*—would tell someone high up in the Reich Chancellery.[5]

That is, if the crown prince did not tell Hitler himself. Wilhelm was an early Nazi fellow traveler and could often be seen wearing his brown SA uniform before the Nazis seized power in March 1933. As an avid automobile enthusiast, he had joined the SA's motor division, under the command of his Nazi cousin, Duke Carl Edouard of Saxe-Coburg and Gotha. He was also friendly with Ernst Röhm and Adolf Hitler and had served as Göring's commander in the Great War.[6]

CROWN PRINCE WILHELM was delighted by Princess Stephanie's approach on behalf of Lord Rothermere. It meant that Rothermere had not given up on the idea of restoration of the central European monarchies in some form. Rothermere's campaign for Hungary was common knowledge and viewed positively in Habsburg, Wittelsbach, and Hohenzollern royal circles. What the Crown Prince would not have realized was that Rothermere's interventions were increasingly frowned upon by Hitler because some Habsburgs and Wittelsbachs did not wholly agree with the führer's desire for *one Reich* under his absolute control. Undoubtedly, the crown prince had no idea that Hitler saw the Hohenzollerns as pawns on his personal chessboard.

Wilhelm, like Ribbentrop, thought Hitler wished to build bridges with the British royal family, too. Since first dining at the Ribbentrops' Dahlem villa in the spring of 1932, Ribbentrop had fed Hitler ample portions of misinformation about the British aristocracy, its "way of life, parliamentary institutions, the City with its trade, and Empire policy. . . . Hitler was particularly interested in what influential Englishmen thought about National Socialism," Ribbentrop wrote. "It was the harmony of our views about England which . . . created the seed of confidence between Hitler and myself."[7]

And so, in April 1933, arrangements were made to receive Princess Stephanie and Lord Rothermere at Cecilienhof Palace near Potsdam, the 1917 English Tudor revival modeled on Bidston Court in Birkenhead.* What could be more fitting? The crown prince ensured that it was an evening intended for a king, since he knew Rothermere had been entertained at Buckingham Palace several times. The finest table was laid, fresh flowers scented the air, and golden goblets filled with the best wines were only the beginning. The meal, though never described, would have been in the most sumptuous German royal traditions. The conversation was, of course, distinctly slanted to dynastic and royal issues. To be in a German royal palace so redolent of the reign of Queen Elizabeth I certainly made dining at Cecilienhof one of Rothermere's "happiest evenings of his rich and eventful life." Unfortunately, neither Rothermere nor Stephanie recorded who else was present. (Stephanie's archive was heavily culled.) Had they discussed the violent one-day Jewish boycott? Or had they talked of the ceremonial opening of Dachau concentration camp, which also occurred on April 1, 1933?[8]

The record did explain how "long after midnight," when Rothermere and Stephanie were shown to their rooms after a splendid evening, "the Crown Prince suggested that Lord Rothermere should see the Vice-Chancellor, Franz von Papen, before his departure to London." His lordship naturally agreed, and Wilhelm promised this would be arranged for the following day. By the time they left the next morning, Papen had agreed to meet at Rothermere's convenience. Stephanie would act as his interpreter.

Wilhelm, delighted with the outcome of this initial meeting, presented Lord Rothermere with "an enchanting 18th century pendule [sic] a sort of elaborate Rococo chronometer" as an exquisite souvenir of Frederician Potsdam. Rothermere was so moved that he became "almost

---

* Cecilienhof would later become famous as the site of the 1945 Potsdam Conference.

inarticulate" and promised in all sincerity, "It shall be my worthy task, Your Imperial Highness, to restore you to the throne. Should I die before this is accomplished, my son will continue to the happy end."[9]

ROTHERMERE MET WITH the vice chancellor later that day. Franz von Papen had played a critical role in overcoming President Hindenburg's reticence toward Hitler, by framing General Schleicher for the misuse of agrarian funds (the *Osthilfe*),thus forcing Schleicher to resign.[10] Hindenburg, already descending into senility, was easily tricked by Papen's lies.[11] Rothermere, too, was unaware of Papen's treachery and his lack of political conviction that made him act as nothing more than a mouthpiece for Hitler.

His lordship wrongly believed the ease with which the crown prince had arranged the meeting demonstrated the closeness of the Nazi cabinet to the Hohenzollern monarchy. So Rothermere engaged in a no-holds-barred conversation with Papen on dynastic issues. According to Stephanie, Rothermere turned to her gravely afterward, calling Papen an ineffectual "yes man," whereas Hitler was "a great man."[12]

A month later, Princess Stephanie was invited to Wilhelm's Kronprinzenpalais in Berlin as Rothermere's ambassadress. Again, the princess did not mention the public book burnings of "un-German books" that took place that month, nor the spectacle of their huge bonfires in Berlin and university cities. When Albert Einstein heard of this final barbarity, he renounced his German citizenship. Yet Stephanie made no remark about the increased brutality of Nazi rule.

Wilhelm impetuously picked up the telephone and left a message at the Reich Chancellery that it would be beneficial for the führer to meet the princess. Stephanie wrote that she had protested and would need to consult with Rothermere before she did any such thing. But when Stephanie reached the Hotel Adlon, there were two messages from the chief of the Reich Chancellery, Dr. Hans Lammers. She claimed that Lammers telephoned a third time before her call to Rothermere could be placed. Her possible objections were waved aside as immaterial by the efficient Lammers, since both Crown Prince Wilhelm and Hitler wished to meet *her*.[13]

Stephanie was whisked off by a chauffeur-driven car from the Hotel Adlon to the Reich Chancellery, a mere block away. During this meeting, she learned that Adolf Hitler's government was *not* to be a transitional government toward reinstatement of the monarchy. And yet she did not inform Rothermere. Could this have been the moment when she agreed to work for Hitler, too? We may never know. Later, she wrote disparagingly in her memoir that there was nothing significant about Hitler as a person. He could have been a schoolteacher, or a minor bank clerk. Unlike others, she did not mention his mesmerizing gaze.

The princess did note that the führer was extremely courteous, kissing her hand. He was fastidiously clean with a delicate complexion, a nervous habit of running his thumb along his index finger, and that his hands were the beautiful hands of an artist. But the most striking thing about her first visit to see Hitler in his lair was that they had a lengthy conversation. "I mean one where both parties speak in turn," she wrote. She had already heard about Hitler's ranting or remaining sulkily silent in the company of his cohorts, but apparently she had no such experience. Although the princess likened his accent and manner of speech to a "servant putting on the dog," one thing was certain: Princess Stephanie had fascinated Hitler.[14] Why? Was it her ability to converse sensually as taught to virginal aristocratic ladies at the *contessen soirées* all those years earlier, reminding Hitler of a youth forbidden to him? Or was it her position close to the powerful Rothermere?[15] Whatever memories were stirred, as with the Hohenzollerns, it undoubtedly crossed his scheming mind that she might just be *the* emissary he had been searching for to persuade the British aristocracy into supporting him.

"Hurrah for the Blackshirts!"

Because Fascism comes from Italy, shortsighted people in this
country think they show a sturdy national spirit by deriding it.
—Lord Rothermere,
Daily Mail, January 15, 1934

Rothermere never questioned why Princess Stephanie had been so
warmly received. As an arch-monarchist, he believed with all his soul
that by reinstating the Hohenzollern and Habsburg monarchies again,
Europe would find its equilibrium. Hitler had said repeatedly he would
restore the Hohenzollerns, and Rothermere—mistaking Hitler for an
English gentleman—thought Hitler's word was his bond. But then, even
in Rothermere's circles, the English gentleman was a dying breed.

Like most of the world's aristocrats, Rothermere firmly thought that
communism was the root of all evil and Hitler was a bulwark against its
malevolence. Confusing trade unionism with communism, he believed
that Britain's general strike of 1926 was a communist-inspired plot. And
the socialists were no better. As a powerful conservative press baron,
Rothermere disliked the conservative leader Stanley Baldwin's hold on
power, too, calling him a "crypto-socialist." He blamed Baldwin—"an
ironmonger's son"—for his poor understanding of foreign policy, not
seeing that this was endemic among the country's leadership. In his first
term as prime minister, Baldwin, in an interview with the right-wing
People Sunday newspaper, reciprocated Rothermere's dislike, saying
that the press barons Rothermere and Beaverbrook "are men I would
not have in my house. I do not respect them."[1]

When Baldwin was the leader of the opposition between 1929 and 1931, Rothermere's press savagely attacked him through its "empire crusade."[2]* Lord Beaverbrook had formed (very briefly) the United Empire Party, promoting free trade within the empire to try to remove Baldwin as head of the Conservative Party. Rothermere lent his support since he knew that whenever foreign affairs came up in the cabinet, Baldwin would slouch down, close his eyes, and say, "wake me when it's all over." Then, too, Baldwin often "yawned in disgust and weariness at discussing for so long so unpleasing a subject."[3] Interestingly, Baldwin never revealed that the British banker and industrialist Ernest Tennant had been singled out by Ribbentrop to invite him to meet Hitler in December 1933. Baldwin, of course, declined.[4]

George Ward Price, the *Daily Mail* journalist who was close to Rothermere, had become the press baron's unofficial mouthpiece. Back in January 1930, Price wrote, "the conviction was fast spreading among Conservatives that their next leader must be found outside the established hierarchy." Price proposed Lord Beaverbrook for the job. Baldwin replied to the haranguing in the Rothermere press as libelous, and that the aim of "the proprietorship of these papers . . . is power . . . the prerogative of the harlot throughout the Middle Ages."[5]

IN 1931, WHEN a financially distressed Winston Churchill was refused a cabinet position in Ramsay MacDonald's "all party government," Lord Rothermere's son Esmond offered a byline (and lifeline) to Churchill

---

* Stanley Baldwin (Conservative) and James Ramsay MacDonald (Labour) alternated as prime minister through much of the interwar period. Baldwin was prime minister three times: May 22, 1923–January 21, 1924; November 4, 1924–June 4, 1929; and from November 14, 1935, until his retirement in May 1937, when Neville Chamberlain took over as leader of the Conservative Party and thereby became prime minister. MacDonald's first Labour government was from January to November 1924; then he served at the head of a minority government from May 1931 to June 1935. In this period, MacDonald and Baldwin would swap jobs as number one and number two in the government, acting effectively as heads of "national governments" (source: Oxford Dictionary of National Biography).

in a lucrative contract for a reported eight thousand pounds a year.* Churchill and Rothermere shared the same dark view of their party leader and the British government, particularly when it came to the rearmament of Britain. To those in favor of rearmament, MacDonald and Baldwin seemed to be spineless hypocrites, who ignored significant arguments about the poor quality of existing armaments or the real dangers of disarmament. Instead, they concentrated on the financial crisis "and steadfastly closed their eyes and ears to the disquieting symptoms in Europe."[6] Rothermere and Beaverbrook were disconsolate; Churchill, outraged. "Mr. Baldwin," Churchill wrote, "preferred the substance to the form of power, and reigned placidly in the background."

Churchill pounded away in article after article and speech after speech about the Nazis and the need to rearm. It was evident to him that the hardworking Neville Chamberlain would succeed Philip Snowden as chancellor of the exchequer, since Chamberlain seemed to be handling just about everything else on the domestic front.[7] But here again, Chamberlain lacked any experience in foreign affairs. To Churchill, such blatant neglect when the Nazis were on the rise could prove fatal to Britain. There, Rothermere and Churchill parted company. Churchill, unlike Rothermere, viewed Hitler as *the* greatest threat to peace.

Still, both Rothermere and Beaverbrook were the loudest voices in the British press in favor of rearmament. *The Times* assiduously skirted around party lines, by quoting Churchill on liberty: "Neither the French nor the English could agree to live in a world where there was neither liberty of conscience, of thought, and of speech, nor equality of races and classes. These common interests explain the spirit of sympathy and understanding existing between France and England."[8]

At that stage, too, the BBC (broadcasting only on radio) was the "new boy" to news gathering, having set up its first news editing bureau in 1927 with its own news agency tape machine. Its first foreign correspondent, Vernon Bartlett (who had worked on both the *Daily Mail* and *The Times*), only arrived at the BBC in 1933. While there, he

---

* Churchill's contract was worth just over £576,300 or approximately $443,308 at an exchange rate of $1.3 to one pound.

provoked a furor of complaints since he was "not beastly enough" when reporting on Hitler's leaving the League of Nations that October. Bartlett had argued that Hitler was right to walk out of the disarmament conference.[9]

From November 1932, Churchill used his *Daily Mail* column to push for a greater expansion of the Royal Air Force. He advocated "measures necessary to place our Air Force in such a condition of power and efficiency that it will not be worth anyone's while to come here and kill our women and children in the hope that they may blackmail us into surrender." Rothermere, like Churchill, felt that the only way to secure Britain's future was to build its air force, but again, as Churchill pointed out to his wife, "Rothermere wants us to be very strongly armed and frightfully obsequious at the same time" in the hope of averting another war.[10]

In Rothermere's infamous July 1933 headline "YOUTH TRIUMPHANT," written from "Somewhere in Naziland," he praised the Nazi regime "for its internal accomplishments, both spiritual and material." And he asserted that, while there may have been "minor misdeeds of individual Nazis," he was convinced that these must be "submerged by the immense benefits that the new regime is already bestowing upon Germany." The "minor misdeeds" did not refer to the opening of the concentration camps at Dachau or Oranienburg for the internment and torture of political prisoners but, rather, the beating up of communists and Jews in the streets.[11] Churchill wrote to his wife, Clementine, "I was disgusted by the *Daily Mail*'s boosting of Hitler."

LIKE CHURCHILL, ROTHERMERE, and Beaverbrook, the haughty and impeccably dressed British air minister, Charles "Charley" Vane-Tempest-Stewart, 7th Marquess of Londonderry, also wanted to push for a real expansion to the Royal Air Force. Unlike Churchill, Londonderry "saw no danger from Germany in the coming five years," and strongly disagreed with Churchill's warning that Germany had been rearming for some considerable time. Churchill had questioned Undersecretary for Air Sir Philip Sassoon's air estimates, which he voiced on Londonderry's behalf in the Commons, making for an awkward moment. Londonderry had to appear supportive of MacDonald's disarmament plan (intended to save money and win votes) while also fighting a rearguard action to stop cuts to the antiquated British biplane air force.

Yet Charley Londonderry was an ineffective advocate to promote a modernization of the air fleet. Following a visit to the Middle East earlier that year, Londonderry's primary concern seems to have been a requirement for a modern air force (including bombers) to maintain order "for police purposes in unruly parts of the Empire."[12] Much was done to tar Churchill as an adventurer, a lone voice in the wilderness of Parliament, isolated from the government's desire to accommodate Germany. The word appeasement had not yet slipped effortlessly into the English language.

In part, Londonderry's ineffectiveness was due to the political prefer-ment granted by the friendship of Prime Minister MacDonald through Londonderry's wife, Edith. The slim, six-foot-tall Londonderry could be "extraordinarily pleasant" when he wanted, but had to be reminded that it was his duty to act in that way. And Edith wanted him to be pleasant to MacDonald since it had been *she* who had created all the opportunities for both Charley's political and social advancement. She was ambitious for him, and without her, it is doubtful that he would have ever held any cabinet position. It was her flirtatious and calcu-lated friendship with Ramsay MacDonald that advanced Londonderry to the position of air minister, giving rise to the joke "he catered his way to Cabinet."

Londonderry was not henpecked, but rather a noted philanderer. Edith was wounded by his affairs, but never stopped loving him. She steadfastly stood by him, despite the birth of his daughter by another woman. She promoted her husband's career unfailingly from MacDon-ald's first term as prime minister in 1924, when she was seated next to MacDonald at a Buckingham Palace dinner. MacDonald made sure that the couple were among the first to visit him at Chequers, the prime minister's country home in Buckinghamshire.

By and large, the Londonderry fortune had been built upon the roy-alties derived from coal production in County Durham. This made the sight of the Labour prime minister (and son of a Highlands crofter), who had battled for the rights of coal miners against absentee landlords his entire life, most incongruous. But MacDonald seemed happiest at the side of Edith, "standing at the top of the grand staircase in Londonderry House" on Park Lane to greet guests at her glittering receptions, which branded the prime minister "a traitor to his class."[13]

Despite Edith Londonderry's perceived influence over the aging MacDonald, there had been a sea change in the electorate that was entirely unforeseen. Not only had the ultraright found a hero in the inspiring rhetoric of Sir Oswald Mosley and his British Union of Fascists (BUF) a year earlier, but the enlarged electorate encompassing *all* men and women over the age of twenty-one had fractured the British vote and society.

A startling pacifist victory in a by-election in October 1933 was the signal for MacDonald to dismantle and "abolish the whole dreadful equipment of war."[14] Londonderry would need to content himself with the stance of "equality of armed status as a means of defusing German grievances."[15] So, when the German delegation stormed out in a huff from the Disarmament Conference in Geneva in October 1933, Londonderry blamed its failure on the "obdurate French" who were "not prepared to play." It never occurred to him that Germany's abandonment of the disarmament talks was merely a disgraceful strategy.[16]

Yet the German walkout presented a unique opportunity in Londonderry's eyes to press for a proper expansion of the Royal Air Force and enhance his own importance. Baldwin immediately quashed the idea, saying it would send the wrong signals.[17] Londonderry never argued that Germany presented a threat to world order. Simply put, he was not the right man for the job, or open to new ideas. Like a petulant teenager, he blamed the Foreign Office for failing in negotiations with Germany yet dared not speak out or resign in disgust.

TOM MOSLEY, ON the other hand, had not only seen the political landscape changing, but was at its very heart. For some while, both Rothermere and Mosley had viewed the national government of Conservative and Labour leaders as "boneless wonders." Unperturbed by how his change of party—not once or twice but now three times—was seen by others, Mosley was known above all else as an intelligent and forceful politician. His wife, Cimmie, had become painfully accustomed to his "little frolicsome ways," as she called his serial philandering, while other men frankly envied his successes with women.

His lifestyle made Mosley unconvincing as a fascist leader to many of his friends. With his film-star good looks and military bearing (and a war wound that gave him a romantic limp), most voters were more interested in his playboy exploits than his latest hobby horse, fascism. After all, he had gone from the Conservative benches to Labour, then formed his New Party and now headed up the British Union of Fascists. With his inherited wealth, and his wife Cimmie's American fortune, Mosley preferred the company of his fellow aristocrats and a hedonistic lifestyle. It was hardly the image of an *homme du peuple*. For Mussolini, it simply would not do to have the fascist leader of Great Britain spending the summer sunning himself on the French Riviera or lolling in a gondola in Venice with his latest paramour. "It's not a place for serious reformers to linger in villas or grand hotels for more than a few days," Mussolini complained to the British fascist sympathizer Gerrard V. Wallop, Viscount Lymington, MP.[18]

Mosley's January 1932 Italian expedition with Harold Nicolson had opened his eyes to fascism. What Mosley wanted, Nicolson wrote in his diary, "would be to lie low till the autumn, write a book, then rope in Winston Churchill . . . [and] Rothermere and if possible Beaverbrook, into a League of Youth. . . . He fears, however, that the Harmsworths, being restless folk, cannot be 'kept on ice for so long as the autumn.'"[19] Mosley's League of Youth was rapidly converted to fascism—as suggested by Mussolini.

On his return to England in April 1932, Mosley's New Party was formally disbanded, and his political association with Nicolson ended abruptly. "I do not believe in fascism for England," Nicolson wrote to a friend, "and cannot consent to be identified with anything of the sort." For Nicolson, it was the end of the road: "I again say that I do not believe this country will ever stand for violence, and that by resorting to violence he will make himself detested by a few and ridiculed by many."[20]

By 1933, UNEMPLOYMENT in Britain had reached nearly three million, exports had halved, the budget deficit stood at a high £170 million. This was on top of the humiliating abandonment of the gold standard a year earlier. Britons were starving in ways not seen since the enactment of the Poor Law in 1834.* And so, Tom Mosley sought direct contact with the unhappy public: "he conceives of great mass meetings with loud-speakers—50,000 at a time," Nicolson wrote.[21]

The year 1932 had been a pivotal one for Mosley. He had not only been charmed by Mussolini, who warned against "attempting a military stunt in England," but also he had met and fallen in love with Diana Guinness, née Mitford. Diana, the twenty-two-year-old wife of Bryan Guinness and mother of his two sons, believed in Mosley as the future leader of the nation. Their affair began that spring (while he was also juggling a dalliance with his sister-in-law, Lady Alexandra "Baba" Metcalfe). But even two mistresses and an ailing wife did not prevent Mosley from honing his interest in fascism.

As Cimmie's health faded after the birth of her third child, Michael, Mosley published his "lucid logical, forceful and persuasive" manifesto *The Greater Britain*, which married the economic strategy of the New Party with a case for his brand of British fascism.[22†]

ALTHOUGH THE FIRST meeting of the British Union of Fascists took place in Trafalgar Square on October 15, 1932, Rothermere had offered the "whole of the Harmsworth press at [Mosley's] disposal" over a year earlier. Mosley's change to fascism did nothing to dissuade the press baron from backing what seemed a "sound, commonsense, Conservative doctrine." To Rothermere, Mosley was as exciting as a panther strutting across a stage, a man he could harness to conservative ideals and rejuvenate the party. Whomever Rothermere thought he was seeing, it

---

* The Poor Law of 1834 provided that, in exchange for being housed in workhouses, clothed, and fed, the poor would need to give their work for free. It was intended as a means of solving the problem of starvation among the extreme poor but, in fact, created a situation where many workhouses became "Prisons for the Poor," according to many, and workhouses were the dread of every poor person (source: The National Archives, Kew).

† Cimmie Mosley died in April 1933. Mosley continued his affairs with both Diana Guinness and his sister-in-law, Alexandra "Baba" Metcalfe, for another three years.

was not Mosley. "Better the great adventure, better the great attempt for England's sake," Mosley told a crowd. "Better defeat, disaster, better far the end of that trivial thing called a political career than stifling in a uniform of blue and gold, strutting and posturing on the stage of little England," he said.[23] These were the words of a brilliant buccaneer, not a politician.

Rothermere could not see that Mosley had already spurned parliamentary tradition. Nor could he understand he was egging Mosley on: "It is a bore being thus dependent on the prima donnas of the Press," the observant Harold Nicolson confided in his diary.[24] Nor could Rothermere see that Mosley would ever be his puppet, particularly when it came to reinstating the monarchies of Central Europe.

In fact, Rothermere was Mosley's tool. Shortly before Cimmie's final illness, Tom and Cimmie visited Italy together to celebrate the International Fascist Exhibition in Rome, where Mosley's "Blackshirt" fascists carried their banners alongside the Italian contingents. The Mosleys viewed the proceedings from the balcony of Palazzo Venezia with Mussolini standing beside them, and Mosley was amply rewarded with a monthly payment from mid-1933 of five thousand pounds from Il Duce.[25]* It was Mussolini who insisted that Mosley use the term "fascist" for his movement.

Rothermere hadn't recognized that Mosley viewed him as an "Albert Hall supporter" whose conventionality did little to endear himself. The *Manchester Guardian* called Mosley "a raider, a corsair." His fascist oratory was only rivaled by the twenty-seven-year-old William Joyce, the street-brawling son of southern Irish loyalists who had recently joined the BUF, abandoning his earlier fascist incarnation with the British Fascisti Party. By November 1933, with Italian money, Mosley was able to recruit the skilled propagandist A. K. Chesterton as editor of his magazine *The Blackshirt*.† Eventually, Chesterton would become Mosley's director of propaganda. John Beckett, the former Labour MP, joined the following year, and acted as the BUF's director of publicity. Although

---

* This fact was not known until well after the declaration of war by Britain in September 1939.

† He was the cousin of novelist G. K., creator of Father Brown.

Mosley later claimed he was no anti-Semite, he incorporated his first anti-Semitic slur against Jews at the October 1932 meeting at Memorial Hall, on Farringdon Street in London. The additions of Joyce, Chesterton, and Beckett accounted for the BUF's increasingly anti-Semitic stance.[26]

Rothermere, however, seemed unaware of this momentous change in direction. Mussolini's fascism was not based on Jews being an inferior race. Yet Nazi influences had already crept into Mosley's thinking and oratory even before Hitler came to power. In his defense of Mosley's Blackshirts, Rothermere wrote, "The Socialists, especially, who jeer at the Blackshirts as being of foreign origin, forget that the founder and High Priest of their own creed was the German Jew Karl Marx." Further on in his *Daily Mail* puff for Mosley, Rothermere asserted that "Blackshirts proclaim a fact which politicians dating from pre-war days will never face—that the new age requires new methods and new men."[27] His Jewish advertisers were unimpressed, and threats to remove their advertising became a cause célèbre.*

Mosley's acceptance of the corporate state as implemented by Mussolini did not immediately attract Hitler. In fact, Mosley sought to distance himself from the Nazis, saying that "their methods are German methods. . . . If a Blackshirt Government came into power in this country they would continue to be different in character."[28] His viewpoint would soon change.

---

* The war of words continued throughout the 1930s. The American Jewish community had begun to militate against the Nazi diatribes, and the British Jewish community was organizing to try to provide a haven for the many thousands of Jewish immigrants.

Corralling the Malcontents

We could have got a dictator a lot easier than Germany got Hitler.
—General Hugh S. Johnson,
Head of the National Recovery Administration

Fascism was on the rise in the United States, too. By 1933, there were the Silver Shirts (officially called the Silver Legion of America), led by William Dudley Pelley and based in Asheville, North Carolina. The Crusader White Shirts of Chattanooga, Tennessee, had been founded by New York–born George Christians, too. The National Gentile League, "true blue" Americans, came slightly later—in 1934—and was led by Donald Shea of Maryland. The secretary of his association, Lois de Lafayette Washburn, who signed her letters "T.N.T.," spread the word from Chicago, Illinois, to Tacoma, Washington. There was also the German American Bund, neat in their silver-gray shirts and black trousers, led by the Munich-born Fritz Kuhn.* The Bund did not shilly-shally with niceties: it sought to establish "a powerful sabotage machine" and "a vast spy net."[1] Inspired by Henry Ford and his *Dearborn Independent* that praised Hitler, Kuhn saw himself as America's natural "führer." But there were others who harbored the same aspirations.

Putzi Hanfstaengl's nemesis, Kurt Lüdecke, had come to the United States in 1924 as a traveling salesman, spreading Nazi propaganda everywhere he went and recruiting members to the National Socialist

---

* Kuhn had immigrated to Michigan in 1928 and worked at the Henry Ford Hospital and later at the laboratory of the Ford Motor Company.

cause. Heinz Spanknoebel followed fast on Lüdecke's heels, initially as part of the Free Society of Teutonia.* All these bodies were white supremacist, fascist, seditious, and, naturally, anti-Semitic.

Although "the shirts" were the most visible sign of the rise of fascism in America, the defenders of the Christian word were by far the most successful. Father Charles E. Coughlin's Detroit radio pulpit reached millions of regular listeners who heeded his call. From Kansas, the evangelist Gerald B. Winrod preached fascism and racial hatred through his popular newspaper *The Defender* and developed a strong following among the German-speaking Mennonites of his state. Between Coughlin and Winrod, millions came to believe President Roosevelt was a purveyor of communist propaganda, the devil incarnate, and an "upstart dictator."[2] They found a natural fellow traveler of the right in the various chapters of the Ku Klux Klan.

Malcontents on the left were targeted by Soviet intelligence operatives already active in the United States. Stalin believed the innocence and moral commitment of these "do-gooders" against fascism would help the communist international movement. Soviet intelligence files are replete with failed—and successful—attempts to recruit those holding "romantic antifascist views."[3]

"I do not think it is too much to say," Rex Tugwell, a member of FDR's Brain Trust, wrote, "that on March 4 [election day] we were confronted with a choice between an orderly revolution—a peaceful and rapid departure from past concepts—and a violent and disorderly overthrow of the whole capitalist structure."[4] Worse still, there were malcontents among the elite. The banks and big business were agog. Angry. Bemused. Defiant. Surely, they could cajole Roosevelt into forgetting his "forgotten man." Surely, he remained one of *them* despite the legislation.

JUST PRIOR TO Roosevelt's taking office, Princess Stephanie had spent some weeks in the United States. Her first stop was New York, where she stayed with her friends Cathleen Vanderbilt and her husband, Harry

---

* Spanknoebel and Kuhn knew each other since their days together at Teutonia in 1924.

Cushing Jr. Next, she joined John Charles Martin and his wife in Philadelphia. Martin ran both *The Philadelphia Inquirer* and *The Saturday Evening Post,* as well as three other journals purchased by his wife's stepfather, publisher Cyrus Curtis. Martin was also second after Pierre S. du Pont on America's rich list. Although Stephanie was no longer working exclusively for Rothermere, he undoubtedly wished her to gauge the temperature among the American conservatives toward Hitler and about his dream of reinstating the monarchies during her visit.[5] The burning question was, however, had Hitler paid Stephanie to contact American "aristocrats" too?

Stephanie did not visit the car manufacturer Henry Ford, who was the only man Hitler admired in America, "not so much as an industrial wonder-worker but rather as a reputed anti-Semite and a possible source of funds."[6] Her mission was purely aristocratic in nature, and she was aware that there was a close link between the aristocratic and the economic in the United States. Industrialists, railroad barons, and investment bankers were all worried that Roosevelt might betray their class.

BETWEEN STEPHANIE'S APRIL and May 1933 trips to Berlin, she made the rounds among the aristocratic circles in London, too. Lady Ethel Snowden, who wrote a column for Rothermere, and her friend Lady Margot Asquith, Countess of Oxford and Asquith, were Princess Stephanie's "sponsors." Soon enough, Stephanie frequented all the best drawing rooms, social occasions, and soirées London had to offer, flaunting her Continental title, jewels, and furs. Naturally, a busy social whirl required a sumptuous wardrobe, as did meetings with heads of state.

But she still had to economize. The princess had heard about the skillful (and relatively inexpensive) hands of the White Russian couturiere Anna Wolkoff, and about how Anna had done wonders for "poor Mrs. Simpson's" fashions. In fact, aristocratic London had been abuzz with rumors of an affair between the slender, angular American from Baltimore and the Prince of Wales ever since Wallis had gone to the prince's home, Fort Belvedere, that January without her husband, Ernest.

And so Stephanie, who was never shy of making a grand entrance, presented herself at Anna de Wolkoff Haute Couture Modes in London's West End, in a flourish of furs and smiles, saying something like, "Make me beautiful clothes like you do for Mrs. Simpson." Enchanted, Wolkoff and Stephanie spoke about the "old days" during Stephanie's numerous fittings, and how they both hated the Bolsheviks. It may not have occurred to Wolkoff—yet—that Edward's circle of friends already revolved around Wallis or, indeed, that *he* would be responsible for Wolkoff losing the American lady's patronage by paying for a Parisian wardrobe. By the time Stephanie crossed the couturiere's threshold, Thelma Furness,* Edward's previous paramour, had been brutally dismissed by a tearful royal telephone operator, who had been forbidden to put Thelma through to the prince.[7]

PRINCESS STEPHANIE WAS disappointed that Hitler's letter inviting Lord Rothermere to meet had not arrived by June 1934. She may even have wondered if her boss's commissioning of an executive monoplane, which he called "Britain first," had offended Hitler.† If she had given in to any doubts about her persuasiveness or her ability to charm Hitler, at least she could comfort herself that British fascism was on the march in London, as Price's article in the *Daily Mail* on June 8 made clear.

Tom Mosley had presided over a crowd of nearly fifteen thousand at the Olympia exhibition hall in London that had degenerated into a riot. The newspapers blamed the communists. Price declared, "The Red Hooligans . . . got what they deserved. Olympia has been the scene of many assemblies and many great fights, but never had it offered the

---

* She was the identical twin sister of Gloria Morgan Vanderbilt and maternal aunt of Gloria Vanderbilt the author, fashion designer, and socialite.

† Fed up with the government refusal to create a viable air force, Rothermere was determined to show Baldwin up and approached the Bristol Aeroplane Company to build an executive airplane that was "faster than anything available elsewhere" in March 1934. It evolved into the Blenheim bomber. Tom Mosley would claim that the airplane's name was taken from the Blackshirt motto "Britain First." It was only the first of several maneuvers to make Britain "air savvy" (source: Taylor, *Great Outsiders*, 308–09).

spectacle of so many fights mixed up with a meeting."[8] The rally began half an hour late because of "disturbances" outside the exhibition hall. Primed for any confrontation, the BUF's boys had been trained in military tactics and street fighting at the party's Black House headquarters in Chelsea. Mosley's "Gothic Madonna," Diana Guinness, was not there due to illness, but her sister Nancy was. Seated toward the front was Mosley's other mistress, Lady Alexandra "Baba" Metcalfe (nicknamed "Baba Blackshirt").

To a fanfare of trumpets and a blaze of white light, Mosley strutted forward like a corsair, flanked by his youthful BUF soldiers. They were "preceded by a long procession of Union Jacks and Blackshirt banners" as they "advanced down the whole length of the 200-yard central aisle to the high platform at the far end." It was a Nuremberg rally in miniature. There were two and a half thousand communist agitators seated, spread out in small clusters. As Mosley opened his mouth to speak, a quartet of young communists chanted: "Hitler and Mosley, what are they for? Thuggery, buggery, hunger and war." Mosley's men pounced. The communists responded, armed for the occasion.

One such communist, Esmond Romilly (who later eloped with Diana Guinness's younger sister Jessica), had come armed with knuckledusters. Hundreds were beaten. Some were treated at makeshift first-aid facilities just outside the hall. Over sixty protesters were taken to the hospital, where medical staff confirmed injuries from razors and other improvised weapons. Nancy Mitford, who had called the BUF "the hope of the future" in an article written a few weeks earlier for the July issue of *Vanguard*, was sickened. The Blackshirts were nothing more than a private army of hooligans, and Nancy felt she had to repudiate them. The middle-class audience was outraged by the violence.[9]

Rothermere was aghast. A twenty-year-old *Daily Mail* journalist who worked in Berlin received a telegram from London: "The Blackshirts are in the wash and the colour is running very fast." So, in Berlin, Rothermere's people put away their Blackshirt uniforms, heeding the tip-off.[10]

Many years later, Mosley claimed an anxious Rothermere informed him in person that the *Daily Mail* was "pulling out" of backing the BUF, blaming its Jewish advertisers. Mosley, knowing Rothermere still felt overshadowed by his dead brother, Lord Northcliffe, who owned the *Daily Mail* and the *Daily Mirror*, replied: "Do you know what Northcliffe would have done? He would have said, 'One more word from you, and the *Daily Mail* placards tomorrow will carry the words 'Jews threaten British press' and you will have no further trouble."

A correspondence between them ensued, which Rothermere published in the *Daily Mail* on July 19. Mosley explained that it was his "task to convert the British people to the new faith" and blamed the Jews for attacking fascists in an internationally organized movement. Rothermere politely replied that "I have also made it quite clear in my conversations with you that I never could support any movement with an anti-semitic [sic] bias . . . or any movement which will substitute a 'Corporate State' for Parliamentary institutions in this country."[11] With the withdrawal of the *Daily Mail*'s patronage, the BUF membership plummeted from its height of fifty thousand members.

THREE WEEKS LATER, Ernest Tennant was dining in Joachim von Ribbentrop's Dahlem garden with Heinrich Himmler. According to Tennant, a kinsman of Margot, Lady Oxford and Asquith, the purpose of the dinner was to talk to Heinrich Himmler. Apparently, Lady Oxford and her daughter, Princess Elizabeth Bibesco, had passed a list of names across to Tennant of those "who were in concentration camps." They wished to see these people liberated, Tennant said.

Tennant "took the opportunity of going through the list name by name." Himmler rounded on him, saying, "I don't remember that during the South African war the Germans were invited to inspect your concentration camps," he shouted. Everyone fell silent. "I don't remember that when Hitler was in prison any of you English showed any interest in how he was treated—you ought to go down on your knees and thank God that we have got those scum under control," Himmler screamed, nearly choking on his food.[12]* As soon as his breathing was back under control, Himmler sprang to his feet and left without a word. Tennant

---

* One of the names on the list was Georgi Dimitroff, the Bulgarian communist, accused of participating in the Reichstag fire.

was unable to understand the remark about getting "those scum un- der control" or other references to enemies of the state. Ribbentrop was even more shocked than Tennant, since Himmler suddenly ranted that Röhm was "as good as dead," too. Ribbentrop feared that his friendship with the SA leader may implicate him in some plot of which he had no knowledge.[13]

OF COURSE, HIMMLER was referring to the bloodbath that took place the following evening—the "Night of the Long Knives." On the peace- ful shores at Wiessee on the Tegernsee in Bavaria, Ernst Röhm, along with seventy-seven of his SA supporters, were arrested and butchered. Simultaneous arrests occurred throughout Germany. Although the fi- nal death toll was never published, it is believed another two hundred people were executed, most notably General von Schleicher (and his wife), Vice Chancellor Papen's outspoken associates, the former head of the police department of the Prussian interior ministry, and the leading representative of the Catholic lay group Catholic Action.

Two weeks later, Hitler addressed the Reichstag: "Mutinies are sup- pressed in accordance with laws of iron which are eternally the same. If anyone reproaches me and asks why I did not resort to the regular Courts of Justice for conviction of the offenders, then all that I can say to him is this: In this hour I was responsible for the fate of the Ger- man people, and thereby I became the supreme Justiciar of the German people," Hitler declared. "I gave the order to shoot those who were the ringleaders in this treason."[14]

June 30 became the date to settle old scores, too. Gustav Ritter von Kahr, who was instrumental in the failure of the November 1923 putsch, was killed. Publisher Fritz Gerlich, who strongly criticized the Nazis, was executed. Gregor Strasser, too, who had allied himself with Schleicher, was murdered for his bad judgment. Some of the assassinations bene- fited Göring, but most helped Heinrich Himmler, who had taken over the SS. During a twenty-four-hour period, Himmler had demonstrated his absolute loyalty to Hitler, and his SS had emerged "as a new power centre within the regime and as the real victor" of the "Röhm affair."[15]

An unwitting Putzi Hanfstaengl was in Newport, Rhode Island, attending the society wedding of John Jacob Astor VI to Miss Ellen Tuck French. Although Putzi was pressed to comment, he had known nothing about Hitler's coup. To make matters worse, tales of a "Second Revolution" and "the leaders' indulgence to the rebels" filled thousands of column inches in America without his input. On July 2, Putzi made his first statement, having cleared it with Berlin, "There will be others who will fill their places. . . . Hitler has averted chaos, and he has not only averted ruin for Germany, but for the entire civilized world."[16]

Men on White Horses

I do not often envy other countries, but I say that if this country
ever needed a Mussolini it needs one now.
—Senator Edward Reed of Pennsylvania,
72nd Congress, 1st Session, May 5, 1932

By March 1934, Pecora, the president's New Deal, and Roosevelt's "forgotten man" generated tremendous anger and despair among America's "aristocrats." Some of their private correspondence found its way
into the public arena, most notably between Robert R. M. Carpenter, a
retired vice president of DuPont, and John J. Raskob, the current vice
president of DuPont and close friend of Pierre du Pont. Raskob disliked
Roosevelt intensely. "You haven't much to do," Raskob suggested to Carpenter, "and I know of no one that could better take the lead in trying to
induce the DuPont and General Motors groups, followed by other big
industries, to definitely organize to protect society from the suffering
which it is bound to endure if we allow communistic elements to lead
the people to believe that all businessmen are crooks, not to be trusted,
and that no one should be allowed to get rich." After all, Raskob noted,
Pierre and Irenée du Pont were "in a position to talk directly with a
group that controls a larger share of industry . . . than any other group
in the United States."[1]

Was he advocating that American industry should resort to some
sort of fascist coup? On August 14, 1934, after consultations with his colleagues, Raskob chartered the American Liberty League in Washington,

D.C., to "teach the necessity of respect for the rights of persons and property . . . and . . . the duty of government to encourage" such rights in the acquisition of wealth. From its inception to its quiet death in 1940, DuPont and General Motors financially backed Raskob's American Liberty League to the hilt.[2]

The organization promoted the philosophy and ideals of rugged individualism along with old and established traditions, debunking the new social, political, and economic imperatives of Great Depression America. It cloaked itself in a respectable past of humanitarianism and American philanthropy that could not stand the scrutiny of the Roosevelt administration. It did not care about Roosevelt's "forgotten man" or hopes of economic or racial equality or about Roosevelt's initiatives to get America back to work.

While the Liberty League was wholly American in character, it caused worry in both Germany and the Soviet Union. *Izvestia* scathingly reported from Moscow that the league "aimed to conquer the masses." Hitler sniggered from Berlin because *he* had conquered his industrialists by using their own organizational network and fear of a return to chaos.

Incredibly, the Liberty League quoted the Constitution while plotting to overthrow the president and take control of the government of the United States. But to succeed, it needed to find "a man on a white horse," a man who could ride over the horizon with the fifth cavalry to rescue America. With the recent violent "Röhm Affair" in Germany as the model, perhaps the league members—all wealthy Wall Streeters and captains of industry—could eliminate the threat that Franklin Roosevelt represented. But who could be their "man on a white horse?"[3] Apparently, Colonel Charles A. Lindbergh was considered, but ultimately he was rejected because he was on the Morgan preferred list of investors. To boot, they believed the rank-and-file soldier would not follow one of the flying glamour boys.

Instead, retired Marine Corps general Smedley Darlington Butler was selected but, unknown to the industrialists, secretly refused to play ball. Butler testified before the McCormack-Dickstein House Special Committee on Un-American Activities in New York City on November

20, 1934.* The following day, Butler was front-page news across the country. The *New York Times* headline read "GENERAL BUTLER BARES 'FASCIST PLOT' TO SEIZE GOVERNMENT BY FORCE." If truth is stranger than fiction, General Butler's story had to beat any fairy tale by a country mile. He said that because of his popularity with soldiers from the Great War over his stance about their receiving bonus pay from the government (which Roosevelt was against), he had been singled out by prominent American financiers J. P. Morgan Jr., Thomas W. Lamont, Grayson M. P. Murphy, the du Pont family, Robert Sterling Clark (heir to the Singer sewing machine fortune), and former presidential candidate Al Smith, among others, to be their "man on a white horse" and lead an army of half a million soldiers to seize power in Washington. As details of the fascist plot unfolded, it became apparent that Congress, too, would be put under the control of a caretaker dictator.

General Hugh S. Johnson, former head of the National Recovery Administration, would become the financiers' dictator. It was hoped that "President Roosevelt would 'go along' as the King of Italy did with Mussolini." If he didn't, then the president and vice president would be forced to resign. Butler made it clear that he had several approaches from Gerald P. MacGuire, a stockbroker for the firm of Grayson M. P. Murphy & Company, and that he had strung MacGuire along to see where the plot was heading.[4]

"Perfect moonshine! Too unutterably ridiculous to comment upon," Morgan's Tom Lamont commented, nonetheless. Hadn't the Glass-Steagall Act forced Morgan to divest itself of its commercial holdings and create Morgan Guaranty Trust Bank as a separate entity? Besides, Butler was a highly decorated soldier, known as "the fighting Quaker" and the recipient of the Army Distinct Service Award, the Navy Distinct Service Award, and twice decorated with the Congressional Medal of Honor for his acts of bravery.[5]

It was also true that Butler had taken the unprecedented step of

---

* Established to investigate propaganda by foreign powers and influences they may have in America to promote fascism, until Butler's testimony, the committee had almost entirely devoted its efforts to the Communist Party.

speaking out against the Italian dictator Benito Mussolini in 1931 and faced a potential court-martial for his actions. The charges were dropped, and Butler resigned in disgust, becoming a champion for the bonus payments to soldiers from the war. In the summer of 1932, he spoke to the "Bonus Army" during their march on Washington. This led the plotters to believe that Butler was the only man who could raise an army of five hundred thousand men needed to overthrow the government.*

In early 1933, Gerald MacGuire approached Butler, proposing that he go to Chicago to address the American Legion. Butler stalled. That August, MacGuire told Butler that he had access to $42,000 in an account with Grayson Murphy that he could put at Butler's disposal. So Butler led him on, he told the committee. At a later meeting in Butler's hotel room in Newark, New Jersey, MacGuire tossed $18,000 onto the general's bed "to pay his expenses" and showed Butler a bankbook with $64,000 in deposits to back the movement.†

Of course, everyone named by Butler declared their innocence. MacGuire, who testified that same November afternoon, said, "It's a joke—a publicity stunt!" Of course, he was unable to answer who would benefit from such publicity. Grayson Murphy, using his former military title of colonel in his rebuttal, said, "It's a fantasy! I can't imagine how anyone could produce it or any sane person believe it."[6]

Nonetheless, Butler's testimony was damning. He quoted MacGuire as saying, "You know the president is weak. He will come right along with us. He was born in this class and he will come back. In the end he will come around." Since DuPont owned the Remington Arms Factory, MacGuire allegedly drew comfort from the fact that the financial backers of the American Liberty League would have no problem in arming the insurgent army.[7]

Then, unexpectedly, the *Philadelphia Inquirer* journalist Paul Comly French testified under oath that Butler's earlier testimony was entirely accurate. Apparently, MacGuire had told French on September 13, 1934,

---

* General Douglas MacArthur dispersed the Bonus Army from the capital.
† With inflation at approximately 1,852 percent since 1934, that would make the $18,000 worth approximately $333,360 and the bank balance $1,185,280 (source: www.in2013dollars.com/inflation-rate-in-1934).

that "we need a fascist government in this country to save the Nation from the communists who want to tear it down and wreck all that we have built in America." MacGuire had regaled French with his eyewitness accounts fresh from Germany. "It was a plan that Hitler had used in Germany [with the SA] in putting all the unemployed in labor camps and barracks. That would solve it [our unemployment] overnight, and when we get into power that is what we will do." MacGuire confirmed to French, too, that Smedley Butler was the only man who could get "a million men" to follow him.[8]

Butler's and French's testimonies were unsettling. Congressman John W. McCormack commented in his Irish lilt that it was disconcerting that "persons possessing tremendous wealth" may have planned an assault on "our democratic institutions." The American Liberty League harbored not only members from the banking sector but also heavy hitters in industry other than John J. Raskob and the du Ponts. Alfred P. Sloan and William S. Knudsen of General Motors, Edward F. Hutton and Colby M. Chester of General Foods, J. Howard Pew of Sun Oil, and Sewell L. Avery of Montgomery Ward were only the tip of the iceberg. Board members of U.S. Steel, Heinz, Colgate, Birds Eye, and Maxwell House were also implicated.

WHEN THE PRESIDENT was asked at a press conference later if he had any problem with the principles of the league, Roosevelt replied, "An organization that only advocates two or three out of the Ten Commandments may be a perfectly good organization in the sense that you couldn't object to the two or three out of the Ten Commandments," but it left open the issues of teaching respect for the right of individuals "against those who sought to enrich themselves at the expense of their fellow citizens." It also ignored the duty of government to find employment for all those who wished to work. Roosevelt added with some wry humor that the founders of the American Liberty League were "deeply moved by the Constitution of the United States. They had just discovered it."[9]

By using wit and satire to belittle the most powerful people in America, and with help from General Smedley D. Butler and Paul Comly French,

Roosevelt had seen off a fascist-inspired coup with not much more than a tickle under their chins. Whatever the McCormack-Dickstein findings would be against the American Liberty League and its backers no longer mattered.[10]* Roosevelt had resolved not to take any further action. If there was only a grain of truth in Butler's and French's testimonies (which the president believed there was), Roosevelt had met the American Liberty League members on his terms and made it synonymous with greedy fascist moneybags for hire.

Roosevelt would not be drawn into an open argument with members of what he called the "I Can't Take It Club" and continued to neutralize the same big guns that had taken aim at his administration with laughter. Some bright spark in the press corps asked the president toward the end of the year if the directors had invited him to join the American Liberty League. "I don't think they did," Roosevelt replied, laughing. "Must have been an oversight."[11]

---

* It was discovered later that Dickstein was a paid undercover agent of the Soviets, nicknamed "Crook" for his avarice.

Hitler's "Listening Posts"

You are the listening posts, for ahead of the front you have definite
undertakings to prepare.
— Adolf Hitler to the Auslands Organization, November 1934

Roosevelt's laughter in Washington, D.C., was putting a brave face on
the threat of fascism in America. Hitler's former propagandist Kurt
Lüdecke willingly testified before the McCormack-Dickstein Committee in a closed session in September 1934 and recounted the tale of his
months as the unwilling guest of the Nazis at Oranienburg concentration camp. Through cunning, Lüdecke had managed a daring escape
to the United States. And yet the specifics of what he said to the committee never made it into the final report. Just the same, Hanfstaengl
and Goebbels were enraged, since Lüdecke knew their plans to infiltrate
aristocratic society throughout Europe and the Americas.[1]

Naturally, Roosevelt was unaware that Rothermere had instructed
Princess Stephanie in November 1933 to meet with Adolf Hitler, or that
she had already captivated Captain Fritz Wiedemann, Hitler's personal
adjutant.[2] Dr. Abraham Flexner wrote from Austria in July 1934 to
Thomas J. Jones, "The folly and stupidity of men seem boundless. Never
has this feeling weighed upon me more strongly than these days spent
in Austria. These people are better educated than we. But they have absolutely no political sense or experience."*

---

* Flexner was the director of the Institute for Advanced Study at Princeton, and Jones
was the former deputy cabinet secretary to four British prime ministers.

In London, Churchill, the main dissenter against Hitler in Parliament, believed the skies over the Continent had darkened. The assassination of the Austrian chancellor, Engelbert Dollfuss, on July 25, 1934, led by the Nazi infiltrator and Austrian politician Anton von Rintelen, had shown Hitler's hand. Mussolini reacted swiftly, dispatching three Italian divisions to the Brenner Pass to protect his borders.* Hitler recoiled from attacking and recalled or dismissed any German official implicated in the coup d'état. However, his "yes man" Papen was appointed as the new German ambassador. Churchill was in no doubt that Papen's "explicit purpose" was to organize "the overthrow of the Austrian Republic."[3]

The attempted coup in Austria was followed almost immediately by the long-expected death of President Hindenburg on August 3. Hitler "was now the Sovereign of Germany," leaving Churchill certain that the führer's "bargain with the Reichswehr had been sealed and kept by the blood-purge [Night of the Long Knives]. The Brownshirts had been reduced to obedience and reaffirmed their loyalty to the Fuehrer," as Churchill wrote. "All foes and potential rivals had been extirpated from their ranks."[4] Incredibly, Hitler's subsequent assumption of the titles as both president and chancellor of the Third Reich was not commented on by the British government. Instead, Stanley Baldwin was battling to keep Churchill out of the cabinet and fighting him on the India Act that was soon to be discussed in Parliament. Like America, but for different reasons, the British leadership slept.

All the same, relations between British and German businesses became frayed due to Germany's lack of foreign exchange. German companies found it hard to pay for deliveries of foreign goods. "How her essential imports are to be paid for once the reserves of gold and foreign exchange are exhausted," Ernest Tennant wrote to the Foreign Office in March 1934, "is a problem which remains unsolved. Leading industrialists are alarmed at the outlook." By June 1934, matters had deteriorated further.[5] Even the cordial relationship between Montagu Norman and Hjalmar Schacht had become strained.

A year earlier, in May 1933, Hitler sent the party ideologue, Alfred Rosenberg, to London. Rosenberg had been appointed the first chief of

---

* Dr. Kurt Schuschnigg replaced the disgraced Rintelen.

the NSDAP's *Aussenpolitisches Amt* (APA).* Rosenberg's aim was to influence the men in power in Great Britain and to "sell" them on the Nazi ethos in a concerted public relations exercise. Even so, Rosenberg was utterly tactless. Among his litany of faux pas was laying a huge swastika wreath at the Cenotaph, the revered British memorial dedicated to the fallen from all wars.

Nonetheless, Rosenberg did make contact within government circles. Among the men approached was Alan Barlow, principal private secretary to Prime Minister MacDonald. Sir Robert Vansittart in the British Foreign Office feared that Barlow "had been suborned by the Nazis" as a result. Rosenberg's main object, however, remained the Royal Air Force, and he hoped to recruit British spies who would reveal secrets about rearmament—not that there were any secrets to be had at that stage.[6]

Although Hanfstaengl and Ribbentrop disliked each other, they each worked in their own mysterious ways to persuade Hitler that sending Rosenberg to England had been a serious misstep. As a fluent English speaker, Ribbentrop became an ideal candidate to replace the trenchant Rosenberg. His facility with the language also marked him out for rapid promotion within Hitler's foreign organization.[†]

AND SO, VOILÀ! Princess Stephanie mysteriously arranged for Rothermere to invite Joachim von Ribbentrop to England as Hitler's newly appointed commissioner at the foreign office (*Auswärtiges Amt*). Ribbentrop was effectively Hitler's personal spy inside the foreign ministry, feeding him daily critical reports of the aristocratic diplomats whom the führer so vehemently mistrusted. Ribbentrop's reward was to head his own organization, Büro Ribbentrop, with a staff of fourteen people. Located across the road from the British Foreign Office at 64 Wilhelmstrasse, it would later become the grander Dienststelle Ribbentrop,

---

* The Nazi Party foreign office ran in parallel to the state foreign office, where Freiherr Konstantin von Neurath was the respected foreign minister abroad.
† Ribbentrop had spent several years in England and then Canada in his youth, and had played ice hockey for Canada in the Stanley Cup.

a private fiefdom that rivaled the *Auswärtiges Amt* and the Nazi Party's Auslands Organization.

Ribbentrop was invited in August 1934 for a weekend at Rothermere's country home, the 2,230-acre estate and new-build mansion Stody Lodge at Melton Constable in Norfolk—nicknamed the "king's county"—for a spot of hunting, shooting, and some of the best trout fishing in England.*

Ribbentrop was in his element, since he always loved to portray himself as an English gentleman. Rothermere was quite evidently sympathetic to the Nazi regime and ensured that Ribbentrop was treated as a "polished emissary of the Führer." Also present were several pro-German businessmen (like Ernest Tennant), who were anxious to protect their Anglo-German trade and find out more about the nasty rumors concerning the June murders. Since Rothermere and his wife had been estranged for many years, it would have been in keeping for Princess Stephanie to act as his hostess and translator when German was spoken in asides. Queen Mary's brother, Alexander Cambridge, 1st Earl of Athlone, who had been the governor-general of South Africa (1924–1930), was present, too. Of course, Ribbentrop knew the earl's brother-in-law, Carl Edouard, the Nazi-loving Duke of Saxe-Coburg and Gotha, but was rather surprised that Athlone seemed to know so little about the Third Reich.[7]

On his return to Germany, Ribbentrop reported that foreign policy in Britain appeared to be pro-French because of a "clique led by the Foreign Office," yet the elite class of people he had met far preferred to be supportive of Germany. Nonetheless, what seemed to worry them all was the "energy" of the new Germany and reports of widespread violence against Jews, Catholics, and the June assassinations.

Ribbentrop proposed to address these issues in a few ways. First, Germany could neutralize any opposition from big business by granting credits to German firms wishing to buy British raw materials, effectively guaranteeing payments. Second, based solely on his conversation with

---

* My thanks to Adrian Tinniswood, delightful author and country house expert extraordinaire, for helping me to ferret out the truth of Rothermere's home in England at the time. The "Stody Estate" was sold by the Marquis of Lothian in 1931 (source: Tinniswood: *Country Life*, May 16, 1931, and October 22, 1948; *The Journal* [Norfolk], September 22, 1934).

the Earl of Athlone, he wrongly advised Hitler that all members of the royal family should be regarded as "the Crown." He emphatically stated that "the Crown" had a "much stronger influence in England" than had previously been believed and naturally hoped to resume its strong and sympathetic relations with Germany. Surely Carl Edouard could do something about reawakening the link between "the Crown" and its German outcasts? Lastly, and most significantly, with Rothermere on their side, Ribbentrop believed they could use the whole of the British press to their advantage.[8]

That was hogwash. Lord Beaverbrook (whose *Daily Express* had the largest circulation within the British Isles by 1937) challenged Conservative thinking but had a popular, aggressive tone and lively features so indicative of the new journalism. Although he kept a close rein on his journalists, Beaverbrook never actively sought the return of the European monarchies as did Rothermere.[9] The Berry brothers (Lords Camrose and Kemsley), Waldorf Astor, and his cousin John Jacob Astor V owned major newspapers, too, and had not adopted the same freewheeling diplomacy as Rothermere or Beaverbrook, generally supporting the national government of the day. Lady Lucy Houston, the former chorus girl who married wisely three times, was the septuagenarian owner of the *Saturday Review*. Lady Houston had a healthy dislike of "the Teuton," exclaiming "stand up to him, and he behaves himself; give him an inch . . . and he will take the whole measuring tape."[10]

STUDIOUS CENSORSHIP OF news from Germany was to blame in part for a lack of consensus in the conservative press. Not all foreign journalists or publishers, including Rothermere, understood that the German news agencies had changed almost imperceptibly since Hitler seized power. At the beginning of 1933, there were four German news agencies: Ullstein, Wolff, Transozean, Alfred Hugenberg's Telegrafen-Union.

When Hitler became chancellor, Wolff was viewed as "suspect" since it had democratic sympathies and a fair number of Jews working for it. The Nazis held up "official reports for hours or even days," T. J. Breen of *The Times* wrote from Berlin. "A favorite trick was to withhold the text of Hitler's speeches on the ground that they needed revision. In the meantime, the *Telegrafen-Union* agency was able to publish." By the end of 1933, Goebbels replaced all news agencies with his mighty Deutsches Nachrichtenbüro, or DNB, which would always sing from the Nazi hymn sheet.

One of the first casualties of the Wolff agency in London was a popular figure among the English, Iona von Ustinow, who was replaced by the patrician Fritz Hesse. On secretly becoming a British citizen with the help of the permanent secretary to the Foreign Office, Sir Robert Vansittart, Ustinow changed his name to Jona Ustinov. He was the father of the author, raconteur, director, and Oscar-winning actor Sir Peter Ustinov. Jona also became a British spy, known as "Klop" or agent "U.35."[11]

By and large, the British were blissfully unaware of the active Nazi plots to infiltrate its newspapers and high society. Ribbentrop returned to London for most of November 1934 and resided at the fashionable Brown's Hotel. He knew that ministers Stanley Baldwin and Ramsay MacDonald had been reluctant to agree with him about Hitler's peaceful intentions and resolved to concentrate his efforts on business leaders, the press, and royal circles.

Soon enough, Ribbentrop became the "must have" figure at all social occasions. Foremost among those entertaining him were Lady Edith Londonderry, Lady Maud "Emerald" Cunard, Lady Sybil Colefax, Mrs. Ronnie Greville, and Lady Nancy Astor—the "queen bees" of London society. Ambassadors from around the world flocked to their drawing rooms, where all the great, good, and fellow aristocrats were entertained lavishly. It was in their homes that informal propaganda webs were spun by the invited guests, with or without the hostess's knowledge.

Nonetheless, Ribbentrop had a steep hill to climb to successfully ensnare these powerful women. The handsome, charming, and undoubtedly aristocratic Count Dino Grandi, the Italian minister in London from 1932, had a head start in wooing London's society hostesses. Grandi was adored by all women. Tall, handsome, charming, with a pointed black beard and dark, intelligent eyes, he was the darling of what became known as Nancy Astor's "Cliveden Set." Understanding that he represented a fascist government in the home of democracy, he and his long-suffering wife, Antonietta, entertained frequently at the sumptuously decorated Italian embassy in Grosvenor Square. On display were tapestries and mirrors that had once belonged to the Medicis, "on loan" from the Uffizi Gallery; a silver candelabra made for the Neapolitan Bourbon kings; and some fifty pictures, including two by Titian. The embassy's entry hall had a lapis lazuli and agate table from the Barberini Palace. An ancient statue of a boy riding a seahorse spoke of Roman art and opulence. These were the accoutrements of the highest civilization, meant to be regarded with envy and proof that fascists were not barbarians.

Grandi conquered many of London's hostesses, including Emerald Cunard.* Known for her biting wit, shocking remarks, charm, and championing of Mrs. Simpson in society, Emerald claimed to be bored with Christmas, which was looming once again, saying it was celebrated "only for servants." At a luncheon party with Grandi at her home, she teased him "unmercifully," accusing him of being the *real* leader of Mussolini's March on Rome. The diarist and MP Chips Channon roared with laughter, realizing that Grandi's charm was "just a trifle too great to be entirely unselfconscious . . ." and noted how all the women hung on his every movement and word, save Alfred Duff Cooper's wife, Diana.[12]

Even sensible Irene Curzon, the eldest daughter of the former viceroy of India and Mosley's sister-in-law, had fallen under Grandi's spell. Irene had met Grandi at a dinner at Cliveden, where he was "thrilling on Tom [Mosley]. He watches every move of Tom's and as the press gives no fair verdict of his speeches, writes home himself the truth. He predicted the spread of fascism here after a Labour government." Knowing his audience, Grandi also spoke reverently of Irene's dead sister, Cimmie. All the while, Nancy Astor and her sister Phyllis fumed that Irene's youngest sister, Baba Metcalfe (who was still Tom Mosley's mistress) had conquered the Italian minister, too.[13]

Baba's husband, Edward, known to all as "Fruity," had been an officer in the Indian army, and was the Prince of Wales's equerry and boon

---

* "Emerald" was born Maude Burke in San Francisco (1872–1948). She was brought up in New York and married Sir Bache Cunard, 3rd Baronet Cunard and grandson of the founder of the Cunard shipping line. They had one daughter, Nancy, who was immensely talented and terribly lonely. She loathed her mother almost as much as her mother hated her. Nancy was an indefatigable patron of Black artists.

companion. Fruity had no money and was not very bright but was a thoroughly likable chap. Quite tall, handsome, and a keen sportsman, Fruity was a man's man, and counted himself lucky to be married to the beautiful and bright Baba. But unlike Tom Mosley, Baba found it difficult to juggle two lovers, a husband, and children all at once. Naturally, Fruity suffered most.

Mosley, on the other hand, was readily able to leave his three children in the care of his sister-in-law Irene and handle both Baba and Diana Guinness. Indeed, when Mussolini later lost faith with Mosley for criticizing the Italian invasion of Abyssinia in October 1935, Mosley seamlessly switched his attentions to the ravishing Diana and her sister Unity Mitford, since both had become cozy with Hitler.[14]

BRITISH SOCIETY HOSTESSES and their husbands were attracted in varying degrees to the dictators: Hitler, Mussolini, and Stalin. Nancy Astor was fascinated by Stalin and went to the Soviet Union in 1931 with her husband, Waldorf. Accustomed to entertaining royalty, statesmen, people of influence, literary lions, and even presidents, Nancy could not leave Moscow until she had personally met the Soviet leader. After an hourlong talk, Stalin asked the Astors to remain while *he* asked *them* questions. Nancy could not recall what those questions were, except for one: "whether in our opinion" Winston Churchill "would regain position and influence." For Nancy, it was *the* most irksome question, since, as a teetotaler, Winston's drinking habits distressed her. She entirely missed Stalin's point. Winston was a man to be feared.[15]

Waldorf had met Hitler in September 1933, not out of admiration, but rather as the leader of a delegation to complain about the treatment of the Christian Science Church in Germany. Wilhelm Frick, minister of the interior, offered comforting words: as long as the church did not get involved in politics, Christian Scientists would not be excluded from society. (They already were.) Waldorf said that he would believe those words from the chancellor himself, and so a twenty-minute interview with Hitler was arranged. Waldorf left the meeting satisfied that Hitler was a man of his word.[16]

It was no secret that London's leading society hostesses were agog at the possibility of meeting the dictators, often moving mountains to do so. The American hostess Laura Corrigan, who was famed for her malapropisms, had made meeting the dictators her personal quest. From March to May 1932, she was in Rome and procured a lengthy audience with a "pompous" Mussolini and a more rewarding interview with Pope Pius XI. When Mrs. Corrigan returned to England, she was staying at Cliveden at the same time as Count Grandi. He made an off-color remark about Il Duce aimed at Mrs. Corrigan and was rounded on by Lady Astor. "Young man," she admonished, "please remember that in this house nothing *ever* is said against Signor Mussolini."[17]

THIS WAS THE environment into which Ribbentrop descended during a November 1934 visit to cultivate the British aristocracy. He offered countless opportunities for the hostesses to arrange future visits to meet Hitler. Mrs. Ronnie Greville had entertained Ribbentrop at her London home in November 1932 (listing him as "Baron Ribbendrop") and invited him again later that month, along with Lady Emerald Cunard, the Aga Khan, and Lady Churchill. Nancy Astor, too, nurtured him in society. Ribbentrop saw Lady Astor as a strong link to Philip Kerr, 11th Marquess of Lothian,* as well as numerous other parliamentarians.

He was particularly interested in cozying up to Lord and Lady Londonderry, too, whose political receptions were *the* go-to event. His wishes were fulfilled. Edith Londonderry introduced him to George Bernard Shaw and the archbishop of Canterbury and facilitated meetings with statesmen like Sir Austen Chamberlain, the former foreign secretary. Hitler encouraged Ribbentrop to act independently of the German ambassador, Leopold von Hoesch, who had been left in place since the Weimar days. Authorized to entertain as lavishly as he had been wined and dined by others, Ribbentrop gladly did as he was told.

---

* Kerr became the 11th Marquess of Lothian after the death of his cousin Robert Schomberg Kerr in March 1930. He had been a devout Catholic, who once thought of becoming a priest, but eventually converted to Christian Science under the overwhelming influence of Nancy Astor.

He even extended all-expenses-paid trips to attend the Nuremberg rally in September 1935.[18]

Lady Emerald Cunard referred to Ribbentrop as a "delicious, real life Nazi" and was especially entranced with "Ribbentrop's dimple."[19] In fact, the American ambassador between 1933 and 1937, Robert Worth Bingham, called Lady Cunard's set a "pro-German cabal." Not that Emerald was the most pro-German among those in her ranks. That dubious honor fell to Edward, Prince of Wales. "The Prince was not a man for abstract ideas or ponderous thought," Wallis, Duchess of Windsor, wrote later.[20] She should have known best, since she led him by the nose.

EDWARD'S PRINCIPAL THOUGHT for the future was already wrapped up in Wallis. In January 1935, Emerald introduced Mrs. Simpson to others in her set, including Princess Stephanie. "She is a nice, quiet, well-bred mouse of a woman with large startled eyes and a huge, huge mole," Chips Channon wrote after lunching with Wallis at Emerald's home. "I think she is surprised and rather conscience-stricken by her present position and the limelight. . . . Emerald dominated the conversation with her brilliance, her *mots* and epigrams, some mild, some penetrating, darted like flashes from a crystal *girandole*."[21]

The Prince of Wales was a Nazi admirer. Although he appreciated what Hitler had done for housing, employment, and nourishment of Germany's poor, he, like so many others, refused to see the brutality of the regime. Since summer 1934, all that really mattered was Wallis. Wallis and Edward. Nothing else. Edward did not want to follow in his father's footsteps and become king, feeling he simply could not be that man. He preferred the idea of a modern monarch, with a private life all his own (of course even more impossible today), and the ability to champion "common people." His special interest was improving low-cost housing.

Edward never hid the fact that he hated society and court life, and yet he spent all his time with society people. He wanted to promote youth (like Hitler) and change the monarchy into something vibrant and modern, possibly for fear of people losing interest in it otherwise. "Even if there had been no Mrs Simpson," his biographer, Philip Ziegler, wrote, "a clash between the King and the Establishment was inevitable." Writer H. G. Wells (who had a Soviet spy, Baroness Moura Budberg, as his long-term mistress) called Edward a "gadfly reformer" who spread terror among those who liked the conventional and believed tradition was a stabilizing factor.* Emerald Cunard told the prince that he was "the most modernistic man in England," to which he replied, "No, Emerald, I am not a modernist, since I am not a highbrow. All I try to do is move with the times."[22] The simpler and truer fact was that Edward found "princing"—as he was to later find "kinging" (to use his words)—tedious. He had not realized that it was his position and good looks that made him "highbrow" and a trendsetter.

Before Wallis, Edward had had other married mistresses, many with an American connection. He positively loved American women. Freda Dudley Ward, who had been his mistress (with intermissions) for sixteen years, had an American mother. Her replacement, the lovely Thelma Furness, née Morgan, was the twin sister of Gloria Vanderbilt. When Thelma asked her fellow married American friend, Wallis Simpson, to look after "the little man" (meaning Edward) while she had to go to New York to support her sister in the public custody battle for little Gloria, Wallis took over Thelma's position as *maîtresse-en-titre*.

IN NOVEMBER 1934, Ribbentrop found England all abuzz, buoyant, and euphoric as the economic recovery seemed to finally take hold. Edward and Wallis had crossed a line in their relationship the previous summer. Understandably, she was awed by the opulence, the splendor, and the thought of never having to scrape and "make do" ever again. But was that more important than being in love with her prince? Wallis thought (wrongly) that she could keep a good husband and an overzealous lover satisfied, as any good society woman could do. And so she invited her childhood friend Mary Raffray to London as a pleasant diversion for her husband, Ernest.

---

* For more on Baroness Moura Budberg, read Deborah McDonald and Jeremy Dronfield's *A Very Dangerous Woman: The Lives, Loves and Lies of Russia's Most Seductive Spy* (London: Oneworld, 2016).

Ribbentrop would, of course, interpret the gossip surrounding Wallis in high society to his own ends. Had he heard, too, about the proposed Christmas gifts of fifty thousand pounds' worth of jewels, to be followed by sixty thousand pounds of more jewels for New Year's? Or the skiing holiday in Austria in February 1935? Certainly, Ribbentrop hoped that the pair would get married so he could have an easier time spreading the Nazi word in America through Wallis.[23]

As Hitler's roving ambassador, Ribbentrop had probably overheard, too, how George V had taken Wallis off the list of invited guests for Prince George's wedding. Edward had reinstated Wallis without his father's knowledge. And why not? Edward had saved George, the "royal bad boy" of the 1920s, from scandalous behavior: the rakish Prince George, Duke of Kent and youngest son of George V and Queen Mary, was bisexual and a former heroin addict. Edward nursed him away from that addiction and helped to restore his brother to a meaningful role in society.[24]

That November, in a grand royal ceremony with all the accompanying panoply, George married the penniless and beautiful Princess Marina of Greece for love. Perhaps Marina did not know about George and his affair with Princess Mira Romanovsky Koutousov, who claimed he was the father of her little girl, Nadia, born in July 1933. But even if Marina had known, would it have mattered? The Kents, Mira, and her husband, Prince Dimitri, a younger son of Grand Duchess Xenia of Russia, remained close friends in the early years of the Kents' marriage.[25]

Like the new Princess of Kent, Princess Dimitri, as the White Russian Mira Romanovsky Koutousov was called, had known financial hardship and exile. Until recently, Prince Dimitri and his wife had resided in a grace-and-favor dwelling in Windsor Great Park,* but now found themselves in a small house near Gloucester Road in West London. The Kents could hardly be alarmed that Princess Dimitri traveled in White Russian circles, nor that she was friendly with Princess Stephanie's couturiere, Anna Wolkoff.

Why should they be? After all, the Prince of Wales played golf with

---

* They were briefly at Frogmore House, the home renovated for the Duke and Duchess of Sussex.

Princess Stephanie, and White Russians were by and large distant relations of the House of Windsor. They, like the Nazis, hated the communists and couldn't possibly betray Great Britain, which had given them sanctuary. Nobody thought society hostesses, British aristocrats, or White émigrés could be Hitler's "listening posts." What's more, most would not have known that the Russian émigrés had been the founders of Hitler's political ideology through the Aufbau in the 1920s and acted as a bulwark for Nazism.

Man of Peace

The Gods love and bless him who seems to demand the impossible.
—Adolf Hitler to Lord Rothermere, May 3, 1935

Joachim and Annalies von Ribbentrop returned to Berlin for Hitler's first dinner party at the Reichskanzlei on December 19, 1934. Industrialist Ernest Tennant arrived with them by car. Lord Rothermere and his son Esmond Harmsworth, accompanied by George Ward Price, alighted from their motorcar at the same time. SS men in full uniform acted as valet parking attendants.

Hitler wore a tailcoat and white tie like most of the men. Hermann Göring wore his Luftwaffe sky-blue uniform with gold braid, his ample chest covered in medals, and an oversized sword strapped to his side. As Hitler shook hands with each guest, addressing them by name, the Englishmen were told that they were the first foreigners Hitler had invited for dinner. Certainly, Rothermere, Tennant, and Price were impressed. Other invited guests included Göring's fiancée, the actress Emmy Sonnemann; Baron von Neurath and his wife; Joseph and Magda Goebbels; Hitler's chief adjutant, Herr Wilhelm Brückner; Dr. Hans Lammers and his wife; and several musicians and singers, who entertained the twenty-three guests after dinner.[1]

They waited for the other guests in the vast reception hall. No drinks were served. An immense Persian rug was the room's most outstanding adornment, along with outsized golden candlesticks. Tennant asked Hitler about the rug. While sniffing the air for the scent of white lilac and red lilies, Hitler hesitated before he laughingly replied that it had been ordered for the new headquarters of the League of Nations in Geneva, but there had been a delivery delay. So he took it. Germany had, of course, abandoned the League of Nations in October 1933, but the allusion seems to have been lost on Tennant.[2] Rothermere resolved then to send Hitler a Gobelin tapestry as proof of his friendship.

The dinner was austere, if well cooked: potato soup, roast chicken, and an assortment of vegetables, followed by a sorbet and cheese and crackers. Only one glass of red or white wine, according to taste, along with a single glass of water accompanied it. Hitler told his guests that the evening was a special occasion for him as it was the tenth anniversary of his release from Landsberg prison. "But by then," Hitler explained, "I had converted all the warders and people who were looking after me to National Socialism." Rothermere was entranced.[3]

LESS THAN A month later, "The good Catholics and workers of the Saar voted themselves back into the Reich," William Shirer wrote in his *Berlin Diary* on January 14, 1935. With over 90 percent voting for reunion, there was little that France or the other Allies from the Great War could do. In Hitler's broadcast, he claimed that the final "bone of contention with France" had been removed.[4] With much of the population being of socialist, communist, or Catholic persuasions, they were bound to be disappointed shortly.

Not understanding the true significance of the Saar plebiscite, the British and French governments issued a joint communiqué in early February calling for "the re-establishment of confidence" and "a general settlement freely entered into between Germany and the other powers," with a specific reference to "the need for an agreement to limit the air forces." Ribbentrop urged Hitler to issue a noncommittal reply solely to the British. It was a crude but effective attempt to split the Anglo-French alliance.[5]

The British plowed on and accepted Hitler's invitation for talks, announcing they would send the British foreign minister, Sir John Simon, to Berlin, accompanied by Anthony Eden, the Lord Privy Seal, and a roving ambassador for the Foreign Office.* Britain proposed to offer Germany freedom from the disarmament provisions of the hated Versailles Treaty in exchange for German promises to accept Austrian and the Little Entente countries' independence, seemingly unaware that Hitler had already been "rapidly freeing himself" from those very provisions. As William Shirer observed, "And simple Simon has fallen for the bait."[6]

AMBASSADOR WILLIAM E. Dodd was in the United States at the time, slack-jawed at the Senate defeat of Roosevelt's request for America to enter the World Court. Senators William Borah, Hiram Johnson, and William McAdoo were the ringleaders for American isolationism, with Johnson shouting loudest about the war debts from the Great War remaining unpaid, and McAdoo mouthing off "under the Hearst banner." Dodd considered publicly resigning and denouncing these mood makers for not speaking out against the dictatorships of Mussolini and Hitler and for then waving their flags of allegiance to William Randolph Hearst, Father Coughlin, and the "Louisiana pirate" Huey Long.

But, instead, Dodd summarized Hearst's support of Mussolini for the past "five or six years" to Representative Edward John Lewis. Apparently, Hearst struck a bargain with Goebbels in September 1934 to get Germany's European news first.[7†] With advance news taken by the Hearst newspaper and magazine empire, Dodd felt that the American publisher represented a credible Nazi propaganda threat to the nation since it is always the "breaking story" that everyone remembers.

After his meeting with Lewis, Dodd was shocked to hear an unnamed

---

* Robert Anthony Eden (1897–1977) was a gifted and promising diplomat at the time and later foreign secretary and prime minister during the Suez crisis. He was credited with narrowly averting another "Sarajevo," referring to the assassinations of Duke Franz Ferdinand and his wife in that city following the assassination of King Alexander of Yugoslavia in October 1934. In the Balkan crisis of 1934, he acted on behalf of the League of Nations (source: Oxford Dictionary of National Biography).

† Edward John Lewis (Democrat from Maryland's Sixth District) served on the House Ways and Means Committee and introduced the Social Security Bill to the House on January 17, 1935, days before his meeting with Dodd. Lewis promised to maintain Dodd's anonymity.

senator during a dinner in Washington explaining how he favored German domination of all Europe and U.S. domination of North and South America, with Canada subservient to the United States. Most of his senatorial dinner companions agreed wholeheartedly, based on their bias against "England and France," their ignorance of cultural differences, and their obliviousness to the lessons of history. Dodd was chilled by their broadcasting Nazi disinformation.

When Dodd met with the president a few days later, he was surprised to learn that Roosevelt was aware of the sentiments emanating from this "particular senatorial group" and even guessed correctly when he said, "It sounds like Senator X—." Roosevelt knew, too, that Senator Huey Long planned to run for the presidency in 1936 in order "to be a candidate of the Hitler type" and that Long hoped to bring the southern states and midwestern progressives along with him. Dodd was relieved that Roosevelt had his finger on the pulse. When he warned the president that he believed "Hearst to be an ally of Nazi Germany," Roosevelt listened intently. Could Dodd send him proof of Hearst's help to Mussolini on his return to Berlin? Despite the president's support, Dodd came away from the meeting feeling that the generation of a "minority of old-timers in the Senate" would continue to misdirect American foreign policy.[8]

NEVERTHELESS, AMBASSADOR DODD was unaware that his daughter, Martha, was having an affair with the Soviet diplomat Boris Vinogradov in Berlin, and that by March 1934 their relationship had blossomed enough for Moscow to order Vinogradov to cultivate Martha as a Soviet agent. "According to our data," the NKVD order begins, "the mood of his acquaintance (Martha Dodd) is quite ripe for finally drawing her into our work."* Vinogradov invited her, as ordered, to Paris that spring. That summer they met again in Moscow.[9]

Afterward, Martha toured Russia extensively and fell in love with the idea of the Soviets' attempts to help their millions of poor and starving masses. She concluded that Russia was a democratic country in its

---

* The NKVD was the precursor to the KGB.

"spirit and plans" and that the dictatorship was helping the people to get "a squarer deal." For her there was no comparison to be made between the Soviet dictatorship and Nazi Germany—the former was slowly succeeding, whereas the latter was failing.[10]

Her rose-tinted perspective failed to see the racial discrimination in the Soviet Union against Jews and other minority groups. She claimed that freedom of worship was still allowed, whereas in Germany it "was being liquidated." She believed Hitler had duped Germany with his "fake socialism" and "hysterical fear." She repeatedly said that "Russia made no threats, either direct or implied, against other nations despite its powerful Red Army."[11]

Later, Martha bragged to the NKVD about her very close contacts with the international journalists in Berlin—in the main, who gathered at the Taverne—a *Ristorante Italiano* owned by Willy Lehman, an enormous "bluff German with nothing Italian about him." It was here that the British and American correspondents ate, drank, and talked informally until the wee hours of the morning. As with the Round Table at the Algonquin Hotel in New York, they had their own *Stammtisch*, or "reserved table," where gripes were aired, wisdom imparted, and private jokes tested out on the other habitués. Although she had left her journalistic job, Martha Dodd, "pretty, vivacious, and a mighty arguer," was often among them.[12]

THE BRITISH JOURNALISTS' conversations that February and March were about stories London would *not* print from its *Times* correspondent Norman Ebbutt. Stories ranged from the "bad side" of Nazi Germany to the Prince of Wales's thinly veiled relationship with the married Wallis Simpson—currently on a monthlong skiing holiday *à deux*. Any journalist worth his or her salt would have been debating the prince's alleged attitudes to the unification of Austria and Germany, too. Only two years earlier, the Prince of Wales told Count Mensdorff, the former Austrian ambassador to the Court of St. James's, that he had tremendous sympathy for the Nazi Party since they were the bulwark against communism. "Of course . . . we will have to come to it [fascism], as we are in great danger from the Communists too," the prince said. Around the same time, he told Prince Louis Ferdinand of Prussia that he did not see where the issue of "the dictators" were anyone's business outside of Italy or Germany, adding that dictators are "very popular these days and that we might want one in England before long."[13]

Even so, the British ambassador to Austria in February 1935 believed that the Prince of Wales's presence shortly after the attempted German coup "gave support" to the beleaguered country. When asked if he would visit the Rathaus (city hall) in Vienna, Edward allegedly exclaimed to his barber at the Hotel Bristol, "Good God no! What on earth would my workers think of me in London if I went to that place which the Fascists took away from the Socialists?" All socialist Vienna oozed admiration for the Prince of Wales thereafter.

Put into context, these diverging viewpoints from the same man do make sense. The balance of power in Europe—the nexus of British foreign policy for hundreds of years—had been disrupted by Versailles. France was viewed as enfeebled, degenerate, toying with socialism, and as having a series of unsteady governments. Hitler's Germany was on the rise. Edward admired the achievements of the Nazis in creating housing for the poor and Hitler's reversal of unemployment. After all, better housing had been a cause Edward had taken up in England. But Edward was never a deep thinker. The prince assumed that the thuggery and brutality were somehow necessary. He assumed that there was a tint of communist disinformation about any news report that criticized the Nazis. He made the same anti-Semitic remarks that many of his friends made, without considering the wider implications. It never occurred to him that genocide or severe racial discrimination had already taken place. Above all else, Edward fervently believed that "a close relationship between England and Germany" was essential for the security of Europe.[14]

THOSE WHO OBSERVED the brutality and rearmament within Germany knew that the peace and security of Europe was already under threat. On a very wet March 1, 1935, the Germans formally reoccupied the Saar territory. American journalist William Shirer was present, watching the pomp and ceremony of this momentous occasion. He was standing next to "Werner von Fritsch, commander-in-chief of the Reichswehr and the brains of the growing German army." Shirer wrote that he was a "little surprised" by Fritsch's loose talk, noting that Fritsch "kept up a running fire of very sarcastic remarks—about the S.S., the party, and various party leaders as they appeared" in the march past the podium. His contempt for them all was unconcealed. When Hitler appeared, Fritsch grunted and shuffled into place behind the führer for the military review.[15]*

Then, unexpectedly, Sir John Simon's previously announced trip to Berlin was postponed. Wilhelmstrasse, as the leaky government foreign office sieve Hitler so loathed was informally called, revealed it was a "code diplomatique." Five days later, in breach of the Versailles Treaty, Hermann Göring publicly announced the existence of the Luftwaffe air force. Rothermere's *Daily Mail* broke the news with Price reporting as their "wonderful Nazi mouthpiece and sounding-board." Although it had long been suspected, it was the first time Göring publicly admitted the Luftwaffe's existence. The *Daily Mail* also carried the story that Göring, as minister for air, would serve under Blomberg, minister of defense, "thus putting the stamp of approval of the army on his job."† In retaliation, the French National Assembly decided to increase the length of military service from one to two years.

A day later, Hitler staged another major propaganda coup. Again, in breach of Versailles, Germany reintroduced conscription to build an army of 550,000 men. Astonishingly, the British Foreign Office meekly asked if Simon and Eden could still come to Berlin. Hitler was nonplussed. From that moment, he knew the British would do nothing while Germany rearmed.[16]

And so the meetings finally went ahead, but the British government had given away its negotiating position. Having come out with a highly varnished version of the truth about rearmament (which of course had

---

* Werner von Fritsch would be falsely accused by Hitler of being a homosexual in February 1938 and removed from his command. Recalled in March 1939 as the colonel in chief of the Twelfth Artillery Regiment in Poland, he died in battle in September 1939.

† Blomberg, too, would be removed in February 1938 to enable Hitler to gain better control of the army.

been going on since the early days of Weimar, thanks to Krupp), Hitler wanted more. A naval agreement with the mighty British navy and Britain's willingness to negotiate one made the führer tremble with delight during their talks. Although these were wide-ranging, with Hitler descending into lengthy tirades against bolshevism, he was a master at deflecting any questions relating to the security of Europe. What he wanted, and revealed, was parity with Britain, an air and naval pact, and Britain's acceptance of Germany's expansion in the east.

Finally, Simon asked the key question about the strength of Germany's Luftwaffe. Hitler hesitated after Dr. Paul Schmidt translated for him, then smiled thinly, saying, "We have already attained parity with Great Britain." Churchill, who had bedeviled the government on this very issue, had been saying for some months that the British estimates were wrong, and that Germany's airplanes were newer and better equipped.* Although Anthony Eden claimed in his memoir that Hitler's remark filled him with "grim foreboding," it was more probably Churchill's insistence that Britain's weakness had already reached a critical state that hit him like a thunderbolt.

Simon and Eden carried that thunderbolt back to Whitehall. The country was gravely weak and, given the rate of rearmament in the air by Germany, a projected first-line strength of 1,330 aircraft by the end of 1938 would leave Britain vulnerable to attack. What Hitler had not revealed was that he had ordered a hundred new tanks from Krupp in March 1934 and expected delivery of another six hundred and fifty by the time of his announcement. The German navy had also ordered six new submarines, with a view to prepare for a "sub-a-month" program by the summer of 1935.[17]

Londonderry's Under-Secretary for Air, Sir Philip Sassoon, had been outgunned by Churchill in the Commons debate on his air estimates. Of course, Londonderry tried desperately to recover his position, pleading with Churchill (who was his cousin) by telephone not to renew

---

* At the time, it was estimated that Germany had around eight hundred operational aircraft, but some were not deemed "first line" by the British. Four months earlier, Baldwin had stated that the British had 880 first-line aircraft, when in fact it was no more than 453 aircraft (source: Kershaw, *Making Friends with Hitler*, 101–02).

his attack about air strength again. But Churchill would not be cowed. Londonderry's estimates were derived from military intelligence. Churchill's numbers were from private sources reporting to him based on industrial intelligence. Since he relied on the building program for armaments in Germany, Churchill knew his estimates were more accurate. Londonderry was "running a frightful risk with the life of the State" and may, so Churchill told him after a sharp exchange of words, "at any moment . . . become the political victim of national alarm."[18]

While London trembled, there was a tremendous rejoicing throughout the Reich. The Reichswehr was renamed the Wehrmacht. Its navy, known as the Marineleitung ("Maritime Forces"), became the Kriegsmarine ("War Navy"). The new names were more than window dressing. They were forceful, youthful, and Teutonic and struck a chord with most Germans. When William Shirer attended the official ceremony at the Kroll Opera House, he witnessed a "scene which Germany had not seen since 1914. . . . Strong lights played on the stage, where young officers stood like marble statues holding upright the nation's war flags. . . . Ostensibly this was a ceremony to honour Germany's war dead. It turned out to be a jubilant celebration of the death of Versailles and the rebirth of the conscript German army."[19]

Londonderry's efforts to defend himself against his misreading the tea leaves took several forms. He revised his air estimates, deploring Whitehall's "panic" over German air strength. He saw "intrigues" against him at every glance and defended an indefensible past when the future mattered most. The new estimates *did* admit to German superiority "of two to one over the Royal Air Force by 1937," but Londonderry went on to assert that Britain *could* achieve parity again . . . in 1942. "The Air Ministry did not realise that a new inheritance awaited them," Churchill later wrote. "The Treasury's fetters were broken. They had but to ask for more."

Londonderry had not asked for enough. Rothermere's press was joined by Beaverbrook's *Daily Express* in smearing him. Stanley Baldwin, son of a Worcestershire ironmaster, forever sporting his pipe and tweeds to make the picture of the solid country squire, knew that MacDonald's health was poor and that the prime minister was hanging on until George V's Jubilee celebrations that May had concluded. Baldwin also knew that he would become MacDonald's successor as prime minister. He knew that a tougher, more dynamic man needed to occupy Londonderry's office, and the candidate had to sit in the House of Commons rather than the House of Lords.

Londonderry wrote to the prime minister, claiming that "these damnable attacks" were made by those who resented his "independence," that he had been badly let down in his "single-handed battle to save the Royal Air Force," and that he had even acted against some of his cabinet colleagues, in particular Stanley Baldwin. Lady Londonderry, of course, tried to boost her husband's morale and put about in society that Rothermere's "constant belittling" and Churchill's belligerence were causing her husband undue anxiety. His defense, however, was feeble given that Baldwin had already told the Commons in November 1934 that air parity with Germany was impossible.[20]

THAT APRIL, HITLER had summoned his *liebe Prinzessin*, Stephanie Hohenlohe, to Berlin. She carried a letter and a priceless jade bowl from Lord Rothermere as well as firsthand gossip from Lady Londonderry's social set about how unfair criticisms of her husband had been. The princess answered Hitler's questions at the direction of her newest lover, Hitler's adjutant, Captain Fritz Wiedemann, about the Prince of Wales and other aristocrats in Stephanie's social set.

Hitler thanked Rothermere in a letter dated May 3, which Stephanie hand-delivered to London. It was a long and rambling document about how Britain and Germany had been natural allies, reminding Rothermere that "for 500 years the two Germanic peoples have lived close together without having become involved in any serious military difference." He lamented how the Great War had washed away "the pick of manhood of both nations" but also "severely hit Germany's influence in Europe" and "left behind a legacy of prejudice and passion." In a statement that could have been written by the old Aufbau or his White Russian friends, Hitler lamented that "Bolshevism tears away a mighty slice of European-Asiatic breathing-space [Lebensraum]. . . . The safety of the British Empire, which is to the interest of the whole White race is weakened."

The solution to today's problems could not be resolved by "day-by-day politicians, whose horizon is frequently limited," Hitler wrote. Indeed, were there an Anglo-German understanding in Europe that "extended by the joining-up of the American nation, then it would indeed be hard to see who in the world could disturb peace without wilfully and consciously neglecting the interests of the White race."[21] The letter makes several references to white supremacy rather than Aryanism, in an attempt by Hitler to broaden the concept to include his Anglo-Saxon reader.

There is no doubt Hitler expected Rothermere to circulate the letter privately among the powers that be. He may have hoped for Rothermere to print it in the *Daily Mail*, too. It was shown to the cabinet office, and King George V "cooly received" it. The words not only contradicted Hitler's actions—he claimed that Germany's rearmament was merely a building block to regaining its honor—but also subliminally demanded the British forfeit friendly relations with the French.

Londonderry thought Hitler made sense. With Britain having lost the air battle before it had even begun, a rapprochement with the Germans became his preferred road to the future. Londonderry, like Lothian, hoped to "be successful in converting the Germans into helpful partners in the scheme of the world."[22]

A stronger believer in the Hitler letter was the Liberal Party peer Philip Kerr, 11th Marquess of Lothian. He had been friendly with the Astors, had served as Lloyd George's private secretary when the Welshman was prime minister (1916–22), and had served in the national government in 1931–32 as the chancellor of the Duchy of Lancaster and undersecretary for India. He had also met with Hitler; deputy leader of the Nazi Party, Rudolf Hess; and Ribbentrop—using historian Philip Conwell-Evans as his interpreter on January 29 that same year. Lothian's "oratorical temperament," recently channeled into Christian Science; distinguished appearance; and tendency to deal "only with matters of major importance" labeled him an "incurably superficial Johnny know-all," despite his apparent gullibility.

Rather misguidedly, Lothian believed, too, that the United States would follow any foreign policy action Britain would take in the future. Above all else, he believed in the British Empire as a force for good and reasoned that a "less emollient approach to France and winning German cooperation through giving Germany 'a square deal in Central Europe' was the best way of preserving the Empire." Admittedly, Lothian spoke no German, did not know the German people, and, like many aristocrats, wrongly believed Hitler to be an English gentleman.[23]

IT WAS AGAINST this background that, on the evening of May 21, Hitler made his "grandiose 'peace' speech in the Reichstag." William Shirer was there and wrote that he feared "it will impress world opinion and especially British opinion more than it should." Hitler was in fine form. An impassioned orator, he spoke to his "hand-picked Reichstag, with its six hundred or so sausage-necked, shaved-headed, brown-clad yes-men, who rise and shout almost every time Hitler pauses for breath" and laid out his convincing program for peace. "Germany needs peace. . . . Germany wants peace. . . . No one of us means to threaten anybody," Hitler screamed. He denied having anything to do with the Dollfuss murder or an attempted coup d'état in Austria, since "Germany neither intends nor wishes to interfere in the internal affairs of Austria, to annex Austria or to conclude an Anschluss."[24]

The diplomatic box was jampacked with ambassadors from Britain, France, Italy, Japan, and Poland in the front row. Ambassador Dodd was squeezed into the third row after an uncomfortable chair had been rejected by him. Although Shirer took Dodd's demotion as a diplomatic affront against the United States, Dodd was quite happy with his improved view of the proceedings. As Hitler rampaged about the "wicked Versailles Treaty," he watched the French ambassador squirm—particularly after the mention that President Wilson's Fourteen Points were inspired by the French. The last hour of Hitler's address dealt with the "severe blows of the League of Nations and Communism" against Germany, for which Dodd had some sympathy. All the same, when Hitler turned his attention to "Lithuania and eastern border troubles" he said that he would never "surrender his hope of annexations." The return of Germany's colonies was far less important and "annexations of regions of half-industrialized peoples like Lithuanians, western Poles and Esthonians [sic] must be made."

Dodd made no comment about Hitler's Thirteen Points, which stressed that Germany would never return to the disarmament conference in Geneva or the League of Nations but that Germany would "scrupulously maintain any treaty voluntarily signed." At the end of the speech, Hitler said, "Something should be done to prohibit the poisoning of public opinion among the nations by irresponsible elements orally or in writing, and in the theatre or the cinema" against Germany.

Later that evening at the *Stammtisch* at the Taverne, Shirer noted that most of the international correspondents believed that this speech paved the way for many years of peace to come. Dodd knew otherwise. Despite assurances from Hitler that he "would throw any German official into the North Sea if he sent propaganda to the United States," there had been a concerted effort that March to show Leni Riefenstahl's *Triumph of the Will,* which filmed the 1934 *Partei Tag* (Party Day), in American and European movie houses. German officials in America had also confirmed that there was no propaganda campaign in the United States. "But there are now 600 employees in the foreign propaganda division now active in Berlin," Dodd expressed, to his grief. "This is one of many evidences of the complete insincerity of their promises. . . . I believe all the powers of Europe must unite and keep united and armed to the limit."[25]

Party Day Propaganda

The masses need an idol.

—Adolf Hitler

In September at Nuremberg, Nazi Party members celebrated a joyous expression of the "national community" in what was known as *Partei Tag,* or Party Day. Initially designed to whip up enthusiasm for the invented myth of the ancient Aryan people, this mass demonstration was the most lavish of Nazi festivals. Of course, there were local and regional mass meetings and propaganda campaigns frequently staged throughout the Reich, but it was Party Day that became the international symbol of the strength of feeling and love ordinary Germans had for their führer. Nonetheless, the 1935 Party Day was designed to attract Hitler's aristocrats to the spectacle, too.

By Hitler's second year in power, Nazi rituals and propaganda were everywhere. The ubiquitous posters, banners, and a "saying of the week" were only the beginning. Newsstands were flooded with "approved" magazines and newspapers. Copies of the rabid anti-Semitic *Der Stürmer,* edited by Julius Streicher (who claimed he could *smell* a Jew but failed to sniff out his Jewish interpreter at Nuremberg);* the Nazi Party's *Völkischer Beobachter*; and Goebbels's Berlin newspaper, *Der Angriff,*

---

* 2011 author telephone interview with Howard Triest, interpreter at Nuremberg for psychiatrist Colonel Douglas Kelly. For an in-depth account of Howard's story, read Helen Fry's *Inside Nuremberg Prison: A Biography of Howard Triest* (CreateSpace, 2012). Streicher's claims can be found on pages 133–34.

were always placed prominently. Catholics, Jews, and political opponents were silenced. Many "enemies of the state" simply disappeared
into the concentration camps of Oranienburg and Dachau.

In April 1935, the president of the Reich press chamber, publisher
Max Amann, a German Nazi of Baltic Russian origin, issued several
edicts allowing him to shut down any newspaper publisher to "obviate unhealthy conditions of competition." Catholic papers or those that
ignored the Nazi mantra were either ordered to close or were sold to
the Nazi Party's publishing house, Eher-Verlag, run by Amann. Ambassador Dodd wrote to Secretary of State Hull that at the Conference of
Bishops at Fulda a pastoral letter was published for the faithful "to stand
firm as the number of enemies of the Christian faith and the Catholic
Church have become legion." Eventually, the Nazi Party would own 80
percent of all newspapers.

A new language began to appear, too. Streets and squares were renamed to bring everyday Nazi terminology into common usage. Advertising—be it window displays or written advertising—had to conform
to the Nazi ideal of graphic and visual arts. Even women's fashion had to
be Aryanized, eliminating the particularly nefarious influence of Paris
and its "un-German" designs. Alternative public opinions were brutally
quashed. Radios relentlessly blared Nazi propaganda, thinly veiled as
news and denouncing "enemies of the Reich." Eyewitness accounts of
atrocities against Germans and interviews with famous people of the
day completed the radio programs, which held a dramatic stranglehold
on the private space.

In July 1935, Victor Klemperer, a lecturer at Dresden's Technical
University and a Jew who had converted to Protestantism in 1912,
found himself forcibly retired as a non-Aryan and was awaiting his "retirement pay." His diary *I Will Bear Witness* sums up the frustrations
"enemies of the Reich" experienced: "I said (as Montesquieu puts it in
his diaries when an aperçu follows) . . . we are sitting here as *in a besieged fortress, within which the plague is raging.*"[1]

ONE OF THE Nazis' most powerful propaganda tools was filmmaking. In
the 1920s, German cinema had been at the forefront of groundbreaking

movies, with Robert Wiene's *The Cabinet of Dr. Caligari* and Fritz Lang's
Metropolis. Under Hitler, such films and directors became "un-German."
In 1930, Goebbels personally targeted the American film *All Quiet on
the Western Front,* which was based on Erich Maria Remarque's antiwar novel of the same name. Goebbels attended the screening with a
large cohort of his followers shortly after its release and led the chants
shouting anti-Jewish slurs. Within "only 10 minutes the cinema is like a
madhouse. The police are powerless," Goebbels wrote. He had whipped
them up into a frenzy about how Jewish Hollywood producers had
made this anti-German propaganda. The screening (as well as the next
one) had to be canceled. Goebbels focused on other movie theaters, too,
until the film was banned because it "was a threat to German prestige."[2]

By 1935, Joseph Goebbels was the national propaganda master-
mind on how to dominate the public sphere within the Reich. He had
gained influence over Hitler with his absolute devotion and gradually
shoved the insufferable Alfred Rosenberg aside. That said, Goebbels
had no international experience like Ribbentrop or Hanfstaengl, nor
any idea how to sell the "New Germany" to a worldwide audience.
He also had no background in filmmaking. Such niceties were left to
Alfred Hugenberg, who had bought the main German movie studio,
Ufa, in March 1927 as an open challenge to Weimar to further the
right-wing cause. Unlike all French, British, and American studios,
Ufa had been created as a propaganda tool in 1917, under the auspices
of General Erich Ludendorff and the German high command. Since
1927, Ufa's creditor banks were the industrialists and nationalists of
the far right, so making movies that promoted Nazi philosophies was
good business.

One of the studio's leading female stars was Leni Riefenstahl, although she was outshone by Pola Negri, Henny Porten (the "German
Mary Pickford"), and Yvette Guilbert. A very young Marlene Dietrich
was her greatest rival for parts in the early days—and Leni watched
helplessly as Marlene soared to international stardom with the Para-
mount/Ufa 1930 coproduction of Josef von Sternberg's *The Blue Angel*.
Born Helene Amalie Bertha Riefenstahl on the outskirts of Berlin, Leni
grew up in a city where modernity reigned supreme. Expressionism
in all art forms, outlawed under the Nazis, had flourished. In the film

world, exciting new directors like Robert Wiene (a Protestant having converted from Judaism), Fritz Lang, and Billy Wilder were compelled to flee, like many other talented "un-Germans." But Leni remained and became a big German star, always denying parts of her past that she found "forgettable." After World War II, she would always deny acting as Hitler's propagandist, too.[3]

Leni directed the Party Day propaganda films in 1933 and 1934. *Triumph of the Will* was released in cinemas throughout Europe in March 1935, but was not well received, despite the *London Observer*'s noting, "It is certainly to be hoped that this film will be shown in all cinemas outside Germany, if one wishes to understand the intoxicating spirit which is moving Germany these days."[4] Nonetheless, Hitler's choice of Leni to portray his most important national Party Day showed her to be a director of rare genius, and *Triumph* remains one of the most definitive and artistic propaganda films ever made.

To Joseph Goebbels's chagrin, Leni refused to work for him. Hitler agreed that she must have full artistic control, despite Goebbels's near monopoly on propaganda. At the helm of all radio programing, Goebbels controlled the theaters and the Reich film chamber, too, which led to the corporate restructuring of the entire cultural sector. What made Leni's independence even more remarkable was that it was Goebbels who had suggested that she should make "a Hitler film" in the first place.[5] Of course, he tried to dethrone Germany's new queen of propaganda with rumor and innuendo (Was she Jewish? Would the men on set take orders from a woman?), but Hitler refused to discuss such things about her. She could thus claim, or so she thought, that Goebbels represented propaganda and, therefore, she was an artiste.[6]

PUTZI HANFSTAENGL COULD only sit back, arms crossed, in admiration of her success. It was quite a coup, though Putzi doubted even Leni realized just how much of a triumph of wills she had achieved. Hanfstaengl loathed Goebbels for his interference in his own film about Horst Wessel. Putzi had composed the music and acted as the movie's assistant producer. When a rough cut of the film was shown to Hitler; his photographer, Heinrich Hoffmann; and Dr. Schacht, they were impressed.

A gala opening at the Capitol Cinema in Berlin was booked for October 3, 1933. Hearst International News Service described it as "the most important premiere for the German film industry" of the year. Goebbels allowed the premiere but then banned the film six days later (the anniversary of Wessel's birthday) on the grounds that it undermined the National Socialist movement and "endangered the vital interests of the state and Germany's image."

Naturally, Hanfstaengl objected vociferously to Hitler. He then appealed to Goebbels. The film could be shown again only after twenty-seven further approved cuts and was rebranded to be about a fictitious character, Hans Westmar. Hanfstaengl lost a fortune.[7] No wonder Putzi called Goebbels the "limping doctor," a "mocking, jealous, vicious, satanically gifted dwarf," or the "pilot-fish of the Hitler shark." Even Magda Goebbels did not escape Putzi's venom. He mocked her for calling her husband "*Engelchen*"—meaning "little angel" or "cherub." Nor was Putzi discreet. "Magda calls out 'Engelchen,' but who should come round the corner but the old black devil himself, club foot and all," Putzi roared. Then too, he also called Goebbels "Gobbespierre" (comparing him to Robespierre of the Terror of the French Revolution).[8]

PREPARATIONS TO INVITE the international elite for Party Day 1935 were made by Hitler's diplomats a year earlier. Yet the greatest contribution to the guest list of influencers from Britain came from two women: Princess Stephanie and Dr. Margarete Gärtner. Princess Stephanie had become a decorative addition to the Lady Cunard set. As directed by Hitler's adjutant, Captain Fritz Wiedemann, Stephanie disseminated pro-Nazi propaganda in an informal context, reassuring her drawing room listeners that Hitler was a man of peace. That year would be her first Party Day, too. Her well-established relationship with Lord Rothermere and European royalty opened most doors, and she had tons of gossipy information she wished to share with Hitler in person.

Dr. Margarete Gärtner took a more serious approach. She had made the greatest inroads into the wider British press and politics. Although the Nazi Party was decidedly antifeminist, she had been a pioneer of pro-German propaganda in Britain since 1922. Seemingly, the Nazi seizure of power did nothing to dissuade her. Gärtner enlisted reasonable support from members of Parliament, the British press, and most "other organizations in Britain active in this hey-day" promoting goodwill and understanding between the two countries.

It was under Gärtner's influence that the Anglo-German Group was established in 1933, under the chairmanship of Lord Allen of Hurtwood, a former chairman of the Independent Labour Party.[9] Always a pacifist, Hurtwood believed Hitler's "man of peace" message, as did other prominent members of the House of Lords. Through him and his fellow traveler Lord Lothian, the Liberal Party peer, Sir Walter Layton, chairman of the *News Chronicle* and editor of *The Economist*; Vernon Bartlett, formerly of the *Daily Mail* and the BBC; Wilson Harris, editor of *The Spectator*; historian John Wheeler-Bennett of the Royal Institute of International Affairs; the Ulster Unionist MP Vyvyan Adams; and W. Arnold-Foster of the League of Nations Union joined the group. Lothian also introduced Dr. Gärtner to those members of Parliament whom he thought would be interested in her ideas. All these names were put forward to attend the 1935 Party Day.[10]

NOTWITHSTANDING THE LADIES' influence, Joachim von Ribbentrop, too, was instrumental in issuing invitations to the British visitors. The rapid expansion of his role as Hitler's ambassador at large also saw his *Büro*'s name change to the larger and more significant *Dienststelle*. He hired Karlfried, Graf von Dürckheim-Montmartin, a former professor of international relations at Kiel University and pro-British champion in international affairs, to head the English section of the enlarged *Dienststelle*. Evidently, Ribbentrop hadn't done his homework, since von Dürckheim-Montmartin—who would become Ribbentrop's sole eyes and ears on the ground in Britain in 1935—was an ardent Nazi but also one-quarter Jewish.* Indeed, Dürckheim would facilitate the meeting between Max Beaverbrook and Hitler that year.

---

* In Nazi speak, this made Dürckheim a second-degree *Mischling*, or "of mixed race," since one or more of his grandparents was Jewish. In 1938, Ribbentrop, fearing that Dürckheim would be recalled to Germany and put into a concentration camp, created

Through Ribbentrop's budding friendship with Ernest Tennant and Gärtner's Anglo-German Group, the Anglo-German Fellowship was formed, with Lord Mount Temple (father-in-law of Lord Mountbatten) serving as its chairman and fifty members of the two houses of Parliament signing up. Carl Edouard, the Duke of Saxe-Coburg and Gotha, who was also Tennant's school-days friend from Eton, became the leader of its German counterpart, the Deutsch-Englische Gesellschaft.[11] Ribbentrop believed the duke's involvement would guarantee the attendance of those in society, particularly in the Prince of Wales's circle and Emerald Cunard's set.

Apparently, Ribbentrop had not yet met either Unity Mitford or her sister Diana Guinness. Born Unity Valkyrie, the youngest Mitford sister would never become a society hostess, even in Germany.* She was conceived in a cabin in a small mining town called Swastika, Northern Ontario, Canada. (Poor girl never stood a chance with such antecedents, did she?) Her father and mother were mining for gold at the time, and true to David's perpetual streak of bad financial luck, they struck mud while the adjacent concession made Harry Oakes—later Sir Harry—a multimillionaire.[12] David Freeman-Mitford, a second son, who inherited his older brother Clement's intended title Lord Redesdale after his death, continued to misspend and poorly invest the family fortune for the rest of his life.[13]

As Unity was the seventh child and the youngest of six sisters (brother Tom Mitford was the third eldest child), it would always be problematic for Unity to shine in such a beautiful, older, and talented sisterhood. Unity found it difficult to make her mark, in part due to a half-hearted smattering of education at a girls' school but mostly because she had run wild on the family's Swinbrook, Oxfordshire, estate. Coming "from a ruck of children in a large family," Unity, according to biographer David Pryce-Jones, explained her decidedly odd behavior by her decision "that she was going to form a personality against everything."[14]

---

a new post for him in Japan, where Dürckheim sat out the war, eventually becoming a Zen master.

* Her mother named her Unity after her favorite actress. Her Mitford grandfather asked that she have the name Valkyrie as an homage to his good friend Richard Wagner, a biography of whom he had written.

Unity also considered herself a failure. She failed at art school. She failed to attract a husband during her 1932 debutante season, in the main because she hadn't wanted to. She had been banned from seeing her "shameful" sister, Diana, in light of her affair with Mosley, making Diana forbidden fruit that must be eaten, no matter the cost. Of course, Unity became part of Diana's glamorous "Eatonery" setup—as Diana's home on Eaton Square was called. With access to Mosley, it was no accident that Unity fixated on the Nazis in general and specifically on Hitler. In April 1934, she went to live in Munich, ostensibly to attend Baroness Laroche's finishing school's summer term. Thereafter, Unity referred to the Mitfords as "pure bred Aryans."[15]

Precisely when and where Unity resolved to marry Hitler is unrecorded. Later, Princess Stephanie claimed to have suggested that Unity camp out ostentatiously at the Osteria Bavaria in Munich, where Hitler lunched, until she was asked to join his table. This is, indeed, how Unity finally achieved her success, but it is doubtful that Stephanie had anything to do with Unity's perseverance. Diana, when asked about what Unity (already something of an "*animal curieux*") did when she didn't see Hitler, Diana replied, "She thinks of him."[16] Hitler, however, merely saw Unity as a British aristocrat and prime example of Aryan womanhood, who was to be used to help him achieve his aims.*

Putzi Hanfstaengl thought Unity would make an inappropriate wife for the führer and secretly set out to foil her plan. When he introduced the American ambassador's daughter, Martha Dodd, to the führer, Putzi was certain they would make a wonderful couple. Neither Hitler nor Martha, however, agreed.

HITLER ATTACHED THE greatest significance to British royalty, and in particular to the Prince of Wales. Misled by his British "expert" Ribbentrop, neither man understood how a constitutional monarchy worked. Nor would Hitler heed his ambassador, Leopold von Hoesch, whom he mistrusted as a remnant of Weimar, disbelieving that Hoesch had successfully cultivated Edward. In an official cable to Berlin, Hoesch

---

* His involvement with Eva Braun was known but not discussed publicly.

described the prince as "being critical of the Foreign Office's one-sided attitude on German affairs" and said that "once again [he] showed his complete understanding of Germany's position and aspirations." So Ribbentrop was dispatched to verify the statement. He met the Prince of Wales at Lady Cunard's, and he agreed. "After all, he [Edward] is half a German," Ribbentrop concluded.[17]

Edward's sympathies alarmed the British, too. Sir Clive Wigram, private secretary to the monarch, reported Edward's attitude to George V. Although the prince's sympathy for Germany was in some ways natural, it was decidedly reckless, too. Edward was noted for making "startling indiscretions" on most matters, and when it came to foreign policy, he earnestly felt that there was a great deal of right on Germany's side. At a dinner at Lady Sybil Colefax's home, he made his feelings abundantly clear. Others present were Brendan Bracken, MP, whom Baldwin called a "faithful *chela*,"* and the former diplomat turned journalist Robert Bruce Lockhart. Bracken was "very anti-German and warlike" and Bruce Lockhart "rather anti-French," Wigram reported.†

Edward "came out very strong for friendship with Germany: never heard him talk so definitely about the subject before." By the end of the year, American ambassador Robert W. Bingham wrote to the president that "[t]he Prince of Wales has become the German protagonist" and is easily influenced by his friends.[18] The German ambassador to Washington, Hans Luther, also reported (via thirdhand information) that Edward did not share his father's viewpoint and that it was the king's duty to "intervene" if he felt that the cabinet acted in a manner detrimental to British interests. The Prince of Wales had no idea that he was helping formulate Nazi thinking about roseate possibilities once he became king.

IN THE SPRING of 1935, London's aristocrats continued to lunch together, play golf together, gamble together, attend one another's London

---

* *Chela* is Hindi for "flea." The statement referred to Bracken's devotion to Churchill.
† Robert Bruce Lockhart was a Scot and held the post of acting consul general to Russia during the last years of the czars. He returned to Russia as the British representative to Lenin's government after the October 1917 Revolution and was imprisoned, then deported. In 1935, he was a journalist for Beaverbrook's *Evening Standard*.

Season balls, and, above all, gossip. Wallis Simpson was their preferred subject, since the Prince of Wales had decreed that all London must "do a politesse" to her as his *maîtresse-en-titre*.

"She is a jolly, plain, intelligent, quiet, unpretentious and unprepossessing little woman," Chips Channon confided to his diary, "but as I wrote to Paul of Yugoslavia today, she has already the air of a personage who walks into a room as though she almost expected to be curtsied to. . . . She has complete power over the Prince of Wales, who is trying to launch her socially."[19]

That June, Edward addressed the British Legion and proposed that its members should visit Germany. The idea had emanated from Ribbentrop earlier in the year. As the patron of the British Legion, the prince suggested that "there could be no more suitable body or organization of men to stretch forth the hand of friendship to the Germans than we ex-servicemen, who fought them and have now forgotten all about it and the Great War." The following day, Robert Bruce Lockhart lunched at the Lady Dalkeith's London home and was admonished. "All London was saying that I had influenced him," Lockhart wrote in his diary, referring to the incident at Lady Colefax's, when he defended Edward against Brendan Bracken. "It is quite untrue. The Prince of Wales has been playing about with this pro-German idea long before our conversation."[20]

When George V heard about Edward's public proclamation, he sent for his son and lambasted him for sharing his personal viewpoint in contradiction of Foreign Office policy. The king reminded Edward that, in a constitutional monarchy, he must never express his views on such controversial matters without consultation. At a Court ball two days later, Edward was in a "very bad temper," still shocked by his father's reaction. He told Ambassador Hoesch that he was "not retracting and was convinced that he was doing the right thing."[21]

That July, the German visit by the British Legion occurred after their German counterparts, the Deutsche Frontkämpfer (German front-line soldiers), came to England. The British were treated to a nearly two-hour interview with Hitler and a visit to Dachau concentration camp, where the guards posed as prisoners while the inmates were herded underground. The pièce de resistance of the visit was a family supper with the Himmlers. The British Legion would return several times more before the outbreak of war. Although Anthony Eden had warned that they would be used for propaganda purposes, their spokesmen "declared at public functions throughout Germany" that the Great War had been "a colossal blunder." So many people fell for Hitler's sincerity as a man of peace.[22]

EFFORTS TO ATTRACT Americans were more problematic. Ambassador Luther had written to the German foreign office that Americans feared involvement in yet another of Europe's countless conflicts. He noted that recent "events" like the announcement of the Luftwaffe, the drafting of a new German army, and the Allies' concerned rumblings at their conference at Stresa "are being presented by the American press in its own peculiar manner and are being compared to the events of the decade 1904–1914. . . . The question of whether there will be war in Europe . . . has recently also become the subject of daily conversation. This question is on everyone's lips."[23]

Not wishing to take any chances on another European war, Congress passed the Neutrality Act of 1935, preventing the shipment of all armaments, steel, oil, and chemicals to belligerent nations in the event of a future war. Avery Brundage, president of the American Olympics Committee, visited Germany and believed the assurances of the Hitler regime that the Nazis would adhere to the Olympic rules and regulations, despite his sports commissar's declaration that "German sports are for Aryans . . . not for Jews."[24] While recommending the United States appear in the 1936 Berlin summer games, he remained silent about whether Jewish athletes would be allowed to participate. Previously, Olympic athletes, university professors, congressmen and senators, journalists, and intellectuals had drawn a woeful picture of the German Reich's attitude toward its Jews.

The United States' reaction to the European situation was entirely reasonable when considered from the domestic viewpoint. Roosevelt faced reelection in 1936 and had still not completed his battles for rural electrification, reforestation, the great dams of the West, unionization and unemployment, control of fair dealing on the stock exchange, and, most important of all, the building of bridges with big business. In the year before an election, foreign entanglements would be a nightmare. Besides, there was a great deal of talk about how the ungrateful Allies—including Great Britain—had failed to repay their Great War debts.

Hitler hopped on the bandwagon, too. No one spoke of an abhorrence of war more than he. Never mind that he had unilaterally torn up Versailles with the announcement of the Luftwaffe and the half million men in the new German army. To further confuse the former Allies, he suggested nonaggression pacts with all Germany's neighbors, apart from Lithuania.* Hitler even claimed to be a great Wilsonian, believing in collective security. That sold the British government into signing a naval treaty with Germany in June 1935 to take advantage of the new spirit of cooperation and to counter the threat of Mussolini turning the Mediterranean into an "Italian lake."

BEHIND THE SCENES, however, Göring, Schacht, Krupp, and the new chief executive of I.G. Farben, Hermann Schmitz,† were working feverishly to convert the rearmament program across all the armed services. Max Ilgner had been working with the Wehrmacht since late 1934, tantalizing the Nazis with how I.G.'s synthetic fuels would transform the forthcoming war for Germany. Like Krupp, I.G. would become fully integrated in the government's processes, acting as a quasi-governmental department. Through 1935, I.G. became increasingly dependent on government funding for its research and development. The head of its research and development division, Carl Krauch, became the key architect of the relationship with the German government and the man responsible for the urgent, strategic need to ensure Germany's self-sufficiency and prepare the country for war.[25]

---

* Lithuania still occupied Memel, a Baltic port city. Today it is known as Klaipeda, Lithuania.
† Carl Duisberg died in March. Carl Bosch became chairman of the company, surrendering his CEO position to Hermann Schmitz. Bosch had refused to become a Nazi Party member, whereas Schmitz was very pro-Nazi.

• • •

SINCE THAT SPRING, Mussolini's desire to re-create an Italian empire in Africa had thrust him onto the world stage. Throughout the summer, he clashed with the members of the League of Nations to enforce his will. August brought threats of sanctions from Britain, and for a while no one concentrated on Hitler or his all-important 1935 Party Day.

Princess Stephanie attended at Hitler's personal invitation, along with Lady Ethel Snowden, the wife of the former chancellor of the exchequer in the Labour governments of 1924 and 1929. Lady Snowden followed up the Party Day visit with several pieces for the *Daily Mail,* which Ernest Tennant applauded. He cabled her that the articles "would greatly encourage British friends of Germany."[26] Diana Guinness and her sister Unity were present, too, promoting Tom Mosley and his Blackshirts. They were among the thousands who cheered the announcement of the Nuremberg Race Laws that September 15, outlawing mixed marriages and the institutionalizing guidelines defining what made someone a Jew.

When Mussolini invaded Abyssinia on October 3, 1935, Hitler decided at first to remain neutral. In fact, as Mussolini later admitted, this was the precise moment when the concept of the Rome-Berlin axis was born. In the coming year, however, Hitler would become the dominant partner. Although Nazi Germany was not yet ready to embark on its war, Mussolini's timing helped to solidify the alliance that would propel Europe into the abyss.

PART III

JUGGERNAUT

There is no better proof of the innate love of peace of
the German people than the fact that despite its
ability and its bravery . . . it has secured for itself only
such a modest share of space for living.

—Adolf Hitler, address to the Reichstag, March 7, 1936

Inevitability of War

Those who make peace revolution impossible, make violent revolution inevitable.

—John F. Kennedy

On December 18, 1935, Charles A. Lindbergh told his wife, Anne, "Be ready to go by the end of the week—at twenty-four hours' notice." They sailed for England on December 21, leaving their forwarding address as "care of Morgan, Grenfell & Co., London, England." Arriving ten days later at Liverpool, Charles held his son Jon in his arms as they descended the gangplank. Anne walked meekly behind them. The sensational New York newspapers' headlines had followed, greeting them on docking. And yet, as they drove to their hoped-for obscurity, Anne felt reassured by the "trams, buses, chimneypots, red-cheeked children, women in shawls, nursemaids wheeling prams, brick houses, raincoats, and drably dressed women." It was all so very English.[1]

Unwittingly, the American press had conspired to give Hitler his greatest American propaganda coup. Charles A. Lindbergh had left the United States for England with his wife and child in disgust.* He had had enough harassment by the press, enough of 24–7 guards at their Next

---

* "Lucky Lindy," so the first man to fly solo across the Atlantic was nicknamed, and his reserved wife, Anne Morrow Lindbergh, had suffered a tremendous tragedy. In March 1932, their twenty-month-old son, Charles Jr., had been kidnapped. The toddler's body was found two months later, some four miles from the family home in Highfields, New Jersey. Bruno Hauptmann, found guilty of the kidnapping and murder, was executed.

Day Hill home, and quite enough of the threatening letters claiming that Bruno Richard Hauptmann was innocent of the kidnap and murder of his toddler son. Lindbergh was on the path to become the Nazis' most ardent American admirer.

THE YEAR 1936 would be an extraordinary one. Even Hitler, who was behind much of the international chaos, could not believe the outcome of all the momentous events. With the disreputable Hoare-Laval Pact of December 1935 throwing Britain and France into political turmoil in their international affairs, 1936 looked as if it would be another great year for Nazi Germany.* On January 7, Mussolini told the German ambassador in Rome, Ulrich von Hassell, that he had no objection to Austria becoming a de facto satellite of the Third Reich. Why? Italy needed a closer relationship with Germany due to sanctions imposed for its invasion of Abyssinia.

In February, a minor setback came when the left won the Spanish elections by a narrow margin. Hitler and Mussolini agreed they could use Spain as a proving ground for new armaments and military training. America's Second Neutrality Act came into effect at the end of the month, strengthening its embargo provisions and linking aid to repayment of the war debt from the Great War. Hitler knew Republican Spain would be most affected and smelled yet another fascist victory.

ASIDE FROM THE German American community in the United States, Hitler had made very little impact on the sympathies of the average American. Jewish organizations were vocal about the plight of refugees from Nazi atrocities and saw the opportunity to create a Jewish homeland

---

* Initially secret, the Hoare-Laval Pact (between Sir Samuel Hoare and Pierre Laval of France) effectively agreed that France and Britain would be happy for Abyssinia to become an Italian colony. When it was leaked, the British public was outraged, and Hoare was forced to resign. Léon Blum, Popular Front leader in France, was livid, accusing Laval of wanting to have his cake and eat it.

in Palestine as the main solution.* America and Britain talked about helping the refugees; but that January, the governments were still trying to understand the ramifications of the Nuremberg Race Laws and what the difference between full, half, and quarter Jewish designations meant financially to the individuals and to the countries where they would seek asylum.[2]

Then, too, Hitler failed to comprehend the significance of President Roosevelt's State of the Union speech before Congress on January 3. His words were not from a neutral or neutered leader but, rather, those from a man aware of the coming dangers and alert to finding a solution—so he hoped—short of war. "Nations, seeking expansion, seeking the rectification of injustice springing from former wars, seeking outlets for trade, for population or even for their own peaceful contributions to the progress of civilization," Roosevelt said, "fail to demonstrate that patience necessary to attain reasonable and legitimate objectives by peaceful negotiation or by an appeal to the finer instincts of world justice."[3]

Roosevelt bemoaned the need to address foreign affairs in just a paragraph—as he had done in his inaugural speech in 1933. His words—"chosen with deliberation"—were aimed at Germany, for its ambitions and mistreatment of segments of its own population as enemies of the state; Japan, for its invasion of Manchukuo (Manchuria); and Italy, for its invasion of Abyssinia. But was the president's speech an empty outcry? "The evidence before us clearly proves that autocracy in world affairs endangers peace and that such threats do not spring from those nations devoted to the democratic ideal," Roosevelt concluded.[4]

That January, too, the disgraced Samuel Hoare resigned and was replaced by Anthony Eden as Britain's new foreign secretary. Norman H. Davis, chairman of the American delegation at the London Naval

---

* Rabbi Stephen S. Wise, the founder of the Zionist Organization of America who had been the president of the American Jewish Congress, wrote to Roosevelt about the United Palestine Appeal Conference in Washington to mobilize American Jewry behind a "constructive effort to further the rebuilding of the Jewish homeland in Palestine on February 1, 1936 (source: Edgar B. Nixon, ed., *Franklin D. Roosevelt and Foreign Affairs*, vol. 3, *September 1935–1937* [Cambridge: The Belknap Press of Harvard University Press, 1969], 181).

Conference, noted that "our relations with the British have improved remarkably since last year. . . . Whatever tendency there was before to coddle Japan, in the hope of thus placating her, has disappeared."* Davis referred to Eden as "a real friend of ours" and reported that he had over-ruled the admiralty on matters of international agreements.[5]

THE POLITICAL AND cultural landscapes were changing. On January 18, British newspapers reported "The King—A Cold" and the death of Rud-yard Kipling. Alfred Duff Cooper had lunched with the Prince of Wales at Windsor two days earlier and despite the snowy weather, thought Edward was "in the highest spirits." After Duff Cooper left, Queen Mary sent Edward a message that his father, while in no immediate danger, was breathless and had no energy. That Saturday night, Edward wrote to Wallis after seeing his father, to inform her that all hope for his recovery had been abandoned. "You are all and everything I have in life and WE (Wallis and Edward) must hold each other so tight. . . . It will all work out right for us." The next morning, Edward drove back to London to warn Prime Minister Baldwin of his father's imminent death. Afterward, Baldwin told Tom Jones, "He had been to see Mrs S before he came to see me. . . . The subject [of Wallis] is never mentioned between us."[6]

George V's death was recorded at 11:05 P.M., conveniently for *The Times*'s deadline.[7] Finally, so Ribbentrop assured Hitler, Germany would get the relationship it craved with Great Britain. The British nation mourned the passing of the old king, never giving Germany a thought, with Chips Channon noting that even Hyde Park was "full of black crows." On January 21, the House of Commons was summoned by gunfire at six P.M. and around "400 MPs out of 615 turned up." At St. James's Palace nearby, Edward VIII took his oath of office dressed in his admiral's uni-form, "solemn, grave, sad and dignified" before "60 or 70 patriarchs, and

---

* The London Naval Conference of 1935–36 was intended to prolong the 1922 Wash-ington Treaty prohibiting the construction of more capital ships and was specifically set against the rise of tensions in the Pacific. Italy, one of the four Allied powers from the Great War, refused to sign any agreement, since sanctions had been imposed against it by the League of Nations for its invasion of Abyssinia.

grandees, in levée dress or uniform, presided over by Ramsay MacDonald as Lord President of the Council."[8] Prime Minister Baldwin spoke to the nation on radio, calling George V "a wise and loving friend and counsellor" who gallantly played his part in a mad, "raving world." Two days later, the House of Commons met, and Baldwin proposed a vote of condolence before speaking for around twenty minutes with "great simplicity" about the king.*

The burning question was how Edward VIII would organize his court, and what role Mrs. Simpson would play. As the date of the king's funeral drew near, the buzz became nearly deafening for those in Edward's social set. Yet, nothing changed immediately. Or so it seemed. Many, like Edward's boon companion Fruity Metcalfe, waited impatiently for promised positions at court. Emerald Cunard, too, had hopes of being appointed mistress of the robes so she could preside over "a court where poets musicians and artists held sway," forgetting, of course, that her remark may well have reached Queen Mary's ears, who believed that Lady Cunard "has done David [Edward] a great deal of harm as there is no doubt she was great friends with Mrs S and gave parties for her."[9] Others, like Princess Stephanie, were promoting Hitler's message that he was the European peacemaker at dinner parties and weekend retreats, feeding tidbits about Hitler's high regard for the British through her lover and the führer's adjutant, Fritz Wiedemann.

"In foreign affairs," Leopold von Hoesch, the German ambassador in London, wrote to his foreign ministry, "Edward VIII shares his father's conviction of the absolute necessity of preserving peace for his people. . . . King Edward, quite generally, feels warm sympathy for Germany." A few days before the death of George V, Edward reassured Hoesch that "it was his firm intention to go to Berlin next summer for the Olympic Games. . . . I am convinced that his friendly attitude towards Germany might in time come to exercise a certain amount of influence on the shaping of British foreign policy."[10]

---

* It had been a trying day for the prime minister. That morning, he had been a pallbearer for his cousin, Rudyard Kipling.

• • •

AN "INNOCENT" LUNCH took place with Duff Cooper* at the Duke and
Duchess of Althone's London home shortly before George V's funeral.
"The point of it was to meet the Duke of Coburg [Saxe-Coburg and
Gotha], her brother," Duff Cooper wrote rather dismissively. "It was a
gloomy little party—so like a small German bourgeois household." Of
course, Duff Cooper knew that Carl Edouard was a fervent Nazi and
had been president of the German Red Cross since 1933. After the luncheon, Duff Cooper was "tactfully" left with Charles Edouard, who explained "the present situation in Germany and assured me of Hitler's
pacific intentions." But Duff Cooper was not taken in. In fact, he was
shocked when the Duchess of Athlone entered to ask Carl Edouard his
opinion about the ribbon to go on the wreath for the king's funeral and
he "dismissed her with a volley of muttered German curses and was
afterwards unable to pick up the thread of his argument."[11]

Three days later, George V's funeral took place. Chips Channon and
his wife, Honor, went to St. James's Palace. "Half the house had been
commandeered for Mrs Simpson and her party." This struck some
(though not Channon) as untoward, especially since the dead king had
refused to have her in his home. Channon remarked that as "the monarch of the world" lay in that small coffin proceeding down the Mall,
the new King Edward VIII looked up, "no doubt seeking Mrs Simpson
at the window" of St. James's Palace. Behind Edward were his "brothers and the Princes and the Kings." Royalty from throughout Europe,
too, were in attendance. Among them shuffled one shabby figure: Carl
Edouard, Duke of Saxe-Coburg and Gotha, shambling along arthrit-
ically in his German soldier's uniform and helmet. It was a pointed,
misguided, and false statement to the country of his birth: he had been
deprived of his British titles and honors, and only had his German war
uniform to wear.[12] He could have worn his Nazi dress uniform.

Harold Nicolson stayed away, hearing "the minute-guns firing dole-
fully in the distance." He sensed that the changes that were coming

---

* Alfred Duff Cooper was serving as the secretary of state for war since November
1935.

would be momentous. At noon, Nicolson went to see Betty Morrow and Anne Lindbergh at the Ritz Hotel, noticing the streets "strewn thick with waste paper."* During his brief visit, Harold may well have told them he feared he and Vita might have to sell their former home, Long Barn. Days later, Vita's mother, Lady Sackville, died, and he was able to offer the house to Anne for the Lindberghs to rent. By March, the Lindberghs accepted his offer, and Nicolson made the postmistress of the village promise that they "shall not stare at the poor people."[13]

THE DAY AFTER George V's funeral, Lord and Lady Londonderry and their daughter, Lady Mairi, boarded a Junkers Ju-52 at Croydon airport that was sent to ferry them to Germany in comfort. The trip was in response to a German charm offensive, led by Göring's representatives to show how much Germany appreciated Londonderry's efforts as air minister before his sacking in June 1935.

Göring's agents met them at Berlin's Tegel airport and stayed with them throughout the trip at Hotel Adlon, Berlin's best hotel (and Hitler's favorite). The following day, Londonderry reviewed the Luftwaffe installations and fighter squadrons situated near Berlin with the British air attaché from the British embassy, Group Captain Don, in tow. That evening, they were invited to the Reich chancellery on the Wilhelmstrasse to view a torchlight parade of many thousand stormtroopers celebrating the third anniversary of Hitler's accession as chancellor. Lady Mairi thought it was spectacular, "the most impressive sight" ever. Yet she overheard her mother say to her father, "This means war, Charley." Londonderry knew Britain did not possess an air force anywhere near the strength or capability of Germany's.

---

* Harold Nicolson and his wife, Vita Sackville-West, met the Lindberghs in 1934 while staying at the Waldorf-Astoria Hotel. Nicolson was later commissioned by Morgan Grenfell to write the biography of Anne's father, Dwight Morrow, and was staying with the couple during the Bruno Hauptmann trial. He was struck by Charles's apparent disinterest. "It *must* mean something to him," Nicolson wrote, "yet he never glances at them [the newspapers] and chatters quite happily to me about Roosevelt" (source: Stanley Olson, ed., *Harold Nicolson Diaries and Letters, 1930–1964* [London: Penguin Books, 1968], 72).

They dined with Hermann and Emmy Göring at the Reichstag president's palace. Bluff, jovial, dressed more like Robin Hood than Germany's second most important man, Göring made a great impression on his guests. The next day, he took the Londonderrys hunting at Karinhall, his country estate north of Berlin. Göring sported a stick that looked like an ancient Germanic spear and laughed like a child as he shot dead an enormous bison.

At tea, Göring talked business, reassuring Londonderry that he wanted an Anglo-German pact. Britain should be wary of France, which refused to accept "Germany's legitimate aims and aspirations," he added. In response, Londonderry suggested that Germany should make some goodwill gesture to the French by accepting the demilitarized zone and that, in return, France might adopt a similar zone at its border with Germany. Göring tacitly accepted this approach, and said he'd pass it along to Hitler, but it was only a cynical device to woo the Englishman.[14]

On February 2, the Londonderrys were entertained at lunch at the Ribbentrops' villa in Dahlem. Among the twenty-five other guests were Dr. Schmidt, acting as interpreter, and Rudolf Hess, Hitler's deputy in Nazi Party matters. The desire for an Anglo-German pact was brought up again by Hess. Ribbentrop steered the conversation to the benefits Britain could achieve by allowing Germany its eastern expansion.* After all, Germany was a bulwark against the spread of bolshevism, he asserted. Afterward, Londonderry said that he found the conversation "somewhat disturbing, as if my worst fears of this development of German strength would be directed to this expansion in Europe and that no nation would be in a position to object."[15] There was no doubt in Edith's mind that the couple were meant to bring this message back to the government, and the new king.

Indeed, Germany was busy in its attempts to groom those close to power. With Duff Cooper, through Charles Edouard, they failed, but Londonderry was—as Harold Nicolson described him—"a real gent," who remained in the 1760s despite the year being 1936. Londonderry's

---

* Ribbentrop had successfully negotiated the naval pact with Britain in June 1935, in direct contravention of Versailles, where the Germans could rearm to the strength of 35 percent of the Royal Navy.

patrician attitude skewed his thinking and made him an unreliable eye-witness about the new Germany. When he met Hitler (with Hess and Ribbentrop in tow), Londonderry was taken in by Hitler's "feigned diffidence," awkwardness, and apparent "ordinariness," never realizing that his behavior was a calculated act to convey humility and make his opposite number trust him.[16] Putzi Hanfstaengl had schooled Hitler well.

Their discussion centered on Germany as the only opponent of bolshevism on the Continent. When Londonderry tentatively ventured that the League of Nations had already carved out this role, Hitler was polite but dismissive. "The League of Nations would finally become just a paper illusion," Hitler replied. By admitting the Soviet Union, it had allowed "germ carriers" to infect and destroy it. Not wishing Londonderry to leave on a negative note, however, Hitler reiterated his "desire for a 'close friendly alliance with England'" to prevent a return to the madness of war. Londonderry left the meeting "visibly impressed."[17]

The wooing of Londonderry continued with endless rounds of receptions, inspections of air force installations, more meetings with the German hierarchy, and visits with the German arm of the Anglo-German Fellowship. Afterward, they were flown by Göring's private plane to Berchtesgaden before traveling on to Munich, then to the winter Olympic games at Garmisch-Partenkirchen for the week. They met Hitler and Göring again and were deeply impressed by the heartfelt reception given to Hitler at the closing ceremony. It was "one of the most remarkable demonstrations I have ever seen," Londonderry told everyone. By the time Charley and Edith returned home, they were utterly bedazzled.[18]

AND SO THEY went to work for Hitler. Before going public with their impressions, they involved their vast social and political set. Their elder daughter, Lady Maureen Stanley (married to Oliver Stanley, MP), was roped in for an "at home" intimate reception with only a few select guests. Harold Nicolson, who deeply disapproved of "ex-Cabinet Ministers trotting across to Germany at this moment" was one, and a "dear little woman in black," the other. She recognized Nicolson at once and reminded him that they had met in Berlin, though she did not say when that was. It was only when a third guest arrived, and she curtsied to the "dear little woman in black," that Nicolson realized he was sitting next to Elizabeth, Duchess of York, the wife of the new king's brother, "Bertie," who was next in line for the throne.

It was widely rumored that Bertie (later George VI) and his wife had taken against Mrs. Simpson and were certainly opposed to a rapprochement with Germany. But one wonders if the Duchess of York had heard Wallis's remark about not liking to wear mourning and not having sported black stockings since she gave up dancing the cancan? Whatever pro-German remarks were made that day, however, they did not prevent Harold Nicolson from giving a shrewd assessment of Anglo-German relations to the Foreign Affairs Committee a few days later. As far as Nicolson was concerned, there would be war against Germany in 1939 or 1940.[19]

On February 22, the German ambassador advised the foreign ministry that Lord and Lady Londonderry had formed the "most favourable impressions" of Germany, but that they would not be issuing a press statement. Hoesch was wrong. In fact, on the very day Hoesch sent his cable to foreign minister Neurath, Londonderry's press statement about Germany was unequivocal: he had encountered "a very friendly feeling towards this country, and a very strong desire for the friendship of Great Britain and France." He concluded with his belief that Hitler was a man of peace. Really, France? Londonderry must have felt he was entitled to some poetic license.

The press release was followed up a few days later with a speech at Durham, where Londonderry referred to Hitler as a "kindly man" and said that, should there be another war and Britain found itself on the opposite side from Germany, it would show an appalling lack of statesmanship. The independent *Manchester Guardian* referred to Londonderry as "an innocent" and stated that after the Durham speech, "most people will be more than ever grateful to Mr Baldwin for having pushed him out of the National Government." It rightly concluded that "because Herr Hitler has said it, Lord Londonderry believes."

Unrepentant, Londonderry followed Ribbentrop's suggestion and joined the Anglo-German Fellowship, aimed at influencing the rich and powerful. And why not? It boasted MPs, generals, admirals, businessmen, and bankers. Financial institutions like Schroeder, Lazard, and Midland Bank held a corporate membership. Industrial giants such as Unilever, Dunlop, and Firth-Vickers Stainless Steels were also corporate members. The governor of the Bank of England was a member, as were the board directors of Imperial Chemical Industries (ICI), the sugar manufacturer Tate and Lyle, and the Distillers Company. The largest donors were Unilever and ICI.[20]

GERMANY'S RELATIONSHIP WITH France remained strained because of the French reluctance to ease the provisions of Versailles and Hitler's stated ambitions for Lebensraum.* On February 11, the debate on ratification of the Franco-Soviet Pact opened in the Chamber of Deputies in Paris. Two weeks later, France declared that such a pact would be entirely in keeping with Locarno. A few days earlier, the Soviet Union had signed a similar pact with Czechoslovakia, giving Hitler every reason to bemoan encirclement, reminiscent of the geopolitical causes of the Great War. The Franco-Soviet agreement was passed on February 27, to a huge outcry in the Reich gazettes: *"An act fraught with consequences!"*

On the morning of March 2, the French ambassador, André François-Poncet, was summoned to an audience with a decidedly annoyed and impatient Hitler. François-Poncet was duly dressed down and reported to his government that Hitler viewed France's actions as naked aggression.[21] Five days later, the Reich war minister and commander in chief of the Wehrmacht, General Wilhelm Keitel, advised that "The Rhineland will be occupied in the course of March 7 and 8 by nineteen battalions and thirteen artillery units from the centre of Germany. . . . In the case of enquiries the Air Attachés will be briefed directly by the Luftwaffe."

But was the French action a casus belli for Germany to remilitarize? Frantic meetings were scheduled for March 10 in Paris, where the French premier muttered, "We are not inclined to leave Strasbourg

---

* The Locarno Pact, signed in London in December 1925, was intended to ease tensions between the two countries and required France to eventually dissolve its *cordon sanitaire*. Signatories to the Locarno agreements were Germany, France, Belgium, Great Britain, and Italy.

exposed to the fire of German guns." But despite the bluster, nothing was done. The French hadn't known that German troops were "under strict orders to beat a hasty retreat if the French army opposed them in any way," according to journalist William Shirer.

Winston Churchill felt compelled to address the Commons on March 26. "There is an extra ordinary volume of German propaganda in this country, of mis-statements made on the highest authority—which everyone knows could be easily disproved—which obtain currency, and which because they are not contradicted are accepted as part of the regular facts on which the public may rely," Churchill said. [22]

Churchill was unaware, however, that Edward VIII had made his first intervention in foreign policy during the Rhineland crisis. According to the German press attaché in London, Fritz Hesse, Ambassador Hoesch had been a friend of the king for some years and had gone to visit Edward in secret. A day or so later, Hesse was listening on a call from the king to Hoesch as a witness. Edward VIII had rung the German ambassador and said, "Hallo. Is that Leo? David speaking. I sent for the Prime Minister and gave him a piece of my mind. I told the old so-and-so that I would abdicate if he made war. There was a frightful scene. But you needn't worry. There won't be a war."

Hoesch was reportedly so excited that he waltzed around his office chanting, "I've done it. I've outwitted them all. There won't be a war. Herr Hesse, we've done it!"[23]

Upping the Ante

It is better to be feared than loved if you cannot be both.
—Niccolò Machiavelli, *The Prince*

On March 22, 1936, Mosley addressed a meeting of the British Union of Fascists at Albert Hall, calling for the country to align itself with Germany. While he roused high emotions, Mosley knew full well that his British Union of Fascists had lost its momentum during 1935, leading Mussolini to reduce his payments and the BUF struggling to survive.

The main source of Mussolini's disenchantment with Mosley was Count Dino Grandi—who was having an affair with Baba Metcalfe, one of Mosley's lovers. Grandi had been grumbling about the BUF to Mussolini throughout 1935, claiming, "with a tenth of what you give Mosley, I feel I could produce a result ten times better." The Italian stipend for the BUF was then reduced to a monthly one thousand pounds. But Diana Guinness had already developed a strong relationship with Hitler. To remain solvent, Mosley sent her to Berlin to ask Hitler to financially back his fascists instead. Hitler was happy to comply by the end of the month.

German backing upped the ante. That April, the party was placed under the direction of Neil Francis-Hawkins, publishing *The Blackshirt* for its working-class readers and launching *Action*, theoretically for its more educated readers, under the editorship of John Beckett. Together, these papers had a circulation of nearly fifty thousand.[1] Mosley then surrounded himself with pro-Nazi rather than pro-Mussolini cohorts like William Joyce, A. K. Chesterton, and Major General John Fuller.

The BUF's rapprochement to the Nazis meant an increase in its anti-Semitic rhetoric and Jew baiting. Its spokesman, William Joyce, exclaimed time and again, "I don't regard Jews as a class, I regard them as a privileged misfortune." As the year progressed, regular complaints piled up on the home secretary's desk. With each attempt by the police to halt the verbal and physical violence, Joyce said, "luminous with hate," that "Britain is today under a hidden dictatorship far harsher than that in Germany and Italy."[2]

There was a strong lobby among the elite in Britain, which felt France was decadent, too, and that Germany had been wronged for far too long. Many were members of the Anglo-German Fellowship or flirted with becoming members. Harold Nicolson concluded that the House of Commons was "terribly 'pro-German', which means afraid of war."[3]

THE NEW KING, however, was oblivious. On a chilly early February evening, Edward VIII invited Ernest Simpson and his friend Bernard Rickatson-Hatt, who was editor in chief at Reuters, to his York House home. After dinner, Ernest turned to Edward and said that it was quite evident Wallis would need to choose between her marriage and His Majesty. Everyone in society, even if Edward was unaware of it, knew about their affair. "What did the King mean to do about it? Did he intend to marry her?" Ernest asked. Edward rose from his chair and replied, "Do you really think I would be crowned without Wallis at my side?"[4]

Wallis Simpson had indeed become indispensable to Edward. She was behind much of the modernizing that offended the old guard, including the "undignified" sight of asking—and getting—the king to call a taxi for her at St. James's Palace. But above all else, it was Wallis's sense of ownership that most offended the old guard, with her gauche we "were so glad you could come" or showing long-standing retainers parts of Windsor castle they knew better than their own names.

Worst of all, it had not gone unnoticed that Wallis was bossy. Diana Cooper heard her reprimanding Edward in front of guests to stop insisting on having his official papers and documents read to him and to simply learn to master the essential points. "She is right of course as he made haste to say," Diana wrote of Edward. "Wallis is quite right," he repeated. "She always is. I shall learn it quite soon." No wonder the "queen bees" of society like Emerald Cunard, Sybil Colefax, and Nancy Astor assumed that Wallis would become queen and assured their fellow aristocrats that they would need to cut their cloth to suit the new court.[5] Tittle-tattle rushed like a spring stream through London society and straight back to Berlin.

Most disconcerting, however, was Edward's inability to make up his own mind without Wallis advising him. State papers were left lying around his home Fort Belvedere or returned with telltale rings from glasses or cups on them. Some dispatch boxes were lost entirely. Who could have been responsible for spiriting them away? "It was not long before the royal household wondered if Princess Stephanie and Wallis Simpson were working hand in glove," biographer Andrew Morton wrote in his book *17 Carnations*. Princess Stephanie was Hitler's "secret weapon in the battle for the political heart and mind of the future king. Her title gave her access, while her vivacious personality and flirtatious charm provided an effective means of persuasion."[6]

Alec Hardinge, Edward's private secretary, despaired. Alan "Tommy" Lascelles, who had resigned from royal service seven years earlier because he "disapproved of the Prince of Wales" and had only recently returned to royal service as the assistant private secretary to George V, convinced Hardinge to tell the prime minister about Edward's dereliction of duty. An enraged Baldwin decided to show only documents to Edward that required his royal signature.[7] The king, of course, never noticed. Making Wallis his queen was all that mattered.

Wallis was in Paris buying her spring wardrobe at Mainbocher's when her future was decided by the two men in her life.* If she felt trapped, it was a sentiment shared equally by the prime minister and his advisers. "Mrs S," according to a memorandum by Lord Davidson, Baldwin's firm ally, "is very close to Hoesch and has, if she likes to read them access to all Secret and Cabinet papers!!!!!"[8]

---

* Chicagoan Main Bocher (who styled himself Mainbocher once he became a couturier) had wanted to be an opera singer but lacked the lungs and began work at *Vogue* as an illustrator before becoming a designer. Wallis's wedding-trousseau commission would become his most famous collection (source: Susan Ronald, *Condé Nast: A Biography* [New York: St. Martin's Press, 2019], 184–185).

Wallis may have been close to Hoesch (who deplored Hitler's march into the Rhineland), but when he died suddenly on April 11, it was Stephanie's old friend and chargé d'affaires, Prince Otto Christian Archibald von Bismarck, who temporarily replaced him.* Stephanie had attended many embassy events over her years in London. She had also gone to the opera with Bismarck's Swedish wife, Princess Ann-Mari, and their mutual friend Emerald Cunard, gossiping in their private boxes.[9] Unknown to Wallis, her former couturiere, Anna Wolkoff, and her near neighbor Princess Stephanie (now living at 14 Bryanston Square, a block and a half away) had been reporting on Wallis and Edward to their handlers for some time. Princess Dimitri, that pretty addition to "the Ritz Set," was always hard up for cash and sang her own song to the Italians and Germans, too.

ALTHOUGH HOESCH'S SUDDEN death did not occur until mid-April, Hans-Heinrich Dieckhoff, Joachim von Ribbentrop's brother-in-law, had been signing documents in London since March 22 as "The Acting Head of the German Delegation." Three days later, the first letter addressed to Ribbentrop as "The Head of the German Delegation in London" arrived from Neurath. It seems Hoesch had been summarily recalled but said nothing to his staff.[10†] Ribbentrop's appointment as German ambassador to the Court of St. James's was finally announced at the end of May, but Bismarck remained in charge of the embassy until Ribbentrop took up his post in October.

Meanwhile, Princess Stephanie had allied herself to the most agreeable Bismarcks. Ann-Mari reminded Göring of his beloved Karin, and he often reiterated how the beautiful Swede who spoke fluent English and German had become the most enchanting "publicity agent" the Reich possessed in London. Loved by Lady Astor, and a frequent visitor at the Astors' Sandwich getaway, Ann-Mari's handsome children wore

---

* He was the grandson of the great chancellor Count Otto von Bismarck-Schönhausen, who unified Germany.
† The sequence of events gave rise to rumors of Hoesch's possible suicide or murder by the Gestapo.

bathing suits with a swastika embroidered on their left breasts when they swam in the Channel.[11]

Under Ribbentrop, the German charm offensive would take on a new dimension. Although he reluctantly took up his ambassadorship (not trusting Hitler to make the "right" decisions without him at his side), Ribbentrop made several trips to England in the spring of 1936. In April, he conveyed Hitler's convoluted "peace plan" to the Foreign Office, but when clarification was sought by the British, Hitler became annoyed and dropped it.

That May, T. J. Jones was invited to visit Ribbentrop's Dahlem home, as a prelude to inviting the prime minister to see Hitler. Jones was quite taken with it since "one might be in Surrey or Sussex." He dutifully noted books by T. E. Lawrence, Lytton Strachey, and George Bernard Shaw sharing shelf space with signed photographs of Hitler and Göring in the study. Their discussions were wide ranging, but Ribbentrop was at pains to explain that neither leader should trust the "professional diplomats."[12]

On May 29, Ribbentrop and his wife returned to London bearing official invitations to the forthcoming Berlin Olympics to "spread influence." That evening, they dined at the American Laura Corrigan's home along with the Londonderrys and the Channons. It had been prearranged for Mrs. Corrigan to fly with the Ribbentrops to the Londonderrys' home, Mount Stewart, in Northern Ireland the next day. Chips, never one to withhold his opinion, thought that Annelies von Ribbentrop had "intelligent eyes" but wore "appalling khaki-coloured clothes and an un-powdered, unpainted face." His thoughts on Ribbentrop were equally condescending: "He, Ribbentrop, looks like the captain of someone's yacht, square, breezy, and with a sea-going look. . . . He is not quite without charm, but shakes hands in an over-hearty way, and his accent is Long Island without a trace of Teutonic flavour." The recently retired prime minister, Ramsay MacDonald, had said of Ribbentrop that he had "stuck a label on his chest: 'I am von Germany.'"[13]

Lord and Lady Londonderry remained avid supporters of the Nazi regime. They shared the German view that the Franco-Soviet pact was the impetus for the remilitarization of the Rhineland and received thanks from Hermann Göring "for all your endeavours for the peace of our countries." Separately, Göring wrote to Edith "how much the Leader [the führer] and all of us desire and love peace" but are stymied time and again by the "irreconcilable attitude of the French." Göring expressed his gratitude for Londonderry's defense of an Anglo-German rapprochement, saying, "we shall never forget that he has pronounced his point of view so clearly and independently." Magda Goebbels and Emmy Göring also wrote to Edith about their hope to "knit the bond of friendship between Great Britain and Germany."

In response, Edith published her own eulogy of Hitler and Nazi Germany in the *Sunday Sun* newspaper. She explained how she, too, had gone to Germany "full of prejudice" and came away a devoted, even religious, convert. In Hitler, she "beheld a man of arresting personality—a man with farseeing eyes" who was "beloved of modern Germany." Her article concluded that Britain should look to revising its foreign policy "so that we come to know that peace we all so greatly desire." A copy was sent directly to Ribbentrop.

Shortly after, Göring wrote to Edith in the hope that *she* could change British foreign policy to favor Germany over France. He painted a dire, and oddly accurate, geopolitical landscape. Italy had prevailed in Abyssinia and was building up its navy. Mussolini was keen to do all in his power to assure a long-term friendship with Germany, too.* An Italo-German pact would represent a threat to the British Empire in the Mediterranean and the Middle East, and threatened Egypt and the Suez Canal, its main artery to the empire in the East. Göring then claimed that the League of Nations was severely compromised, and the Bolsheviks were in the ascendant. Spain had narrowly elected a communist government that was hell-bent on breaking the bonds of the Catholic Church, and France was strongly under the influence of its left and communistic influences. So why insist on this outdated and outmoded alliance with France, Göring asked, when Germany represented the only European "bulwark against Bolshevism and for peace and quiet?" When Baldwin had the same picture painted by T. J. Jones, he consulted

---

* Göring, of course, did not reveal that the rapprochement was due to the League of Nations sanctions against Italy for invading Abyssinia, depriving it of gasoline, or that Mussolini was anxious to get access to I.G. Farben's synthetic fuels.

with Eden, who warned that "the object of German policy was to divide us from the French."[14]

AND SO THE Ribbentrops, his two adjutants, Heinz Thorner and Georg von Wussow, and the American hostess Mrs. Corrigan flew to Mount Stewart in the ambassador's black-and-silver Junkers Ju-52 passenger plane, the *Wilhelm Siegert*. Another invitee was Rothermere's foreign correspondent George Ward Price, one of Hitler's greatest apologists in Britain. Price stood among the journalists to meet the *Wilhelm Siegert* on landing. He reported later that Ribbentrop declared he was "a great friend of Lord Londonderry."

No wonder the London wits nicknamed Ribbentrop "The Londonderry Herr," after the folk song "The Londonderry Air." Both Ribbentrop and Londonderry were at great pains to declare that they were merely having a relaxing break, that there was "no connection whatever with any public matter," and that there was "nothing mysterious" about the visit.

As *The Star* newspaper reported: "Lord Londonderry may assert to his heart's content that at his weekend party . . . Herr von Ribbentrop and the chief of our air staff, Sir Edward Ellington, never had any intention of discussing public matters. But who will believe that these two men would come together at such a juncture in Anglo-German relations as the present one and confine themselves to the discussion of the weather?"[15]*

No record was made of any discussions that weekend. Golf was played (poorly by Ribbentrop), food eaten, and plenty of wine and champagne drunk. On the Sunday, a prearranged visit by three squadrons of RAF planes flew into Newtownards aerodrome from Glasgow, Edinburgh, and Durham. Thirty-six military aircraft, including two Hawker Hart two-seater biplanes, landed in perfect formation, taking up docking positions near Ribbentrop's Junkers. The leader of the Glasgow squadron was none other than the Marquess of Clydesdale, Londonderry's great

---

* The air marshal Sir Edward Ellington was chief of staff of the Royal Air Force and also a house guest.

friend and later Duke of Hamilton.* Clydesdale was also a celebrity for having flown over the peak of Everest in 1933. Ribbentrop inquired if this gathering was a regular occurrence. Londonderry lied, saying that it happened about once a month. In fact, it was laid on to show the prowess of the RAF in the hope that Ribbentrop would take that message back to Germany.[16]

On his return to London, Ribbentrop stayed on to meet with "friends" sympathetic to Germany: Geoffrey Dawson, the formidable editor of *The Times*, T. J. Jones, and Lord Lothian. Shortly after, Jones told Ribbentrop that Baldwin felt that if the right moment presented itself to go to Berlin, the trip would need to be "a straightforward official visit arranged through embassy channels, and that he would have to be accompanied by Eden." Jones protested. Involving the Foreign Office would be disastrous, and "I have taken the matter as far as I can without damage to the cause we both have so much at heart," he wrote to Ribbentrop on June 18. "You will, I hope, come over as soon as you can to see Eden yourself and put to him what you have put to me with so much conviction." Ribbentrop despaired, telling the British ambassador to Germany, Sir Eric Phipps, "Great Britain . . . persisted in maintaining a 'Versailles' attitude." It was the beginning of his disenchantment with Britain, which would develop into hateful antagonism.[17] In fact, Ribbentrop feared he had let Hitler down.†

WITH HOPES OF a British understanding stalling, Ribbentrop contented himself instead with hosting his "English friends" at the Olympics. Top of his list was, of course, Edward VIII and Mrs. Simpson, who had promised to attend. But Edward's priority remained Wallis *über alles*. On June 10, the recently bereaved Sybil Colefax was preparing to move from her

---

* As the Duke of Hamilton, he would be the object of Rudolf Hess's ill-fated May 1941 flight to Scotland. He was also a member of the Anglo-German Fellowship. So was Geoffrey Dawson of *The Times*.
† Ribbentrop's only salvation in 1936 would be to pull off the Anti-Comintern Pact with Japan (negotiated by Hermann von Raumer on his behalf, and eventually signed in November 1936). Bringing Imperial Japan to the table would be the work of German ambassador Herbert von Dirksen in Tokyo.

Chelsea home and invited the king and Mrs. Simpson as her principal guests. Others present were Winston and Clementine Churchill; Noël Coward; Harold Nicolson; Robert Bruce Lockhart; Kenneth Clark and his wife; Robert Vansittart and his wife; Tom Lamont of J.P. Morgan; the piano virtuoso Arturo Rubinstein; the socialite Daisy Fellowes; Daisy's aunt, Winnaretta Singer, the Princesse de Polignac; the Londonderrys' daughter Lady Maureen Stanley and her husband, Oliver Stanley, who was minister for education and generally viewed as "lacking in vim."

Harold Nicolson and Edward discussed his dinner at the Lindberghs', with Edward declaring that it had been a great success. Anne had been rather shy at first, "but with my well-known charm I put her at ease and liked her very much." Sir Robert Vansittart listened carefully to the king's enthusiasm for a rapprochement with Nazis, passing on his view privately that as a reigning monarch, the king was required to avoid any political comment in public.

After dinner, Sybil invited Rubinstein to play the piano, an event the Princesse de Polignac, who led the most famous Parisian salon for music, relished. Rubinstein played Chopin's Barcarolle, followed by two other pieces of classical music. He was about to play a fourth piece when the king jumped up, crossed the room, and stopped him. "We enjoyed that very much, Mr Rubinstein," and nodded to Wallis that it was time to leave. Rubinstein was offended but relinquished his place at the piano. The Princesse de Polignac "must have thought us a race of barbarians," Nicolson wrote. Edward said good night to the assembled guests, just as Noël Coward leapt onto the piano bench and began to sing and play "Mad Dogs and Englishmen." Edward and Wallis remained for another hour to listen to several encores of popular tunes sung by Coward, adding insult to injury to the Jewish Rubinstein.[18]

Tom Lamont, for one, feigned not to have noticed. After all, he was in England to see those aristocrats whom the bank represented, like Waldorf and Nancy Astor, but also to sound out those whom he hoped had the power to begin repaying the American debt. In fact, Tom Lamont had just come from Cliveden. His friendship and banking relationship with the Astors extended back some years. He corresponded regularly with Nancy, and, as with Lothian, there was a romantic hue in Lamont's prose, like calling Nancy "the girl I love most." He showered her with gifts and did not shrink from using their "special relationship" to his, Morgan's, and America's advantage. Nancy, as an MP and aristocrat, was a useful ally in fighting his corner.

Lamont and the Astors were like-minded. The British Empire could (and should) coexist with the Nazis. They supported the policies of Stanley Baldwin and Neville Chamberlain, whom everyone treated as a prime minister in waiting. At times, their views of the fascists were benign; at others, admiring. Both Lamont and the Astors shuddered at Churchill's warnings about German rearmament and ridiculed his stance.

The Astors had five sons, and like so many of the British, still felt that the European dictators could be held at bay through intelligent diplomacy, meaning appeasement. And yet Lamont recognized that neither Hitler nor Mussolini seemed "to have changed their spots very much, but I seem to think that raging at them will do no good," Lamont wrote to Nancy with an oblique reference to Churchill, "and if there is a possibility of methods of appeasement, these are our only chance." Therefore, Lamont urged Nancy to lobby the Foreign Office to placate it over Mussolini's conquest of Abyssinia.[19]

THEN, ON JULY 17, the Spanish Civil War erupted when General Francisco Franco led the military revolt against the Spanish Popular Front government. Five days later, Franco pleaded with Hitler for assistance. Hitler agreed to send the Condor Legion, a Luftwaffe unit that could test out the new air force and bombs manufactured by Krupp and I.G. Farben. As nonintervention talks were slated to take place in London, Hitler invested half a billion dollars on war materiel for Franco to use in Spain as a training ground for Krupp's stunningly successful eighty-eight anti-aircraft and anti-tank guns. Over 150,000 Italian and German troops and ten thousand technicians would soon be fighting for the rebel nationalists under Franco. The Soviet Union sent two thousand technicians and money and arms, but no soldiers. Some fifty thousand foreigners would join the fight on the side of the Loyalists and duly elected government—forty thousand of whom served in international brigades. Throughout that fateful summer, France was up in arms, crying out that if other Western countries (meaning Great Britain) gave aid to the Loyalists, the war would spread to the rest of Europe.[20]*

Simultaneously, Charles Lindbergh accepted an invitation from Major Truman Smith (formerly Captain Truman Smith, who had introduced Putzi Hanfstaengl to Hitler, now the American military attaché in Berlin) to visit Germany to report on the German air strength, with the approval of Hermann Göring. He would be accompanied by his wife, Anne. Whatever grandiose plan Göring may have had to capitalize on Lindbergh's fame was slightly dampened by Lindbergh's acceptance. "What I am most anxious to avoid," Lindbergh replied, "is the sensational and stupid publicity which we have so frequently encountered in the past; and the difficulty and unpleasantness which invariably accompany it."[21]

German hospitality at the highest levels was thrown open to the Lindberghs. The Smiths and Lindberghs paid a social call on Hermann Göring at Karinhall after inspecting several aviation facilities and attending a seemingly countless round of social functions jam-packed with government officials. For a man wishing to avoid press attention—and who had moved countries to live quietly only six months earlier—it was an unusual turn of events. Of course, the American press reported his travel itinerary and wondered why his five-hour tour of an aeronautics research center should take place "almost secretly" on the outskirts of Berlin.[22] Lindbergh never once commented that Germany had supplied arms and war materiel to the Spanish rebels. Nor had he stopped to think that he was being used by the Nazis as their best international publicity agent capable of frightening the world into letting the Germans achieve their expansionist dreams.

---

* Four batteries (sixteen guns) were originally sent to Spain with the Condor Legion. The official name was the 8.8cm Flak 36, which was later improved into the Flak 37 and the Flak 41 (the numbers denoting the date of launch). Flak, meaning anti-aircraft fire, came into the English language from the German, *Fliegerabwehrkanone* or *Flakabwehrkanone,* meaning "anti-aircraft cannon."

Olympians and Titans

Choose your penance . . . destruction or sacrifice.
—Hades, *Clash of the Titans*

Lindbergh "became so interested" in Germany's rejuvenation "that he decided to accept the invitation of the German government to stay for the opening day" of the Olympics as a guest in Hitler's box. (Apparently, no one thought to introduce them. . . .) In London, *The Times* wrote that Lindbergh was "intensely pleased by what he had observed" of Germany's aircraft production. Privately, he believed that "Hitler must have far more character and vision than I thought existed in the German leader," who had been painted "in so many different ways" in the English and American press.[1] Had Lindbergh known that Goebbels ordered all the anti-Jewish placards to be torn down in preparation for the Olympics? Surely, Truman Smith would have told him?

That July, too, Hitler secretly approached Hermann Göring to lead his Four-Year Plan. The immediate beneficiaries were I.G. Farben, Krupp, and other German industrial giants.* Schacht had resigned in disgust, but Hitler told his economics minister that Adolf Hitler *is* Germany. The Olympics would be Germany's crowning glory, and Schacht would need to remain at his post.

The XI Olympiad had already given the Third Reich unprecedented publicity, propaganda, and, most of all, much-needed foreign exchange.[2]

---

* Contemporary art, previously scorned and burned by the Nazis, was being converted to a huge export market to fund the future war under Göring's tutelage, too.

It would enhance their youth culture, symbolized by the Olympians, waging their war against the older, outmoded ideologies of modern society: capitalism, democracy, and liberalism. It would undoubtedly showcase Aryan superiority and show, too, the Third Reich's accomplishments and political values.

Foreign sponsorship from multinationals like Coca-Cola and Standard Oil were warmly welcomed. Standard Oil's Hamburg operations had been active in supervising test runs, assessing airplane engines, writing an aviation handbook, and supplying gasoline to German aircraft manufacturing facilities, especially for its largest clients, Focke-Wulf and Göring Corporation. During the Olympiad flying rally, the German pilot, Ludwig Vogel, won. He was the same pilot who would fly Ribbentrop to Moscow in August 1939 to sign the Molotov-Ribbentrop Pact.[3]

Despite thousands of articles and organizations protesting American participation in the games, the president of the International Olympic Committee, Avery Brundage (the only American to hold that position), was determined the United States should participate. It was an election year, and Brundage believed that neither the president nor the State Department would take an active interest. He was right. The protests died down as positive publicity surrounding the athletes themselves and the commercial opportunities took off. Brundage had argued throughout the various committee meetings that the 1932 Los Angeles games, with their Hollywood flair, had changed the complexion of the Olympics forever. He ignored the fact that Nazi persecution extended to "Protestant and Catholic churches and against professors, artists, industrialists and persons of every category of political and social reason."[4]

NONETHELESS, THE CURIOUS, the supportive, the athletic, and, above all, the world's elite flocked to Berlin that August. Fritz Kuhn, the former Ford Motor Company employee and "American fuehrer," visited Ambassador Dodd as part of Kuhn's guided tour around Germany with some two hundred visitors "to convince them that Nazism is the salvation of modern peoples." Only days later, Dodd learned that Kuhn's junket had been paid for by Ernst Bohle, who "worked at the foreign Office of the Nazi Party," the Auslands Organization (AO). After the war, it emerged during Bohle's interrogation that the AO had been "engaged in a struggle" against Ribbentrop, and that Bohle had placed "men of confidence" (read: party propagandists) in key cities throughout the United States as consular officials by 1935.[5]*

During the games, Goebbels hobnobbed with the Bulgarian czar, Boris III; the Italian crown prince, Dino Alfieri (the Italian minister of propaganda); and Sir Robert Vansittart, the undersecretary of state at the British Foreign Office and supporter of Churchill's anti-German stance. Vansittart was the brother-in-law of the British ambassador, Sir Eric Phipps, and attended Dr. Goebbels's phantasmagoric party at the close of the games.

The Goebbels extravaganza at "Peacock Island" on the river Havel (formerly the home and mansion of a Jewish family) was breathtaking. The entire diplomatic corps and most gauleiters and Nazi Party leaders were among the three thousand guests. The island was accessed by a pontoon bridge built by the Wehrmacht Pioneer Corps that was "hung with festive lanterns," like all the trees. The guests crossed the bridge to the airs played by the Berlin regional orchestra. Three more dance bands and the German Opera House Ballet also entertained the assembled company after the lavish supper. Fireworks lasting half an hour sounded like gunshots raining down on the crowd, with many people "complaining at this form of war propaganda," according to Ambassador Dodd.[6]

Despite Goebbels's claiming the Olympics was his personal propaganda coup, Göring knew better. One and a half million reichsmarks had been awarded to Leni Riefenstahl to produce her film *Olympia* as the lasting record. On Hitler's personal order, a further three hundred thousand reichsmarks was allocated to Riefenstahl during the editing stages from the budget of the propaganda ministry. Goebbels was furious.

---

* The Auslands Organization (AO) of the NSDAP was officially dissolved in the United States in 1933 by Rudolf Hess but was, in fact, folded into the German foreign ministry. Hess's brother Alfred was Bohle's assistant. Bohle's brother was in the overseas division of Siemens and worked closely with Westinghouse (source: OSS Secret Intelligence Reports, M1934, RG 226, Roll 0009, NARA Catalog 4504574, 117–20; Nuernberg Interrogation Records, M 1270, NARA Catalog 647749, RG 238, Roll 0002, 12).

· · ·

As EXPECTED, GÖRING's celebrations at his palace on the Leipziger Platz were over the top. He engaged Albert Speer to transform its enormous garden into a venue "worthy of a Borgia prince," which included some of his art treasures that had been brought into Berlin from Karinhall. He created a replica of the Munich Oktoberfest beer garden with a fairground at its center and served light and dark beer on tap and typical German fare at the buffet of delicious sausages, roast game, corn on the cob, and mountains of sauerkraut and mashed potatoes. Dancers from the corps de ballet of the Berlin opera entertained the crowd, while pilot Ernst Udet gave a heart-stopping display of aerial aerobatics. Despite the cool evening, "everyone was determined to have fun and they were very cheerful and happy," Göring's Swedish stepson, Thomas von Kantzow, said, "winning big prizes at the shooting galleries, riding on the roundabouts, the giant wheel and a crazy airplane" were just some of the attractions. Although Chips Channon and his British friends thoroughly enjoyed themselves among Göring's seven or eight hundred guests, someone said, "There has never been anything like this since the days of Louis Quatorze," to which Channon replied, "Not since Nero."

Indeed, Chips concluded "there is something un-Christian about Goering, a strong pagan streak, a touch of the arena, though perhaps, like many who are libidinous-minded like myself, he actually does very little. People say that he can be very hard and ruthless . . . but outwardly he seems all vanity and childish love of display." In fact, Chips reflected later that the show put on by the Nazis reminded him of the "French Directoire and the Consulate" of the 1790s.

Chips was awestruck by the outstanding showmanship. "Berlin has not known anything like this since the war," he wrote admiringly. "One felt the effort to show the world the grandeur, the permanency, the respectability of the new regime." Princess Stephanie described the games and the September 1936 Party Day as "tribal excitement" and "an orgy of dedication" to the new Germany.[7] Neither recognized that Hitler had already decided to unleash the Holocaust.

. . .

OF COURSE, GOEBBELS, Göring, and Ribbentrop were constantly vying for the position of second in command to Hitler, and each attempted to seduce "aristocratic" foreigners to the Nazi *Weltanschauung* through their entertainments. Göring told his Swedish stepson that he was not too worried about "the little doctor's" party, even though it had Hollywood-style fairy dust with its sprinkling of Germany's favorite starlets. Göring "had his spies out and learned that his two principal rivals" would not pose too great a threat to his own plans. He belittled Ribbentrop's party as a simple ox roast with champagne: "It will be burned to a frazzle and the champagne will be that well-known piss."[8]

And so the Ribbentrops received their six hundred guests in a "fairyland" marquee in their garden. The swimming pool was filled with blossoming water lilies, with thousands of Christmas-tree lights and candles strategically placed in the tented area and the grounds. After midnight, as the older generation drifted away, the swimming pool was covered with a dance floor and a band began to play. A cocktail bar was set up, and the champagne flowed freely. Chips sidled up to Hermann Göring for a chat. "Goering, his merry eyes twinkling," Chips remarked. "He seems a loveably disarming man."

Naturally, everyone agreed that Göring had eclipsed Ribbentrop. Then, too, only the Nazi top brass knew that Hitler had to blackmail Ribbentrop into announcing his appointment as ambassador to Britain at the Olympics. If Ribbentrop refused to announce it, then Hitler would decline to meet or receive the distinguished guests Ribbentrop had invited. And so a glum Ribbentrop announced his ambassadorship to London on August 11, the eve of his entertainments. Everyone who congratulated him could not help remarking on his despondency, despite the grand occasion. No wonder rumors about his being out of favor to the "dignified banishment" of London circulated widely.

Ribbentrop's only hopeful sign that evening was that Sir Robert Vansittart had accepted his invitation, since Ribbentrop knew full well that he, like Churchill, opposed Nazi Germany's policies. What Ribbentrop hadn't understood was that Vansittart had come to observe "the enemy" on his home ground. Vansittart would report to the

Foreign Office that the new German ambassador had "the sore vanity of a peacock in permanent moult" and that Ribbentrop was "shallow, self-seeking and not really friendly. . . . He was most markedly unenthusiastic about his London appointment, of which I spoke to him without a flicker of response."[9]

Chips Channon was enamored with the invitation list, which included the kaiser's son (though he fails to mention which one) and daughter, Princess Victoria. He was equally amazed by the "tonic" and "revelation" of it all. Over a hundred peers and MPs and their wives were there. Kenneth Lindsay, the Labour MP for Kilmarnock in Scotland (who always depressed Chips by his stupidity), sidled up to him and suggested to form "a small pro-German, or Friends of Germany [group]" in the House of Commons to offset the "Francomaniacs, who are so dangerous to the peace of Europe."[10]

UNDOUBTEDLY, THE OLYMPICS were an astounding success. For the Germans, there was a great deal to celebrate. Hitler's bid for recognition on the world stage had shown that Germany was no longer a beaten and downtrodden nation. Order, crowd control, and fantastical displays with torchlit parades crowned the achievements within the stadium. The German display of power as a people was complete, despite Hitler deprecating America's use of Black and Jewish athletes. Throughout the games, he continually ranted that such "animals" should not have been allowed to participate. Nonetheless, Germany came first in the competition, with thirty-three gold, twenty-six silver, and thirty bronze medals. Yet, it was the prowess and remarkable achievements of the Black Olympians, most notably James Cleveland "Jesse" Owens, with his four Olympic gold medals,* that drew the greatest positive press attention.[11]

THERE WERE THOSE who refused to attend on principle, too. Harold Nicolson even avoided traveling through Germany. He did, however,

---

* Owens won gold medals in the 100 meter, the long jump (8.06m and Olympic record), the 200 meter, and the 4-by-100-meter relay. There were seventeen other Black

join the Channons and their party at Schloss St. Martin in Upper Austria after the close of the games. Chips said he was weary of all the anti-Nazi talk by his friends, while Nicolson felt "the Channons have fallen much under the champagne-like influence of Ribbentrop and the youthful influence of the Brunswicks, the Wittelsbachs and the House of Hesse Cassel." In fact, Nicolson was troubled that they hadn't been "in the least disconcerted" by Goebbels or Goering and that they considered Ribbentrop "a fine man." Worse still, Honor and Chips believed that Britain should allow Germany to "glut her fill of reds" and compel France to toe the line while Hitler consumed the Soviet Union and its satellites.

Naturally, Nicolson protested. "We stand for tolerance, truth, liberty and good humour." How could the British stand aside when Hitler's mob stood for deceit, oppression, and violence, Nicolson asked? Chips was irate, insisting that Britain had no right to criticize either the thought or form of government of another country. Nicolson, Colin Davidson, and Lalli Horstmann* agreed that Chips had been brainwashed. It was not the best way to begin a relaxing holiday but was emblematic of other conversations throughout Europe, as innocent people were impelled by Germany's rhetoric and actions to take sides.

Chips felt he was on the right side of history. He was disappointed, too, when the king sent a cable apologizing that he and Wallis couldn't join their party at Schloss St. Martin. Apparently, both Edward and Wallis were having "daily treatment" from Dr. Neumann, the renowned

---

members of the U.S. team: high jumpers David Albritton (high-jump silver), Delos Thurber (high-jump bronze), and Cornelius Johnson (high-jump gold); sprinters Ralph Metcalfe and Mack Robinson; runners Archie Williams (400-meter gold) and John Woodruff (800-meter gold); boxer Jim Clark; weightlifter John Terry; long jumper John Brooks; Willis Johnson; Howell King; James LuValle; Art Oliver; Fritz Pollard Jr.; and two women, hurdler Tidye Pickett and track and fielder Louise Stokes (source: www.ushmm.org/exhibition/olympics/?content=aa_athletes&lang=en).
* Lieutenant Colonel Colin Keppel Davidson was killed in action on March 2, 1943, in Tunisia (Seventy-seventh Royal Army Anti-Tank Regiment). Leonie "Lalli" Horstmann was the wife of diplomat Frederick Horstmann, who had been "retired" by the Nazis in 1933. He was arrested by the Soviet NKVD in 1947 for allegedly publishing a newspaper that supported National Socialism and died at Camp 7, Sachsenhausen-Oranienburg. His reputation was only restored in 1995 by the Russian Federation.

audiologist (not a sex-therapy doctor, as others have claimed) for their ears. But that was a lie.[12]

PRIOR TO BECOMING king, Edward had promised to attend the Olympics and planned to join the Channons afterward in Austria. It seems Wallis had no intention of going, so their plans changed. Her preferred option was to rent a villa at Cannes, but that had been deemed "too dangerous" by special branch due to the war in Spain. After much indecision, it was decided to charter Lady Yule's yacht, the *Nahlin*, despite its being furnished "rather like a Calais whore-shop." An apt description, considering that two of the passengers—the king and Hugh Molyneux, 7th Earl of Sefton— "were cohabiting with other men's wives." The guest list ebbed and flowed from port to port, but the constants were Mrs. Simpson; Alfred Duff and Lady Diana Cooper; Lord Sefton and his mistress, Helen Fitzgerald; and John Aird and Tommy Lascelles from the king's household.

For security reasons, it was decided that the king would travel incognito as the Duke of Lancaster—a common enough occurrence, but the ruse was hardly credible given that the yacht was shadowed by two British destroyers throughout its voyage. In fact, "the image of the *Nahlin* cruise imprinted on the public mind," according to the king's biographer Philip Ziegler, "is of the King, his mistress and a group of disreputable hangers-on carousing around the eastern Mediterranean, invariably under-dressed, usually drunk, shocking the local inhabitants and causing any Englishman who met them to hang his head in shame."[13]

The American ambassador in Belgrade reported Edward was clearly in Yugoslavia to enjoy himself, and that any political motivation to improve Anglo-Yugoslav relations was an afterthought. From Athens, the American minister made no such caveat, hailing Edward's passage a tremendous diplomatic success. In Ankara, the American embassy translated the Italian press's outrage that this tour of the eastern Mediterranean was simply to promote a new alliance against Italy. Kemal Atatürk, the first president of modern Turkey, remarked on Edward's "uncommon charm" while also noting that the king was "obviously enslaved" by Mrs. Simpson and would "lose his throne because of her."

After ten days aboard the *Nahlin*, Diana Cooper felt her patience with

Mrs. Simpson wane considerably. Comparing Wallis to Becky Sharp in Thackeray's *Vanity Fair* and mocking her for her insistent references to "the King and myself," as well as her diet of whisky and water, Diana couldn't help remarking about Wallis and her friend Katherine Rogers, "goodness how common they are . . . they each have a pair of those immense field glasses which they glued to their eyes all saying 'I don't see any hotel. Do you think that's one?' For all the world," Diana, who was, after all, the daughter of a duchess, "as if they had just come off the Gobi Desert after weeks of a yak milk diet." As far as Duff was concerned, Wallis was "as hard as nails, and she doesn't love him."[14]

Once the cruise was over, Edward and Wallis traveled to Vienna. His canceled plans to join the Channons in Austria had nothing to do with Dr. Neumann, or indeed his enlightening talk with the chancellor of Austria, Kurt von Schuschnigg. It was Wallis. On September 16, Wallis wrote to Edward that she had decided that she should return to Ernest, that she would "only create disaster" for the king. The letter concluded, "I want you to be happy. I feel sure that I can't make you so, and I honestly don't think you can me."

Edward's response to her letter was to telephone and threaten Wallis that he would slit his throat if she did not go to Balmoral with him. Of course, she did, with Hermann and Katherine Rogers as her chaperones. Obsessed, Edward shirked his duty to open a new state-of-the-art hospital in Aberdeen, sending the Duke and Duchess of York in his place, while he was seen expectantly awaiting the arrival of Mrs. Simpson's train.

Edward had paid scant, if any, attention to the fall of San Sebastian in Spain to the rebels that September. Nor had he seen anything untoward with the reoccupation of the Rhineland. The American presidential election in five weeks' time was deemed unimportant. However, news of Wallis's impending divorce, to be heard at the Ipswich Assizes in October, swept through Whitehall like an arctic storm. Sir Horace Wilson (a rabid anti-Semite, admirer of the new Germany, and senior government adviser to Stanley Baldwin) was dispatched to see the prime minister at Chequers to inform him that "he *must* now intervene."[15]

Fifth Columnists

I am counting on four columns of troops outside Madrid and another column of persons hiding within the city who would join us as we enter the capital.
—General Emilio Mola, rebel leader of the Northern Army,
October 16, 1936

Neither the British nor the Americans were aware that a new Fifth Column was established again on their shores that September. Shortly after the Olympics, Nikolaus von Ritter, the German émigré who had first settled in New York in 1924, was summoned to the Hamburg headquarters of the Abwehr. Age thirty-eight, Ritter was surprised to learn that he was to head a new office of air intelligence at *Abwehrstelle* (or *Ast*), in Hamburg, with his primary object being military espionage against Great Britain and the Americas (north and south). His primary duty was to create a web of covert agents to provide the Luftwaffe with details of "everything that could be procured in terms of technical and military information . . . to make up for lost time."

The FBI report, dated September 2, 1945, and the British Secret Intelligence Service (SIS) referred to Ritter as "one of the leading lights of the German overseas secret service based in Hamburg." A British secret agent reported that, "He is like a Middle-West businessman speaks fluent English with a strong American accent and scarcely drinks at all and talks very little . . . and he does command respect." Ritter later claimed that he was answerable only to Hermann Göring.[1] With his American accent, international contacts, and understanding of how Americans thought, Ritter was a born undercover operative. His first goal was to "look around for a man whom I could train as an agent with a secret transmitter."

Ritter's first port of call in the United States was Rudolf Ilgner, brother of Max Ilgner, the I.G. Farben man who set up their espionage company Chemnyco in New York City. Max Ilgner, who had been the main liaison between I.G. and the Wehrmacht since 1934, not only became the main purveyor of "information regarding the financial and industrial conditions in the United States" but also "I. G. Farben's official link and paymaster to the Nazi hierarchy."[2] In New York, Rudolf Ilgner knew which firms were susceptible to Nazi influence, which wanted to expand into the German market, and how to approach any individuals concerned.

Chemnyco had already become I.G.'s American intelligence service in the business world. "The representatives of Chemnyco negotiated with leading American companies in connection with licensing them under patents and processes owned by I. G. Farben," the postwar OSS report on the company confirmed. "Chemnyco's Statistical Department, through access to United States Government information agencies as well as to other public and private sources . . . was able to amass reports more impressive than anything that could be obtained by an American company." This meant that Chemnyco's real significance was in its ability to gear its propaganda to American businessmen and industrialists.[3]

Of course, there were other financial and corporate insiders, too. Since 1934, the Hamburg-America Line had provided free passage to Germany for journalists willing to write favorable articles about Hitler. Hapag North German Lloyd soon joined the game. J.P. Morgan & Co. were their bankers, and Hamburg-America Line became the designated instrument to buy back—at a discount—the Dawes and Young Plan loans from the bank, enabling Morgan to recover some of its losses.* Although this was not propaganda in the truest sense, Dr. Schacht figured that he needed friends in high places in American finance who

---

* The Dawes Plan of 1924 did not reduce Germany's indebtedness but spread out payments over a longer period of time. It was credited for ending the diplomatic crisis with the Allies.

would look to the bottom line and not balk about where the money came from or whether payments received were from Germany's refugee "flight tax."[4]*

Throughout the 1930s and on into 1942, Brown Brothers Harriman's director, Prescott Bush, was managing the affairs of steel magnate Fritz Thyssen in the United States. Both Bush and Roland Harriman served as Thyssen shareholding nominees in the New York–based shell holding company United Banking Corporation (UBC), which they ran on behalf of Thyssen while the steelmaker was producing all manner of armaments for Hitler. UBC was a wholly owned subsidiary of a Rotterdam-based, Thyssen-controlled bank, Bank voor Handel en Scheepvaart, directed by Mr. Hans A. Kouwenhoven.

Until December 7, 1941, none of these activities were against the law in America. Nonetheless, they were instrumental in assisting Nazi Germany with obtaining foreign exchange—over $3 million was shipped abroad by the end of 1933—and helped build up Germany's war machine. The companies managed by Brown Brothers Harriman would later be employers of slave labor at Auschwitz. It is interesting to note that Mr. John A. Kouwenhoven, who was the main director of Voor Handel in Rotterdam, became the chosen author of Brown Brothers Harriman's book, *Partners in Banking: An Historical Portrait of a Great Private Bank Brown Brothers Harriman & Co., 1818–1968*. John is the anglicized version of the name Hans. Kouwenhoven does not mention Thyssen or, indeed, the firm's other German connections during the Nazi era.[5]

NOTWITHSTANDING THESE BUSINESS connections, by 1936 Father Charles E. Coughlin was the most persuasive of the fifth columnists in America, with a radio audience of over ten million listeners imbibing his profascist and anti-Roosevelt messages regularly. Millions became members of his People's Lobby and partly funded his hookup with

---

* The "flight tax" was effectively confiscation of Jewish assets in all but name. Essentially it meant that Jews fleeing the Nazis could only leave the country with the clothes they wore and one suitcase they could carry. Bank accounts and investments within Germany were automatically forfeited.

thirty-five radio stations across America. He told his listeners that the president was a communist sympathizer and nicknamed him a "great betrayer and liar."

Coughlin had been hell-bent on using his profascist pulpit to keep Roosevelt from reelection. As the New Deal took shape and Benito Mussolini, Adolf Hitler, and Louisiana's demagogue senator Huey Long attracted Coughlin's admiration, the radio priest turned like a rabid dog on his former Democrat allies. Nothing would stop his repeated poisonous condemnations—not even Long's assassination in 1935. He even set up his "apolitical" National Union for Social Justice platform and whipped up a frenzy of support for his new presidential candidate.

That's when August T. Gausebeck, Reichsmarschall Göring's banker in America, who ran a Wall Street company called Robert C. Mayer, knocked on Coughlin's door.* If the good father agreed to take off the gloves and land firm punches against Roosevelt, Gausebeck would fund any shortfall Coughlin might experience—in untraceable donations of five- and ten-dollar notes. Freed from any financial worries (and pocketing hefty sums along the way), Coughlin went on the attack. With the Catholic vote deemed essential to winning the 1936 campaign, Roosevelt agreed that Joe Kennedy would be his best antidote to the priest's poison. Not only did Kennedy take to the airwaves to counter the renegade priest's rhetoric, but he pounded away at Bishop Francis Spellman of New York to do something—anything—about the obstreperous Coughlin. Spellman informed his good friends at the Vatican, the secretary of state Cardinal Eugenio Pacelli and his confidant Enrico Galeazzi, and Coughlin soon found himself a bargaining chip in international politics.[6]

---

* Gausebeck's Robert C. Mayer was one of several institutions handling the return of German citizens living in America in a highly questionable financial system called the Rückwanderer Mark Scheme. Other institutions were J. Henry Schroder Banking Corporation, Chase National Bank, Deutsche Handels- und Wirtschaftsdienst, and New York Overseas Corporation. Under the terms of the scheme, returning German citizens could cash in their dollars at the top exchange rate of 4.50 reichsmarks to the dollar (instead of 2.10 to the dollar). The difference was funded by the capital stolen from refugees compelled to leave Germany.

. . .

NONETHELESS, THE AMERICAN press was divided on Hitler. The mighty William Randolph Hearst, who preferred democracy to anything else and particularly cherished his own freedom of speech, had inadvertently jumped onto Hitler's bandwagon. Hearst was the father of all isolationists, using his influence in Congress against any interventionist or internationalist stance Roosevelt took during his first term. Hearst, with the help of his close friend Republican Senator Hiram Johnson (the former governor and then current senator for California) and aided by a torrent of telegrams from Father Coughlin's listeners, defeated the president's bill for the United States's entry into the World Court.

Hearst was an isolationist, but not a fascist. He certainly feared the spread of communism, equating it to the loss of *his* personal property and freedoms. What he hadn't recognized was that his anticommunist rhetoric had been interpreted by the Farmer-Labor Party of Minnesota, the American Federation of Teachers, and the anti-interventionist League Against War and Fascism as his being "the vilest racketeer of them all" and "Hitler's man in America."[7]

Hearst had always courted the public's outrage. Accused by the National Educational Association's Dr. Charles Beard (a Hearst victim) as having "pandered to depraved tastes and [having] been an enemy of everything that is noblest and best in our American tradition," Beard ordered a series of antifascist articles. Italy "has suppressed all freedom and thought and expression, has drilled and dragooned all independent industry and all prosperity out of the country," an early article declared. In Germany, "not only is all liberty lost, and all modern ideas of freedom of thought and speech and publication ended, but as further evidence of complete return to the Dark Ages, the Nazi Government has revived medieval methods of execution and political practices of wholesale assassination."[8]

It became a widespread practice to hiss in movie houses when the Hearst-Metrotone logo appeared on screen. Metrotone was compelled to delete the Hearst name in 1936. A boycott of Hearst newspapers was called, urging "Buy a paper, but don't buy a Hearst paper!" Newsagents and organizations against Hearst handed out stickers proclaiming, "I don't read Hearst." Despite his long-professed isolationism, Hearst had become the bogeyman of conservatives and the sacrificial lamb of liberals and radicals.

Of course, Hearst had been unpopular in the past and reckoned that this was just another blip on his horizon. He hadn't seen that a puff from his newspapers in the forthcoming presidential election for any candidate would be the kiss of death. There was no way Hearst would back Roosevelt for reelection, so he decided to go to Topeka, Kansas, to "size up" Governor Alf Landon on his way back to California.

Hearst traveled with his editor, Arthur Brisbane, and the owner of *The Washington Herald*, Cissy Patterson, in her private railway carriage.* If *she* backed Landon, because her newspaper was the most widely read in Washington, D.C., both Roosevelt and his secretary of the interior, Harold Ickes, knew there would be hell to pay. Luckily, Ickes was friendly with Cissy socially. Considering that Ickes was noted for his dour nature and skeptical eyes that peered over his rimless glasses, he cherished his gentle friendship with Cissy and reassured Roosevelt they would know the lay of the land soon enough.[9]

"Everybody was taking stock of everybody else," Cissy wrote later, "saying one thing and thinking several times another." But had Landon, "this clean-living, simple man the power to win him to guide our sorely troubled country out of its present wilderness?" she asked. Granted, Landon had been a fine governor and had reduced state taxes—a subject near and dear to Hearst's heart. After the meeting, Cissy told Hearst that Landon was "simply grand." Yet within weeks of Hearst and Patterson throwing their substantial weight behind Landon, he had lost his shine. His speeches were dull and fell flat. So Hearst attacked Roosevelt harder, while Patterson toned down her criticisms in *The Washington Herald*, believing they had simply backed the wrong horse.

On November 3, despite the combined efforts of Father Coughlin (on behalf of his presidential candidate, William Lemke), the Hearst newspapers, *The Washington Herald*, and the German American Bund

---

* Cissy Patterson was the former wife of Princess Stephanie's first important lover, Count Gizycki, a Hungarian.

in backing Kansas governor Alf Landon on the Republican ticket, Franklin Roosevelt was reelected by 55 percent of the popular vote, winning forty-six of the forty-eight states and the electoral college by 523 votes to Landon's 8. Hitler's propagandists had singularly failed to dent the president's popularity by not having a cohesive plan across its Fifth Column aimed at charming the American public.

HITLER DESPAIRED. HANFSTAENGL had failed to suppress the negative press he received overseas. "The whole art [of propaganda] consists in doing this so skilfully that everyone will be convinced that the fact is real, the process necessary, the necessity correct, etc.," he had written in *Mein Kampf*. "The art of propaganda lies in understanding the emotional ideas of the great masses and finding, through a psychologically correct form, the way to . . . the heart of the broad masses."[10] What a fool Hearst was, Hitler ranted. Instead of appealing to the unions and the masses, Hearst had made enemies of them. Hitler wondered why Hanfstaengl had not been able to control the mighty American publisher.

BY THE AUTUMN of 1936, the only foreign press that Hitler had come to trust was Lord Rothermere's, thanks to Princess Stephanie. What Hitler had not known was that Rothermere had grown tired of Stephanie's financial demands, complaining endlessly about her impoverished state. Wasn't his lordship aware that she must have a fitting wardrobe to attend the opera with Emerald Cunard or go to country house weekends at Cliveden? Didn't he recognize that she had to return their lavish hospitality to be useful to him and to Hitler? After Rothermere paid her bills and suggested that even "the ex-Queen of Wurtemberg travels second class on the railways and keeps no motor car," Stephanie wrote three days later that she needed more cash. Her son, Franzi, was at Oxford, and his future was uncertain. Rothermere replied, "When your boy leaves Oxford send him to me. I can make him useful."[11]

Rothermere's problem with Stephanie was complex. His original stance for the restoration of the Hohenzollern monarchy in Germany lay in tatters after the remilitarization of the Rhineland, but he would not be deterred from maintaining a friendly stance toward Hitler. Stephanie knew everything about his dealings in Hungary and Germany and had become indispensable as his courier, interpreter, introducer, and educator regarding Central and Eastern European affairs. Together with Lady Ethel Snowden, they painted the precise picture that Rothermere (and Hitler) wished to convey about Germany in the *Daily Mail*.

Yet gnawing away at him was the lack of preparedness for war at home. The "build-up" of the Royal Air Force was, to say the least, languishing, with the chancellor of the exchequer, Neville Chamberlain, admitting to Rothermere only months earlier that he found "the information about German air strength very confusing and contradictory, but a figure of eleven thousand aeroplanes appears to me quite incomprehensible." Baldwin had told the House of Commons in March 1935, "We adhere to the position of equality with any Power which may be within striking distance." Nevertheless, precious little had been done in the intervening eighteen months. Londonderry was among those who accused Rothermere of only being interested in boosting the readership of his newspapers. In fact, Rothermere's air-rearmament stance cost the *Daily Mail* much of its circulation. In 1936, the *Daily Mail* produced a pamphlet, *Arming in the Air: The Daily Mail Campaign; Warnings of Three Wasted Years*.

And so, at the very time Rothermere wished to dispense with Stephanie's services—or rather her outrageous expenses—he found himself under attack by the government and other newspapers. The *News Chronicle* (owned by the Quaker industrialist Cadbury family) claimed, "There is nothing in modern politics—even in German politics—to match the crude confusion of the Rothermere mentality as revealed in the Rothermere Press. It blesses and encourages every swashbuckler who threatens the peace of Europe."[12]

Rothermere was determined to carry on just as he had begun. Once again, he sent Princess Stephanie to the Party Day (known as "The Rally of Honor") that September. Hitler ensured that she was treated with the utmost respect and gave her a large, autographed photo to *"Mein Liebe Prinzessin"* of himself in a silver frame. Stephanie mingled with the former cabinet secretary T. J. Jones, Lord Dawson of Penn, and the gentlemen who would become known as "Ribbentrop's Kindergarten": Lord Allen of Hurtwood and Admiral Sir Barry Domvile.

On October 18, Hitler proclaimed Reichsmarschall Göring as plenipotentiary of the Four-Year Plan with authority to issue decrees for the "strict coordination of all competent authorities in the party and state." Göring's actions put Germany firmly into a war economy. Along with rearmament, the development of synthetics, particularly in fuel, rubber, copper, tin, and even textiles, became Germany's top priority. His new duties, however, resulted in his responsibilities for the police to pass to Heinrich Himmler. From this point on, Himmler's fiefdom encompassed the SS, the Gestapo, and concentration camps.[13]

AT PARTY DAY 1936, Unity Mitford glared at Princess Stephanie and the British contingent from a short distance away. Of course, the besotted Unity was outraged by Stephanie's purported influence on Hitler, just as she was jealous of "this Eva Braun . . . what does she have that I don't?" Ever since Stephanie's first Party Day in 1935, Unity had been badmouthing Stephanie as a Jewess. So, too, had Putzi Hanfstaengl. Yet Hitler ignored them both, for good reason.

Unlike Rothermere, Stephanie had no dying loyalty to Britain. She was forty-seven years old and had developed a certain aristocratic lifestyle that she had every intention of maintaining. Naturally, that meant she was constantly short of cash. Earlier that year, when her English chauffeur had taken possession of her car until she paid his back wages, she complained to the police. They said that the chauffeur was entirely within his rights. And so, rather than curtail her spending while Rothermere refused to pay her outrageous expenses, Stephanie turned to Hitler's adjutant, Captain Fritz Wiedemann. He dutifully arranged for a German bank loan and paid the endless barrage of her bills that landed on his desk. The bank loan soon was paid off and Stephanie was given a salary of twenty thousand reichsmarks per month, straight from the Reich Chancellery account.[14]

By October 1936, Stephanie was not only in the pay of Hitler but also continued to represent Rothermere's interests. Was she a spy? Yes, despite her lifelong protestations to the contrary. But neither Unity nor Putzi had the wit to realize that she had been spying for Hitler. Neither saw the tremendous propaganda value that Stephanie represented with the British aristocracy and Rothermere's press. While Hitler would remain fond of Unity and was helpful to her, Putzi's outspoken views and clownish behavior had already begun to displease the führer—mainly because Putzi had singly failed to control or even tame the international press.

EVEN SO, UNITY had her purposes, too. Shortly after Party Day, on October 6, 1936, Unity's sister Diana Guinness and Tom Mosley were married at the home of Joseph and Magda Goebbels. Hitler attended, but the marriage was to remain secret, since Mosley had insisted.* The timing also provided Hitler, so he thought, with another propaganda route into Britain. Mosley was already preaching the Nazi creed. What Hitler hadn't understood was that the infamous BUF "Battle of Cable Street" two days earlier, when Mosley's Blackshirts marched through the East End of London and were blocked by some fifty thousand people, was a turning point in the British leader's fortunes. Mosley, and all BUF candidates running to become members of Parliament, had become unelectable.[15]

After the wedding ceremony, Hitler suggested that Diana give him the marriage certificate for safekeeping. He had long been intrigued by the beguilingly beautiful Diana and was thrilled to hear at the wedding breakfast Diana's blow-by-blow description of the scandal brewing in royal circles: Edward VIII was madly in love with the American Wallis Simpson, and Wallis had recently filed for divorce. Hitler determined then that his new ambassador Ribbentrop must, without further prevarication, head to London.

---

* BUF director Bill Allen was one of Mosley's witnesses, and Bobby Gordon-Canning was his best man. Unity was the other witness. Diana told her parents and her brother, Tom, about the wedding but said nothing to Nancy, Pam, Jessica, or Deborah. All parties were sworn to secrecy.

. . .

So, AT LONG last, on October 25, the Ribbentrops set out for London, traveling like royalty with their retinue of forty-four people. Annalies von Ribbentrop immediately determined that the German embassy on Carlton Terrace overlooking the Mall would need to be entirely revamped, and she arranged to lease the home of Neville Chamberlain in Eaton Square. At all costs, the embassy must be ready for Edward's May 1937 coronation.

Dashed Dreams

Is England prepared to take any action ... or must the boiler eventually burst?

—Sir Eric Phipps, British ambassador to Germany,
December 1936

Of course, Edward VIII abdicated on December 11, 1936, announcing to the world, "I have found it impossible to carry the heavy burden of responsibility and to discharge my duties as King as I would wish to do without the help and support of the woman I love."

Ribbentrop was apoplectic with rage. "Don't you know what expectations the Führer has placed on the King's support in the coming negotiations?" he asked his secretaries incredulously. "Don't you think the whole affair is an intrigue of our enemies to rob us of one of the last big positions we hold in this country? You'll see, the King will marry Wally and the two will tell Baldwin and his whole gang to go to the devil."

Ribbentrop did not ask Rothermere or Lothian, or even Prince Louis of Hesse (one of his junior secretaries and a great-grandson of Queen Victoria), to discover the truth of the matter. While lunching with J. C. C. Davidson, Conservative Party chairman and one of Baldwin's closest confidants on the day of the abdication, Ribbentrop predicted "that this was the end of Baldwin, that there will be shooting in the streets, that the King's Party would eventually restore Edward VIII to the throne."[1] Ribbentrop reported this fairy tale back to Hitler.

But was there a grain of truth to Ribbentrop's paranoia? Surely Edward VIII's support for Germany gave cause for concern. Only a month earlier, foreign secretary Anthony Eden admitted to Jan Masaryk, the Czech ambassador, that Edward had only taken a "desultory interest" in his official boxes, yet he sought to interfere with cabinet decisions, most notably over the Rhineland. General Stuart Menzies, head of the Secret Intelligence Service (SIS, which later became MI6), had reported to Baldwin that "leakages of the contents of State Papers had been traced to the King."

In searching for the truth, Wallis had been put under surveillance. As she was constantly with the king, it meant that he, too, was being carefully watched. Princess Stephanie now lived at 14 Bryanston Square, a short walk from Wallis's Bryanston Court flat, and it had not gone unnoticed that the king and Wallis, the Kents, Lord and Lady Londonderry, the Duke of Westminster, Lady Oxford, and Stephanie's good friend Lady Emerald Cunard frequented the princess's flat, just as she did theirs. In fact, her flat was later described in the *New York Mirror* as "the focus for those British aristocrats who have a friendly stance towards Nazi Germany." There, too, she prominently displayed Hitler's photograph to "*Mein Liebe Prinzessin*."[2] This may well be the reason why a large portion of Princess Stephanie's MI5 file will not be opened to scrutiny by historians until 2060.

Edward repeatedly annoyed the government, too, by speaking out on political matters. He would not forego his criticisms about slums and unemployment, nor would he stop his incessant moaning about modernizing the Crown. Neville Chamberlain (who would become prime minister shortly after George VI's coronation in May 1937) believed that unless the king "pulled up his socks he will soon pull down the throne."[3] Baldwin's usual response that problems will take care of themselves was no longer an option.

The fact was, many in Britain preferred the Germans—even under Hitler—to their French allies, who had signed a pact that year with the Soviets. Most of those were at the heart of the years of appeasement that followed. They were the elite, the aristocrats, and the ones who sought to avoid war above all else. They were the *comme il faut* of the country.

. . .

On December 3, the British media broke its silence. Headlines in Lord Camrose's *Daily Telegraph* cataloged the problem as "THE PRIME MINISTER AND THE CRISIS" or "NO CONSTITUTIONAL DIFFICULTY AT PRESENT" or "MRS SIMPSON INDISPOSED." Several series of articles had to explain who this Mrs. Simpson was, too. The Northern Ireland *Belfast Telegraph* opted for a more truthful headline: "KING AND HIS MINISTERS— CONSTITUTIONAL CRISIS DEVELOPS OVER HIS DESIRE TO MARRY AMERICAN LADY MENTIONED—REFUSAL TO ACCEPT GUIDANCE."[4] The media frenzy and the hate mail erupted into an unbearable ordeal, and Wallis was secretly taken by car to the South of France and the refuge of the Cannes home of her friend Katherine Rogers.* On December 10, Edward signed the Instrument of Abdication, and Parliament passed His Majesty's Declaration of Abdication Act, naming his brother Bertie his successor as King George VI. Separately, Edward agreed to leave the country for a few years and go into exile.

When Lord Rothermere fired off a raft of questions to Hitler as the news of the possible abdication broke, Hitler replied with an invitation to Rothermere and Princess Stephanie to come to Obersalzberg January 5–8 "to answer the numerous and varied questions which Princess Hohenlohe has submitted to me."[5] Of course, Stephanie had already disabused Hitler of Ribbentrop's interpretation of the events surrounding the abdication.

Rothermere was delighted to accept. The führer's private train was sent to meet them at the Austrian border. At the Berghof, they were greeted by Hitler and Joseph and Magda Goebbels. (Eva Braun was also in the house, but she did not join the others.) Stephanie remarked afterward that Hitler's face was quite puffy, presuming he was taking drugs. Although she was naturally observant, chances are that Wiedemann, and others, would have whispered about Hitler's addiction to the multiple daily injections (which Hitler believed to be "miracle cures") by his personal physician, Dr. Theodor Morrell.

The next morning at breakfast, Stephanie observed Hitler filling his teacup with sugar lumps before having the tea poured on top. He also

---

* Much later, Beaverbrook admitted that he was behind most of the unseemly attacks on Mrs. Simpson. It made for wonderful press, he thought.

ate three slices of cake. Unfortunately, there is no record of their discussions that day, even in Dr. Paul Schmidt's memoirs, who was present to translate for Hitler. Stephanie alleged later that Hitler raised the "Jewish question" and that Britain had fallen into the trap of an anti-Nazi campaign by Winston Churchill, backed by powerful Jews.

Who was Hitler to believe about the abdication? Ribbentrop or Rothermere? It suited him to believe the former, but he needed to manipulate Rothermere into pressing his government into an alliance with Germany to achieve his aims. During his long walk with Rothermere after lunch, Hitler blamed Churchill, too, and his pugnacious opposition to the Nazis in Britain for a breakdown in the relationship between their respective countries.

Goebbels's diary entry for that time states, "Lord Rothermere and Princess Hohenlohe are here. . . . Enquires in detail about German press policy. Strongly anti-Jewish. The Princess is very pushy. After lunch we retire for a chat." Goebbels recorded that the subject of Spain came up—not the eight thousand Germans who were engaged there—but rather Hitler's inability to tolerate "a hotbed of communism in Europe."

Stephanie and Goebbels circled around each other the entire visit like two wrestlers in the ring, with Goebbels seething over Hitler's obvious fondness for the princess. Before everyone parted company, Hitler ordered a photograph to be taken. He would later send Stephanie a copy as a remembrance of her "visit to Berchtesgaden." During the visit, Hitler had made up his mind about Stephanie and decided that he had not been using the princess to his full advantage. He resolved to correct this oversight.[6]

The Boiling Cauldron

There is a pro-German cabal led by Lord Lothian and actively fostered by the Waldorf Astors.

—U.S. ambassador Robert W. Bingham,
September 4, 1936

"England turns the corner of the new year congratulating herself upon the manner, economically and politically, in which she has come through 1936," Ambassador Bingham wrote to the reelected President Roosevelt on January 5, 1937. Two weeks later, in his inaugural address, the president asked, "Have we found our happy valley?" Roosevelt knew all Americans wanted a job they could count on, a decent and affordable home, and the ability to educate their children. America's happy valley was still out of reach for millions. The president knew, too, that a cauldron was boiling in Europe and the Pacific. He suspected he would be compelled to renew the Neutrality Act against his better judgment, but foreign wars and entanglements were not what the American public wanted or needed to hear.

Ambassador Bingham had warned Roosevelt during 1936 about the potential powder keg in Europe, too. "The situation in Spain, as you know, is very grave," Bingham wrote on September 4. Spain was the shell-shocked heart—microcosm of the 1930s—beating strongly to uphold its democracy, pleading for help from the former Great War Allies. But the Allies refused aid, fearing an all-out European war.[1] This was the moment when isolationists became anti-interventionists.

On August 23, the Soviet Union joined the Anglo-French Non-Intervention Committee while its long-standing ambassador, Ivan Maisky, had been on home leave. By December, Lord Lothian's Germanophilia had cooled. At a lunch with Maisky, Lothian confided, "All intelligent people understand that we are currently seeing in Spain the first serious duel between the USSR on the one side and Germany and Italy on the other. Much depends on the outcome of this test of strength, including the future orientation of British policy."[2]

France, too, was teetering on yet another change in government. There had been eighteen different prime ministers since January 1930, although several had been prime minister more than once. More worrying was the fact that most of their governments were from the Radical-Socialist Party and had a distinct socialist agenda. "There is grave reason to apprehend a blow-up in France," Bingham lamented. "A weak France means a strong Germany. A serious outbreak there might mean immediate hostile action by Germany."[3] By June 1937, the government of Léon Blum would fall, making Bingham's predictions a gloomy reality.

The invasion of Manchuria by the Japanese in 1931 finally caused the eruption of the Second Sino-Japanese War in July 1937, which had racism at its core. The Japanese had long believed the Chinese to be racially inferior. In the war of words, the Chinese military leader Chiang Kai-shek called the Japanese invaders "dwarf bandits" and declared the conflict a "war of resistance to the end." China was fractured by not only the brutal Japanese regime but also Soviet influences, and a confusing mosaic of local warlords.[4]

At the same time, Joseph Stalin had begun his "Great Purge," which lasted into 1938. Not only did he eliminate his top military brass, Communist Party officials, and millions of innocent citizens (mostly Ukrainians, whom he labeled *kulaks,* defined as the oxymoron "wealthy peasants," or those who owned an acre or more of land). Stalin's sole purpose was to obliterate all political, cultural, and social opposition. His actions fed ample portions of the "red scare" to Hitler, Mussolini, and lesser dictators throughout Europe, like Hungary's Admiral Horthy. When the führer addressed the Reichstag on the fourth anniversary of taking power, he proclaimed that Germany's "national honour had been restored and the battle for German equality among the Great Powers won." Hitler also told a grateful Reichstag that "the time of so-called surprises has ended."[5]

IT WAS ANOTHER Hitler lie. The Spanish Civil War had reached a stalemate by March 1937. General Mola's boast about his Fifth Column only served to guarantee a relentless search for "spies, scare-mongers, defeatists—those who, concealed in their hiding places, are awaiting the order to rush out onto the streets." The propagandists for the rebel General Franco were most feared by the Republican government. Fearing the worst, the Loyalists summarily executed some two thousand rebel-supporting fifth columnist prisoners—clergy, military advisers, and wealthy landowners—in one month.[6] In response, Hitler and Göring stepped up their campaign in the proxy war.

The Basque country became the testing ground for Hitler's advanced technologies. Göring ordered five thousand men and a hundred planes of the Luftwaffe's Condor Legion to be deployed to northern Spain while Republican forces were kept busy in the south. This attack became a world first, better known today as aerial carpet bombing. The campaign began in late March, with General Mola's offensive against Durango.[7]

Then, around 4:30 P.M. on the afternoon of Monday, April 26, a single medium-range bomber that had been designed to release its payload while flying horizontally (most likely a Heinkel He 111), zeroed in on the undefended "spiritual centre" of the Basque country, the historic town of Guernica and its 7,500 inhabitants. His target was the Rentería Bridge. He missed. Wildly. Instead, he bombed the railway-station plaza. Minutes later, a clutch of other medium-range bombers—which had the same instructions to blow up the bridge—landed direct hits on the candy factory. It erupted into an inferno and spread immediately to nearby buildings.

By the time the plodding Junkers Ju-52s arrived, "nobody could recognize the streets, bridge, and suburb [on the other side of the bridge]," the Condor Legion commander, Wolfram Freiherr von Richthofen, recorded in his diary. "We therefore dropped the bombs right into the midst of things." Soon enough, the Heinkel He 51 fighters and the new and unproven Messerschmitt Me 109 joined in. The Messerschmitt's mounted machine guns and lobbed hand grenades were particularly effective in the carnage. Around 70 percent of the buildings were destroyed, miraculously leaving the Casa de Juntas archives, the ancient Basque parliament building, and the sacred tree of liberty—the Guernica Oak—defiantly standing. The number of animals slaughtered as they were driven to market that day is uncertain, as were the number of people killed. Estimates vary between 300 and 1,700 souls.[8]

Guernica was front-page news in both London and New York. British war correspondent G. L. Steer wrote in London's *The Times* that the "object of the bombardment was seemingly the demoralization of the civil population and destruction of the cradle of the Basque race. Every fact bears out this appreciation, beginning with the day the deed was done." Market day. The *New York Times* headline made grim reading: "HISTORIC BASQUE TOWN WIPED OUT—REBEL FLIERS MACHINE-GUN CIVILIANS—WAVES OF GERMAN-TYPE PLANES FLING THOUSANDS OF BOMBS AND INCENDIARY PROJECTILES ON GUERNICA, BEHIND ENEMY LINES, AS PRIESTS BLESS PEASANTS FILLING TOWN ON MARKET DAY." In London, the Foreign Office rightly concluded, "Guernica has taught us what to expect from the Germans."

Berlin, however, viewed the mission as a limited success. Although the town was destroyed, its sole military target—the bridge—was left intact. The aircraft manufacturer Ernst Heinkel told Göring that the bombers lacked an accurate bombsight. Word soon reached the new member of the Auslands Organization of the Nazi Party, Nikolaus Ritter, who thought he held the solution. A man known only as "Pop" had sent over a package of bombsight blueprints from New York, assuring him that these "were of the utmost importance." Ritter thought "it would be well worth our effort to send somebody over to establish personal contact."[9] Why? Because no one in the Luftwaffe could read them.

AMERICA'S ANTI-INTERVENTIONIST CONGRESS pushed through the Second Neutrality Act that May. Roosevelt was obliged to sign it since the United States was unprepared both mentally and militarily to assist any ally. The new act prohibited American citizens from traveling on belligerent nations' ships and American merchant ships from transporting arms to belligerents "even if those arms were produced outside of the United States." Civil wars were included in the term "belligerents." That said, Roosevelt was able to negotiate a significant improvement from the previous Neutrality Act: belligerents were allowed "at the discretion of the President" to purchase items except arms and carry these on non-American ships in a "cash-and-carry" clause. Vital resources, such as oil and engine parts, were not considered "implements of war" and were excluded.[10] While America slept, Roosevelt was already preparing the nation to help Britain and France. Throughout 1937 he would receive important British visitors seeking to establish a closer relationship between the two countries.

THIS SNAPSHOT OF the worldwide turmoil at the outset of George VI's reign omits other issues within the British Empire, like the Arab uprising in Palestine, Zionist lobbying for a separate Jewish state, the influx of mainly Jewish refugees from Germany, and the utter lack of military preparedness for war. Nor were relations with the United States what they should have been. The chancellor of the exchequer, Neville Chamberlain, wrote to his sister Hilda, "We ought to know by this time that USA will give us no undertaking to resist by force any action by Japan short of an attack on Hawaii or Honolulu." Goodwill and fair words would be uttered, but the president would invariably take refuge behind Congress. "We have the misfortune to be dealing with a nation of cads," Chamberlain added.[11]

Churchill referred to 1937 as the "loaded pause" with all guns cocked. "We cannot tell whether Hitler will be the man who will once again let loose upon the world another war in which civilization will irretrievably succumb," he wrote in his *Great Contemporaries*, "or whether he will go down in history as the man who restored honour and peace of mind to the great Germanic nation and brought it back serene, helpful and strong, to the forefront of the European family circle." Despite the accommodating tone, Churchill added, "[W]e are forced to dwell upon the darker side of his work and creed. . . . Adolf Hitler was the child of the rage and grief of a mighty empire and race which had suffered overwhelming defeat in war." But Churchill was still out of government. His final remark that the Allies were rapidly becoming the vanquished through Hitler's actions and Britain's inaction went unnoticed.[12]

A petulant Joachim von Ribbentrop returned from Germany on February 2, 1937, feeding healthy portions of the "red scare" to everyone he met, even going so far as to complain to the British foreign minister, Anthony Eden, that the Soviets were intervening in Spanish affairs on behalf of its Popular Front Republic. (Nothing was said of the Italian and German legions fighting for the rebels.) Since Edward VIII was reduced to the status of the Duke of Windsor, Ribbentrop's bitterness knew no bounds. Six years after his appointment to London, while serving as Germany's foreign minister, he told Prince Regent Cyrill of Bulgaria, "Seldom in history has greater baseness been shown than by the circles around Edward VIII whose work finally led to his being deprived of the English throne." He would also erroneously claim that the idea of marrying Mrs. Simpson was trumped up by Lady Diana Cooper aboard the *Nahlin*.

Hitler had made his "period of so-called surprises is over" speech three days before Ribbentrop's return to London. On presenting his credentials to George VI on February 4, 1937, Ribbentrop broke with court etiquette to make idle friendly remarks and said, "the Führer, since the beginning of his political career, had pursued the aim of German-British understanding." George VI agreed that such an aim was reciprocated. But then, for reasons that remain Ribbentrop's own, he began to enlighten the new monarch about workers' housing projects in Nazi Germany and how the führer took the workers' housing to heart. His Majesty turned to speak to the German senior counselor, Dr. Ernst Woermann, when Ribbentrop's arm shot out in the *Hitlergruss* (full Nazi salute) mere inches from George VI's nose. "The King was so startled," Wolfgang zu Putlitz recalled, "that I feared he would lose his balance." George VI, however, acted as if nothing had happened. The marshal of the diplomatic corps wrote afterward to Ribbentrop asking him to please "give prior warning whenever he intended to repeat this performance in future." Five days later, at a court levée at St. James's Palace, Ribbentrop gave the "half-heil" salute instead.

Ribbentrop seethed and eventually lodged an official complaint in person to the Foreign Office. Edward Wood, Lord Halifax, was acting as foreign secretary in Anthony Eden's absence. "The first National Socialist Ambassador to the Court of St James has been described by part of the press with deliberate distortions and stupid comments . . . I must sharply reject such machinations and," Ribbentrop spat, "must attribute them to the agitation conducted by irresponsible elements against National Socialism and Germany." What could Halifax reply, other than that there was freedom of the press in Britain?[13]

When Ribbentrop returned to Germany at the end of February, Goebbels was delighted to write in his diary that after four months on the job, Ribbentrop had proved incompetent. On March 1, the ambassador spoke at the Leipzig Fair, making veiled threats against the British, blaming Versailles for Germany's current economic woes, and stating that the only way peace could be achieved would be "by means of the German people's own strength." The speech reestablished him in Hitler's favor but read to the British as an unpleasant "undated ultimatum." Goebbels wondered, incredulous, "Why must an ambassador say such things, thus committing himself and closing off all options?"[14]

DURING THE REFURBISHMENT of the German embassy in London, Hitler's architect, Albert Speer, noticed that Ribbentrop "was always in a bad temper upon receiving cabled instructions" from the foreign minister, Neurath. "This he regarded as pure meddling and would irritably and loudly declare that he [Ribbentrop] cleared his actions with Hitler personally."[15] By the time the finished German embassy was unveiled for the coronation party on May 13, Annelies's Parisian wardrobe and Joachim's extravagant lifestyle were mocked incessantly in the British press. With each offending article, the Ribbentrops' "hostility towards Britain and the British grew accordingly," Third Secretary Reinhard Spitzy wrote, "and before long this hostility turned into a dangerous hatred. From that point onwards Frau von Ribbentrop began to work on her husband in an attempt to steer him towards the promotion of an anti-British policy."

Ribbentrop was at pains to remind everyone at the embassy that only he could bring about an Anglo-German agreement. Since that no longer seemed possible, "he must now think of his own career and become the leading advocate of an anti-British coalition." And so the dispatches from London became laced with Ribbentrop's lies that the ruling classes were in the pockets of the Jews and how the country was ruled by Freemasons. Apparently, too, Britain was also a "fertile breeding ground for Communism." Eventually, Ribbentrop realized that Captain Wiedemann and Princess Stephanie were presenting an entirely different picture to Hitler, namely that Germanophilia was in the ascendant. Rather than engage in diplomacy as his role dictated, Ribbentrop let his hatred for the British, Stephanie, and Wiedemann fester and intensify.[16]

THAT SPRING, LONDON was awash with precoronation parties. At each one, the topic of whether one was for or against "the Windsor solution" reigned supreme. Only a few palace officials knew that while Edward had been king, he maintained a secret conduit to Hitler through his cousin, Carl Edouard, Duke of Saxe-Coburg and Gotha. It was Carl Edouard who pressed Edward to arrange a meeting with Baldwin, to which Edward replied, "I myself wish to talk with Hitler and will do so here or in Germany. Tell him that please." Carl Edouard dutifully reported back to Hitler that the king's "sincere resolve to bring Germany and England together would be made more difficult if it were made public too early" and that he agreed to visit Edward, subject to Hitler's approval, at any time the führer wished.[17]

Since his abdication, Edward, now as Duke of Windsor, resided at Baron Eugène and Kitty von Rothschild's estate at Schloss Enzesfeld in Austria under strict instructions that he was not to see Mrs. Simpson until her divorce decree absolute had been granted. There could be no hint of scandal, and so Wallis remained with her friends Herman and Katherine Rogers at Lou Viei in Cannes. "When I saw him at Enzesfeld, he had turned into something quite different," Edward's equerry wrote. "It was as if he had crossed an alien frontier. He never again thought for himself or had a mind of his own." Baba Metcalfe said later that "he hears with her [Wallis's] ears, sees with her eyes, and speaks through her mouth." Naturally, the highlight of Edward's empty days were his telephone calls to Wallis.

Worse, he had become a skinflint like Wallis. Fruity Metcalfe, as Edward's faithful friend, paid an extended visit to Edward at Schloss Enzesfeld. He wrote to Baba, "He won't pay for anything—it's become a mania with him." The telephone bill amounting to some four thousand dollars was left for the Rothschilds to pay. Between this and Edward's unkind treatment of Kitty Rothschild, Edward was compelled to move to the hotel at Villa Appesbach to await his reunion with Wallis.

Meanwhile, Katherine Rogers wrote to her friend Fern Bedaux that it would be "intolerable" for Wallis and Edward to marry at Lou Viei, given the constant barrage of the press and death threats they received. There were officers from the French *Sûreté* guarding the home, and Herman slept with a pistol under his pillow. Fern Bedaux replied in January 1937 that she and her husband, Charles, a dual national of France and America with substantial connections to Nazi Germany, would be delighted to host Wallis and Edward at their Château de Candé in the Loire for their wedding in June. Surrounded by acres of land and its own eighteen-hole golf course, Wallis jumped at the chance. Naturally, the British Secret Intelligence Service made inquiries about Bedaux and Candé; however, their findings have been "heavily weeded" out of Charles Bedaux's MI5 file.[18] Shortly after April 27, the date when Wallis's decree absolute was granted, Edward and Wallis were reunited at Candé and set the wedding date for June 3.

AND SO, ON May 12, the coronation of George VI took place in the best of British traditions. The BBC had begun broadcasting for two hours daily in November 1936, and the coronation was the first event to be covered outdoors. By the time of the coronation party at the embassy, Ribbentrop had decided that Stephanie and Wiedemann were plotting against him, and he would get his revenge by more than simply expunging her name from the Court Circular. But for now he had to accept the pair at *his* reception.

Ribbentrop did not understand that it was Hitler's need for another viewpoint about the British ruling classes that empowered Wiedemann and Princess Stephanie. Equally, Ribbentrop was unaware that in addition to the Gobelin tapestry given to Hitler during Lord Rothermere's visit to Berchtesgaden the previous January, Princess Stephanie had personally delivered a priceless and ancient jade bowl from Rothermere at Easter. The thank-you note from Hitler was effusive: "Your precious token will be an ornament for my rooms on the Obersalzberg and for me a lasting remembrance of your friendship and esteem." Hitler was mindful of Rothermere's tremendous efforts to establish a "true German-English friendship" and that the editorials he had published within the past weeks echoed Hitler's own sentiments. "The new Germany has no more sincere and warm-hearted friend in England than you," he wrote.[19] Hitler's warmth extended to Princess Stephanie, as she was providing him with alternative intelligence about the British aristocracy.

Then, too, Ribbentrop's attitude about the coronation party had upset many in Berlin. Not only had he taken against Wiedemann, but Goebbels had come to think of Ribbentrop as "a liability" and that his "only talent is for ruthless self-advancement." Göring was furious that he had been prevented by Ribbentrop from attending—an affront he would never forget.[20]

Within the week, Ribbentrop lost interest in his London posting, communicating with Berlin primarily by telephone until he left in August on home leave.[21]* Stanley Baldwin, worn out by his service to the government, surrendered his seals of office to George VI. His advice on the next prime minister was simple: send for the chancellor of the exchequer, Neville Chamberlain. After years of being de facto prime minister, Chamberlain would no longer have to be obsequious to anyone, saying "Have you thought . . ." or "What would you say if . . ." as he had written to his sister Hilda back in March 1935, when he first became "a sort of Acting P.M."[22] In May 1937, Neville Chamberlain was sixty-eight and had all the self-importance of someone who had been waiting in the wings far too long.

Chamberlain had suffered his entire life as the younger son by a second marriage of a man who made the political weather in his heyday, Joseph Chamberlain. His older half-brother, Sir Austen Chamberlain,

---

* Ribbentrop only signed one telegram between May 22 and August 30. During this same period, Woermann reported on the renewed and important Anglo-Soviet discussions about a proposed naval agreement.

had been destined for politics from an early age, and in the eyes of their father, "had been born to the red dispatch box." Austen held several government posts during his long career but assured his legacy as a successful foreign secretary under Baldwin between 1924 and 1929. Neville, six years younger than Austen, had his future mapped out as the family businessman. But that endeavor was doomed to failure and then, finally, in December 1918 Chamberlain won his seat as an MP for Birmingham, Ladywood. He served thereafter in a variety of ministries in both Ramsay MacDonald's and Stanley Baldwin's governments throughout the 1920s and 1930s.[23]

Chamberlain had a rather lugubrious appearance: tall but stooped, rarely smiling, with a hawklike nose and dark, sullen eyes peering steadfastly from beneath bushy eyebrows. His Victorian wing-collared shirts and dark, fusty-looking suits made him resemble an undertaker, and he was often called that (or "the Coroner") behind his back.

His manner was brusque, too. Where Baldwin had been considered emollient in opposition, Chamberlain was a "cruel debater" who delighted in dissecting the opposition "almost like a vivisectionist." He loathed the Labour Party and thought they were ineffective and muddle-headed and treated them terribly, even though "Stanley [Baldwin] begged me to remember that I was addressing a meeting of gentlemen. I always gave him the impression, he said, when I spoke in the H. of C. that I looked upon the Labour Party as dirt. . . . [W]ith a few exceptions, they *are* dirt."

For a leader who begged the nation to engage in international understanding and conciliation with the dictators, he was fatally flawed. In his private correspondence, he was broadly silent on German domestic issues, including the treatment of the Jews, but had long before understood that "Germany is the bully of Europe." Worse, Chamberlain had resolved that *he* would direct foreign policy, despite his half-brother chiding him that he knew nothing of foreign affairs.[24] His biggest mistake was yet to come. Chamberlain believed he could, through "careful diplomacy," bring Hitler to heel and trusted that he was a man of his word.

Princess Stephanie zu Hohenlohe circa 1937.
(Granger Historical Picture Archive)

Princess Stephanie as a
young girl on horseback
(née Stephanie Richter).
*(Granger Historical
Picture Archive)*

Princess Stephanie with
Captain Fritz Wiedemann
in San Francisco.
(Shutterstock.com)

Princess Stephanie in profile circa 1940.
(Spartacus Educational)

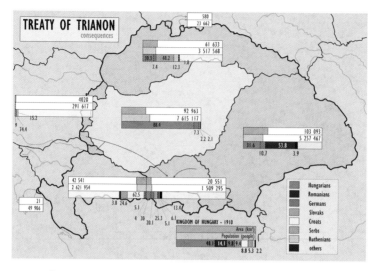

Map of Hungary post–Treaty of Trianon showing lost populations and territory. *(Public domain)*

January 1937: Princess Stephanie, left, seated next to Magda Goebbels. Behind (l-r): Lord Rothermere, George Ward Price, Adolf Hitler, Fritz Wiedemann, and Joseph Goebbels. *(Spartacus Educational)*

January 1937, Berchtestaden: Chancellor Adolf Hitler with Lord Rothermere. *(Alamy)*

Waldorf, Viscount Astor and his wife Nancy, Lady Astor in New York. *(Getty Images)*

Henry "Chips" Channon, diarist and member of Parliament, 1934. *(Getty Images)*

Lady Ethel Snowden circa 1930. She was a colleague and good friend of Princess Stephanie. *(Alamy)*

Lady Margot Asquith, the widow of Prince Minister H. H. Asquith and friend of Princess Stephanie. *(Alamy)*

Lady Maud "Emerald" Cunard, who was taken with Ribbentrop's dimple, October 1933. *(Getty Images)*

Reichsmarschall Hermann Göring presenting a ceremonial sword to Charles A. Lindbergh, July 1936. Anne Morrow Lindbergh is on the far left. *(Alamy)*

Three Mitford sisters: (l-r) Unity, Diana, and Nancy. *(Getty Images)*

Harold Nicolson and his wife, Vita Sackville-West, arriving in New York 1933, when they first met the Lindberghs. *(Getty Images)*

Alfred Duff Cooper and his wife, Lady Diana Cooper, on the cover of *Sketch*, 1931. *(Age of Photostock/Illustrated London News)*

Adolf Hitler bowing to kiss the Duchess of Windsor's hand while the Duke of Windsor looks on, October 1937. *(Getty Images)*

The Duke and Duchess of Windsor with Adolf Hitler (center) and Dr. Robert Ley (on the right). *(Getty Images/ Daily Herald Archives)*

The Duke and Duchess of Windsor's wedding at La Candé. Herman Rogers, left, and "Fruity" Metcalfe on the right. *(Getty Images)*

Thelma Furness, American-born mistress of Edward VIII before Wallis Simpson. *(Granger Historical Picture Archive)*

Adolf Hitler relaxing with Unity Valkyrie Mitford at Bayreuth, 1936. *(Alamy)*

Ernst "Putzi" Hanfstaengl playing piano, 1936. He was betrayed the following year by Unity Mitford and her sister Diana Mosley. *(Alamy)*

Sir Oswald "Tom" Mosley in uniform giving and receiving the Nazi salute in London. *(Getty Images)*

Mosley speaking at the Royal Albert Hall in London. *(Alamy)*

I.G. Farben defendants at Nuremberg: (front l-r) Carl Krauch, Hermann Schmitz, Georg von Schnitzler, Fritz Gajewski; (back l-r) Paul Häflinger, Max Ilgner, Friedrich Jähne, Hans Kühne. *(Getty Images)*

Nikolaus Ritter, Nazi spymaster. *(German National Archives)*

Thomas J. Lamont, J. P. Morgan, and Owen D. Young in Paris to advise on the negotiation of the Treaty of Versailles. *(Getty Images)*

Dusko Popov, the British double agent known as JOHNNY to the Nazis and SKOOT or TRICYCLE to MI5 and MI6. *(Public domain)*

Count Dino Grandi, 1st Conte di Mordano, Italian ambassador to the UK from 1932 to1939. *(Alamy)*

Galeazzo Ciano, foreign minister and Mussolini's son-in-law, with Hitler. He was executed by the Germans in 1943. *(Alamy)*

Leopoldskron, once the home of Max Reinhardt, given to Princess Stephanie by Hitler between 1937 and 1939. *(Simon Bernd Kranzer, Alamy)*

Appeasement

"Appeasement" is the policy of feeding your friends to a crocodile, one at a time, in hopes that the crocodile will eat you last.
—President Franklin D. Roosevelt

Now that a new Napoleon had appeared and was rearming quickly, Chamberlain's message became "the appeasement of Europe as a whole." When Hitler remilitarized the Rhineland, Secretary Eden spoke of not reacting precipitously, of gleaning a "breathing space," which meant acting solely through diplomacy while Britain built stronger defenses in the event of attack.[1] What Eden could not say was that Britain's commitment to the League of Nations had been eroded by Chamberlain's appeasement policy. The new prime minister aimed to "correct" Eden's misguided view. When writing to a distant relation in Boston, Massachusetts, Chamberlain claimed, "The dictators are too often regarded as though they were entirely inhuman. I believe this idea to be quite erroneous."

It is a poignant letter, showing Chamberlain's disappointment in America, his pragmatism, and his humanity. He is all too aware that "many people are haunted by a constantly recurring fear of war" and that "we are too close to danger spots for any but a few cranks to hope that we could remain safe in isolation." And so, "in the absence of any powerful ally, and until our armaments are completed, we must adjust our foreign policy to our circumstances, and even bear with patience and good humor actions which we should like to treat in a very different fashion." For these reasons, "I am about to enter upon a fresh attempt to reach a reasonable understanding with both Germany and Italy," Chamberlain wrote, "and I am by no means unhopeful of getting results. I have an idea that when we have done a certain amount of spade-work here we may want help from U.S.A." and require America's "helping hand."[2]

For all his frank understanding of Britain's perilous situation, Chamberlain never admitted to any dereliction of duty during the Baldwin years, precisely because he *was* de facto prime minister. He did not see that precious little progress had been made to quell Germany's outrage about Versailles in the 1920s, when it was still possible to do something concrete about its real grievances. The only "diplomatic" breakthrough had been in 1935, when the Anglo-German Naval Pact was signed, to the general disbelief of the opposing party in Parliament, Churchill, and the world. Nor did Chamberlain seem to understand that within the early months of his tenure as prime minister, much had happened to further weaken Britain's position, both at home and abroad, by virtue of Hitler's—and Mussolini's—superior propaganda.

IN MARCH 1937, Mosley's British Union of Fascists (BUF) ran a populist campaign contesting the elections of the London County Council. William Joyce was one of several candidates. The BUF held around 150 election meetings that had an average attendance of 1,400, claiming its candidates were "watchdogs" to "keep a sharp look-out that no grafter of Right or Left takes advantage of the present rotten system to fill his pockets." It promised to abolish the current property tax system and replace it with a tax based on the services supplied and the wealth of the occupant. This redistribution of wealth was a guiding principle of National Socialism, and Mosley made it his creed, too. The privileged must "be made to recognize his social obligations and assist those who are less fortunately situated," he said. Despite all manner of infringements of electoral law, the party did not win a single seat.[3]

William Joyce, John Beckett, and A. K. Chesterton were furious. They accused Mosley of putting a break on their electioneering against the steady influx of Jewish refugees. Given the election fiasco, too, Mosley could no longer afford to pay salaries, and both Joyce and Beckett quit the BUF. Within the month, they formed the National Socialist League.

Other right-wing anti-Semitic groups spread like a rash of poison ivy. Viscount Gerard Lymington's, the English Array, gave its back-to-the-land message with a pro-Nazi twist. In December 1938, he would publish the *New Pioneer*, which had a blueblood roll call of British fascists as his correspondents.

A more serious addition was the Link. Active from July 1937, the Link was founded by the deeply disturbed Admiral Sir Barry Domvile, who had had a distinguished career as Commissioner of Imperial Defence, 1914–1915, and Director of Naval Intelligence, 1927–1930. Domvile had become fixated on the Nazi creed of a Jewish and Masonic conspiracy against all Christians, and in 1936 he published his book, *By and Large*, praising Hitler and the new Germany. The Link was openly pro-Nazi and differed from both the BUF and the Anglo-German Fellowship, since it stressed views that were neither populist nor elitist. As a former member of the Anglo-German Fellowship's council, he admitted he was never very happy about that organization because it "catered mainly for the well-to-do, and was largely supported by big business firms, interested in clearing the ground for an extension of commercial relations. . . . Membership of the 'Link' was open to all."

The Anglo-German Brotherhood had been founded by Baron Friedrich von der Ropp in June 1936 as an apologist organization for the Nazi persecution of the church. By 1938, an undercover reporter for the *Daily Worker* wrote that it had become a wholly Nazi organization, holding prayer meetings at Strand House in which the congregants prayed for Hitler, since he "is carrying on the Messianic work of Christ."

Then there was the White Knights of Britain, also called "the Hooded Men"—the British version of the Ku Klux Klan. Their stated purpose was to "rid the world of the merciless Jewish reign of terror," but it was, in fact, "an occult body with secretive passwords and much mumbo jumbo." As the Nordic League, an association of "race-conscious Britons," took hold in 1937, the "Hooded Men" melted away into it or the Link. The Nordic League's counterpart in Germany, the Nordische Gesellschaft, applauded the British group's services, which were "engaged in exposing and frustrating the Jewish stranglehold on our Nordic realm."

The Nordic League's meetings had an unusual number of women from the upper-middle class, described by infiltrators as "expensively dressed society ladies." Its speakers were notably extreme and included men like William Joyce; A. K. Chesterton; Captain Archibald Maule Ramsay, MP; Lord Redesdale (father of the Mitford girls); and a clutch of retired British generals. Member Freda Dudley Ward, the Duke of Windsor's former lover, was quite keen to hire the film on Jewish ritual slaughter of cattle for a private showing at her home. She later wrote a book, published in 1944, titled *Jewish "Kosher,"* in which she claimed, "there is money in Kosher. . . . Itchy palms; ferocious vested interests."[4]

Naturally, these organizations heralded a new rise in anti-Semitism. It worried the police, if not the prime minister. Increased violence beginning in April 1937 in the East End of London directly contravened the previous January's Public Order Act, prohibiting "Jew-baiting." It reached a crescendo when the chief commissioner warned that anti-Semitic propaganda (much of it written by the German news agency in London) would no longer be tolerated, nor would the use of "grossly abusive language." And yet the popular historian Arthur Bryant, who was employed by the Conservative Central Office and a close associate of both Stanley Baldwin and Neville Chamberlain, was responsible for some of the most poisonous tracts that blamed the Jews for Germany's moral decline.[5]

ALL THESE ORGANIZATIONS were nothing in propaganda terms compared to Chamberlain's control and manipulation of the press, which had become a fine art form by May 1937. The press office of 10 Downing Street, under Chamberlain's sole control, became the filter to convey messages to the nation. While it made perfect sense to have a direct link between the prime minister's office and newspapers, precisely how the Downing Street press office developed is obscure, since both George Steward (under Ramsay MacDonald) and his successor, Major Sir Joseph Ball, destroyed its files. The only thing that is certain is that George

Steward revised admission to "the Lobby" to a group of select political journalists.

Steward was a master magician. While appearing to "help the press in its search for information," he had erected an invisible ten-foot wall between the press and the government. "The change of power and status was implicit, the old-style competitive outsiders were converted into a fraternity of organized insiders." The Lobby briefing became the primary source of a political correspondent's news.[6]

For busy journalists, constantly working under tight deadlines, the new system seemed to work in their favor. As Chamberlain's term in office took hold, however, Lobby journalists began to observe that the prime minister's briefings were "patently contrary to all other existing evidence." If Lobby journalists dissented with a statement, they would be met with "a cold arrogance and intolerance." If they "expressed suspicions about Hitler's or Mussolini's intentions that differed from Chamberlain's own views," the prime minister answered, "he was surprised that such an experienced journalist was susceptible to Jewish-Communist propaganda."[7]

Steward's successor, Major Sir Joseph Ball, had been recruited from MI5 by the Conservative Party chairman, J. C. C. Davidson, in 1924 to run a "little intelligence service" as an independent arm within the main Conservative Central Office organization. In 1930, Ball became the director of the new Conservative Research Department and Chamberlain's closest and most indispensable political adviser.* He was the "quintessential éminence grise," whose influence on world affairs "cannot be measured by the brevity of the printed references to him." During Chamberlain's premiership, he used Ball (or was it the other way around?) to disseminate anti-Semitic propaganda in Ball's journal, *The Truth*. Ball's "papers," representing over thirty years of service as a senior civil servant, are constricted to a mere .77 meters, or 2.53 linear feet—the rest was destroyed.[8]

Ball's mastery of the Lobby upset many in the Foreign Office, but

---

* Ball was also an anti-Semite, who, shortly before his death in 1961, maintained that his views against the Jews were well founded.

none more so than Sir Robert Vansittart, who began his own shadow group called "z Organization," an intelligence service that ran in conjunction with the head of the Secret Intelligence Service to keep him advised of developments inside Nazi Germany. Vansittart was particularly close to *The Manchester Guardian*'s F. A. Voigt, who had been a Berlin correspondent and introduced the minister to his contacts regularly.* Rex Leeper, who ran the Foreign Office News Department, was also an admirer of Eden and very "anti-Chamberlain" because he felt that the prime minister was "splitting the country" with his politics.[9] Through them, select journalists were given a different picture of the news coming from Germany. In March 1938, Vansittart would be "kicked upstairs" to a meaningless position in the Foreign Office, and Leeper was moved to the BBC.

The great provincial newspapers *The Manchester Guardian* and *The Yorkshire Post* became the bastions of independent reporting. Given that *The Observer* was owned by the Waldorf Astors and that Geoffrey Dawson, editor of *The Times,* was their close friend, combined with the fact that Lords Beaverbrook and Rothermere were unwilling to question Hitler's motives, unbiased news became a rara avis.

THERE HAD BEEN a virtual news blackout in Britain about the ex-king during his months spent in exile. Nonetheless, in the spring of 1937 Edward and Charles Bedaux (pretending to have a strong relationship with the Nazi hierarchy) had several conversations about the duke visiting Germany. Edward inanely believed that he could meet Hitler traveling incognito—something Bedaux always maintained would lead to a disastrous farce. Any visit to Germany must be accompanied by a "worldwide investigation of the working classes," Bedaux counseled, adding it would help the duke's public profile if he visited the United States.

But Bedaux's entrée to Hitler was not what he claimed. The story goes that while at the Bad Reichenhall spa for his bronchial condition,

---

* The Germans tried to assassinate Voigt in Paris. Vansittart later discovered that the Gestapo had almost verbatim transcripts of Voigt's conversations with fellow journalists at the Café Royal in Piccadilly.

Bedaux received the visit of Anna Hoefken-Hempel, the mistress of Hjalmar Schacht, who had sculpted busts of Charles and Fern Bedaux and a small piece entitled *Love* as a wedding present for the duke and duchess. Bedaux asked the sculptress if she knew the best person to approach about the duke's desired visit to Germany and, as a quid pro quo, promised to arrange a show of her work at the Galerie Charpentier in Paris for her help.* It would have been entirely understandable for Hoefken-Hempel to ask what Bedaux's interest was. Bedaux said that she, through Schacht, would introduce Bedaux to the powers that be within I.G. Farben as his reward.

A week later, Hoefken-Hempel returned with her other reputed lover, Captain Fritz Wiedemann, in tow. Wiedemann listened to Bedaux's request, knowing the tremendous propaganda value the duke's visit would create. After, Wiedemann merely said that he would see what he could do. According to Princess Stephanie's biographers Rudolf Stoiber and Boris Celovsky, the princess and Wiedemann viewed this "coup" as the highlight of their secret diplomacy together, with Wiedemann "pulling the strings" behind the scenes. A few days later, after clearing his bases with Hitler, Wiedemann returned. Not wishing to appear overanxious, Wiedemann suggested that Bedaux contact Dr. Robert Ley, a former chemist with I.G. Farben, who had since become the head of the Nazi Labor Front. Ley would arrange the duke's social visit. Bedaux could claim, too, that through Schacht's introduction, I.G. Farben had become his client.[10]

Edward knew that a trip to Nazi Germany would create a furor. Six months earlier, while Baldwin was still prime minister, he had been told that "prolonged visits or close contacts in Fascist countries would be unwise," particularly as it would make his return to Britain more difficult. Even so, Edward wanted no advice from Baldwin or Chamberlain and asked no questions.

In the weeks preceding Edward and Wallis's wedding, the ever loyal and "fine fellow" Fruity Metcalfe contacted the U.S. ambassador in London asking if Bingham could not possibly arrange a visit on behalf of the

---

* During the war, the Galerie Charpentier was a hotbed for the sale of looted art.

Duke and Duchess of Windsor to the United States.* Bingham, ter-
minally ill, delayed several months before advising Roosevelt about
Fruity's request, having already replied that it would be "a great mistake
for a long time to come." This was echoed immediately by the Roosevelt
administration in writing to Bedaux. In the meantime, Edward had
pressed ahead with Bedaux to arrange his tour of Germany.[11]

DID ANYONE IN Chamberlain's government know or care what Edward
did? Walter Monckton, appointed as attorney general to the Duchy
of Cornwall while Edward was king, had been Edward's most trusted
confidant. Monckton most certainly knew about Edward's hopes to visit
Germany when he saw George VI in August 1937 and told the new king,
"They are not considering the possibility of a return [to Britain] within
5 years."

Monckton had been one of the men to screen Edward's mail at
Candé before the wedding, too. After all, Wallis had been the subject
of several death threats. The question is, had Monckton seen the letter from Oscar Solbert, a Swedish-born retired American army officer?
Solbert had been a military attaché at the U.S. embassy in London after
the Great War and had served as an assistant to Edward during his 1924
trip to the United States. Solbert's letter was important because it asked
the duke to "head up and consolidate the many and varied peace movements throughout the world" and stressed that such a world peace organization had the enthusiastic support of "Mr. Axel Wenner-Gren, the
most successful captain of industry in Sweden."† Wenner-Gren wanted
to back Edward as its leader with "a considerable sum of money." Certainly, Monckton had no idea that Wenner-Gren bragged about his
close friendship with Hermann Göring. Seemingly, it hadn't occurred
to Edward that Wenner-Gren's "peace initiative" was a surreptitious tool

---

* The wedding was a sorry affair with no royal family member in attendance and only
Randolph Churchill and the Metcalfes present from England. The Duke of Kent sent
a Fabergé egg as a wedding present, which Edward unceremoniously returned.
† Axel Wenner-Gren was the founder of Electrolux and invented the solid-state re-
frigerator and the electric vacuum cleaner. He settled in the Bahamas on Hog Island
after the outbreak of war.

of the Nazis when he asked Bedaux to handle matters with Solbert and Wenner-Gren. The proposition offered Edward a purpose—he would be the envoy of peace.[12]

Edward had been deeply wounded by the abdication and his family's withholding of the title "Her Royal Highness" to Wallis. So he decided that the German trip would become a *royal tour* to make Wallis feel every inch the queen. Acrimony had built up over his reduced financial settlement, too, and the letter from Solbert provided a solution of sorts for a man who had never worked outside "princing" or "kinging."

With the backing of Wenner-Gren's peace initiative, Edward could replenish his diminishing coffers and make a good start to his new "peace emissary" role. When, precisely, any financial arrangement did—or did not—begin between the duke and the Swede is still a matter of guesswork. Soon enough, Edward learned that Wenner-Gren was undoubtedly a Nazi sympathizer and knew that the Swede was acting as banker to Göring in Mexico.[13]

WHILE THE WINDSORS were on their honeymoon in Austria and Hungary, Bedaux made the final arrangements for their German trip. On Monday, October 18, the day after their train left Leipzig cheered by crowds, the duke published an official statement that his forthcoming tour of the United States would be arranged entirely by Mr. Bedaux and that the industrialist and his wife would accompany the duke and duchess on their "private visit." The trip, as outlined in the press, never took place, of course, because of the belated reply from the State Department. Seemingly, Wallis did not want to return to the United States to live, and the decision to stay in France "for the foreseeable" had been made before the German tour.[14]

Three days later, the British press reported on the Windsors' meeting Herr Hitler in a stub article below headlines of "KING AND QUEEN ALMOST MOBBED" (referring to their tour of Yorkshire) and "DUKE OF KENT MAKES TOUR IN ILLUMINATED CAR" (when he visited Blackpool, greeting tens of thousands of well-wishers). By Saturday, the Windsors' visit to Berchtesgaden, described beneath the headline "DUKE OF WINDSOR AND HITLER EXCHANGE SALUTES," was front-page news in Britain. *The New*

York Times preferred to note that "the former British king must have realized that his host evidently makes a distinction between abdicated royalty and reigning monarchs or dictators" by the simplicity of their two-hour visit with the führer. Despite the press coverage, the precise content of their interview went unreported. The British article implied a warmth of purpose, backed up by the famous photograph of Hitler clasping the duchess's hands in his. The American article made them seem as if they were grasping at the limelight. Privately, Hitler said that the duchess "would have made a good queen."[15]

DURING THE WINDSORS' honeymoon that July, Japan had renewed hostilities in China, leading to the occupation of Peking, Tientsin, Kalgan, and Paoting* and Japan's landing in Shanghai, the British stronghold. By August, the Japanese had blockaded all Southern China. President Roosevelt wrote to Chamberlain toward the end of 1937 suggesting that the United States and Britain combine their forces in the Far East to protect their territories and avoid a global conflagration. The president received a sniffy reply dated January 14, 1938, from Chamberlain that he was "greatly encouraged to know that world affairs were engaging his attention so directly for so courageous an initiative" but refused FDR's kind offer. Privately, Chamberlain seethed at the "American bomb" hurled across the Atlantic, ruining his own appeasement plans for a rapprochement with Germany.[16]

Roosevelt was out of step, out of time with Chamberlain. The president had applauded Eden's initiative the previous September at the Nyon Conference, when he secured the protection of Mediterranean shipping routes against Italian piracy. Chamberlain chafed that the mere hint of Italian piracy would ruin Anglo-Italian relations. In London, Sir Joseph Ball conducted talks that summer with Count Dino Grandi. But above all else, Chamberlain told Ball, "If only we could get on terms with the Germans I would not care a rap for Mussolini."[17]

On October 5, 1937, while dedicating a bridge between the north and south ends of Lake Shore Drive in Chicago, Roosevelt hit out against

---

* These cities are now called Beijing, Tianjin, Zhangjiakou, and Baoding respectively.

the dictators. For the sake of America's future, it was crucial for him "as the responsible executive head of the Nation" to choose this occasion to speak out about "the present reign of terror and international lawlessness" that was based on "unjustified interference in the internal affairs of other nations or the invasion of alien territory in violation of treaties," Roosevelt explained. Law, order, and justice were being eradicated. Indeed, "nations claiming freedom for themselves deny it to others." While America plowed on to build its infrastructure "and many other kinds of useful works," Germany, Italy, and Japan were building "huge standing armies and vast supplies of implements of war" and counseled "a quarantine . . . to protect the health of the community against the spread of the disease."[18]

Roosevelt's solution meant no trade, no sustenance for their policies, and no money in something that became known as the Welles Plan, named after the assistant secretary of state, Sumner Welles. Chamberlain was incandescent. Eden and his supporters, referred to disparagingly by Chamberlain and his followers as "the Glamour Boys," were thankful for the president's interest and hoped that it might turn the tide of Chamberlain's misguided appeasement policy.

A month later, Chamberlain was unperturbed by the Anti-Comintern Pact signed between Germany, Italy, and Japan, effectively establishing the Axis Powers. Churchill could barely believe that the president's proposal for a fresh conference in Washington about the European situation on January 12, 1938, had gone unanswered, despite Eden and the British ambassador, Sir Ronald Lindsay, strongly advising it. Churchill could only shake his head in despair at the leadership of "blind and obstinate men."

Espionage

When sorrows come, they come not single spies, but in battalions.
—William Shakespeare, *Hamlet*, act 4, scene 5

Putzi von Hanfstaengl's troubles began shortly before his fiftieth birthday and were instigated by Unity Mitford. She had come a long way since the 1934 Party Day, when Putzi told Unity and Diana to "wipe some of that stuff off your faces" if they wanted to meet Hitler. Göring and Goebbels had agreed that there was no way "such painted hussies" should be allowed to see the führer. As Hanfstaengl would later tell Unity's biographer, David Pryce-Jones, "a remark of Unity Mitford started the chain of events."

Ever since Diana, the more beautiful and poised sister, had married Sir Oswald Mosley, Unity, deluded or not, had set her heart on marrying Hitler. As Unity grew closer to Hitler, Putzi imbued her with his "own ideas in the hope that she would repeat them" to Hitler and claimed that "I may have gone too far one day." While they were out picnicking with Putzi's son, he was "railing away" about other advisers when Unity rounded on him and spat, "If you think this you have no right to go on being his foreign press chief."

Unity was in Hitler's thrall, but aside from her representation of the pure Valkyrie type, he was indifferent to her. To ingratiate herself to the führer, she passed along comments she had either overheard or ideas that she had deduced—for example, that Princess Stephanie was Jewish. "She spent her time snooping," Putzi said. "She hated Americans, and she was a fanatical Jew-hater, always on about it, boring me with

Jews. . . . Her importance was that she fed him [Hitler] all the gossipy stories." In fact, "Hitler knew that if he wanted something broadcast, he had only to talk in front of Unity." She would repeat everything at the British consulate in Munich, Winifred Wagner recalled. For Unity, it was telling tales to please her would-be lover. For her victims, it was life changing.[1]

Putzi's "railing," aimed at the nefarious influences of Goebbels and Rosenberg, asserted that if Hitler continued to listen to them, there would be another war. By repeating his indiscretion to Hitler and Goebbels, Unity had given them the necessary ammunition needed to eliminate Hanfstaengl. "Goebbels began casting aspersions on Hanfstaengl's character," Albert Speer recalled of the luncheons in Hitler's dining room, nicknamed the "Merry Chancellor's Restaurant." Goebbels "had once brought in a phonograph record to show that Hanfstaengl had stolen the melody for "a popular march he had composed" from an English song. From such beginnings, Goebbels was able to poison Hitler against his foreign press chief by saying that Putzi had "made adverse remarks about the fighting spirit of the German soldiers in combat" in Spain and needed to be taught a lesson.

Hitler agreed to a "practical joke" arranged by Goebbels to judge Hanfstaengl's prowess under fire. Putzi had been planning his fiftieth birthday party for February 11, 1937, at his home in Munich. His previous birthday parties in Berlin had been an annual highlight for the American expatriate community. That is, until Fritz Wiedemann telephoned Putzi. "You are urgently requested to come to Berlin," Wiedemann ordered. "Flight Captain Baur has been instructed to bring you by special plane from the Munich airport." Putzi thought his disagreement with Hitler over Kurt Lüdecke's betrayal might be the motivation for the summons and reluctantly obeyed.

In Berlin, Hanfstaengl met with Wiedemann, not Hitler. Earlier, Martha Dodd had judged Wiedemann to be a man whose natural charm and a welcoming smile hid the "shrewdness and cunning of an animal. Wiedemann was a dangerous man to cross, for despite his social naiveté and beguiling clumsiness, he was as ruthless a fighter and schemer as some of his compatriots." He also never questioned Hitler's orders and was "a political trusty."[2]

Wiedemann ordered Hanfstaengl to fly to Spain immediately and liaise with the German journalists reporting on the civil war. Putzi was enraged: "Suddenly such an important thing? You are nice people; tomorrow I am fifty years old, and you send me to Spain on my birthday?" Wiedemann smiled, putting a hand on Putzi's shoulder. "Many of us miss having you here quite a lot. If you succeed in this mission, the Führer will no doubt want to have you back here again." Then, in case Putzi had missed the message that matters were at a crossroads at the Reichskanzlei, he added, "Your influence would be very valuable."[3]

Wiedemann revealed no more about the mission and sent Hanfstaengl across the street to the ministry for propaganda, where he would be filled in on its technical details. Seemingly, American journalists had better access to the frontline fighting, and it was up to Putzi to change that. He would be attached to the Nazi covert organization HISMA, fly to Salamanca, and stay at the Grand Hotel during his negotiations. Then he was warned that there existed the real danger his plane could be shot down. He went back to Wiedemann and asked for more time to put his affairs in order, but Hitler's adjutant was undeterred. "You will leave here tomorrow afternoon at four. You will be picked up at three by car, which will take you to the airport. By that time I shall have fixed your papers and all the formalities."

Hanfstaengl was fearful, even before he was driven to the military airfield at Staaken. He was carrying a fake passport in the name of Ernst Lehmann, who was allegedly a painter and decorator. As he was shunted aboard, he was ordered to put on a parachute, in case the plane came under fire and he had to jump. Within ten minutes of takeoff the pilot told him that their destination was not Salamanca but Barcelona. Nonplussed, Putzi spluttered that something must be wrong. He was going to Salamanca. The pilot confirmed that his orders came direct from General Karl-Heinrich Bodenschatz, Göring's adjutant, with whom Hanfstaengl had spent the previous evening. Already panicked, Putzi was then told by the pilot that he would have to parachute over Barcelona, as he was being inserted into the Spanish campaign as a secret agent.

Putzi staggered back to his seat, finally aware that this was his death sentence. He had been awkward, outspoken, and Hitler had ordered a "hero's death" to be rid of a troublesome friend. He imagined his obituary in the *Beobachter* praising him for his courage. Then, suddenly, the engines began to rattle, and the pilot called out that they were landing to investigate the trouble. The aircraft set down at a small airstrip between Leipzig and Dresden.

Feigning airsickness, Putzi miraculously slipped away and asked a local peasant where the nearest train station was located. Luckily it was only a mile away, and a train came through almost immediately, headed for Leipzig. He hopped on, unnoticed by anyone. On arrival in Leipzig, Putzi climbed onto another train, then stumbled off on the other side, thinking he could cover his tracks like a character in a detective novel. Then he spotted a night train leaving for Munich, and he jumped aboard. From Munich, he escaped to Zurich in Switzerland (eventually with his son in tow). The Gestapo contacted him there, but Putzi refused to return to Germany. Then Göring sent Bodenschatz to meet with him, assuring Hanfstaengl it was all a harmless joke. "I assure you on my word of honor that you can remain here amongst us as you always have done in complete freedom. Forget your suspicions and act reasonably," Bodenschatz cajoled.

But Putzi knew better. Later that spring, Hanfstaengl and his son escaped to London.[4] The British secret services needed to discern if Putzi Hanfstaengl—with his fantastical story—was a Nazi spy or if he could be "turned" into a British asset.

OF COURSE, WIEDEMANN would not be blamed for the aircraft's engine trouble or Hanfstaengl's escape. Throughout 1937, Wiedemann acted as Hitler's diplomatic face for sensitive projects. On November 20, 1937, fresh from their victorious and undoubtedly stressful machinations behind the scenes of the Duke and Duchess of Windsor's German sojourn, Princess Stephanie, Fritz Wiedemann, and his long-suffering wife, Anna-Luise, boarded the Hamburg-America line's flagship *Europa* at Cherbourg, bound for New York. On board, Stephanie occupied

herself "romantically" with forty-one-year-old American baritone Lawrence Tibbett, who had captivated European audiences.*

On arrival in New York, Wiedemann made a reluctant statement to
the American press at the pier that they were merely vacationing in the
United States—an extravagance in those days—but that he might see
President Roosevelt during the Washington, D.C., portion of their stay.
When asked if he believed the prospect of peace was damaged by the
fighting in the Far East, he replied, Stephanie acting as his translator,
"I am convinced that there is a better prospect of peace in Europe than
there was a year ago."[5]

In fact, the trip had been suggested by Princess Stephanie to Hitler.
Despite Wiedemann's protestations to the contrary, it had all the hall-
marks of an official mission with "travels to Washington for the purpose
of consultation with the German embassy in the interest of the Reich."
Given that Wiedemann paid for all expenses from his "special fund" for
himself, his wife, Princess Stephanie, and Stephanie's parlormaid, Wally
Oeler—with the führer's blessing—it certainly smelled like a significant
fact-finding mission.[6] Any dalliance with Lawrence Tibbett (attested to
later by the talkative Oeler) would have allowed Stephanie to learn who
he, having toured throughout Europe and America, thought the friends
and enemies of the new Germany were. Eventually, news of the relationship between Tibbett and the princess would find its way to the FBI files
on May 21, 1940.[7]

In New York, the Wiedemanns stayed with the German consul, Dr.
Hans Borchers, at his residence. Wiedemann's schedule was extremely
busy, since New York was a hotbed of "special projects." His aim was
to understand the setup for pro-German propaganda in the United
States and to gauge who might make the best secret operatives. After,

---

* Tibbett was a lead baritone with the Metropolitan Opera in New York. In January
1937, he accidently stabbed a member of the chorus in a fight scene, who died later
that same day. The European tour was meant to put some distance between the terrible incident and Tibbett, in the hope that Americans would forget it by the time
he returned. He would only remain with the Met for another three months before
continuing his world tour in Australia and New Zealand (source: *New York Times*,
January 27, 1937, and November 26, 1937).

Wiedemann reported his findings back to Hitler personally, suggesting how to improve propaganda and infiltration into the country.

After consulting with Borchers, Wiedemann met with Dr. Friedhelm Draeger, who reported directly to Ernst Bohle in Hamburg and ran the Nazi Party's Auslands Organization (AO) in the United States. Wiedemann also met with Captain Friedrich Mensing of the North German Lloyd line to discuss the undercover operatives on board their ships—generally, hairdressers, barbers, and wait staff. Wiedemann also examined the workings of the "haul" of three to five million dollars secreted into the United States by the "quiet and deadly efficient" Italian courier Luigi Podestà. The money was used by the Reich to pay fifth columnists for their propaganda work. A separate fund of thirty thousand dollars, directed by Ferdinand Hansen, had already been allocated to pay off anti-interventionist congressmen.[8]* It is likely, too, that Dr. Herbert Scholtz, the Gestapo agent based in Boston, where he was known as consul general, came to New York to see Wiedemann.[9]

Unusually, Princess Stephanie kept a very low profile during her stay, and her papers make little mention of what she did in New York. Her oldest American friend, Cathleen Vanderbilt, had married her second husband, a CBS Radio vice president, Lawrence Wise Lowman. Of course, the CBS Radio connection was one she would attempt to nurture, but one she would not be able to exploit. Instead, it was "Farben men" who reintroduced the princess to New York society, through Chemnyco's naturalized American boss, Rudolf Ilgner.[10]

By 1937, Chemnyco had become a "potent instrument and conduit of economic warfare between nations." Through its close affiliation with I.G. Farben, and by "taking advantage of the friends it made in the ordinary course of business," Chemnyco transmitted to Germany "tons of material ranging from samples of newly discovered chemicals to photographs, blueprints, and detailed descriptions of whole industrial

---

* Podestà would be expelled from the United States in 1941, along with German embassy and consulate officials, and go on to fight for Mussolini. After the war, he would reenter the United States with the assistance of Myron C. Taylor, the U.S. representative to the Vatican, to attempt to evade Italian justice (source: OSS Secret Intelligence Records, NARA, M1934, RG 226, microfilm 0001, 89).

developments." These were forwarded on to I.G. Farben using mail drops and foreign addresses.

Its operations gave American "industrial and economic vital statistics whose German counterpart our military and administrative authorities would give much to possess." As an American company, albeit controlled by Germans, Chemnyco had access to government sources and accurate information indicating all principal electrical power sources and proposed developments nationally, copies of the American rail network and its methods and regulations for the transportation of explosives, and a survey of all mines across the United States. It only had to pay fifteen cents for the information from each of the associations approached: the cost of a self-addressed, stamped envelope's postage.[11] Stephanie was in awe of all that Rudolf Ilgner had achieved.

Additionally, there were other German companies that colluded with their government in gathering intelligence and the proliferation of Nazi propaganda. Ernst Bohle's brother administered the overseas division of Siemens. However, the AO's Ernst Bohle was the person who placed "appropriate" party members in the overseas offices of Siemens. At the time, Siemens had successfully concluded twenty-one licensing agreements with American firms for the manufacture of everything from spark plugs and oil measuring devices to mercury-arc rectifiers, turbines, and electronic tubes. Its main American partner was Westinghouse. Although Rudolf Hess had publicly dissolved the AO in America in 1933, none of its "employees" had been fired. Instead, they became employees of various consulates, private German firms like Hamburg-America Line or the North German Lloyd line, or Americanized firms like Chemnyco. The heads of the AO in most American cities were the consuls. The German Red Cross, with Carl Edouard, Duke of Saxe-Coburg and Gotha, as its president, became an active propagandist in the United States, too. From time to time, some of their employees also engaged in sabotage.[12]

STEPHANIE ACCOMPANIED THE Wiedemanns in the guise of interpreter since the captain's English was not as reliable as it should be. Their journey took them on to Washington to meet with the German ambassador.

But who they really wanted to see was cultural attaché Ulrich von Gienanth. Wiedemann, in his new role as vice president of the Reich Film Chamber, which had an overarching duty concerning censorship, worked together with Gienanth to arrange for Leni Riefenstahl to come to America in 1938, since Hitler had decreed that her film *Olympia* must be widely distributed in American movie houses.

Gienanth's real value, however, was that he had special relationships with the Westermann Bookstore in New York and all other German-language bookstores in the United States. He financed magazines like the *Pilgrim Father's Circular* and the *Winona Wisconsin Weekly*; acted as paymaster to a variety of pro-Nazi organizations in America; under-took developing "special relationships" with sympathetic, high-profile Americans; acted as a courier to several consulates; funneled sensitive mail through Portugal; and undertook "special projects"—like report-ing on Nelson D. Rockefeller's movements in the years leading up to his appointment as the U.S. government's coordinator for inter-American affairs in South America and passing this information on to Germany's South American embassies. His current target was the American avi-atrix Laura Houghtaling Ingalls. It was agreed with Wiedemann that she would be paid two hundred and fifty dollars a month to barnstorm around the country spouting praise for the Nazis.[13]*

From Washington, the party traveled back to New York briefly, then on to Chicago, San Francisco, Los Angeles, and back to New York to board the ocean liner home. In Chicago, Wiedemann learned that the *Chicago Daily News,* owned by Colonel Frank Knox, was not pro-German and that the Hearst-owned *Chicago Herald-Examiner* had hired an anti-Nazi, Austrian-born reporter named Joseph Roos. The Midwest, always a beacon of German propaganda, was under attack. More than likely, no one informed Wiedemann that Roos, at the instigation of his publisher

---

* Laura Houghtaling Ingalls was an American aviatrix who won the coveted Harmon Trophy in 1934 when she flew the Lockheed Air Express route from Mexico to Chile, becoming the first woman to fly over the Andes. She was a distant cousin of Laura In-galls Wilder of *Little House on the Prairie* fame and was friendly with Wilder's daugh-ter, Rose Wilder Lane. In September 1939 she flew over Washington, D.C., dropping anti-intervention leaflets on the capital, and was imprisoned as an undeclared agent of a foreign country.

and Colonel George C. Marshall (the future U.S. Army chief of staff and secretary of state), had been contacted by Leon Lewis, a dogged Jewish lawyer, to help investigate the German fifth column in Los Angeles.[14]

From San Francisco, Wiedemann reported back to Hitler that Freiherr Manfred von Killinger, who had narrowly escaped being murdered for his affiliation with Ernst Röhm in the Night of the Long Knives, was heartily disliked. Wiedemann told the Los Angeles German consul Georg Gyssling that he had come to assess the positive Nazi assets in Southern California and to deliver new orders to both Gyssling and local Bund leaders.

Gyssling was informed that Joseph Goebbels expected him to pass on the message that the United States was to remain neutral for as long as possible in the coming war. Hollywood also needed to be "encouraged" to stop producing films against Hitler's Germany. Wiedemann reiterated his message from when he became vice president of the Reich Film Chamber in April 1937: "There is no such thing as public taste; we can shape that as we will. We have determined political taste; we can do the same with artistic taste."

Wiedemann decided after the whistle-stop journey across America that the West Coast was incredibly important to Germany. Not only was it the halfway point between Berlin and Tokyo and the major center for America's film and defense production, but it offered untold opportunities for taming anti-Nazi sentiment. The port of Los Angeles at San Pedro Bay was relatively unmonitored, and German and Japanese spies could use it to enter the country and send intelligence back to their masters at will.[15] Then, too, the Port of San Francisco provided a vital link to Japan. It was during this journey that Stephanie's and Wiedemann's roles changed from propagandists, influencers, and listening posts to spies. For her work as an influencer and listening post, Hitler had rewarded the princess with the Honorary Cross of the German Red Cross. More Nazi honors would come her way for her espionage work.

BEFORE WIEDEMANN AND Stephanie arrived in America, the Abwehr had decided, too, that it was time to initiate a new action. Eleven days before their departure, Nikolaus von Ritter was strolling on the deck of the SS *Bremen* gazing at the Statue of Liberty. It was a red-letter day for him. Not only had he been put in charge of establishing his own spy network from scratch in New York, but his divorce from his American wife had been granted. She had "no understanding for my kind of work nor for the extraordinary stress to which I was exposed as a result of my duties," Ritter wrote later. He entered the United States using his real name and under orders not to go anywhere near the German embassy or its consulates. Ritter did not know that Wiedemann was handling those spy networks instead.

As part of Ritter's briefing, he knew the Office of Naval Intelligence (ONI) was understaffed. The military intelligence division—known as G-2—had one officer and two assistants monitoring foreign espionage networks in New York, New Jersey, and Delaware. The FBI was only rarely asked to open counterespionage investigations from the army, navy, or Department of State, giving its long-serving chief, J. Edgar Hoover, little incentive to become involved in tracking down foreign spies or ferreting out homegrown ones.[16]

Ritter knew that Germany wanted America to remain neutral. Orders had gone out to the Bund and other organizations that there can be no sabotage, no disruption of the American way of life. Nonetheless, Ritter's top priority was to understand those blueprints sent to the Abwehr in Hamburg and contact the man known as "Pop." First, however, he registered at the Taft Hotel and reserved a second room at the Wellington Hotel under the name of "Alfred Landing." He then mailed two postcards to himself, one to the Wellington Hotel, and the other to general delivery at a nearby post office. A few days later, Ritter checked out of the Taft Hotel, walked a few blocks, and checked into the Wellington Hotel as Alfred Landing. Retrieving his postcard from reception, he went to the post office and was given the second postcard, also addressed to Landing, using the one from the Wellington as proof of his identification.

Having established his new persona, Ritter headed off to meet Friederich Sohn, aka "Pop," at his Queens home. Pop worked at Carl L. Norden, a U.S. military contractor at 80 Lafayette Street in Lower Manhattan that had developed "the most important military secret project" to date, the Norden bombsight. It was what the Germans needed in the proxy Spanish war. With over thirty patentable components and over two thousand calibrated parts, when the axis of the sight's telescope and the range bar pointer were aligned, it automatically released the aircraft's payload—eliminating human error or hesitation.[17] Carl Norden was a Dutch mechanical engineer and stickler for detail who believed that Northern European craftsmanship was unparalleled. He hired many German Americans who had gone through the European apprenticeship system. Nicknamed "Old Man Dynamite" for his explosive temper, Norden did not suffer any deviations from perfection. That's why the bombsight would revolutionize aerial armed conflict.

Pop suggested that Ritter meet with Hermann W. Lang, who worked on Norden's sixteenth floor, where the bombsights were assembled and completed. Lang, Pop said, would be willing to help the Luftwaffe. Lang was a native Bavarian who lived among like-minded Bavarians in the Ridgewood section of Queens. He had been a Nazi since 1923 and was involved on the periphery of the beer hall putsch. Lang came to America in 1927 and found work as a machinist before starting work at Norden in 1929. Initially a mere bench hand, Lang had become a highly respected staffer and one of four assistant inspectors of the bombsight. Age thirty-six, he was unapologetic about his political beliefs and was a member of the German American Vocational League, which sought to unite workers in America with those of "the homeland" under the leadership of Adolf Hitler.

It was Lang, not Pop, who had secreted the plans out of the building on Lafayette Street and copied them on his kitchen table as his wife slept. Returning to work the following day, he replaced the blueprints before anyone noticed they were missing. Lang was offended when Ritter offered him money for his assistance. He was a German of "the highest humanity" who loved Germany. "If you can bring this kind of instrument to Germany, then Germany will be able to save millions and lots of time," Lang told Ritter. Within the week, copies of the bombsight blueprints began to wend their way to the fatherland.[18]

Before returning on the SS *Europa*—the same vessel the Wiedemanns and Princess Stephanie took home—Ritter had set up a network
stretching between Philadelphia, Saint Louis, Detroit, and Chicago. The
next stop for Ritter, Stephanie, and Wiedemann was London.

Secret Maneuvers

What you read in the papers is all bunk ... a camouflage which
Hitler himself has set up to hide the truth.
—Princess Stephanie to Lord Rothermere,
February 2, 1938

While Stephanie and Wiedemann planned their American outing, others were working to burnish Hitler's halo as a "man of peace." In September 1937, Mussolini and his son-in-law, the foreign minister Galeazzo Ciano, visited Germany. Ribbentrop made sure that he was placed at Hitler's elbow. Ciano was relatively unimpressed, other than seeing the Krupp works at Essen and Frederick the Great's palace, Sanssouci. Ciano claimed the pro-German policy was his idea, saying, "The Rome-Berlin Axis is today a formidable and extremely useful reality. I shall try to draw a line from Rome to Tokyo, and the system will be complete."[1]

While Ribbentrop remained the German ambassador to the Court of St. James's, his crack negotiator Hermann Raumer hammered out the details of a stronger, more meaningful Anti-Comintern Pact with Ciano.* The agreement officially brought Italy into the Axis sphere of influence on November 6, 1937. Mussolini had acceded to Hitler's demands to annex Austria on the promise of a Rome-Berlin-Tokyo axis against

---

* Both Foreign Minister Neurath and the German ambassador Ulrich von Hassell dragged their heels, seeing a stronger alliance as a step closer to war. Ribbentrop's testimony at Nuremberg made it sound as if the whole idea was Raumer's, which may have been true, but Ribbentrop unhesitatingly took the credit for it back in the day.

the spread of communism. In response to the news, Anthony Eden made a hostile speech in the House of Commons about the dangers of the new Rome-Berlin axis, called "a force to reckon with," in Ciano's own words. There was no doubt in the Italian foreign minister's mind that the new pact was "anti-Communist in theory, but in fact unmistakably anti-British."[2] While Parliament debated, Italy eyed up Albania and Corfu for its next conquest.

SIMULTANEOUSLY, REICHSMARSCHALL HERMANN Göring sent an invitation to Lord Halifax (who was also Master of the Hounds in Yorkshire) to join him for a spot of "shooting foxes in Pomerania" through an advertisement in *The Field*. The new British ambassador, Sir Nevile Henderson, encouraged Halifax to accept, "believing appeasement must be the first solution to Europe's woes." At an official dinner of the Yugoslav foreign minister a few days later, both Eden and Chamberlain jointly urged Halifax to accept. So Halifax reluctantly "shot foxes in Pomerania" with Göring and met Hitler.

On his return, he said "Nationalism and Racialism" were "powerful forces" in Germany, and the trip laid the foundations for Halifax's own appeasement policy. Ciano rightly remarked, "Halifax's visit to Germany is a new proof of the anomalies in the Reich's foreign policy. Too many cocks in the hen-house. There are at least four foreign policies— Hitler's, Göring's, Neurath's, Ribbentrop's. Without counting the minor ones. It is difficult to co-ordinate them all properly."[3]

Ciano, whose vanity rivaled Ribbentrop's, understood the dynamics well. On November 10, Hitler convened a strategic group to discuss "his basic ideas concerning the opportunities for the development of our position in the field of foreign affairs." As Hitler stood beneath the oil painting of Bismarck, he swore his military leaders to secrecy. Göring (Luftwaffe chief), Field Marshall von Blomberg (minister of war), Erich Raeder (commander in chief, navy), and Werner von Fritsch (commander in chief, army) all gave their individual viewpoints, with only Göring backing up Hitler. The only one to maintain a stony silence was Neurath, knowing that his days as foreign minister were over.

Hitler said that Germany's eighty-five million people required "living space" to flourish. This principle was linked to the question of whether Germany should pursue self-sufficiency (autarky) or a greater participation in the world economy. Autarky, in the long run, would be unable to satisfy Germany's long-term goals, and with growing animosity toward the Nazi regime by the "hate-inspired" British and French—and, recently, the United States. Their antagonism jeopardized Germany's participation in the world economy in the future. So the question for Germany was "where could she achieve the greatest gain at the lowest cost."

To combat Britain, Hitler proposed to strike at the British Empire's weakest links: the Irish and Indian struggles for independence, the Middle East, and the Mediterranean rivalry between Britain and Italy. Then he gave an assessment of various options regarding France. Known as the Hossbach Memorandum, named after Colonel Hossbach, who took the minutes, the discussion was a complete blueprint for all-out war. It also crystallized the generals' dismay at Hitler's Lebensraum policy and marked the beginning of the *Schwarze Kapelle*'s treasonous plans to overthrow Hitler.*

"All the conservatives are being kicked out," Stephanie wrote to Rothermere on February 2, "and only the extremest extremists have or are taking their places."[4] Two days later, the German nation was told to stand by their cheap, state-manufactured radios. One after another, the household names of Blomberg, Fritsch, Neurath, and thirty-five of Hitler's most illustrious generals were sacked. Hitler declared himself war minister and supreme commander. Göring was promoted to field marshal (Reichsmarschall). Ribbentrop achieved his heart's desire and became foreign minister. A day later, Schacht was replaced as Reichsminister for economics by Walther Funk.†

The three hundred remaining generals (there had only been twenty-three in 1923) were called to the Reichskanzlei that evening to hear

---

* *Schwarze Kapelle* translates as "Black Orchestra" and was the name given by the Gestapo to the aristocratic and military plotters against Hitler.

† At his Nuremberg trial, the American chief prosecutor, Robert Jackson, called Funk "the banker of gold teeth," referring to the nonmonetary gold extracted from the teeth of concentration camp victims and that he arranged for the gold to be melted down by the Reichsbank into bullion.

about Fritsch's and Blomberg's frailties. Hitler, relaxing later with his closest party cronies, said he'd feared they would either "resign en masse or arrest him." Quietly, some generals began to gather around General Ludwig Beck (chief of the general staff of the high command, or OKH), outraged by the trumped-up charges in the Fritsch-Blomberg affair.*

THAT FEBRUARY, TOO, Chamberlain's secret machinations with Joseph Ball in London and his sister-in-law Lady Ivy Chamberlain in Italy boxed Anthony Eden into a corner. Ball and Lady Ivy wanted Chamberlain to recognize the burgeoning Italian Empire. Eden was strongly against it, as was Roosevelt. To his credit, Roosevelt had remained well informed. He knew from the American ambassador in Rome, William Phillips, that Chamberlain was using Lady Ivy as his go-between with Mussolini. In fact, Roosevelt's January summit proposal had been intended to stop Chamberlain from giving in to Italian demands to recognize its "empire" in Abyssinia.

On February 1, 1938, Galeazzo Ciano, the Italian foreign minister, wrote in his diary that he accompanied Lady Ivy to meet with Mussolini and that "Great Britain is ready to formally recognize the [Italian] empire." That same day, Mussolini dictated terms to Lady Ivy that he would be prepared to accept. Outraged at Chamberlain's anti-Wilsonian stance against America and his "secret" negotiations on foreign policy with Lady Ivy, Eden resigned. He was immediately replaced with the competent Edward Wood, Lord Halifax, who was of the same mind as Chamberlain.[5]

Chamberlain never could accept "any decision in the opposite sense" from his own. Damning Eden with faint praise, Chamberlain refuted rumors in the press about serious quarrels, claiming any disagreement they had was merely a matter of "method" rather than principle. It was a diabolical charade. Then the real campaign began against Eden, with whisperings emanating from Downing Street that Eden had suffered a

---

* Hitler had accused Blomberg and Fritsch of hesitancy toward his war preparations and later created trumped-up separate charges of personal impropriety, accusing Blomberg of marrying a common prostitute and Fritsch of being a homosexual.

nervous breakdown. Wiedemann hightailed it to London to report back secretly to Hitler about the furor.[6]

The parliamentary pro-appeasement supporters were elated. "There is jubilation in the House," Chips Channon wrote. "Harold Nicolson attacked Italy in violent, foolish terms and did the cause of peace as much harm as he could. He is a little mad when Germany or Italy are discussed." In disgust, he enumerated Nicolson's supporters, "about fifteen in all," including Churchill. It was preposterous, Channon felt, too, that a group of Labour MPs entered the Lobby demanding Eden's reinstatement.

In fact, Harold Nicolson accused Chamberlain of "butchering Eden" and wrote a biting letter to the papers about the scene that February day in the Commons. "Not that I mind the calm jubilation of Lord Londonderry or Sir Arnold Wilson," Nicolson began. "After all, they have for years waved the swastika aloft and have the right to shout aloud in joy. Nor do I mind the wild-west cries of Lady Astor. She also has fought bravely for Hitler and Mussolini and is entitled, during her fleeting visits to the House of Commons, to indulge in her whoopee."[7] None of this was officially reported to President Roosevelt, since the State Department was fixated on negotiating a new trade agreement with Britain and agreeing on the sovereignty of the Phoenix Islands group in the Pacific, just as soon as its new ambassador arrived.

AMERICAN AMBASSADOR BINGHAM had resigned due to ill health in October 1937. His replacement, Joseph P. Kennedy, docked belatedly on March 1, 1938.* Kennedy had won his ambassadorship partly through hard graft as a Roosevelt supporter but mostly by outmaneuvering the president. Slender, handsome, and an astute businessman who already had earned three fortunes in the stock market, Hollywood movies, and the importing of liquor to America, Kennedy was a man of unbridled

---

* See *The Ambassador: Joseph P. Kennedy at the Court of St. James's, 1938–1940,* by the author for details. Kennedy's arrival was a crucial two months too late to successfully conclude the trade agreement to include movies, and certainly too late for him to grasp the Austrian situation.

ambition for himself and his nine children. He presumed—wrongly—that his ambassadorship would be a dawdle to set him up for a presidential nomination in 1940. That was the first purpose of his mission.

The second was to keep America out of any European war. When he met with Lord Halifax the following day, Kennedy "talked pretty frankly . . . about the isolationist tendencies at home and found him [Halifax] prepared for that point of view." Halifax wrote to the British ambassador in Washington that Kennedy was "in good form and made even more generous use than usual of the American vernacular to emphasize his point." Two days later, Kennedy met with Neville Chamberlain. Kennedy wrote to Roosevelt afterward that "he is a strong decisive man, evidently in full charge of the situation here. Perhaps those at home who regretted the departure of Anthony Eden are backing the wrong horse." What Kennedy hadn't known was that his isolationist rant was music to Chamberlain's ears. The new ambassador and the prime minister would get along just fine.

There were others in Britain who felt Kennedy was "of bad stock," partly for his staunch Catholic and Irish American credentials, and "partly because he had the unpleasant traits of a man permanently on the make."[8] Others, like Churchill, Nicolson, and the anti-appeasers, wondered why America had not sent its best man in these troubled times. It was obvious to them that Kennedy did not have a full grasp of the situation, either about Britain's foreign policy toward Germany or about the possibility that the guns could begin firing at any moment.

A FEW WEEKS before Kennedy's arrival, on February 12, the Austrian chancellor Kurt von Schuschnigg had been summoned to Berchtesgaden by Hitler and given an ultimatum to hand Austria over to Germany. On his return to Vienna, Schuschnigg scheduled a plebiscite for March 13 instead, so that the population could vote on unification with Germany in what became known as the Anschluss. Rumors had already begun to circulate that there were troop movements on the Austrian frontier. These were discounted by the new, belligerent German foreign minister Ribbentrop as mere "spring maneuvers."

On March 10, three days before the scheduled Austrian plebiscite,

Chamberlain hosted a farewell luncheon for Ribbentrop as ambassador to the Court of St. James's. Although Ribbentrop's successor, Herbert von Dirksen, was in attendance, he had not yet presented his credentials. Chamberlain "spent 20 minutes after lunch talking earnestly to Ribbentrop about a better understanding and mutual contributions to peace by Germany and ourselves," during which official news of German troop movements and successive ultimatums to Schuschnigg were handed to him. Seething with rage, Chamberlain called Ribbentrop and Halifax into his private study. "I talked to him [Ribbentrop] most gravely and seriously begging him before it was too late" to persuade Hitler to halt his "swallowing Austria," Chamberlain said. Why was the prime minister so upset, Ribbentrop asked? Chamberlain was rendered speechless by Ribbentrop's self-satisfied, shallow, and "frankly stupid reaction."[9]

Halifax, however, saw the dangers ahead with considerable clarity. "The experience of all history went to show that the pressure of facts was sometimes more powerful than the wills of men," he wrote to the British ambassador in Germany at 11:30 P.M. on March 10, "and if once war should start in Central Europe, it was impossible to say where it might end or who might not become involved."[10]

Joe Kennedy was present at the same luncheon, too, and wrote to President Roosevelt on March 11: "My impression is that Hitler and Mussolini, having done so very well for themselves by bluffing . . . are not going to stop bluffing." Then he went on to say, "If you take my word, these quick bulletins will be newsy but still unimportant as far as the United States of America's policy goes."[11]

At 5:00 A.M. on Saturday, March 12, only a few hours after Kennedy's cable to Roosevelt, three divisions of German infantry and one division of trucks crossed into Austria. The skies over Vienna were darkened by two hundred transport aircraft landing at a rate of fifty planes per hour, carrying German troops to Vienna's Aspern Airport.* The Viennese were deafened by hundreds of German bombers purposely flying low over the city. No bombs, however, were dropped. By 11:00 A.M., forty-five German military planes had landed, and German storm troopers marched down Vienna's streets to a rapturous welcome. Huge swastika

---

* Aspern Airport was replaced by Vienna International Airport in 1954.

flags were unfurled from upper-floor apartment windows, almost touching the pavement below. Flowers were strewn at the goose-stepping soldiers' feet and the *Hitlergruss* was freely given and returned. Gestapo agents armed with Hitler's "Black Book," which held the names of the enemies of the new Ostmark (as Austria would be known), raced into action. Austrian culture would be first subsumed and then eventually obliterated. Arthur Seyss-Inquart, the Austrian Nazi Party leader, replaced Kurt von Schuschnigg with immediate effect.

Instantly, the Third Reich's laws came into effect. Austria's two hundred thousand Jews were made to scrub the streets, to be spat upon and worse, while the Gestapo raided their homes for treasured possessions. Some escaped; most didn't. Vienna's most famous Jew, Sigmund Freud, hurriedly scrawled across a whole page of his diary: *Finis Austriae*— "Austria is finished." The Anschluss was completed by midday. But was the macabre ballet, well planned and minutely rehearsed since 1936, the end of the myth of Hitler as a man of his word, a man of peace?

Evidently, the Austrians were delighted with the turn of events. Two days later, Hitler received a messianic welcome in the land of his birth, his new commander of his personal bodyguard, Colonel Erwin Rommel, at his side.[12] All the generals who had said it could never be done had been wrong. They nicknamed the Anschluss "the Battle of the Flowers" after the blooms strewn in the path of the conquering Nazis. While his generals remained baffled, Hitler immediately began planning "Case Green"—the invasion of Czechoslovakia. By April, General Ludwig Beck thought his only alternative was to resign.[13]

OF COURSE, THERE was a furor in Parliament. Despite Ribbentrop's abandonment of an agreement with Britain, his friend and steadfast supporter Lord Londonderry spoke up for Hitler in the House of Lords. "We know little of the events which have succeeded each other with such amazing rapidity in Austria," he said. "We then understood that Herr Schuschnigg went back to Austria with the intention, in a broadcast of telling the world that he had come to a satisfactory arrangement with Herr Hitler."

Instead, Schuschnigg announced *his* plebiscite, in contravention of

Hitler's desires, Londonderry continued, bringing about these momentous events. On the positive side, "this change [the Anschluss] has
relieved that terrible tension which was in existence in Austria." Warning that Hitler was hardly satiated and that he must be placated, Londonderry declared, "We must also realise another point which is in the
German Chancellor's mind, and that is the question of the German-
speaking people not only in Austria but in other parts of Europe. That
is a matter on which we must very clearly come to an understanding."

Londonderry had declared the day after the Anschluss that "he did
not at all like 'this new aspect of German politics' recognizing the taking
of Austria as 'a victory for more extreme Nazi elements in the German
Government.'" Londonderry blamed Britain for failing to "hold out the
hand of friendship to Germany as a primary cause for Hitler's actions."
His fellow parliamentarians could be forgiven for wondering which
comment represented his true feelings.[14]

Lord Lothian asked the House of Lords whether it was prepared to
accept "any form of national organisation which may prove to be necessary in order to make our armaments effective and to impress other nations with the conviction that this country was willing, if they decided
to resist aggression, to fight and fight successfully?" But was the country
in a position to fight a war? Lothian, and the other law lords, knew that
it was not.

Lord Strabolgi,* after taking a stab at Charley Londonderry and
Waldorf Astor, among others, for "the usual apologia for the German
invasion of Austria," said, "I am sure the Foreign Minister has good reasons for discretion when he returned from his famous visit to Berlin,
but . . . if the Germans are going to misrepresent the conversations he
might find it expedient to give his version." The inference being that
either Hitler or Halifax was lying, and Parliament needed to know the
truth. Strabolgi concluded, "We are faced with a new situation, following on the events of last weekend. We are faced with the new technique

---

* Joseph Montague Kenworthy, 10th Baron Strabolgi, was a Liberal member of the
House of Commons (Hull) and a former naval officer before inheriting his father's
title in 1934 and moving to the House of Lords. He was outspoken about Abyssinia
and the Spanish Civil War and in 1938 became the opposition chief whip in the
House of Lords (source: Oxford Dictionary of National Biography).

of aggression. We are faced with a Germany which presently will be far stronger, materially and militarily."[15]

Lord Redesdale, father of the Mitford girls, joined Lord Tavistock in defending Germany when he declared that "the gratitude of Europe and of the whole world is due to Herr Hitler for averting a possible catastrophe [civil war in Austria] of such magnitude without shedding one drop of blood." Colonel Sir Thomas Moore, also a Germanophile and member of the Anglo-German Fellowship, wrote to *The Times* that Hitler's "bloodless method" should be welcomed.

THERE WERE OTHER dangers, too. "Tory opinion is almost entirely on the run and would willingly let Germany take Russia and over-run the Near East so long as she leaves us alone," Harold Nicolson commented. Appeasement for him and others like Churchill and Eden meant turning a blind eye to your neighbor's home as it burned down. Historically, that had never been Britain's stance. Once the headline "The Rape of Austria" appeared in *The Times,* the article declaring that "by an open exhibition of overbearing force the German Government has compelled the surrender and overthrow of Herr von Schuschnigg's Government." Effectively, the Anschluss had dealt "a blow to the policy of appeasement by leaving it more than doubtful whether appeasement is possible in a continent exposed to the visitations of arbitrary force."[16]

Lord Mount Temple, an aristocrat of the old school who thought socialism was a subversion of British democracy, was also the chairman of the Anglo-German Fellowship. His view was that there was nothing shocking about the Anschluss, since Hitler had always stated it as his aim and the Austrians appeared to be quite happy with the unification of the two German-speaking nations. In fact, Mount Temple said that this represented Hitler's ideal nationhood, and that areas like the Sudetenland in Czechoslovakia, which held some three million German speakers, were "in no danger" from further Nazi expressions of a united Germany. Sir Lambert Ward, MP, questioned the veracity of the German atrocities in Austria. Many pro-German supporters in Britain agreed that the Anschluss had been inevitable. That did not mean Herr Hitler was marching toward war. Chips Channon wrote that Schuschnigg's March

13 plebiscite was unfair "and left Hitler no alternative but to sweep in." After all, Austria was "half-Nazi," and "other parrot cries" claiming "Czechoslovakia will be next" were unduly alarmist.[17]

CHARLES LINDBERGH HAD, up to that point, appreciated his life in England and the opportunity it afforded to live "without worry from politics, press, or fanaticism." His third son, Land, had been born in London on Coronation Day. As the clouds of war gathered in the spring of 1938, Lindbergh decided that "England, aged, saw not the future but the past and had resigned herself to the gardens of her greatness." It worried him that the best replacement propeller he could buy for his Miles Mohawk airplane in England had been in use when he flew air mail flights between Saint Louis and Chicago in 1926—and was obsolete in the United States by the time the *Spirit of St. Louis* had been built.[18] Any talk of war did not bode well.

As Lindbergh continued his travels across Europe, he returned to Germany. Ambassador Dodd echoed Lindbergh's concerns when writing in anticipation of the aviator's next visit: "what dangerous plans lie ahead for poor old Europe. I hope you may render some service in the direction of peace." Lindbergh understood his unique position. He could visit any airfield in the world and would be proudly shown all—from the standing air forces to that country's manufacturing capabilities. He wrote back to Dodd, "It is necessary to be able to enforce peace, and to do away with the advantages which may be obtained by war."

That said, Lindbergh admired Hitler's accomplishments. "Much as I disagree with some of the things which have been done . . . he has done much for Germany," Lindbergh wrote to his friend and mentor, Dr. Alexis Carrel, who had been "nudged" into retirement from the Rockefeller Institute.* To a friend of Anne's, he wrote that he saw "youth, hope

---

* Dr. Alexis Carrel was Lindbergh's mentor in the vast fields of science that interested the two men. Under the new management of Dr. Herbert Gasser, Carrel's scientific image had become tarnished by interpretations put on his writing. He admired Mussolini for building the Italian Empire, which did not sit well after the Abyssinian invasion. Carrel also believed in "voluntary" eugenics to build a stronger human race, too, which may have been one reason behind Lindbergh's "experiments" and his

and vigor in Germany today—and a strength . . . based on one of the strongest of foundations—defeat."

At the end of 1937, Lindbergh was invited to more German airfields and factories. At the Focke-Wulf factory in Bremen, he saw a demonstration of a prototype helicopter. Ernst Udet (who had become a part-time lover of Martha Dodd) showed Lindbergh the Rechlin air-testing station in Pomerania—the most secret aircraft establishment in Germany. There, he examined the Messerschmitt (ME) 109, the Luftwaffe's single-engine fighter, and the Dornier (DO) 17, its bomber-reconnaissance aircraft. He learned, too, that Daimler-Benz engines were used in a new Messerschmitt 110, under development as a twin-engine fighter. Before leaving, Lindbergh helped U.S. military attaché Truman Smith prepare his report number 15540, "General Estimate (of Germany's Air Power) of November 1, 1937." It concluded that the Luftwaffe would reach "full manhood" within three years, outdistancing France and closing the gap with Britain. Lindbergh predicted it would reach parity with the United States in 1941.[19]

At the same time, Charles Lindbergh's good friend and landlord at Long Barn, Harold Nicolson, wrote in his diary, "I am convinced that Germany and Italy are trying to chloroform us while they occupy strategic points to our disadvantage." He was convinced, too, that Eastern Europe had been lost with the Anschluss and the government was wrong not to make the full strength of the British Navy felt in Spain. "It is madness to suppose that Italy and Germany will not obtain from Franco some sort of secret arrangement," just as the Germans offered the Turks in 1913. "*When* war comes, we shall be unable to defend Malta, Cyprus, Egypt or Palestine."[20] Within the week, Nicolson was asked to resign as vice chairman of the Foreign Affairs Committee due to his strident criticism of the government and its lack of preparation for the nation's defense.

That May, the Lindberghs joined the Nicolsons at Sissinghurst.

---

bigamous marriages in Germany after the war, when he married two German women and had children with each one. Lindbergh's wife Anne claimed she knew nothing about these "wives" and sought counseling with Dr. Henry van Dusen in the 1950s to try to understand (source: email exchange with Hugh van Dusen, son of Henry van Dusen).

"Lindbergh is most pessimistic," Harold wrote on May 22, as the Czechs and the Germans massed on the Czech border. Anne Lindbergh noted that her husband was "evidently" pummeling Nicolson "with gloomy aviation data." Not only was Germany's Luftwaffe ten times superior to Russia's, France's, and Great Britain's put together, she recalls his saying, but "our defences are simply futile. . . . He thinks we should just give way" and become Germany's ally. Nicolson was shocked. Lindbergh had been living in Britain for over a year and seemingly understood the British mindset. The only way Nicolson could accept Lindbergh's attitude was to discount him as an aeronautics expert who believed in the superiority of air bombardment. Still, he could not get around Lindbergh's belief "in the Nazi theology." Having observed him for several years through many dark days, Nicolson was convinced that Lindbergh's worldview had been skewed by his hatred of the American public, democracy, and the press.[21]

Soon, Lindbergh would be America's poster boy against the war.

THE ANSCHLUSS CHANGED much of the rhetoric in the British press, with the Nazi apologist T. J. Jones writing to his friend Abraham Flexner in America that "Hitler's aims and his methods and the daily tale of persecution, repression and suicide" is changing attitudes here. That said, Lord Rothermere stood by Hitler and continued to send the führer congratulatory letters and telegrams, despite taking Princess Stephanie off his payroll in January 1938.*

When the Nazis entered Vienna, Rothermere's foreign correspondent, Price, was standing close to Hitler as he addressed the crowds. Both Rothermere and Price remained silent about the barbaric attacks against political enemies and Jews. Rothermere hadn't known that Georg von Schnitzler's Commercial Committee of I.G. Farben—with the full backing of its main board—had agreed to "provide financial support" to Czechoslovakia's pro-German newspapers to ensure that its sales agents

---

* Rothermere sent Stephanie a letter ending their business relationship on January 19, 1938. He did not reply to Stephanie's February 2, 1938, letter. (See appendix I.)

there would campaign for "reconstruction according to the German pattern."[22]

Princess Stephanie was in America when the Anschluss came, absorbed in expanding the network both she and Wiedemann had nurtured at the end of 1937. Within a few months, she would find herself the mistress of Schloss Leopoldskron near Salzburg, a gift from Hitler (confiscated from the Jewish theatrical producer Max Reinhardt) to establish Stephanie with her own salon of international music lovers. In fact, she would make out rather well from the Anschluss, taking money from prominent Austrian Jewish families, including the Austrian Rothschilds, to arrange "safe passage" away from the Hitler juggernaut.[23]

Swapping Horses Midstream

Our Hermann . . . the irresistible Lohengrin . . . there is no other man in Germany of whom the Fuehrer speaks with so much respect, admiration, and gratitude.

—Princess Stephanie

Princess Stephanie was incredulous that Lord Rothermere called a halt to their business relationship without warning in January 1938. "You will have to be very careful in the future," she wrote to Rothermere on February 2. "As a matter of fact, I cannot see how you will be able to support Hitler any longer under these new conditions, and at the same time serve the best interests of your country."[1]

Stephanie was panic-stricken. It was one thing to find herself without a patron saint to pay her enormous bills in England, but quite another to be cast adrift from the *Daily Mail*. It endangered her usefulness to Hitler. However, Fritz Wiedemann claimed she could be just as effective with the British aristocracy by other means. Hadn't she attended the opera repeatedly with Lady Cunard, Sybil Colefax, and Lady Oxford? Was not her good friend Lady Snowden able to pick up the telephone to many top government officials? Was she not known as a great lover of music? Surely, if the princess took over Max Reinhardt's Schloss Leopoldskron, she could invite all the British aristocracy to the great Salzburg music festival that summer. She could also make money "helping" fleeing refugees.[2] And so, unknown to Max Reinhardt or his associate Rudolf Kommer, Wiedemann set in motion the acquisition of the fairytale castle for his princess.

That May, international awareness of the confiscation of Leopoldskron became newsworthy. *The New York Times* reported that one of Reinhardt's tenants was suing him for two hundred dollars because the Nazis had dispossessed him. The same article made it clear that "Jews are not allowed to enter the municipal pawnshop nor are they allowed to acquire unredeemed pledges."[3]*

Much later, according to a letter sent by Rudolf Kommer at Stephanie's request, he stated on the record that Stephanie had intervened on Reinhardt's behalf. By June 1938, she had obtained a lease of five years for the castle estate—saving it from use as an army barracks. Kommer repeated that Princess Stephanie had done this out of friendship, and that she had generously forwarded Reinhardt's and Kommer's "library, books, silver, furniture" at her own expense. He ended his letter of support by writing, "no words [were] good enough to do justice to your attitude." Kommer never learned that it was the Third Reich that ultimately paid for Stephanie's largesse.[4]

As THE DAYS became weeks and then months, Stephanie's cajoling of Rothermere turned to threats, accusing Rothermere of treason. In reply, she received a letter from the *Daily Mail* in which she was reminded that she was almost certainly liable for both "Income Tax and Super Tax" and advised to consult Inland Revenue,† lest she "get into trouble."[5]

Given her profligate lifestyle, Stephanie was once again financially embarrassed—so embarrassed, in fact, that she could not pay her laundry bill for £45 15s. 2d. and a lawsuit had been filed against her. (She would lose and had to pay court costs.)[6] She had no alternative other than to turn to her lover Wiedemann, yet again, for help. Perhaps he could let Rothermere know that she was preparing the lawsuit against him for her loss of reputation and for his reneging on his contract with her, preventing her from making money elsewhere, and inflicting various other perceived wrongs. Surprisingly, Wiedemann told her she would have to wait. Germany needed her.

---

* This meant that they could not redeem any of their pawned belongings for cash.
† The British equivalent of the IRS.

Stephanie was employed to act as hostess to the leader of the Sudeten Germans, Konrad Henlein, during his mid-May visit to London, and to do her damnedest to ensure sympathy for the Sudeten cause. She was under strict instructions that nothing untoward could happen while Henlein was there. Afterward, Wiedemann told her to initiate contact with Halifax to gauge the temperature for a possible meeting with Hitler in London.[7] She was also instructed that Ribbentrop mustn't know.

And so Stephanie approached Oliver Hoare, the younger brother of the home secretary, Sir Samuel Hoare.* Through Hoare, Halifax's permanent secretary, Alexander Cadogan, was approached. Had Wiedemann known that Halifax had come to believe in forbearance and face-to-face negotiation while serving as viceroy in India in the troubled years of 1926–31? Or that Halifax also believed that, whereas the Hindu negotiator was mild mannered, the Prussian was "both alarming and vigorous?"

Halifax was a deeply religious man who was sad-eyed, reed-thin, six foot five inches tall, and born without a left hand. He had become "the priest" to the dour Chamberlain's "undertaker" since taking office.[8] Given that the Czech and German troops were facing off at the border when Stephanie sought the initial meeting, Halifax cautiously accepted the princess's approach—even if it meant only delaying war.

Halifax had conditions, too. Under no circumstances must the meeting become a matter of public record, nor should Rothermere be told. To Alec Cadogan, he made it infinitely clear that Ambassador Kennedy must not be informed either. Rather than report back to Wiedemann in writing or over the telephone, Stephanie—the woman who couldn't pay her laundry bill—flew to Berlin and stayed at Hotel Adlon, Hitler's favorite.

---

* Hoare had become home secretary in 1937. An initial approach through Lady Snowden failed, most likely due to Stephanie's threats against Rothermere. Oliver Hoare was married to Edith and Charley Londonderry's daughter Maureen. Her approach was intended to reach home secretary Samuel Hoare since he was a noted appeaser and would become a primary target for German "peace feelers." Dutifully, Samuel Hoare broached the subject with foreign secretary Halifax (source: Petropoulos, *Royals and the Reich*, 205).

. . .

AT THE SAME time, Kennedy held a series of meetings with the new—but highly experienced—German ambassador in London, Herbert von Dirksen, without informing either the State Department or the White House.* On June 10, Kennedy and his German counterpart exchanged "frank" views about the European situation. Still, Kennedy said nothing to Washington. Ribbentrop, however, received a report from Dirksen that they "discussed the subject of the agitation against us in the American press. The American Ambassador replied that he would do everything in his power to stem this press agitation. . . . His main objective was to keep America out of any conflict in Europe." Kennedy had revealed his poker hand before the bets were in and kept his backers in the dark.[9]

Two days before returning stateside, Kennedy had another meeting with Dirksen at the German embassy. Again, neither the White House nor the State Department were informed (either before or after) of this meeting. "The President desired friendly relations with Germany," Kennedy said. "However there was no one who had come from Europe and spoken a friendly word to him regarding present-day Germany and her government." Dirksen and Kennedy discussed again the poor press Germany was receiving in America. "Most of them [the press] were afraid of the Jews and did not dare say anything good about Germany," Kennedy told Dirksen. "Others did not know any better. . . . In this connection, it was not so much the fact that we wanted to get rid of the Jews that was so harmful to us," Dirksen continued in his report to Berlin, "but rather the loud clamor with which we accompanied this purpose." In fact, Dirksen was convinced that Kennedy was entirely in agreement with Nazi policy concerning the Jews.[10]

BY JUNE, THE Czechs and Germans had retreated from their border confrontation. Stephanie was still in Berlin when she received a cable from

---

* Herbert von Dirksen had been ambassador to both Moscow and Tokyo prior to London. He was from a newly ennobled Prussian family, and his mother was a well-known society hostess in Berlin.

Hermann Göring inviting her to his Karinhall estate. Although Ribbentrop had always been overtly hostile to her, labeling her a "pestilential
intruder" in German affairs, she had never met Göring. Stephanie knew
about the "kaleidoscopic turmoil within the [Nazi] party," as she called
it, and knew that this meeting meant she would have to choose sides in
the internal struggle for power.

Göring greeted the princess wearing a nile green shirt with leg-
o'-mutton sleeves, a green leather waistcoat with gold buttons, a mul-
ticolored tie, and white trousers held up by a vast belt with a golden
gem-studded buckle and white shoes. At his side he wore a large golden
dagger with a sheath "studded with precious stones." Stephanie claimed
she was overwhelmed by this enormous man and his tremendous personality. Göring laughed, duly noting her speechlessness, before saying
he could see she liked gemstones. Then he came to the point. Stephanie had spent four hours with the führer the previous week. Evidently,
Stephanie passed some sort of test in her reply.

Then Göring confided that it was *he* who wished to meet with
Halifax in London, not Hitler. After all, a certain rapport had been
established between the two men during Halifax's shoot in Pomerania in November 1937, and in these troubled times, Göring plausibly
ventured, they should meet again—this time on Halifax's home turf.
Perhaps as part of a shooting party for grouse in Scotland? Certainly
unofficial. Göring presented himself as a counterfoil to Ribbentrop,
Himmler, Goebbels, and Rosenberg—all of whom wanted war. Naturally, the führer could only be informed afterward, or Ribbentrop
would "torpedo" his peace plan. And so, it was decided that Captain
Wiedemann—who had Hitler's ear—would come to London as soon
as practicable to meet with Lord Halifax to make further arrangements.[11]

At least, that is the story Stephanie told later. As Germany actively
prepared to invade Czechoslovakia with Göring's connivance, Wiedemann, Stephanie, and even Hermann Göring needed to be portrayed
as Hitler's "peace faction." Before the London meeting took place, Adolf Hitler awarded Princess Stephanie the Gold Medal of Honor, pin-
ning it personally on her chest. From now on, Princess Stephanie zu

Hohenlohe-Waldenburg-Schillingsfürst would be an honorary Aryan and thus untouchable for her Jewish heritage by her enemies in the Reich.[12]

Of course, Wiedemann came to London with Hitler's full knowledge and consent, not as some undercover representative of the Reichsmarschall. Indeed, when Wiedemann flew into London on July 18 to meet with Halifax and Cadogan at Halifax's home in Eaton Square, Prime Minister Chamberlain was buoyant with hope. Stephanie's presence was required as Wiedemann's translator, even though he understood and spoke English quite well by then.

Wiedemann made a good impression on the British, and Halifax was convinced of his sincerity. The handsome captain said he had come "with the full knowledge of the Führer to enquire about the possibility of Göring coming to London to continue the talks begun by Halifax the previous November." Both Halifax and Cadogan thought that Wiedemann "cooed softly as any dove." When Halifax suggested that perhaps the Czech situation should be resolved first, Wiedemann gave him a "binding assurance" that Hitler was not planning any "forcible action" so long as there were no incidents provoked by the Czechs or any massacres of the Sudeten Germans in their country. Afterward, Halifax told Cadogan that with the resolution of the Czech situation as a precondition, the Göring visit would never happen.

In Captain Wiedemann's written report to Hitler, he quoted Halifax as controversially saying that it would give him great satisfaction to see "the Führer entering London, at the side of the English king, amid acclamations of the English people." If Halifax had said this, it was certainly in the belief that another war in Europe could be averted by the talks initiated at Eaton Square.

AT THE SAME time, Kennedy returned from home leave "with the most roseate accounts of the change in American opinion," Chamberlain wrote to his sister, "and of the president's desire to help. And if it be true that American papers are expressing that sort of view one may be sure the Germans are aware of it."[13] In fact, Kennedy's June 1938 return home was disastrous. His friend Arthur Krock placed a puff piece for Kennedy in *The New York Times* headlined: "BRITISH PRESS SETS TASKS FOR KENNEDY: 'INSIDE' REPORTS SAY ENVOY, ON HIS 9-DAY VISIT IN THE U.S., WILL REVISE OUR FOREIGN POLICY." Roosevelt was angry, believing the article heralded Kennedy's first step to a presidential nomination for 1940.[14]

On his return to London, Kennedy continued his secret meetings with the German ambassador. Dirksen told him that "matters were progressing as planned in Czechoslovakia." Dirksen urged Kennedy to pay no attention to the overblown reports about refugees, and asserted that peace would prevail. But Kennedy replied that "the average American blamed Germany for the general insecurity which prevailed in the world."

Kennedy could remedy that by meeting with Hitler. Dirksen needed to back his "plan to visit Germany in order to establish contact there with the persons in authority." Dirksen cabled Secretary of State Ernst von Weizsäcker about Kennedy's plan to improve German-American relations through his personal diplomacy, making a meeting with Hitler essential. Through a combination of Chamberlain's and Kennedy's wishful thinking and Dirksen's lies, Kennedy wrote to Roosevelt that "the European situation was not as critical" as the president thought. Believing that the meeting with Hitler would go ahead, Kennedy finally told the State Department and Roosevelt about his private discussions, certain that they would be pleased with his "new method" of "investigation and mediation." Neither replied to Kennedy's message.[15] The American ambassador had gone rogue, attempting to establish his own State Department in London, keeping Washington in the dark.

By MID-AUGUST, KENNEDY had embarked on an affair with Marlene Dietrich while on holiday with his family on the French Riviera, just as tensions over Czechoslovakia's Sudeten German population had become nearly intolerable. Unknown to Kennedy, Ewald von Kleist-Schmenzin, a gentleman farmer from Pomerania and secret envoy of the *Schwarze*

Kapelle,* had come to London. Kleist-Schmenzin's mission was clear. He had come to London to warn the British government, as instructed by General Beck and Admiral Wilhelm Canaris, that "through yielding to Hitler the British Government will lose its two main allies" in Germany, "the German General Staff and the German people."

Kleist-Schmenzin told Lord George Ambrose Lloyd, who had close connections with MI6 and the palace, "Everything is decided. . . . [T]he mobilization plans are complete, zero-day is fixed, the army group commanders have their orders. All will run according to plan at the end of September, and no one can stop it unless Britain speaks an open warning to Herr Hitler." Their discussion took place in a private dining room at Claridge's. Lord Lloyd had the food delivered by dumbwaiter since it was rightly suspected that some of the serving staff at Claridge's may have been working for the German secret services.

The next morning, Kleist-Schmenzin met with Sir Robert Vansittart, hoping to strike a bargain about Germany's borders after a successful coup d'état against Hitler. Vansittart later reported to Churchill that he simply responded, "You can have everything, but first bring us Hitler's head."[16]

Kleist-Schmenzin returned to Berlin and told Canaris, "I have found nobody in London who wishes to take this opportunity to wage a preventive war. I have the impression that they wish to avoid war at almost any cost this year. . . . [T]hat it is not possible under the British Constitution to commit themselves on a situation that has not yet arisen."[17] The *Schwarze Kapelle* did not know of Hitler's machinations with Göring to meet with Halifax in London or that after a decent interval, Wiedemann had been instructed to write to Halifax, "given the great uncertainty about Britain—the page had turned once again."[18]

LORD WALTER RUNCIMAN was chosen as Chamberlain's personal envoy to Czechoslovakia to help break the deadlock between the Czech

---

* Among its most prominent members were Admiral Canaris and his second in command, Hans Oster; General Beck; Colonel Graf von Stauffenberg; General von Stülpnagel; and Ernst von Weizsäcker.

government and the Sudeten Germans, arriving in Prague on August 3. An unkind observer remarked that "a stooping, bald-headed man with a clean-shaven beaked-nose face" had been thrust into the most fraught negotiations. Nothing was said of his wife, Hilda, who had served as a Liberal Member of Parliament (St. Ives, Cornwall) in 1928 and who, like her husband, had repudiated the formidable David Lloyd George's policies as Liberal leader.[19] Runciman was quite aware of the "Czecho-phobia" among Britain's pro-German and extreme right circles as well as in Beaverbrook's *Daily Express* and Rothermere's *Daily Mail*. After all, there were nearly fifty members of Parliament and a multitude of cap-tains of industry who could be counted among their number. Runciman was no fool and knew he had accepted an impossible remit.[20]

The newspapers followed the Runciman mission with tormented in-terest. It was alleged that Princess Stephanie took Hilda Runciman for long walks and innocent chats in the gardens of Prince Max-Egon von Hohenlohe-Langenburg's Rothenhaus Castle in northwestern Bohemia while Henlein, Lord Runciman, and the other mediators strolled in the grounds separately. Stephanie, however, would always claim that she had been in Salzburg or Leopoldskron at the time.[21]* Prince Max-Egon, a Lichtenstein national and aristocrat of German blood like many of the Czech landed gentry, favored the separation of the Sudetenland from Czechoslovakia to maintain control of his family's ancestral estates and became a spy for the Nazis in Spain after the outbreak of war.

Clearly, the British feared a stealth attack against Czechoslovakia in September. However, when Hitler spoke at the Party Day closing cere-mony on September 12, 1938, their fears were allayed, simply because Hitler had not made an open declaration of war. "We are confronted by a united front from Bolsheviks down to Democrats," Hitler shouted.

---

* Prince Max-Egon von Hohenlohe-Langenburg was Stephanie's distant cousin by marriage. His wife, Piedita Iturbe, Marquesa de Belvis, came from a fabulously wealthy Mexican-Spanish family and provided Prince Max-Egon not only with the money to buy the family estate (he was the third son) but also with the highest level of contacts in Spanish and Mexican society. In the closed file HO 382/250, an anon-ymous accuser alleges that Prince Max-Egon led all fascist activity in Mexico. Given what is known about the activities of I.G. Farben, he may have been working in con-junction with the conglomerate.

"Today we see how international world democrats work hand in hand with Moscow. This insincerity is simply disgusting." After fulminating against the Jews, whose days as "an alien race" of domination were at an end—as well as prophesizing the end of unrepresentative democracies— Hitler finally made his main point: "I shall not suffer the oppression of the Sudeten Germans. . . . If the democratic countries are of a different opinion, the consequences will be serious. . . . I demand the right of self-determination for three and a half million [Sudeten] Germans."[22]

The speech was broadcast to the United States on CBS Radio. It was the first time most Americans had heard Adolf Hitler's voice.

PART IV

THE UNRAVELING

I shall give a propagandist reason for starting the war,
no matter whether it is plausible or not.

—Adolf Hitler to his generals at the Berghof,
August 22, 1939

Fall from Grace

The German dictator, instead of snatching the victuals from the table, has been content to have them served to him course by course.

—Winston Churchill to the House of Commons,
October 5, 1938

In September 1938, the Duke of Windsor contemplated another visit "to expostulate with Hitler." It was a misplaced effort to eradicate memories of his German trip the previous October. Fortunately, Chamberlain's shuttle diplomacy preempted him. Edward wrote to congratulate the prime minister for following "the dictates of your conscience in the same fearless way in which you have faced up to all the complex phases of foreign politics that have confronted you in the last year." On this, Edward and his brother George VI were agreed. "I really cannot understand our old friend Winston Churchill's attitude," Edward wrote to Walter Monckton, "which is hardly worthy of the brilliant and experienced politician that he is." After all, Russia was more dangerous to Britain than Germany, Edward thought.[1]

AND SO THE world watched helplessly as the aged Chamberlain embarked on the greatest peace objective of his life. Berchtesgaden. Godesberg. Munich. Three grueling journeys by the British prime minister to Germany to ensure his "peace with honour" and "peace for our time." To observers, his eyes became increasingly hollow, his posture ever more bent with each mission. He did not take Halifax with him to help with his burden, opting instead for Sir Horace Wilson. Hitler had brought Captain Wiedemann, who could always be counted on to sincerely state Hitler admired the British and was a man of his word. "Herr Hitler had certain standards," Chamberlain told his cabinet on September 22, "he would not deliberately deceive a man who he respected and with whom he had been in negotiation."

And all the while, Czechoslovakia had been told "to make all the sacrifices so that Europe may have peace." No Czech was present at any of the meetings or consulted in negotiations.[2] Hitler was referred to by the international press as the *Teppichfresser,* or "carpet eater," since witnesses to his rages against the Czechs saw him fling himself on the floor and chew the edges of the carpet. Nonetheless, the "carpet eater" had pulled off yet another stunning victory through propaganda and bluster.[3]*

What no one realized was that Chamberlain had cut the ground from beneath the feet of the conspirators in the *Schwarze Kapelle* when he announced he would go visit Hitler to negotiate a lasting peace between the Czechs and the Sudeten Germans. They had been ready to mount their coup d'état against Hitler by September 15, 1938. Now with Britain believing Hitler's lies that the Sudetenland would be his last acquisition in Europe, they would have to regroup. General Paul von Kleist, who was not part of the rebellion and would go on to loot art and invade Belgium, France, Yugoslavia, and the Soviet Union, commented to the former German ambassador to Rome, Ulrich von Hassell, "If we really had been pushed into war on 28th, there would have been no way to avoid catastrophe for Germany but for the military to arrest leading politicians."[4]†

Most significantly, Lord Halifax had shuddered at Chamberlain's

---

* Under interrogation in London, Putzi von Hanfstaengl maintained that the "carpet eating" stories were untrue (source: The National Archives, London: von Hanfstaengl file KV2–470–71, 61).

† Ambassador Ulrich von Hassell was part of the vast February 1938 reshuffle. He was among the 4,980 victims executed on September 8, 1944, as a member of the Stauffenberg July 20, 1944, plot to kill Hitler. I thank his grandson, Agostino von Hassell, for his support in writing this book.

belief that he had made "peace for our time." Halifax was not a vain man like the prime minister and had come to recognize that appeasement was a futile policy. Henceforth, he would work for rearmament, for surely it was a matter of weeks or months before Hitler would be on the march again.

Alfred Duff Cooper resigned as first lord of the admiralty in disgust, admitting the British were not prepared to fight for Czechoslovakia— referred to by Chamberlain in his radio broadcast as "a faraway country about which we know nothing." Cooper justified his resignation to the Commons by stating he knew war was inevitable. Others would soon realize that "a moment may come when, owing to the invasion of Czechoslovakia, a European war will begin."[5] But which ally would Britain betray the next time? The rump of Czechoslovakia surely. Then Poland? Hungary, under the leadership of Admiral Horthy, was already in the German camp.

JUST BEFORE THE prime minister's treks to Germany, Joe Kennedy had made two statements to the German chargé d'affaires, Theodor Kordt (who was part of the *Schwarze Kapelle* with his brother Eric). First, if Britain went to war, the United States would support her. Second, "if Hitler refrained from bloodshed," the president would be "the first to congratulate Hitler on exercising restraint." Kordt duly forwarded both messages to Berlin. In the immediate aftermath of Chamberlain's return from Munich, President Roosevelt kept his own counsel, refusing to make any statement whatsoever to the press. Kennedy's views were wholly at odds with Roosevelt's.[6]

Following Chamberlain's triumphalist return to London, Kennedy continued to back him. As the first American ambassador to speak at the Navy League's great dinner commemorating the victory of Admiral Horatio Nelson at Trafalgar, Kennedy made "an endorsement of Chamberlain's philosophy of government but being expressly advanced as the Ambassador's personal views."[7] Again, Washington was not amused.

. . .

As with the Anschluss, the theft of the Sudetenland marked a major shift for Hitler's propagandists in Britain. The ruses of the past three years with Rosenberg, Ribbentrop, and Göring could never be repeated. Hitler's hostile Saarbrücken speech on October 8 was aimed at Britain and France, and although he assured them of his goodwill, he stepped up propaganda against Duff Cooper, Churchill, and Eden, claiming their goal was "to begin a new World War at once. They do not beat about the bush, but say so openly."

Hitler had already let it be known privately that he was angry the British prevented him from having his war. Now, he publicly declared war against Britain's non-appeasers.[8] It was time for both Princess Stephanie and Fritz Wiedemann to move on to other pastures—the Americas. The groundwork had been prepared for their departure, and, as before, they would appear to be "friends" of Britain while secretly working for Nazi Germany.

Even so, there were things on Stephanie's "to do" list before she abandoned London. Any change in her British status would affect her son, Prince Franzi, who had been studying at University of Oxford, playing his own role for the not-so-new Germany. Recently he had embarked on a career as an artist, with Stephanie pulling whatever strings she could. His first show was just off St. James's Street. Only a third of his artworks had been bought—by his mother's friends. Seemingly, his artistic talents left much to be desired, as *The Times* reviewed it as "more artistic than art." At Franzi's behest, Stephanie asked Wiedemann if he might be able to get her son a job with I.G. Farben instead.

On October 25, Weidemann wrote that Dr. Max Ilgner would intervene on Franzi's behalf. Franzi was instructed to write a personal note to Dr. Ilgner, mentioning Wiedemann's name, and enclose his résumé and any relevant history. Wiedemann assured him that he had handled Franzi's having had a Jewish grandmother by redacting his Jewish past.[9]

A few days earlier, at a predinner reception at the American embassy in Berlin in honor of Hermann Göring, the Reichsmarschall thrust the *Verdienstkreuz* into a surprised Charles Lindbergh's hand, stating proudly, "by order of the Führer for services to the aviation of the world."* Since Lindbergh had become embroiled in the phony plan to sell the Luftwaffe's newest engines to the French, and he had accepted German hospitality again, he felt it would be inappropriate to hand back the medal then and there. Later, he excused his actions by saying that had he handed it back, he would have no hope of receiving intelligence information about German air strength. It did not seem to occur to Lindbergh that he was being used as a pawn to tell America it would be outgunned in the air if it chose to go to war against Germany. Lindbergh's wife, Anne, understood all too well what was going on and nicknamed the medal "Albatross."

Another "Albatross" had been awarded earlier. On July 30, 1938, at Henry Ford's seventy-fifth birthday party before fifteen hundred prominent Detroiters, the inventor of assembly line production received the Grand Cross of the German Eagle from the German consul. It was the "highest honor given by Germany to distinguished foreigners." Ford's eyes gleamed as he beheld the golden cross surrounded by four small swastikas set in white enamel strung on a red ribbon. Hitler's recognition of Ford was for his "pioneering auto work." Left unsaid was that Ford-Werke AG had become "a symbol of its wholly German identity regulations" and that, in the previous month, the Nazis had placed an order for 3,150 custom-designed three-ton trucks—self-evidently for military use. Also left unsaid was Ford's decades-long contribution to the spread of anti-Semitism in America.[10]

Lindbergh and Henry Ford had been socializing for more than a decade. Lindbergh told friends that "some of Ford's ideas are far out, but they are always stimulating." Later, Ford told Detroit's FBI chief, "when Charles comes out here, we only talk about the Jews." To Ford's mind, Lindbergh was following in the footsteps of his Minnesota congressman father, C. A. Lindbergh, who was a passionate anti-interventionist in the Great War. Ford also told the FBI that "Young Charles accompanied

---

* The *Verdienstkreuz* is still the German Order of Merit. After Henry Ford's Golden Eagle medal was awarded, Professor Heinrich von Moltke of Wayne State University, John Koos and Ernest G. Liebold of the Ford Motor Company, and Thomas J. Watson, president of IBM, also received lesser medals. Watson would return his medal in 1940 (source: Baldwin, *Henry Ford and the Jews*, 285).

his firebrand father barnstorming around the state on some of his campaigns" and that, as adults, the two men were in sympathy for many of the same issues. "A few Jews add strength and character to a country," Lindbergh wrote later, "but too many create chaos."[11]

OF COURSE, HITLER's war plans continued unabated. A raft of new laws governing daily life flowed from his pen throughout 1938. The Ordinance for the Registration of Jewish Property meant that Jews had to itemize all assets worth more than RM 5,000.* Confiscation was redefined as legal government expropriation. All "degenerate" art (meaning all modern, impressionist, or expressionist art) was confiscated. New passports stamped with the infamous red *J* for *Jude* ("Jew") were issued. Polish Jews who had been living in Germany for some while were expelled. The Polish government refused to accept these refugees, and by the end of October tens of thousands of Jews were huddled into freezing "transit camps" in no-man's-land between Germany and Poland with no end to their misery in sight.[12]

On hearing that his parents were among these victims, the distraught seventeen-year-old exile Herschel Grynszpan, then living illegally in Paris as part of a small Yiddish-speaking Polish-Jewish enclave, went to the German embassy on November 7 and shot the first official who came into the reception area—the unwitting Ernst vom Rath, third secretary. As Grynszpan was taken away by the police, he cried out, "Being a Jew is not a crime! I am not a dog!" Vom Rath died two days later of his wounds. Hitler resolved immediately that, like the great German religious leader Martin Luther, who also disliked Jews, he would "with one blow, herald a new dawn." Joseph Goebbels decreed, "The Jews should for once get to feel the anger of the people."

Less than two months after Munich, a vicious wave of Teuton hatred ensued during the night of November 9—the fifteenth anniversary of the failed beer hall putsch and a national holiday. Throughout Germany and Austria, the widespread looting and destruction of Jewish

---

* The reichsmark was valued at RM 2.49 to one dollar, and 12.4 to the British pound sterling.

shops and homes, firebombings of synagogues, and beatings and murder of Jews were declared by Goebbels as nothing more than a nation following its "healthy instincts" in its "spontaneous outburst" and outrage at the murder of Vom Rath. It was not yet named Kristallnacht, or Night of the Broken Glass. A simultaneous Arab uprising took place in Palestine against the British for "terrorization of the Arabs." Almost all Jewish shops throughout the Reich were vandalized, more than 250 synagogues were burned, and thousands of archival and art treasures held by Jews were looted or destroyed. Twenty thousand Jewish men were rounded up and sent to Sachsenhausen, Buchenwald, and Dachau. Immediately, all insurance claims were declared by the government to be null and void.

Dr. Goebbels denied there had been any looting, adding, "If I were a Jew, I would remain silent. There is only one thing Jews can do—shut up and say nothing further about Germany." Goebbels added a warning to American Jews, "The German people are an anti-Semitic people, and will not tolerate having their rights curtailed or being provoked by the parasitic Jewish race." By November 12, the Jewish exclusion from all interaction in German life was complete.[13] The British and American publics were finally awakened to the savagery and barbarism of the Nazi regime.[14]

Kristallnacht peeled away another layer of Nazi support within Britain and the United States. The *News Chronicle* called it a "pogrom hardly surpassed in fury since the Dark Ages." *The Times* reported that "no foreign propagandist bent upon blackening Germany before the world could outdo the tale of burnings and beatings, of blackguardly assaults upon defenseless and innocent people, which disgraced that country yesterday." The editor of the Chamberlain-supporting *Spectator* put it quite succinctly: "the events of the past week have obliterated the word appeasement." A Gallup opinion poll showed that 73 percent of the British people felt that "the persecution of the Jews in Germany is an obstacle to good understanding" between the two countries. Even Lord Londonderry belatedly acknowledged that the persecution of the Jews on Kristallnacht was "medieval in its ferocity." Lord Mount Temple resigned as chairman of the Anglo-German Fellowship. Another fellowship member, Lord Brocket, continued his support, embarking on his planned shooting trip with Göring. He returned home stupidly repeating neither Hitler nor Göring had any inkling about the recent disturbances.[15]

FROM HIS ENFORCED retirement, Ambassador von Hassell wrote on November 24 "under crushing emotions" about the "vile prosecution of the Jews." His shock and horror were palpable: "I am most deeply troubled about the effect on our national life which is dominated ever more inexorably by a system capable of such things." With all synagogues in Germany burning, public opinion among Italians, too, was at its lowest point. Powerless to stop the orgy of looting and murder, the Hassells spent the worst days in Switzerland "in an atmosphere as distinct from this obscenity as fire is from water."[16]

That November, a Gallup poll asked, "should we allow a larger number of Jewish exiles from Germany to come to the United States to live?" Seventy-two percent responded "no." In accordance with the Johnson-Reed 1924 Act for Immigration, 153,000 immigrants would be allowed to enter the United States in any given year. This quota was subdivided into countries of birth (not residence)—an inspiration of the "proponents of eugenics" calculated to enhance the racial mix of Americans from northern and western Europe. Any unused quota from any country could not be carried forward into the next year. Taking in refugees was not a vote winner, and so the United States maintained no official policy regarding refugees during the Nazi era.[17]*

STILL ONE STEP ahead of his adversaries, Hitler had prepared the groundwork for his next propaganda onslaught. On January 20, 1939, he "fired" both Hjalmar Schacht and Captain Fritz Wiedemann. Schacht, who had masterminded Germany's financial recovery in the 1920s, had been at odds with Göring on the economic plans for war. Worse still, Schacht spoke out freely against Goebbels and the state-sponsored terrorism of

---

* Despite the best efforts of many, including President Roosevelt, the Johnson-Reed Act of 1924 was not amended or adjusted from 1933 to 1941. The act remained in place until 1965.

Kristallnacht. Schacht's removal from his post prior to the war saved his life when on trial at Nuremberg, despite his prewar crimes against humanity: the creation of financial vehicles for secret rearmament and his involvement in the refugee "flight tax."

Wiedemann's removal from office would also spare him after the war. There were myriad excuses for "sacking" Hitler's former commanding officer. Goebbels claimed that it was done because of Wiedemann's long association with Princess Stephanie, who was Jewish according to the race laws. Nonetheless, Hitler had protected Stephanie by making her an honorary Aryan. Göring, newly nominated as the leader of the "antiwar" party, thanks to Wiedemann's endeavors the previous summer, claimed Hitler disapproved of his adjutant's womanizing. After all, Wiedemann was a married man. Both Stephanie and Wiedemann later espoused the fairy tale that he was fired because he was against Hitler's war policies. It was an easy lie to tell since Wiedemann's next job was as far away from Berlin as possible—halfway around the world in San Francisco.

Ribbentrop, as the main minister advocating war, may have objected to having Wiedemann "the peacemaker" as the consul general to San Francisco. The animosity between the two men had not diminished, and yet Ribbentrop did not grumble about Wiedemann going to the West Coast of the United States to replace the disliked Consul von Killinger. According to Wiedemann's autobiography, "he [Ribbentrop] was happy to get rid of me in this way."

Captain Wiedemann also described the scene with Hitler. He had just come from seeing a delighted Schacht. "Hitler stood in the winter garden, obviously in the worst of moods. He turned to me and said curtly: 'I cannot stand having people in positions of trust near me (he probably meant Schacht) or in my immediate entourage (as was my case) who do not agree with my politics. I dismiss you as my personal adjutant and appoint you as General Consul in San Francisco. You can accept or reject the appointment. . . . I will always be there in financial matters for you.'"[18]

The New York Times greeted Wiedemann's appointment with guarded enthusiasm. The headline "WIEDEMANN'S APPOINTMENT HELD PLAN TO BETTER RELATIONS" was followed by "Herr Hitler has repeatedly used

him for personal missions such as conveying an invitation to Premier
Mussolini to visit Berlin in 1937, and, particularly in mysterious trips
to London during the Czech crisis." It omitted Wiedemann's presence
in Paris at crucial junctures and, importantly, at Munich. When Wiedemann disembarked from the SS *Hamburg* in New York on March 5, he
declared that "there will be a long period of peace and prosperity, just as
the Fuehrer has said."[19]

Astutely positioned just below the Wiedemann article was the announcement that Princess Stephanie was sailing for New York on the
Normandie on January 28. The princess "who is known as *the* leading
Nazi hostess in London" had not made the purpose of her journey
known, but "it is suggested that she will try to win Americans to a more
sympathetic view of the Nazi regime." Quite deftly, it concluded that she
had spent the last several weeks at Leopoldskron, "formerly the property
of Max Reinhardt, which was placed at her disposal by Herr Hitler."[20] A
week earlier, *The New York Times* noted, "the princess is undoubtedly
a star performer among a number of feminine members of the former
German aristocracy who have been enlisted in various missions—many
of a secret nature by Chancellor Hitler. They have become political in-
formers, propaganda hostesses, social charmers and mystery women."[21]

ACCORDING TO GALLUP's American Institute of Public Opinion, published on the day Fritz Wiedemann arrived in New York, "one of the
most important subjects the public wants investigated is that of foreign
war propaganda in this country." During 1938, the Dies Committee, a
later resurrection of the McCormack-Dickstein Committee, had been
in session primarily exploring communist activities—although much of
its work attacked the Roosevelt administration. It had just won an additional appropriation to continue its investigations for 1939. Incredibly,
the committee remained ignorant of nearly thirty thousand dollars in
bribes paid by I.G. Farben's Chemnyco to isolationist congressmen to
block any intervention against Nazi Germany.[22]

"Much will depend on how the [Dies] Committee goes to work," Dr.
George Gallup told the Associated Press. "Voters are more concerned
about this type of alien activity than either Communist or Nazi-Fascist

activities by themselves." Democrats were more concerned about Nazi propaganda. Republicans feared the communists.[23] But why did an article about the Gallup poll and the Dies Committee show a huge picture of the smiling, relaxed consul general–elect Fritz Wiedemann? Was it a mistake or a subliminal message?

Undoubtedly, the fear that "foreign propaganda" would provoke the United States into another war was palpable. It hadn't helped matters either that Dr. Ernst von Bohle, sporting the title of director of the Institute for Germans Living Abroad, had entered the United States that March, too. (It was known that he traveled on two passports—one diplomatic, the other in an assumed name.) Everyone knew that Bohle's job was to convince the German diaspora that their "first loyalty must be to Hitler and the German people" and that they should "make every possible effort to propagandize on behalf of Naziland," the Anti-Defamation League wrote to the Dies Committee.[24]

Ten days after these articles appeared—and less than six months after Munich—Chamberlain's "peace for our time" was shattered. Hitler's army invaded the remainder of a greatly weakened Czechoslovakia.

Last Throw of the Dice

Among the measures that I feel might well be adopted . . . is the discouragement of all that harmful propaganda which . . . tends to poison the minds of the peoples of the world.

—Edward, Duke of Windsor,
NBC Radio broadcast, May 8, 1939

"Your best advocate, which I claim to have been," a disconsolate Charley Londonderry wrote to Franz von Papen on March 29, "has been completely destroyed by his [Hitler's] policy having been shown to be quite impossible at the present time and probably for many years to come." On March 31, on behalf of both Great Britain and France, Neville Chamberlain was compelled to recognize he had been wrong and announced the government's guarantee to go to war should Germany invade Poland. In late May, Londonderry wrote to Göring proposing to come to Germany in the interests of peace "even though I am certain that on my return I would find it extremely difficult to gain a sympathetic hearing."

Simultaneously, Chamberlain sent word to Mussolini that Britain's "quarrel was not with him but with Hitler." After all, Mussolini had been a tremendous help to wheedle an agreement from Hitler at Munich—never mind that it was broken within six months. Less than a week later, Mussolini invaded Albania, leaving Chamberlain breathless at his betrayal. Scuttling and scurrying became the main mode of transport within the Foreign Office and at Downing Street. Chamberlain backtracked, then inched forward, before finally offering a British guarantee to Greece aimed at Mussolini.[1]

Voices were raised loudly by the old friends of the new Germany attempting to stop the madness. At home, there were more than a dozen extreme-right groups led by powerful men who whooped and hollered. Lord Lymington claimed that Britain was manipulated by American foreign policy to encircle Germany and Italy. Lymington, too, funded the newer right-wing group the British Council Against European Commitments, which had hired a veritable roll call of former BUF leaders: John Beckett, A. K. Chesterton, William Joyce, George Pitt-Rivers, and Major-General John Fuller. Although Mosley and his BUF kept in contact with these organizations, evidently many British fascists had rejected his leadership in favor of strident anti-Semitic propaganda. By April 1939, another political group called the British People's Party, led and paid for by the eccentric Marquess of Tavistock, appeared over the horizon, publishing its *People's Post*.[2]

The most treacherous of these organizations was formed in May 1939 by a relatively obscure Scottish MP, Captain Archibald Henry Maule Ramsay, who hailed from an aristocratic background. (He was a *very distant* cousin of the king.) He had a military mien, claimed to be deeply Christian, was wildly anti-Semitic, and had been awakened to the threat of the international situation, he would later claim, by the Spanish Civil War. Special Branch referred to Captain Ramsay as "definitely unbalanced and suffers from persecution mania so far as the Jewish problem is concerned." Ramsay would become the leading light of a new fascist group, the Right Club. Claiming loyalty to Great Britain, he and his fellow travelers embarked on a "dinner-club" propaganda campaign to keep the peace with Germany. Behind the scenes, they became involved in serious espionage.[3]

Several aristocrats and members of Parliament were sent—or went of their own accord—to Germany that spring and summer. Lord Brocket; the Duke of Buccleuch; Lord Redesdale; Sir Arnold Wilson, MP; Ernest Tennant; the former MP Henry Drummond Wolff; Hugh Grosvenor, Duke of Westminster; Arthur Bryant; and Lord Aberconway. Sir Joseph Ball appears to have been behind much of the back-channel chatter since he believed that "it would be dangerous for such negotiations" to be undertaken directly through Halifax or Chamberlain. They were all ill-conceived and sophomoric attempts at peace. Even Ball acknowledged that Lord Brocket and Walter Buccleuch had told the Germans that Britain will never fight, making them "potentially dangerous."

Buccleuch, Brocket, and the former BUF man Major-General Fuller all accepted invitations to attend Hitler's birthday celebrations in April 1939—directly against the Foreign Office "advice." Buccleuch, who was lord steward of the royal household, should have also consulted Buckingham Palace. He did not. When the palace heard that Buccleuch had left to attend Hitler's celebrations, they cabled an order not to go. Buccleuch's fascist and anti-Semitic pronouncements and his proximity to Hitler and the king were an embarrassment. He was "decidedly *lié* with Hess, if not with Hitler himself, and made no secret . . . of his pro-Nazi sympathies," the king's counselor Tommy Lascelles wrote in his diary. "They led, in fact, to his replacement by Hamilton in the office of Lord Steward."[4]*

Others, like Arthur Bryant, whose fascist sympathies were well known, considered their positions should war break out. And yet Sir Joseph Ball sanctioned and paid for several visits to Germany by Henry Drummond Wolff, the former MP and BUF supporter. In January Hitler had asked for commercial credits, resolution of the "Jewish Problem," and the return of Germany's colonies. By March, Wolff returned, demanding an end to the economic boycott and the encirclement of Germany.[†] Two months later, Wolff met with Helmuth Wohlthat, Hermann Göring's economic adviser, and Göring himself.[5]

AMBASSADOR KENNEDY HAD been badgering Chamberlain about the advantages for such a policy, too, even though it flew against official United States foreign policy. James Mooney, president of General Motors

---

* Richard Scott, 10th Duke of Buccleuch, is an acquaintance and was asked to comment through the offices of his wife whom I know better. Sadly, he declined. Douglas Douglas-Hamilton succeeded his father as the 14th Duke of Hamilton and was the man Rudolph Hess flew to Scotland to see on his abortive peace mission in May 1941.
† The economic boycott of German products began as a sanction for Kristallnacht.

Overseas, was another like-minded individual. On April 25, Mooney paid a courtesy call to Kennedy in London at the behest of Göring. He told Kennedy about his meeting with Helmuth Wohlthat and Emil Puhl, vice president of the Reichsbank and a director of the Bank for International Settlements in Basel, Switzerland. Mooney said that in exchange for a gold loan to the Reich, Hitler would reverse his discriminatory policies against the Jews. "We'd give it all up," Mooney quoted Puhl to Kennedy, "if we thought there was the slightest chance of our negotiating a gold loan and come back into normal trading relations." If only Kennedy would go to Paris to meet with Wohlthat, Mooney grumbled.

Joe Kennedy was never one to hang back. Of course, he would go to Paris, he declared. But when he informed the State Department about the trip, he was barred from going. Instead, Mooney and Kennedy arranged for the meeting with Wohlthat to take place in London—and this time, the ambassador said nothing to his superiors. Wohlthat was a major international economic wizard who had pulled off a huge coup only a month before Mooney visited Kennedy in London—the repatriation of the Czech gold sent to London for its "security"—with the connivance of his friend, the Bank of England governor Montagu Norman.*

Kennedy believed Mooney. But as the recipient of the Order of the German Eagle in 1938, Mooney had ample reasons for lying. He was keeping his German division of General Motors wholly German and profitable by cozying up to the Nazis, rather than thinking about international diplomatic repercussions of his actions. A friend at the State Department described Mooney as "dangerous and destructive" and "eager to see the fall of Britain." Mooney was also considered part of "an Irish Catholic group of influential Americans 'so blind in their hatred of England that they are prepared to sell out their own country in order to bring England down.'"

But Kennedy was a sucker for voices that echoed his own. His eldest

---

* Sir John Simon, then chancellor of the exchequer, lied to Parliament about the status of the Czech gold on deposit at the Bank of England because he was misdirected by Governor Montagu Norman. Norman knew full well that the directors of the Czech National Bank had requested the return of the gold under duress, but Norman, too, was an admirer of Hitler.

son, Joseph Kennedy Jr., wrote after seeing Unity Mitford in Munich, "She believes Hitler to be more than a genius; those who know him well consider him as a God. He can make no mistake and has made none." Did the younger Kennedy know that Unity's apartment in Munich had been "found with Hitler's help"? Did he even inquire if it had belonged to that Jewish couple who had "decided to leave"? More than likely yes to the first question, and as to the second, seemingly neither Joseph Kennedy Jr. nor Unity Mitford cared.[6]

THAT SAME SPRING, Sir Oswald Mosley refused to accept that Germany had not been provoked into action against the rump of Czechoslovakia. He believed the government's guarantee to Poland and Romania was "a suicide pact." Poland was in the pocket of British, American, and French financial interests, and for this reason the Allies of the last war lined up together once again in 1939. On his speaking tour in the north of England, Mosley asked why British blood should be shed for Poland, for the sake of "this rotting confederacy of cash and corruption." Here was a message that respectable, blue-collar Englanders could accept and were prepared to hear.

To unwind the war rhetoric, Mosley suggested to return Germany's colonies and concentrate on "minding Britain's business" of empire in return for a new disarmament pact with Germany. It was an appealing message. By the summer, Special Branch worryingly reported that BUF membership was surging ahead, and Mosley was speaking in London to audiences of around twenty thousand people. Treading a fine line between patriotism and rebellion, his message was, "We fight for Britain, yes, but a million Britons shall never die in your Jews' quarrel."

Mosley and his wife, Diana, had been negotiating with the Germans since 1936 to develop a closer relationship, which would include a new radio station. Diana had asked Hitler to arrange up to a £100,000 credit with the Morgan Bank, but the deal had been nearly two years in the making. On February 7, 1937, Goebbels made an entry in his diary about Diana, whom he refers to as Mrs. Ginnest. She "wants more money. They use up a fortune and accomplish nothing. I am having nothing more to do with this thing. Refer her to Hanke and Wiedemann." This partly explains Wiedemann's repeated visits to Paris until his posting to San Francisco. The deal was finally signed in November 1938, two months after the Munich agreement. When the Germans marched into Poland in September 1939, the radio station was only partially built.[7]

IN THE SPRING of 1939, Edward, Duke of Windsor, believed another war would "see the Democracies go down with the Totalitarian States, and Victory go only to Communism," or at least that is what he told Robert Bruce Lockhart.[8] On May 8, he was invited by NBC in the United States to address the world on the theme of peace. The battlefield at Verdun (where no British or American soldier fought) was chosen, and it seemed that Edward had at last put a foot right. That is, if one accepts the words "encirclement" and "aggression." The BBC asked Alec Hardinge for advice as to whether they should carry the broadcast, and it was decided it would be "inopportune," particularly since King George VI and Queen Elizabeth were en route across the Atlantic for a state visit to Canada and the United States.* "What a fool he [Edward] is and how badly advised," the Duke of Kent wrote to his brother the king, "and everyone is furious he should have done it just after you left."[9]

That may have been Edward's point. His definition of "encirclement" and "aggression" as propaganda was seriously flawed, too. Wasn't the invasion of Czechoslovakia "aggression"? What of the state-sponsored terrorism against Germany's and Austria's Jews? What about the invasion of Albania? The threats to Greece and Poland? Still, the Duke of Windsor would not believe that German aggression was anything other than propaganda. Even the loss of the Spanish republic to yet another dictator, Generalissimo Francisco Franco on June 23, would not dissuade him.

In the last days of peace, Chips Channon wrote despondently that preparations had been made to move the Foreign Office to Cheltenham, the Ministry of Labour to Leamington Spa, the Air Ministry to Worcester and so on. He also recounted the bizarre comings and goings of "A Balt, named Mr D"—who was the Swedish businessman and friend of

---

* Canada, too, refused to broadcast the speech.

Göring's called Birger Dahlerus—and his secret (but bogus) peace missions to London.[10]*

Chips did not know that since May 1939 the Duke of Buccleuch had been Princess Stephanie's main contact back to Hitler. Stephanie later showed an incriminating letter from Buccleuch to a friend, who informed MI5. Written on hotel stationery from The Hague, the letter said, "The Fuehrer told Buccleuch and Ribbentrop that he [Buccleuch] must make it plain to the Prime Minister" to make a significant gesture very soon "independent of the Cabinet if necessary." The "gesture" was to allow Germany to occupy Danzig.[11]

---

* Dahlerus was duped into being used as a decoy for peace on behalf of Göring as Germany prepared for war.

The Exiles

WARSAW THREATENS BOMBARDMENT OF DANZIG—UNBELIEVABLE
AGITATION OF THE POLISH ARCH-MADNESS!
—Headline in *Der Führer*, August 10, 1939

Those not living in Germany had no conception of the steady buildup in propaganda to prepare Germans for war. Hitler had told his commanders at the Berghof on August 22 that he "shall give a propagandist reason for starting the war, no matter whether it is plausible or not." Hitler assured his generals that no one ever asked the victor afterward if he had told the truth. The plan for the invasion of Poland was already underway. It was astounding that both Unity Mitford and her sister Diana Mosley had known of the invasion plan since 1938 and that neither had said a word. That day, too, Leni Riefenstahl, Hitler's beloved propaganda storyteller, agreed to become his war chronicler in Poland. She would film German atrocities and the victorious troops.

On August 23, 1939, the Molotov-Ribbentrop Pact between Germany and the Soviet Union was celebrated in Berlin, while an astonished world reeled in disbelief. An incredulous William L. Shirer and his fellow journalists congregated at the Taverne later that evening. The "virtual alliance" between the arch-enemies included terms that "[invite] Germany to go in and clean up Poland. . . . That Stalin would play such crude power politics and also play into the hands of the Nazis overwhelms the rest of us," he wrote.[1]

Even Lloyd George was aghast. "I've been expecting this for a long time," he told the Soviet ambassador, Ivan Maisky. Churchill and "the war party" had seen it coming, too. The British efforts to create an alliance with the Soviets were less than half-hearted, and always held back by Chamberlain's own mistrust of their motives. Freshly returned from Paris, Churchill told Harold Nicolson that the French were half mobilizing. During the debate in the Commons, Harold Nicolson described the prime minister as "dignified and calm, but without one word" of inspiration: "Exactly like a coroner summing up a case of murder." London, too, prepared for war.[2]

On August 30, Edward R. Murrow broadcast in his "This Is London" at 4 P.M. that on September 1, "It has been decided to start evacuation of school children and other priority classes. . . . School children will be taken by their teachers to homes in safer districts." London's streets leading into the capital were transformed overnight into one-way avenues—all pointing out of the city. An estimated three million children and adults were on the move.

In Washington, President Roosevelt told his postmaster general that Kennedy had taken tea with the king and queen and found them "deeply disturbed." And so they were. The ambassador had not spared the king and queen their blushes. Kennedy was ceaselessly spouting that it was incomprehensible that Poland, with its 33 million souls, should be the subject of so much brouhaha. "They [the British and French] should just let Hitler take over all of Europe since we could not possibly do business with the Russians but could always assassinate Hitler," Kennedy said, should the führer go too far. In Parliament, *The Times* reported that it was agreed "a great evil must be erased from the world."[3] Almost all the fifty MPs who had backed an Anglo-German alliance found their positions untenable.

THE DUKE OF WINDSOR could not have had any idea about Hitler's plans when he sent his telegram to Hitler from the South of France three days later. He called on the führer in his "entirely personal, simple though very earnest appeal for your utmost influence towards a peaceful solution of the present problems." Hitler replied, "You may be sure that my attitude towards England is the same as ever. . . . It depends upon England, however, whether my wishes for the future development of Anglo-German relations materialize."[4]

On the same day, Chamberlain wrote directly to Roosevelt to ask if the British might be able to purchase the new American Norden bombsight, stating that the Royal Air Force had gone through military channels but had been flatly refused.* Roosevelt, too, would turn Chamberlain down. But then again, Roosevelt did not know Nikolaus von Ritter and Hermann W. Lang had given the bombsight's blueprints to the Germans.[5]

THE PROPAGANDA COUP Hitler had planned for the invasion of Poland was simple. At 4:45 A.M. on September 1, the German cruiser *Schleswig-Holstein* opened fire on the heavily fortified port of Danzig. Several dozen "false flag" incidents were given the green light. German commandos led incursions into Poland pretending to be Polish soldiers. The most famous of these was the Gleiwitz incident, during which the SS murdered a German farmer sympathetic to the Poles along with over a hundred concentration camp victims from Dachau who were dressed up as Wehrmacht soldiers and who the Germans would claim had been brutally murdered by the Poles. Since Hitler planned to be the victor, he thought no one would ever discover the truth.[6]

IT WOULD TAKE two more days for Chamberlain to uphold his guarantee. MPs packed into the Commons "like sardines," the Russian ambassador, Ivan Maisky, wrote in his diary. "The atmosphere was heavy, menacing and oppressive. . . . Lady Astor, as is her custom, seemed to be sitting on needles, and looked at me as if she meant to grab me by the hair."[7]

The Duke and Duchess of Windsor were bathing in the swimming pool at their home in Antibes, Château de la Croë, as Chamberlain declared war. Minutes later, the British ambassador in Paris telephoned Edward with the news. When he rejoined Wallis, he said "Great Britain has just declared war on Germany. I'm afraid in the end this may open the way for world Communism." There was no why, when, or how, or any other explanation. Then he dived into their pool.

---

* By then, Chamberlain realized that Kennedy was being circumvented by the White House and State Department.

Evacuation preparations for the Windsors were made by George VI. An airplane was ordered to fly to Nice to pick them and their entourage up. It was arranged for Edward and Wallis to stay at the Metcalfe home in Sussex temporarily. When Edward was told, he ranted that unless the king "was ready to have him and his wife to one of their own houses they would not return to England." The faithful and ever jovial Fruity Metcalfe, who was with the Windsors in Antibes, exploded. "You *only* think of yourselves. You don't realize that there is . . . a war going on, that women and children are being bombed and killed while *you* talk of your PRIDE." It was the first and only time Fruity would raise his voice to Edward. At 8 A.M. the next morning, the Windsors were ready to embark, despite Wallis's fear of flying. But the plane did not arrive.

In London, the question was asked: what *does* one *do* with an ex-king? Sitting out the war in London was not an option. Eventually, some position with the British military mission in France was thought most appropriate, and the offer of the plane was renewed. This time, Wallis demanded a destroyer be provided instead. As Churchill was finally back in government as first lord of the admiralty, he requested Louis Mountbatten's destroyer HMS *Kelly* to be sent to Cherbourg to ferry the couple home. Randolph Churchill, decked out in his Fourth Hussars uniform, attended Edward and Wallis on behalf of his father.

What neither Windsor knew was that the chief of the Imperial General Staff, William Edmund Ironside, expressed some consternation that Edward would have access to secret French war plans if he were given such a position. These would be made known to Wallis, and *she* was not to be trusted. To overcome this possibility, it was decided that Edward should not have access to the *really* secret intelligence.[8]

TWO DAYS AFTER the British and French declaration of war against Germany, President Roosevelt issued two proclamations on American neutrality that "no American citizen could be expected to remain 'neutral in thought.'" Two weeks later he asked the anti-interventionist Congress to lift the international arms embargo attached to the neutrality laws. Roosevelt was determined that America's old allies would not suffer the same fate as Spain.

Journalist Dorothy Thompson had long before taken up the cudgels of her favored themes in her syndicated column "On the Record" and flung them at the cowardly appeasers, isolationists, America firsters, and the "architects of cynicism in American life." She had made many enemies among the sanctimonious and those whose consciences had been dulled. She believed that the world itself "walks in chains. Those who would free it do so at the risk of their own lives." In the press and on the radio, Dorothy ceaselessly campaigned "with a clang like that of a powerfully swung hammer" and "beat upon [the] general confusion of mind till the will to defend democracy was forged." Her wrath was particularly directed against the America First Committee. "It was no American virtue to put 'America First,'" she argued. Democracy was under threat and she believed it was the most perfect form of government. Excusing Hitler by saying he was mad was playing ostrich.

On September 6, she took to the airwaves, proclaiming that the German invasion "moved forward with kaleidoscopic swiftness to the point where we are tonight. . . . [T]he Nazi troops stand at the gates of Warsaw, the French troops at the Western wall of Germany. . . . More than a score of cities and towns have been bombed, the great capitals of Western civilization have been evacuated, millions of children have been put into gas masks" while America sat back as a silent witness.[9]

Five days later, Leni Riefenstahl was in Poland with her specially commissioned war-film unit, and the Germans were in Warsaw. She was meant to film Hitler as he entered the Polish capital. She claimed later, "In Poland, I never saw a corpse, not of a soldier, not of a civilian." And yet she filmed the first known massacre of the war.[10]*

ON SEPTEMBER 15, Colonel Charles A. Lindbergh countered Thompson's criticisms with a speech in defense of the Nazis from Washington.

---

* Known as Bloody Sunday, this was when the German army fired on retreating Polish troops. The outraged Polish population retaliated against the large German population of Bromberg, and when the Germans captured the city on September 3–4, they executed between 600–800 Poles in "revenge." Then, as part of Operation Tannenberg (reprisals against the Poles), a further 1,000–1,300 residents were executed and placed in a mass grave. Leni filmed these acts.

Taking up the gauntlet his father had thrown down as an appeaser in the Great War, Lindbergh began with his own plea: "I speak tonight for those people in the United States who feel that the destiny of this country does not call for our involvement in European wars. . . . We must keep foreign propaganda from pushing our country blindly into another war. Our forebears had fled the constant European conflicts, preferring the wilderness and Native American to their problems," he said slowly, carefully. "It is madness to send our soldiers to be killed, as we did in the last war, if we turn the course of peace over to the greed, the fear, the intrigue of the European nations," Lindbergh continued. Blaming this new war on the wrongs of Versailles and the vestiges of hostility between the former combatants, Lindbergh claimed, too, that "This is simply one more of those age-old quarrels within our family of nations." The implication was that Hitler was not such a bad chap. Peace at any cost was worth the price. "We must not be misguided by this foreign propaganda to the effect that our frontiers lie in Europe."

These were the words from the man who wrote incredulously in his journal on Kristallnacht: "My admiration for the Germans is constantly being dashed against some rock such as this." The words of 1939 were from a different Lindbergh, one who came within a hair's breadth of moving to Berlin, so *The New Yorker* wrote, "presumably occupying a house that once belonged to Jews." But his September 1939 speech was just the first of many in which he would make several anti-Semitic remarks about "the Jews" and the need for "new policies" and "new leadership" to counter Jewish influence. Dorothy Thompson lashed out at Lindbergh, calling him a fascist, a fallen hero, with the "notion to be the American Fuehrer." Privately, Roosevelt labeled him "a Nazi."[11] But what was the person in the street to think when America's only international hero said such things?

ON SEPTEMBER 3, 1939, William Shirer "was standing in the Wilhelmplatz about noon when the loudspeakers suddenly announced that England had declared herself at war with Germany." Berliners "listened attentively to the announcement. When it was finished, there was not a murmur. They just stood there as they were before. Stunned."[12]

The outbreak of war affected many of Hitler's acolytes irretrievably. The self-exiled Unity Mitford had told Hitler that unless he could stop the war, she would have to shoot herself. She had repeated the threat to her friends some four months earlier, brandishing a pistol some thought she had bought on one of her trips to Belgium. On September 3, she wrote to a close friend about her suicide and what he should do with her money and possessions.

Unity had left a package and letter with the gauleiter of Munich, who read it much later. It allegedly contained a "be merciful to my people" plea to Hitler and a simple farewell that "she could not bear a war between England and Germany" and so "she had to put an end to herself." The Sicherheitsdienst (the intelligence agency of the SS and the Nazi Party) was notified, and Unity was eventually found slumped on a bench in the Englischer Garten. She had shot herself in the temple but lived. Diana rushed to Munich and informed their parents.

Erna von Hanfstaengl, Putzi's former wife, had been close with Unity. It was a friend of Erna's who discovered Unity's slumped figure and called immediately for help. Given Putzi's escape to England, Erna felt that she could not "send a message through to Hitler to make sure she [Unity] was properly treated." Gauleiter Wagner did it instead. Hitler was told that Unity had been brought to the university clinic with a gunshot wound to the head, and he immediately confirmed that he would pay all costs, including her removal to a private room. "I had to show no personal attachment . . . now that my influence with Hitler had weakened," Erna confessed. "That's why I never visited Unity in the clinic."[13]

IN LONDON, ERNA's exiled former husband, Putzi, had been near the top of the security services list to be apprehended at the outbreak of war. Hanfstaengl had done little to endear himself to the authorities, spending a great deal of time cooking up a bogus libel claim against the journal *Cavalcade* and Selfridge's department store about his "alleged dismissal and banishment from Germany." Putzi's entire exile saga had been known to MI5 since his arrival in London, including General Bodenschatz's visit to Hanfstaengl in Zurich on March 17, 1937.

Within hours of war being declared, Putzi was taken from his home to Bow Street Alien's Office, where he was registered and allocated the number E.Z. 281247. His son, Egon, was already aboard the *Empress of Britain,* heading for Quebec. Putzi was sent on to Olympia, where a makeshift detention camp had been set up. Then, his home was searched. Two safes and a filing cabinet were locked by the police and the keys sent on to the superintendent of Special Branch.

On examining his papers, they saw that Hitler had promised Frau Winifred Wagner recently that he would write to Hanfstaengl to apologize. There were other enlightening missives, too. In one, the American journalist stationed in Berlin, Louis Lochner, suggested Putzi contact Baroness Budberg, "a very clever Russian" (though he doesn't mention she was the former lover of Robert Bruce Lockhart and the current lover of H. G. Wells). She was a Soviet spy known to MI6 and had asked Lochner "when the grand show" would start, meaning the war. Another letter reported a conversation with Diana Mosley in which Diana admitted having "assisted her friend Captain Wiedemann, her sister Unity, and A.H. (presumably Adolf Hitler) in the perpetration of the harmless joke." MI5 concluded that Hanfstaengl's story was either the sorry truth or an elaborate ploy to set him up as an espionage agent in London.

Of the forty-one men interned at Olympia that day, Putzi was the most famous. They were nearly equally divided between fascists and antifascists. It was a misbegotten policy: the former Jewish Berlin assistant police chief who had fled the Nazis stood next to the man who had signed his arrest warrant. Putzi's lawyers argued for his release. He was just about to write an exposé about Hitler's regime for *Collier's* and Hearst and even sent through a copy of the contract for the dollar-a-word article.[14]

Diana and Oswald Mosley were left unmolested for a further nine months. MI5 and Special Branch were keeping an eye on them, of course, but Mosley had been preaching peace for the previous year, and it would have been a controversial and unpopular move to intern two British aristocrats without trial or reason.

Fritz Thyssen knew war was imminent. On August 15, he went on holiday with his wife to Bad Gastein in the Austrian Alps. He said later that the Molotov-Ribbentrop Pact came as a complete surprise, but Thyssen immediately grasped its significance. On August 25, Thyssen was summoned to Berlin for a meeting of the Reichstag. He knew this was not just "good theatre" for propaganda purposes. He had asked his daughter, her husband, and his two-and-a-half-year-old grandson to join him and his wife at Bad Gastein.

A second summons arrived on August 31 from the gauleiter of Essen. Instead of boarding the plane sent for him, Thyssen sent a cable to Hermann Göring as president of the Reichstag that he was "unable to act on this suggestion owing to unsatisfactory state of health." Afterward, Thyssen said the cable stated, above all, "I am against war. A war will make Germany dependent on Russia for raw materials and Germany will thus forego her position as a world power." Thyssen even refused to listen to the Reichstag meeting on the radio the following day. So what had transformed the arch-Hitler acolyte?

On August 30, Thyssen received a telegram from his sister, Baroness Berg, who lived in Munich. Her son-in-law "and my nephew, von Remnitz, had just died in the Dachau concentration camp," Thyssen wrote. Before the Anschluss, Remnitz had been the leader of the Habsburg monarchists, known as the Austrian legitimists. After that fateful March, the Salzburg Nazis told Remnitz that if he did not pay a "contribution" to the Nazi Party, he would have to suffer the consequences of his anti-Nazi actions. He refused, and the following day he was taken to Dachau. Thyssen said that he had tried to intervene for Remnitz's release but Gauleiter Bürckel, commissioner of the Reich for Austria, ignored him.

Two days later, Hitler said, "He who is not for me is a traitor and will be treated as such." Thyssen knew that included him. After he escaped to France, Thyssen heard Joseph Goebbels over the French broadcasting services say of him, "What is more natural than that an industrialist who has suffered from intense overwork of the past few years should take a few weeks' leave?"[15]

ON SEPTEMBER 13, the War Office had a visit from Mr. H. B. White, the head porter at the Dorchester Hotel. He said it was his patriotic duty to report that someone should interview an Austrian maid, Miss

Anne Stoffl, who had been in the employ of Princess Stephanie for over a year and would soon be taking up a new position in Surrey. An officer duly went to Miss Stoffl's temporary accommodation to interview her. After some reticence to speak out since her mother and sisters still lived in Austria, Stoffl said she was in no doubt whatsoever that Princess Stephanie "was operating in this country and elsewhere as a very active and dangerous agent for the Nazis." Apparently, the princess was currently living at 95 Park Street W1, very close to the Dorchester Hotel. Indeed, Mr. White had seen a man wearing a monocle bow to Stephanie at her front door. The occupant at that address, however, was a Major Harold Wesley Hall, who was a noted ornithologist and philanthropist associated with the Department of Zoology at the Museum of Natural History.[16]*

Princess Stephanie had, of course, been known to the British security services since 1932, and the Hungarian, Austrian, German, and French secret services before that date. In fact, there had been several Home Office warrants issued since 1934 to secretly read Stephanie's mail.† The revelation by White and Stoffl was old news.

More to the point, Stephanie had been preparing her lawsuit against Lord Rothermere since early 1938. The litigation aimed to reestablish, for life, her annual retainer of five thousand pounds, which his lordship had summarily canceled in January 1938. Stephanie also claimed loss of reputation due to Rothermere's not defending her against the 1932 French accusations that she was a German spy. The litigation was a subtle form of blackmail, since Rothermere's friendship with Hitler and his machinations behind the scenes would become public knowledge if heard in court.

Once Rothermere's legal team had seen the claim against him, his lordship had simple choices to make. Try to get the government to stop the proceedings on the grounds of "national security," pay up, or let

---

* Major Harold Wesley Hall's archive at the Museum of Natural History is *closed* to researchers until one hundred years after his death, or 2064. He was born in Australia but made his career in London. Since his profile does not match any of Stephanie's other friends, it is more than likely that Hall had rented out his London home to her for six months in 1939 while he was on one of his expeditions.
† See appendix III.

Princess Stephanie do her worst. So Rothermere instructed his lawyers to put pressure on the government. He believed Hitler would be aghast at Stephanie's flaunting the führer's private missives to him as exhibits in a legal case in London.

Next, Rothermere wrote to Wiedemann. On behalf of Hitler, Wiedemann replied that Stephanie had given him the letters to translate into German, that "the F. [führer] greatly appreciates the work the Princess did to straighten the relations between our two countries," and that the führer was aware of her endeavors "on your behalf and on your instructions." Hitler also knew that Stephanie had laid the groundwork "without your assistance" for the "Munich no more war" agreement. Hitler, being of "chivalresque character" and possessing great "magnanimity . . . besides the real friendship he has for the Princess leave in my mind no doubt that he will grant her any help in her fight to re-establish her personal honour and financial situation. He will grant her permission," Wiedemann continued, "as he will feel it will be a great help for a woman in a fight against a powerful man," despite his aversion to the case being argued in open court.[17] Still, Rothermere would not be moved.

The most damning of the original documents (and there were many) that Stephanie had in her possession were "letters sent to Hitler favouring his marching into Rumania," the cable to Hitler "congratulating him on the annexation of Czechoslovakia," and a copy of the letter to Admiral Horthy "suggesting that Esmond Harmsworth should be made King of Hungary." Apparently, Stephanie had let Rothermere know (more than likely through Lady Snowden) that Henry Luce of *Fortune* and *Time* had offered "a very large sum" to publish exclusively the exhibits she intended to rely on in court, but Stephanie claimed she preferred instead to clear her name.

MI5 had no doubts that Stephanie had been an agent for Admiral Horthy and in the pay of the Hungarian regent when she first approached Rothermere. She had played hostess to the Sudeten leader Konrad Henlein in May 1938 during his London trip and had entertained him with the Astors. MI5 also knew she had a Swiss bank account and that Fritz Wiedemann had counseled her to have her creditors present their unpaid bills to Major General Bodenschatz, Göring's *homme de confiance*, for payment. Worse still, MI5 knew Stephanie had been sent on a mission to the Middle East, visiting Syria, Lebanon, and Istanbul in the winter of 1938–39 with I.G. Farben's head man in Beirut, Wilhelm von Fleugge. In Istanbul, she mixed with the best of Italian society in the company of the son of Marshal Badoglio, the Italian consul general there.

Guy Liddell, MI5's director of counterespionage, wrote in his diary on October 13, "Princess Hohenlohe and her mother have applied for exit permits to proceed to the United States," more than likely to see Wiedemann or to "consult an American crook lawyer in connection with her case against Lord Rothermere." Liddell even speculated that Rothermere "may be paying her to leave the country" because his lordship's "solicitors are trying to persuade the Home Office that the Princess is a dangerous Nazi agent and should be deported." In fact, "Rothermere is considering whether he will now go to the Attorney-General and ask him to give his fiat that the case should be stopped in the national interest," Liddell sizzled with anger. "Personally I think that it would be in the national interest the case should be heard."[18]

Liddell got his wish.* The case was reported internationally, and yet there was no feeding frenzy. There was a war on, and a respected, if not beloved, member of the press establishment was under attack. When Rothermere took the stand on November 14, he said that if one prevented the princess from talking about money, she would be devoid of conversation, and he often felt compelled to send her to Budapest or Berlin just for peace and quiet. His lawyer asked, "wasn't that a bit tough on Hitler?" Rothermere replied, "Hitler richly deserved it. In 1935 I thought Hitler was a man who really wanted peace above everything. I was wrong and so was half the population."

Stephanie did not prove her case. As to the charge that Rothermere had prevented her from suing the French newspapers, he had consulted French lawyers on the princess's behalf back in 1932. Word came back that the French officials "were satisfied with her position." The French lawyers advised against any legal action, and Stephanie had—perhaps reluctantly—accepted this. It had damned her case, too, that she had taken Rothermere's documents illegally. She never had permission to

---

* See appendix III.

take photostats of these, let alone to use them for her personal retribution or "legal" blackmail.[19]

She did, however, succeed in blackening Rothermere's name. There was no question of interning Rothermere without trial under the draconian Defence Regulation 18(b), like Putzi Hanfstaengl. Max Beaverbrook, that mischievous gremlin and Rothermere's friend, had been appointed minister for aircraft production and wired Rothermere that autumn, "I will want your services in America and hope you will go there at once."[20] After the trial, Rothermere made plans to leave the country. Before his departure for Toronto and New York, he took pity on the princess and paid her outstanding legal bills.

On December 7, George Strauss, MP for Lambeth North, asked the home secretary Sir John Anderson "whether, in view of the revelations in a recent high court action of her close association with the German Chancellery, he is considering the deportation of Princess Hohenlohe?" Anderson's reply was, "this Hungarian subject has made arrangements to leave the country by a boat which will be sailing in the next few days."[21] He did not elaborate on the simple fact that her exit visa, along with that of her mother, would be stamped "no return permitted."

The American Dimension

SO2 have asked whether we can supply them with Princess Hohenlohe's letters for publication in America.
                                    —Guy Liddell diaries, April 8, 1941

Lord Rothermere and Princess Stephanie departed for New York at
approximately the same time. Stephanie and her mother arrived on
December 22 aboard the MS *Veendam* of the Holland America Line.*
Rothermere had sailed to Canada first to undertake his mission for
Beaverbrook, then entered the United States at Saint Albans, Vermont.[1]
In November 1940, he traveled with his secretary and granddaughter,
Esme, to Bermuda. Almost immediately, Rothermere was checked into
the King Edward VII Memorial Hospital. Two weeks later, he was dead.[2]

Stephanie traveled accompanied by her mother under the assumed
name of Mrs. Maria Waldenburg and had booked a suite at the Waldorf-
Astoria Hotel. Their visas to the United States were only valid for one
year from the date of their arrival. Stephanie told the immigration officer she had come for a holiday and to visit her son, who was ill. It
would be a short visit. Her 106 pieces of luggage told a different tale.[3]
The FBI was alerted, and Stephanie was put under surveillance. But the

---

* Stephanie arranged for her mother, Ludmilla Richter, to marry the aged and impoverished Hungarian Baron Kálmán Szepessy in November 1938 to avoid her mother's
passport being stamped with the red *J* marking her out as a Jew. In return, Baron
Szepessy would receive 290 pengös a month ($58). By March 1939, Stephanie was
more than one thousand pengös overdue. There were roughly five pengös to the dollar, and twenty to the pound.

princess was no down-and-out, disgruntled has-been. She had come to New York at the request of her literary agent, Curtis Brown, to write her explosive memoirs. Descending the gangplank, she wore a silver-fox turban and three-quarter-length silver-fox coat, a black silk dress, and black kid Perugia sandals with sky-blue platform soles. Diamonds adorned her ears, and she wore a diamond brooch on her dress.[4]

THAT JANUARY, FRITZ Wiedemann was summoned to Washington for a conference of all German consuls in America. Top of the agenda was raising funds to repatriate the stranded crew of the German ship *Columbus*.* The crew had been moved to Angel Island in San Francisco Bay, since the captain had been ordered to scuttle the vessel by his admiral. Apparently, Germany could not "afford to pay for internment or upkeep of boat and crew as this would have to be paid in foreign exchange."[5]

On March 3, 1940, Fritz Wiedemann wrote a letter addressed to "Darling" Stephanie saying he was disappointed she had not been able to come to San Francisco. It seemed to him, however, that her excuses for not leaving New York were flimsy. The plaintive tone was similar to the letter written the previous October, in which he bemoaned that his "Darling" hadn't written and that he was sure something was wrong with the mail. This was no lover's complaint. It was his personal code to let her know his mail was read by the U.S. security services.†

Sometime after Stephanie's arrival in New York, she had written to Wiedemann about her book with reams of questions. "Above all, your questions are worded very cleverly," Fritz wrote. "But before we go into

---

* It was better to destroy a ship worth millions than to "pay a couple hundred thousand dollars which could be used by Germany for the war." Some thirty thousand dollars was raised to repatriate the crew from Angel Island by consuls in various jurisdictions. As Angel Island was in Wiedemann's area, it is assumed that he raised the bulk of the cash (source: *News Research Service*, CRC2–066–22).

† A skeleton operation had been set up in Bermuda from the opening days of the war in Europe. By January 1940, Churchill authorized a full-scale airmail-censorship station in Bermuda that could be on the lookout for any espionage or sensitive military information. Bermuda became "Britain's number one listening post," unmasking several espionage plots and military secrets (https://bernews.com/2019/10/wartime-spies-read-mail-bermuda/).

it any further, we must speak about it first. For you can well imagine that the whole world will know that certain informations you could only have received from me, and you must consider my position."[6] Neither her letter nor her questionnaire has survived.

In fact, Fritz Wiedemann thought he had settled in as consul general in San Francisco quite well.* His predecessor, Killinger, had a name that fitted his primary purpose in life. Killinger, so *The New York Times* reported on June 25, 1937, had directed undercover operatives in Czechoslovakia "to wipe out Marxist, democratic, and Jewish plague spots." Wiedemann's orders were to project the image of the "good German." Here was no gimlet-eyed Prussian. He was more akin to the laughing cavalier. His stern features and low, almost simian forehead disappeared when he smiled—and he smiled frequently. He was affable, knowledgeable, immaculately dressed, and friendly—especially to ladies. He laughed "uproariously" when his English failed him or when asked embarrassing questions, endearing him to most people.

In the same issue of *Life* magazine showing King George VI and Queen Elizabeth waving fond good-byes to the Roosevelts at Hyde Park, an article entitled "CAPTAIN FRITZ: CONSUL WIEDEMANN, HITLER'S OLD SUPERIOR OFFICER, RUNS INTO TROUBLE SELLING NAZISM TO THE WEST" took pride of place. He "chose his friends carefully," *Life* magazine wrote, but it showed Wiedemann in the same picture as Captain Friedrich Mensing, formerly of the North German Lloyd line in New York, now chief of German Steamship Lines in San Francisco and in the pay of Farben's New York company, Chemnyco, for espionage. From his sleepy post, Wiedemann would lay claim to the myth that he was only interested in improving German-American trade. He was, in fact, a Nazi propagandist and spymaster.[7]

Clearly, Hitler's secret policy toward the Americas had matured since Killinger's appointment. Both Killinger and Wiedemann ran fifth columnists in the United States and Latin America, with Wiedemann taking over German government payments to spies and propagandists.

---

* His predecessor, Freiherr Manfred von Killinger, was a fiery Nazi and had been part of the notorious Ehrhardt Freikorps Brigade that was implicated in the murder of Weimar's finance minister Matthias Erzberger.

By June 1941, these would amount to over five million dollars. The smiling consul Wiedemann was head of Nazi undercover operations in the Western Hemisphere, concentrating on the western part of North America, Latin America, and the Pacific and coordinating his actions with Japan and other quasi-governmental organizations like I.G. Farben. His Farben connections dated back to his affair with Georg von Schnitzler's wife, Lily, in 1935, who had recommended the charming Wiedemann to her husband, the powerful main board director of I.G. Farben.[8]

WHILE PRINCESS STEPHANIE's lawsuit was heard in London in November 1939, Fritz Wiedemann was squeezing the German American Bund. In a bizarre act of self-destruction, the San Francisco branch of the German American League for Culture called for Wiedemann to be ordered out of the country as a "dangerous Nazi spy and propagandist." They published a circular that began with the inflammatory phrase, "In the interest of security of the United States" and "of all those who do not want this country undermined by a carefully organized network of spies and saboteurs we should raise our voices and ask for the recall of Captain Fritz Wiedemann." The Bund had turned against Wiedemann because he refused to give them any further clandestine funding. Ernst Bohle, head of the AO in Hamburg, had been disgruntled for years about the Bund's loudmouthed activities, but this particular morsel of counterpropaganda could not go unpunished.[9]

Shortly before Wiedemann came to America, on February 19, 1939, Fritz Kuhn spoke at Madison Square Garden to an at-capacity crowd. "The Bund is an Organization of American Citizens unequivocally committed to the Defense of the Constitution, and Sovereignty of these United States," its handbill for the event claimed. A thirty-by-fourteen-foot portrait of George Washington was erected behind the speaker's platform and adorned on both sides by star-spangled banners *and* swastika-bedecked Bund flags with the letters *AV* on a red background.*

---

* There was nothing truly American about AV, which stood for "Amerikadeutscher Volksbund."

Derogatory references to "President Rosenfeld" and "the Jewish Federal Reserve System" were duly booed while Hitler, Mussolini, and Father Coughlin were cheered.

Dorothy Thompson was in the press box and burst into a long, loud fit of laughter when she heard the Nazi golden rule was to "treat all human beings with a human face." Who could blame her? The Bundists seated near her shouted for Thompson to be removed. "I was immediately seized by two policemen, whose salaries as a New York taxpayer I help to meet, and I was also set upon by a husky uniformed storm trooper, whose movement is following the detailed instructions of a foreign power" before she was "roughly hustled to the door."[10]

The Madison Square Garden event had gone too far. Kuhn was grooming himself to become the American führer, and his actions had deeply displeased Hitler. Wiedemann was under orders to stop him. Since the war in Europe had begun, discrediting the Bund was de rigueur to keep America neutral.

Had Wiedemann tipped off New York Mayor Fiorello La Guardia to raid the Bund's Yorkville offices on the Upper East Side of Manhattan? We may never know. But the diminutive mayor rubbed his hands gleefully as information of Kuhn's embezzlement of funds from his own membership was discovered. After a three-week trial in November 1939, Kuhn was convicted on two counts of grand larceny and three counts of larceny and forgery, the stolen Bund money being used to finance his two mistresses. He was sentenced to between two and a half to five years on December 4 "as an ordinary small-time forger and thief and not because of any gospels of hate or anything of that sort." Sing Sing in Ossining, New York, became his new home.[11] The Bund's leadership fell to Gerhard Wilhelm Kunze, and the Bund began to dissolve. California was one of the first states to ban it as a subversive organization, and local chapters fell away or were merged into other groups.

WIEDEMANN WAS REWARDED with the grateful thanks of his country. His staff more than trebled from eight to nearly thirty employees so he could cope with his expanded portfolio. His extensive geographic remit was not only unusual for a consul general but also indicative of the inordinate trust placed in Wiedemann's discretion and ability to handle a complex operation. His new duties officially placed him in charge of the Orient Gruppe, the Asian-German intelligence network. He became the regional head of the AO, which received much of its funding through I.G. Farben.* Finally, Wiedemann founded the German American Business League, which comprised some thousand small businesses that agreed to boycott Jewish companies.

But all was not plain sailing. Granted, Wiedemann found solace in the anti-Semitic leanings of some *Social Register* dowagers in the San Francisco suburbs of Burlingame and San Mateo, but he was blackballed at Burlingame Country Club. His cocktail parties inviting important local Americans became indefinitely postponed. American naval officers who were happy to shoot the breeze with Wiedemann at local nightclubs were suddenly severely reprimanded by their superior officers, and the same society dowagers began to ask one another, "what do you *do*, my dear, if you found Captain Wiedemann sitting next to you at dinner?"[12]

Superficially, it seems odd that no one thought of approaching Congressman Martin Dies and his House Un-American Activities Committee (HUAC), formed in 1938. Dies, an imposing six foot three with blond hair, had initially been a New Deal supporter, but because of the president's lenient stand on strikes and trade unions and the First Lady's advocacy for antilynching legislation, particularly in the South, Dies became an implacable enemy of the Roosevelt administration. Dies had obtained his federal funding on the basis that the committee carry out its mandate to probe "the extent, character, and object of un-American propaganda activities in the United States." Yet one of his committee members was quoted in *The New York Times* as saying its remit was to root out "the four horsemen of autocracy: Fascism, Nazism, Bolshevism, and New Dealism."[13]

For the first two years of its existence, it turned its sights against the last two "horsemen." According to the secretary of the interior, Harold L. Ickes, Dies's "preposterous committee" had become an "actual menace." The committee had not uncovered or considered any Nazi-supporting

---

* The AO was also the main recruitment and espionage network linking American businessmen to the Reich.

fifth columnist, nor had it proved any link between the American Communist Party and wildcat strikes. As the German threat appeared to be growing, Dies continued to dedicate most of his efforts to the communists, while Roosevelt feared a real and present danger of a Nazi fifth column in America.[14]

By 1938, Roosevelt had arranged a proper investigation of possible sabotage and espionage against the United States through J. Edgar Hoover's FBI instead. Hoover reported directly to the Oval Office on individuals and organizations that he believed to represent a threat. In fact, the Dies Committee went to the FBI to hand over its list of communist subversives. Roosevelt vetoed that idea as a gross violation of civil liberties and refused to implement Dies's seven-point countersubversive program, proposed in 1940. It would have brought forward the horrors of the McCarthy era to the eve of America's entering World War II.[15]

In the spring of 1940, the British SO* wanted sight of Princess Stephanie's letters to uncover Wiedemann's true role. MI5 had already drawn up its own list of the greatest threats, and knew about contacts between bankers at Morgan, Chase, Schroders, and others who had also lent millions to Germany, German schemes in the United States (Rückwanderer Mark Scheme), and German companies.[16] They also knew about Kurt von Schröder's most recent efforts to help the Nazis. But what about Morgan?

THE HOUSE OF Morgan became a staunch supporter of Great Britain once war was declared. Its failed German-loan portfolio was a thing of the past. Much had changed with the curbs and controls put in place in the United States since 1929, too. In fact, no bank was large enough any longer to bankroll multinational conflicts, as the Morgan, Rothschild, and Baring banks had been in their heydays.

Tom Lamont lobbied President Roosevelt to repeal the Neutrality Act, arguing that the embargo only strengthened Germany's hand. Nonetheless, with Ambassador Kennedy and several isolationist senators like

---

* The Foreign Office's clandestine sabotage and subversion department that would later become known as the Special Operations Executive, or SOE.

Robert La Follette Jr. and Burton K. Wheeler against repeal, Roosevelt suffered a humiliating defeat when Congress rebuffed his first cash-and-carry bill in March 1939. Soon enough, however, it became apparent that Hitler was not satiated with his invasion of Poland that autumn. While the debate in Congress remained fierce, Roosevelt eventually won the day. The new neutrality act of November 1939 permitted arms to be exported to belligerents on a cash-and-carry basis as long as they were not transported on American vessels.

To finance their vast purchases of armaments, the British had to sell whatever they could, and nominated the House of Morgan as the country's agent. The British government either commandeered or sold American securities on the strict proviso that the sales should not trigger any sharp decline in stock prices. Morgan shared a similar operation with Lazard Frères in France. The utmost secrecy was required, and only a few people in each brokerage house knew about the operation. Lamont, however, shared his information with the new British ambassador to the United States, Lord Lothian. Like his dear friend Nancy Astor, Lothian felt he had some repenting to do for his vociferous appeasement days. The Astors and Lothian were among the majority who now renounced Hitler.

Even so, despite its support for Britain, Morgan Bank, like the United States government, was opposed to any U.S. entry into the war, primarily because "there were too many of the devils, and they are too competent."[17] It was the same view shared, albeit for different reasons, by Charles Lindbergh.

BACK IN SEPTEMBER 1938, at the behest of Ambassador Kennedy, Charles and Anne Lindbergh had flown to London. Kennedy gave Lindbergh his take on the Czech crisis and asked the aviator to compile a report on the strength of German aviation. Lindbergh had terrified Kennedy with the notion that even the great fleet of the British Empire could not counter the German aerial juggernaut. Britain was in "no shape for war," since it didn't have the men or modern materiel to fight, Lindbergh told Kennedy. "I am afraid," Lindbergh wrote in his journal, "this is the beginning of the end of England as a great power."

Had Kennedy paused to think how much Lindbergh had come to admire the Germans and Germany? Yes. Kennedy planned to use that to his advantage. Lindbergh wrote in his diary on April 2, 1939, "I believe she [Germany] has pursued the only consistent policy in Europe in recent years. . . . The question of right and wrong is one thing by law and another thing by history." Shortly afterward, Lindbergh made up his mind to return to the United States, where he "could exercise a constructive influence . . . by warning people of the danger of the Soviet Union and by explaining that the destruction of Hitler . . . would probably result in enhancing the still-greater menace of Stalin."[18] Lindbergh maintained his stance for Germany, despite the Molotov-Ribbentrop Pact, signed on August 23.

By that fall, Lindbergh was making racist speeches on the radio and in person. On October 13, he urged the "white populations" to see sense and to fight one another only if "the white race is threatened." Evidently, Jews were not "white." In March 1940, the *Atlantic Monthly* quoted him cynically saying that the French and British were fighting for their possessions, whereas the Germans claimed a valid "right of an able and virile nation to expand—to conquer territory and influence by force of arms as other nations have done at one time or another throughout history."

As the shock and awe over the war grew in America, the "Century Group"* was at the forefront of the argument to stop Hitler. Opposing them, Lindbergh found his voice in a Midwest nativism, stronger and more virulent than his own father's populism. He lashed out against the hated "Money Trust and its dark vision of Anglo-American finance." Despite his three years overseas, he had become a hundred percenter, an America firster, an arch-isolationist. Anne could do little but sorrowfully recall her internationalist father, the Morgan partners who were

---

* There were twenty-eight men who comprised the Century Group, so named because their weekly meetings took place at the Century Association. The first meeting took place on July 11, 1940, shortly after the fall of France. They were all men of significant influence who believed deeply that America could not stand on the sidelines as a spectator, assisting FDR in the campaign of destroyers-for-bases deal, among other early interventions on behalf of the British (source: Chadwin, *Hawks of World War II*, 43–73).

her father's lifelong friends, and the discreet, kindly, "warm rich world" her father inhabited with like-minded souls. She reflected on friends she had left behind and where "Daddy would stand" on the international situation. Old friends, like the Jewish Harry Guggenheim, who had sponsored Lindbergh's three-month tour after his solo flight, refused to have anything further to do with him.[19]

Then, on April 7, 1940, Mussolini invaded Albania. Two days later, Hitler invaded Denmark and Norway. The invasion and capitulation of Denmark was named the Six Hour War. Norway was occupied and all resistance quelled by June 10, thanks to the traitor Norwegian politician Vidkun Quisling. The "Phony War" had ended. Germany had no gripe with either country. No large expatriate community lived there, unlike in America. Propaganda and espionage in the Americas would now take on an entirely new dimension.

Mysteries Within an Enigma

It is a riddle wrapped in a mystery inside an enigma; but perhaps there is a key.

—Winston Churchill, BBC broadcast about Russia

Throughout 1939 and 1940, the greatest opposition to the United States's possible involvement in the war in Europe came from the America First Committee, labor unions, German and Italian immigrants, and midwestern farmers. Their favorite spokesman was Charles Lindbergh, setting him on a collision course with Morgan Bank and his mother-in-law, Betty Morrow. Betty believed firmly that her husband would have favored aid for the Allies.

On May 10, 1940, Germany invaded the Netherlands, Belgium, and France. British forces had fought in Norway, and the British Expeditionary Force was in Belgium and France to face the German onslaught. Although there was a bitter vote of confidence in Parliament that Chamberlain narrowly won that same day, he knew he did not have the backing of the country. Lord Halifax was asked if he would like to be prime minister but refused since he knew he was not the man for the job. Halifax also knew appeasement had mainly benefited Germany. Instead, Winston Churchill was summoned by the king and asked to form the next government. At the age of sixty-five, Churchill magnificently assumed the burden of saving Great Britain.

. . .

FIFTH COLUMNISTS WERE feared throughout Europe and the United States. During that March and April, Carl Edouard, Duke of Saxe-Coburg and Gotha, newly arrived from Tokyo,* toured Southern California. The speakers' stage at the recently renamed Hindenburg Park (now La Crescenta Park in Glendale) was decorated with American and Nazi flags and a single Red Cross flag since Carl Edouard was the president of the German Red Cross. The Aryan Bookstore and the Trinity Sales Company each had a stall selling the latest Nazi newspapers and German books provided by Gienanth's Los Angeles office. But Carl Edouard failed to show. Instead, he was meeting with important Nazis in Santa Barbara. After all, the purpose of his visit was to raise money for the German Red Cross—already complicit in crimes against humanity in Poland and those hospitalized in psychiatric institutions.[1]

CHARLES LINDBERGH NEVER believed that there were fifth columnists in the United States, and was vocal against all the "calamitous chatter." On May 19, Lindbergh took to the airwaves, ostensibly to talk about "the air defense of America." It was a menacing speech against "blind selfishness of party politics" and "powerful elements in America" who controlled the "machinery of influence and propaganda." These unnamed powers would "seize every opportunity to push us closer to the edge," and he begged all Americans to "strike down these elements of personal profits and personal interests." He told Americans no foreign power could conquer the country without an accompanying army, which could never invade by air or sea. "There will be no invasion by foreign aircraft and no foreign navy will dare to approach within bombing range of our coasts," Lindbergh said. "No one wishes to attack us, and no one is in a position to do so." The message to those opposed to Germany was clear. The next

---

* Carl Edouard arrived aboard the *Asana Maru* in San Francisco on March 9, 1940. He had traveled from Germany through the Soviet Union aboard the Trans-Siberian Railway. Accompanying him to Los Angeles was the Austrian baroness Felicitas von Reznicek, who was also Wiedemann's new lover (source: UCN: *News Research Service*, CRC2–103–2, 3).

day, President Roosevelt told the Treasury secretary, Henry Morgenthau, "I am absolutely convinced that Lindbergh is a Nazi."[2]

Also, the aviator had lashed out against the "Money Trust," deeply
offending his mother-in-law. Anne, too, was torn between her internationalist father's memory and her isolationist husband's increasingly
nativistic rhetoric. Their British and French friends were dismayed at
Charles's simplistic—wrongheaded—views. Anne's way of coping was
to write her book *The Wave of the Future* in 1940, in which she tried
valiantly to find a middle way. The Allies represented the "Forces of
the Past" and the Nazis "Forces of the Future." Did she know about the
medieval and barbaric treatment the Germans had already meted out
to their enemies? Dorothy Thompson was merciless in her criticism of
Anne's book in *Look* magazine and accosted her "for saying there was
no way of fighting" communism, fascism, and Nazism.

Where Anne sought a middle way, Charles reveled in being the
brighter, stronger image of his isolationist father, C. A. Lindbergh.
The swift defeat of Norway and Denmark echoed on in Holland, Belgium, and France. Betty Morrow asked Tom Lamont at Morgan Bank
in New York to have a word with Charles after her own efforts to calm
his speechifying failed. Lamont tried but was shocked at Lindbergh's response. There would be "chaotic conditions" that would "destroy American moderation," Lindbergh told him. Later, when asked if he still saw
the Lindberghs, Lamont snapped, "I have nothing to do with them."[3]

LINDBERGH WAS WRONG that there were no fifth columnists in America.
Then, too, as late as May 15, 1940, informed Americans carrying out undercover work did not believe that the Norden bombsight had already
fallen into German hands. "The story of the theft of the bomb-sight . . .
is the same old song," Vincent Astor, a knowledgeable and confidential
source to President Roosevelt, wrote. The fairy tale was regarded by a
certain type of person, "the sort Cholly Knickerbocker calls Café Society. In my opinion there is little to it." By July, the president told the
secretary of the navy, Frank Knox, that he was pretty sure the Germans
had it.[4]

The first drawings for the Norden bombsight had sailed with the

Reliance on November 30, 1937, and over the next two years further drawings would be sent cut up and laid in between sheets of newspapers. "The device contains a number of interesting technical solutions," the Luftwaffe wrote to the Abwehr, and "shows a good structural development." Nikolaus von Ritter had scored his greatest success as spymaster.[5]

Then, in February 1939, Ritter had recruited William G. Sebold. Age forty, Sebold was a naturalized American who had recently quit his job and returned to Germany to visit his mother in Mulheim. On his immigration card, Sebold wrote that he was a "mechanic at the Consolidated Aircraft Company plant in San Diego California." The Gestapo immediately wrote to him to come to nearby Düsseldorf "on a matter that would be of advantage to him and also serve Germany." Sebold declined. He was happy as an American. The Gestapo then blackmailed him, claiming it would notify the Americans that he had served time in Germany for smuggling and "other offenses." So Sebold went and reluctantly agreed to spy for Germany. Eventually, Sebold's dossier was sent to Hamburg, where a Dr. Rankin—Nikolaus von Ritter's new code name—took over as Sebold's handler. Ritter never questioned how Sebold had been recruited and sent him on to the spy school in Hamburg.

Sebold proved to be adept at radio transmissions, so his task on his return stateside was to transmit intelligence back to Hamburg. Armed with a forged passport, a false name, and the code name Tramp, Sebold was told to contact four agents once he arrived. His office, the bogus Diesel Research Company, was in suite 627 of the Knickerbocker Building on the corner of Broadway and Forty-Second Street. Hermann Lang of Norden was one of the Nazi spies who passed their information to Sebold for transmission to Hamburg. The others included Everett Minster Roeder, the Abwehr's most prolific draftsman of detailed technical intelligence in the United States; Lilly Stein, a Vienna-born artist's model who headed recruitment for new agents; and Frederick Joubert "Fritz" Duquesne, the leader of what became known as the Duquesne spy ring. Years earlier, Ritter had painstakingly set up a spy ring under Duquesne, a naturalized U.S. citizen and buccaneer of South African origin.

Sebold's channel proved reliable. It operated so seamlessly that other Abwehr officers in Hamburg asked Ritter to allow Sebold to transmit messages from their agents, too. Puffed up with his successes, Ritter agreed. And so Sebold became a major espionage hub. Paul Fehse, head of the marine division of German espionage reporting on ship movements and developing Nazi sympathizers as potential new spies, used Sebold. Others like Carl Reuper, an inspector at Westinghouse Electric Company in Newark, New Jersey, photographed his employer's defense equipment and sent the information through Sebold. Edmund Carl Heine, a suave and sophisticated Ford Motor Company manager since 1920 who had worked in South America, Spain, Germany, and Detroit, was asked by Ferdinand Porsche to get secret information from other automobile and airplane manufacturers, like the Consolidated Aircraft Corporation. Agents had been strategically placed to purloin the Sperry Gyroscope Company's advanced aircraft autopilot, too. And so the list went on. "Sleepers" like Simon Emil Koedel were activated by seemingly innocuous advertisements in *The New York Times* by the use of the simple word "alloy." There were battalions of spies in America.[6] Yet no one suspected that Sebold had become a double agent for the FBI.

Ritter's successes were impressive. Thanks to his perfect English, he became the main spymaster against Great Britain, with subsidiary offices in Spain and Portugal, too. Given the number of agents he ran, a raft of pseudonyms to avoid detection became necessary if an agent had been blown or captured. The most often used were Dr. Rheinhardt, Dr. Rantzau, Dr. Renken, Dr. Rankin, Mr. Richards, Dr. Hansen, or Mr. von Jorgensen.[7]

In London, Ritter ran a select clutch of spies. Among them was a disgruntled, hopelessly immoderate, small Welshman named Arthur Owens, whom Ritter code-named Johnny. Eight days after the declaration of war, Owens was detected and arrested under Emergency Regulation 18(b) for operating a wireless set given to him by the Germans. He was sent to Wandsworth Prison. Owens had only reported to Ritter three times. By September 19, Johnny was out of jail and had become double agent Snow. Under the direction of MI5, Snow began transmitting weather reports to the Germans. By October, Snow had bedded in nicely and recruited a fellow Welshman to accompany him to spy school in Hamburg. The friend established himself in a stamp business, "old school" espionage according to MI5's director of counterintelligence,

Guy Liddell, where the Germans would send messages on the underside of postage stamps in invisible ink. Soon enough, Snow was running agents, too. Walter Dicketts, a former World War I air intelligence officer discharged for dishonesty, became MI5's agent Celery. In fact, it was through the German use of Snow that the British learned about "microphotography" and the microdot.[8]

ONCE THE WAR in the West began, MI5 swooped on other known agents. It had been keeping tabs on the American embassy for quite some time and had become exasperated with Ambassador Joseph P. Kennedy more than once. "It is difficult to know whether this war is being run by Joe Kennedy, the Home Office or the fighting Services," Guy Liddell wrote in his diary nine days after the war began. Apparently, Kennedy had lectured Lord Halifax on September 4, stating that "Great care must be taken by France and ourselves not to set back American opinion by any air action that would enable American opinion to be brought to think that we had been the first to resort to indiscriminate bombardment." Kennedy's remark was made *after* he had been notified of the sinking of the SS *Athenia*, which had thirteen hundred American, Canadian, and refugee civilians on board.

It must have given Liddell enormous pleasure when, on May 19, 1940, Maxwell Knight saw chargé d'affaires Herschel Johnson at the U.S. embassy in London. MI5 had had an American code-room clerk named Tyler Gatewood Kent under surveillance for quite some time, and they had proof that Kent was a close associate of the couturiere and White émigré Anna Wolkoff and Captain Archibald Maule Ramsay, MP, the leading light of the Right Club. Knight told Johnson that MI5 knew for some while that Tyler Kent had been secreting documents out of the embassy and believed they were being leaked to the Italians and Germans.[9] Johnson knew this meant *all* the U.S. embassy codes were compromised, including the supposed unbreakable "gray code" used by the president.

It wasn't the first time Kent had come under suspicion. While stationed in Moscow, the embassy had a tip that Kent was passing intelligence to the Soviets through his Russian girlfriend, Tatiana "Tanya"

Alexandrovna Ilovaiskaya, an agent for the GPU (Soviet secret service). It is hardly surprising that Ambassador William C. Bullitt discovered Kent's complicity with the Soviets, calling him "a complete rotter and always has been." So why had Kent not been dismissed instead of being sent to the most prestigious post as a cipher clerk in the London embassy? Some think it was because his father was a diplomat and known to the U.S. secretary of state, Cordell Hull. But was Kennedy ever informed of Kent's dubious past? These questions, despite a raft of material, remain unanswered.[10]

THE TIMING OF the raid on Kent's address was no accident. Churchill had become prime minister on May 10 and immediately ordered a tightening of security. A panicked Ambassador Kennedy wrote to Hull on May 15: "England will never give up so long as he remains a power in public life . . . even if England is burnt to the ground." Kennedy already knew that there had been direct correspondence between Churchill as first lord of the admiralty and President Roosevelt. He was disconsolate at Churchill's appointment as prime minister, too. That same day, Churchill sent an encoded telegram to Roosevelt that he expected him to deliver on his promise with "everything short of engaging armed forces" and made his first request for "40 or 50 destroyers" and "aircraft, submarines, munitions, and steel" to keep Britain fighting. Roosevelt responded the next day that he was doing his level best in a hostile environment.

The outspoken isolationist senators like William E. Borah (Republican, Idaho), Robert La Follette Jr. (Progressive, Wisconsin), and particularly Gerald Nye (Republican, North Dakota, whose committee studied the causes of the U.S. involvement in the Great War) were being courted by the America First Committee, and its popular voice, Charles Lindbergh. Much about the American system of government remained opaque to an increasingly exasperated British government, too, since it was unable to appreciate the almighty power of the Senate Foreign Relations Committee. Where Chamberlain had been uncaring about the president's difficulties, Churchill struggled to cope with Roosevelt's inability to take decisions simply with his cabinet. He even viewed this sphinx-like committee with some disdain. Roosevelt knew, at best, he could only hope for a majority of thirteen to twelve that May.[11]*

WHEN JOE KENNEDY opened his door on Saturday, May 18, to Captain Maxwell Knight and Herschel Johnson, he had to do some quick thinking. Knight advised that the twenty-nine-year-old Kent was suspected of espionage and involvement with the Right Club; Anna Wolkoff, a known White émigré spy; and the flamboyant Italian military attaché, Duke Francesco del Monte Marigliano.[†] Kent had been a person of interest to MI5 within three days of arriving in London on October 5, 1939. Knight then gave the background to Kent's Soviet espionage work in Moscow.

Immediately, Kennedy felt threatened. He had been an uncompromising and scathing critic of the war. If he handled this incident poorly, not only would his diplomatic career end in dishonor, but his sons'

---

* There were twenty-three senators who served on the Foreign Relations Committee, which had the power to veto the selection of ambassadors and other high officials and to alter, delay, and, in certain political circumstances, veto almost any piece of major legislation or treaty in this field—including joining the League of Nations. The Senate Foreign Relations Committee at the time was composed of fifteen Democrats, seven Republicans, and one Progressive. The Democrats were Connally of Texas (chairman), Barkley of Kentucky, George of Georgia, Glass of Virginia, Thomas of Utah, Wagner of New York, Van Nuys of Indiana, Green of Rhode Island, Reynolds of North Carolina, Guffey of Pennsylvania, Gillette of Iowa, Tunnell of Delaware, Clark of Missouri, Pepper of Florida, Murray of Montana. The Republicans were Johnson of California, Nye of North Dakota, Capper of Kansas, Vandenberg of Michigan, White of Maine, Shipstead of Minnesota, Davis of Pennsylvania. The Progressive member was La Follette of Wisconsin (source: Thomas E. Hachey, "American Profiles on Capitol Hill: A Confidential Study for the British Foreign Office, 1943," *Wisconsin Magazine of History* 57, no. 2 [Winter 1973–74], JSTOR).

† Guy Burgess, the notorious British elite broadcaster, spy, and later diplomat, was working for MI6 at the time and claimed that it was he who had divulged Kent's activities. As a BBC reporter (undercover for MI6), he passed information to Churchill. Given that Burgess was a double agent working for the Soviets, it is fascinating that under *their* orders, he revealed Kent's spy network in London, meaning that the Soviets did *not* want White émigrés plotting against the USSR (source: email correspondence with Paul Willetts, author of *Rendezvous at the Russian Tea Rooms,* and FDR Presidential Library, Small Collections, Memoranda and Notes, Container 3).

political careers would be snuffed out, too. The immediate problem was that only Kennedy could strip Kent of his diplomatic immunity. This was necessary to legally search Kent's home—deemed an extension of the embassy as long as he had immunity. Kennedy's mind raced. It was the eve of the Democratic presidential nominations and Joe Jr. was a novice delegate with the Massachusetts representatives to the convention.

Captain Knight made it quite clear that the British wanted to try Kent and his accomplices under English law, but they needed his cooperation to do so. Kennedy's alternatives were stark. If he chose to "hush it up" or fire Kent, he would be deported by the British publicly as a suspected spy for the Germans. It would be electoral manna for the Republican candidate against Roosevelt. Of course, Joe Jr.'s future mattered more than Kent's, but Kennedy hemmed and hawed, hoping that Knight could keep it out of the press. Knight made no promises.

Kennedy saw that he had no options and agreed to cooperate. While Frank Gowen from the embassy accompanied Knight and his men on their raids of the rooms belonging to Kent and Wolkoff, Kennedy advised Hull of the breach in security. Without delay, Hull designated Herschel Johnson as the sole person to handle sensitive encryption and decryption of messages until further notice.

During the raid on Kent's premises, over two thousand decrypted messages dating from 1938 to the present along with a locked red leather ledger were discovered. The messages effectively dated from a year *before* Kent's employment in London and the whole of Joe Kennedy's term as ambassador. Kent immediately claimed diplomatic immunity and that these were for his "personal use." The most damning was a pencil note Kent had made of "a highly confidential dispatch from the British prime minister to President Roosevelt" decoded in the early hours of May 19–20, found in Kent's jacket pocket. He was due to hand it across to his Italian accomplice that evening. Kent was taken to the embassy, where Kennedy told him he was stripped of all diplomatic privileges, then on to prison. Anna Wolkoff was arrested the same day.

By May 23, the highly confidential cable exchange between Churchill and Roosevelt on May 15 and 16 had been passed from Tyler Kent to Anna Wolkoff and on to the Italians. William Joyce, Oswald Mosley's former ally now exiled in Berlin, broadcasted the gist of some of these in the following days under his new identity as Lord Haw-Haw.[12]*

AN UNINTENDED CONSEQUENCE—PERHAPS—WAS the discussion that took place at MI5 on the evening of May 21. The home secretary, Sir John Anderson; Sir Vernon Kell, director general of MI5; Sir Alexander Maxwell, who was responsible for implementing Defence Regulation 18(b) for the Home Office; Sir Charles Peake, chief press adviser to the Ministry of Information; Sir Alan Brooke, commander of the II Corps of the BEF (British Expeditionary Force); Guy Liddell; and Maxwell Knight were present. The agenda was who should be taken into custody under the terms of Defence Regulation 18(b).

The home secretary found it difficult to imagine that Sir Oswald Mosley or anyone from the BUF would assist the enemy. In a recent edition of *Action,* Mosley quite clearly "had appealed to the patriotism of its members." Knight said it was just another example of Mosley's insincerity and that "many of his supporters simply regarded utterances of that kind as a figure of speech." He then told the others about the "underground activities of the BUF and the recent case against Tyler Kent involving Captain Archibald Ramsay." Knight said that Mosley and Ramsay were "in constant touch with one another" and that many members of the BUF were also members of Ramsay's Right Club. Anderson said that he needed better proof to detain peers of the realm. He got it later that day. Both Ramsay, who Anderson admitted was a grave danger, and Mosley, who he did not, were interned on May 23. Diana Mosley had recently given birth to her son Max but would join her husband in Holloway Prison after the fall of France in June.[13]†

---

* Anna Wolkoff had not known that Tyler Kent was a double agent for the Soviets. I thank Paul Willetts for taking the time to share his research with me in copious correspondence and agree with him that Kent was a double agent. The Soviets also received the cables through Kent.
† By 1940, another Mitford sister, Jessica, known as "Decca" in the family, had moved with her husband and second cousin, Esmond Romilly, to the United States after

Earlier that spring, David Redesdale, the Mitford girls' father, could take no more of the pro-Hitler rantings from his wife or invalid daughter Unity. Although Hitler had paid for Unity to be repatriated via Switzerland, Redesdale felt aristocrats like himself had been led up the proverbial garden path by Hitler's lies. Despite Unity's amazing recovery and the improvement of the paralysis on one side of her body, her hand hung loosely at her side and was barely manageable. Redesdale's beautiful daughter had become loud, careless, and physically gauche. So he moved out, first to Inch Kenneth, an island off the west coast of Scotland, then to Redesdale Cottage in Northumberland. His wife, Sydney, however, stayed and made caring for Unity her life's work. Unity would eventually die in May 1948 from meningitis caused by the bullet wound to her head. Diana never admitted any fault in taking her sister to the first Nuremberg rally in 1933. "The end would have been the same whether I had taken her to Germany or not," she said.[14]

As NEWS OF the arrest and proposed trials of Tyler Kent, Anna Wolkoff, and Captain Archibald Maule Ramsay made headline news, young second lieutenant T. V. W. Willes of the Second Royal Gloucester Hussars felt it was his patriotic duty to notify the authorities about his last encounter with Anna Wolkoff, back in 1936. He alleged to Special Branch in June 1940 that he had met Anna with Princess Mira Romanovsky Koutousov (aka Princess Dimitri) in Austria in the summer of 1936, when the princess had confided to him that she was a spy in the pay of the Italians. Since her husband, Prince Dimitri, was a lieutenant in the Royal Navy stationed at Ramsgate and his duties included contraband control and acting as part of search parties, a warrant was issued. Like so many White émigrés, the princess had been motivated to spy for

---

serving in the Spanish Civil War for the Republicans. The pair led a peripatetic life, traveling from New York to Washington and then to Miami. Romilly volunteered for the Royal Canadian Air Force in 1940 and was shot down and killed in January 1942. Romilly was also Winston Churchill's nephew (source: www.washingtonpost.com /archive/local/1996/07/25/muckraking-author-jessica-mitford-dies/d5aace57–4d0e -49aa-aa63–03827166b729/).

anyone who could return her to Mother Russia and the life she could never live again.

Anna Wolkoff—once couturiere to the princesses Dimitri and Stephanie as well as Wallis Simpson—was sentenced to ten years' imprisonment. Tyler Kent received seven years' imprisonment but was deported to the United States at the end of the war. Captain Archibald Maule Ramsay, despite his aristocratic heritage and position as a member of Parliament, was detained under Defence Regulation 18(b). The ledger obtained in Kent's rooms gave MI5 the complete list of names of members of the Right Club, who were—to varying degrees—put under surveillance or detained.

MI5 had no doubts that Princess Dimitri had been spying back in 1936. That said, "the princess has been revealed as a highly unreliable and undesirable person who periodically pursues alcohol and sex with equal determination and lack of discrimination," the report concluded. Given the close connection to the British royal family, and the fact that nothing concrete against her could be found, the investigation closed without action in 1943. She would divorce her husband shortly after the war and emigrate to the United States. Her last known job was as a saleswoman at Saks Fifth Avenue in New York City.[15]

IN JUNE 1940, as machine guns were mounted into position on the rooftops of Whitehall and signposts were removed from all roads to confuse potential invaders, there were growing calls to round up the "B"- and "C"-class enemy aliens. From the north of Scotland to the English Channel, some three thousand living within twenty miles of the coast were removed from their homes. The category "A"—or the most dangerous prisoners, like Putzi Hanfstaengl—were sent to Canada aboard three ships. Putzi arrived in Quebec that June and was interned at Camp Henry in southwestern Ontario.[16]

June 1940 was to prove a watershed for the Duke and Duchess of Windsor, too. The week after the miraculous rescue of over three hundred thousand Allied troops from Dunkirk, Paris was abandoned by its fearful inhabitants. All roads leading south were jammed with refugees and troops hoping to escape. Undoubtedly, by June 15—five days after the government left Paris—France was falling. Yet Edward dithered. Apparently, he had been waiting for word from London, but none came.

The Duke of Windsor had held the rank of major general to the British Military Mission at French General Headquarters since September 1939 and had remained in Paris with his mission until May 28, 1940, when he requested (and was granted) a transfer to *l'armée des Alpes* on the Italian frontier and close to his home at Antibes. On June 10, the Italians entered the war as Germany's ally and attacked the South of France. They were repulsed, but the duke and duchess's position was precarious. At midday on June 19, just as the French sued for peace, the Windsors set out for Spain with their three Cairn terriers and their driver, George Ladbrook, at the wheel of their Buick. Wallis's maid followed in their Citroën, towing a luggage trailer.* Piper Alistair Fletcher, the duke's manservant, and Marguerite Moulichon, the duchess's French maid, brought up the rear with a hired van containing the Windsors' luggage. The duchess was disconsolate at leaving behind her *maître cuisinier* Pinaudier and his wife, but such were the sacrifices of war.[17]

Edward understood that setting out for Spain on choked roads without the appropriate paperwork was a gamble. Both he and Major Gray Phillips (the duke's comptroller) stood a halfway decent chance of being interned at the border as soldiers on active service attempting to escape to a neutral country—that is, if Spain was still neutral. They decided to follow an inland route and reached Arles by nightfall, setting off early again on June 20 for Barcelona. Despite facing several barricades, the party was waved through each time as the prince announced, "*Je suis le Prince de Galles. Laissez-moi passer s'il vous plaît.*"† Their first real test came at Perpignan, near the Spanish border, where the Spanish consul refused to grant them visas, fearing they would become a charge upon the impoverished Spanish state.

Edward, after "much persuasion," was allowed to cable the Spanish ambassador at Bordeaux and the British ambassador in Madrid (Sir

---

* Fruity Metcalfe had resigned in disgust as the duke's equerry.

† Translated as, "I am the Prince of Wales. Please let me pass." Of course, that title had not been accurate since becoming king and he should have identified himself simply as Edward, Duke of Windsor.

Samuel Hoare, whom Edward had consulted over his abdication), and all roadblocks were cleared, save for George Ladbrook. He was driving the luggage van and was ordered to return to Antibes—and more adventures. By midnight on June 20, the duke's party reached safety and the relative comfort of a hotel in Barcelona.

The following morning, Edward strode to the British consulate general and sent a cable to Churchill, care of the Foreign Office: "HAVING RECEIVED NO INSTRUCTIONS HAVE ARRIVED IN SPAIN TO AVOID CAPTURE. PROCEEDING TO MADRID. EDWARD."[18]

"Willi"

They talked freely of everything except their plans.
—*The New York Times*, June 26, 1940,
of the Duke and Duchess of Windsor

Sir Samuel Hoare, demoted to the post of British ambassador to Spain by Churchill, informed the Foreign Office on the evening of June 20 that he intended to show "His Royal Highness the usual courtesies" and planned to facilitate his passage to neutral Portugal. "In view of the press articles here saying that it is intended to arrest him on arrival in England," Hoare asked, "please confirm by telegram that I am acting correctly." Churchill knew that, while Hoare had made a lamentable foreign minister, he would make a competent ambassador able to play games of intrigue for his country.[1]*

Before the Windsors arrived in Madrid, Hoare informed Churchill, "every kind of rumour was spread by the German Embassy. Under pressure by the Germans, the Spanish press declared that . . . he [Edward] had come here to make a separate peace behind your back, that he had always disapproved of the war . . . etc., etc." On June 23, the Windsors were safely ensconced in Madrid and the Foreign Office cabled Hoare "asking him 'to inform His Royal Highness that a Flying

---

* On another occasion, Sir Samuel Hoare would find himself severely reprimanded by Churchill for meeting with and giving credence to Prince Max-Egon von Hohenlohe-Langenburg, Princess Stephanie's relation by marriage, who was a known spy for the Third Reich in Spain.

Boat is leaving the United Kingdom for Lisbon on June 24' and to 'invite Their Royal Highnesses [sic] to proceed to Lisbon.'"2* Then came the first hitch.

Prince George, Duke of Kent, was scheduled to arrive in Lisbon on June 24 at the head of the British delegation to celebrate eight hundred years of Portuguese independence and the ancient friendship between the two countries since 1373, which no war had affected. So the Windsors were told in no uncertain terms that they would need to remain in Madrid until George departed.

Meanwhile, tales of "the fleeing Windsors" eating only sardines were headlined in *The New York Times*, and the German ambassador, Dr. Eberhard Baron von Stohrer, came under considerable pressure. Remembered by the Nazis for having saved German Jews in Egypt after Hitler came to power, Stohrer's own position within the foreign ministry had only been safeguarded by his close friendship with the parents of Rudolf Hess. He was not an ardent Nazi, but under the kaiser served his country well in Spain. Stohrer formed a good working relationship with Franco's brother-in-law and interior minister, Ramón Serrano Suñer, and together they ensured that German aid to the nationalists was effectively distributed. Nonetheless, the Nazi Party regarded him as suspect, and his embassy was filled with Gestapo agents.

Like so many, Stohrer hated Ribbentrop, particularly as he was attempting to bring Spain into the war. When he received instructions from Ribbentrop that the Windsors were "to be kept in Spain, for Ribbentrop evidently believed that he could play the Duke off against the new King and the existing British Government," Stohrer sighed and nodded for the German propaganda mill to whir away.

Ribbentrop demanded that Edward should remain in Spain. A credible Spanish intermediary was thought necessary, and the hunt was on. Don Javier "Tiger" Bermejillo y Schmidtlein proved to be the perfect go-between. Tiger had been friendly with both Edward as the Prince of Wales and the Ernest Simpsons while he served as secretary to the

---

* The official rebuke of the Foreign Office official who had described the Duchess of Windsor as "royal" can be found in FO800/326/195. This remained a bone of contention for the duke until his death.

Spanish embassy in London. Collectively, they adored him. He was a frequent guest, too, at Fort Belvedere in more halcyon days. When the Spanish Civil War broke out, Tiger was imprisoned by the Republicans and appealed to Edward to help. Soon after, Tiger was evacuated in a refugee exchange.[3]

The trusted Tiger met up with the ducal party in Barcelona and accompanied them to Madrid. Rooms had been booked for them at the Ritz, and Ambassador Hoare greeted them with the first reliable news they had in a month: they would be welcomed home. Still, Edward's old fear of not being useful reemerged. Edward *demanded* to know if he was to have a job back home. Hoare replied, "If he fails to return to England within a few days, all sorts of mischievous rumours will circulate about him."

Hoare advised Churchill that as ambassador he needed to say something about Edward's future *before* departing for Lisbon, otherwise the duke might refuse to return. An exasperated Hoare confided to Lord Halifax, "I feel that you will never have peace and perhaps I shall never get him away from here unless you can find something for him." He also said that unless Edward could be isolated somehow—perhaps a naval command—"there will be a prince over the water who will be a nuisance and possibly an embarrassment."[4]

Simultaneously, Tiger was instructed by Colonel Beigbeder y Atienza at the behest of Ribbentrop to offer a free stay for the duration of the war to the Windsors. They could stay at the Palace of the Moorish Kings (*casa del rey moro*) in the remote mountains of Ronda in Andalusia as the guests of the Spanish government. Living like a king again, at no expense to himself, treated like the royalty he was instead of begging for a job and being cold-shouldered in Britain, would feel sublime. So sublime that Edward cabled Churchill asking, What was the hurry for him to return?

Then Edward made his second misbegotten request. Could Tiger arrange for their properties to be secured against plunder by the occupying forces? Tiger dutifully passed the message on. Ribbentrop's emissary in Paris, Otto Abetz (soon to be named ambassador to occupied France), immediately obeyed the duke's request. In due course, the duchess's hapless maid, Marguerite Moulichon, was on her way to their Boulevard

Suchet home in Paris to retrieve some sought-after linen, furniture, silver, and porcelain—as well as the duke's memorabilia.*

Hoare was right to be nervous about Edward's presence amid the intrigue in Spain. It would have been entirely in character for either the duke or duchess to drop an indiscretion in idle dinner table conversation. All it took was a sympathetic ear and the illusion of privacy. A case in point was when Edward told Alexander Weddell, the U.S. ambassador in Madrid, "the most important thing to be done now was to end the war before thousands more were killed or maimed to save the faces of a few politicians."[5]

The remark was repeated to Churchill. Until recently, Edward's close connection with Charles Bedaux had been unappreciated by MI6 and the American FBI. In 1939, on a "heaven-sent opportunity of visiting the French front," Edward had teased out secrets from the French that their defenses north of the Maginot Line were inadequate to repel tanks. His report found its way onto General Guderian's desk. Shortly after, German Panzers broke through the French lines precisely at this point. "The question that would logically follow," historian Jonathan Petropoulos wrote, "center on whether espionage or indiscretion contributed to this superiority and whether the Windsors were the source of any intelligence." Eventually, suspicion fell on Charles Bedaux, who had been ingratiating himself with the Windsors *and* the Nazis. Edward, however, was the source of the information.

Churchill knew, too, neither the king nor his queen wanted the Windsors back in England. In fact, Alec Hardinge wrote to Churchill that it would be difficult to respond positively to Edward's plea for work "as an ex-King . . . in this country."[6†] A standoff was inevitable. Churchill demanded their return without any preconditions. Edward replied,

---

* Their Parisian home had already been entrusted to the Americans for protection, along with British diplomatic property, and once the United States entered the war, the order was still honored. Marguerite would suffer all sorts of trials in her efforts to please the duchess.

† Today, by comparing the Allied and German records, a convincing case can be made that Edward's careless remarks made in private to "friends" played a part in Hitler's directing his generals to change the battle plan for the invasion of Belgium, Luxembourg, the Netherlands, and France.

demanding meaningful employment. Then the duke upped the ante: he would return if both he *and his wife* were received by the king and queen *and* notice of this "meeting" would appear in the Court Circular. Edward was unprepared that both he and his wife should be "pushed . . . into a bottom drawer." The request received no reply during their nine days in Madrid. Wild rumors swirled in the Spanish press (dictated by the Germans), making the duke and duchess increasingly nervous.[7]

ON JULY 1, Prince George left Lisbon, and the Windsors were free to finish their journey. Hoare warned the Foreign Office that he did not believe "they will return to England without further assurances." Instead, Edward was happy to go to Lisbon and await the reply to his most recent demand. They could always return to Spain and accept the government's generous offer to treat him like the king he once was, he intimated to Hoare. Churchill was dutifully warned that the rift with the family needed to be healed. It was impossible to predict how the Windsors would react—or, indeed, what they might do, Hoare wrote.

In fact, Edward had already told the Spanish that he would only return to England if "his wife were recognized as a member of the Royal Family and he were given an influential post of a military or civil nature." That message arrived on Ribbentrop's desk on July 2, triggering an incredible plot to kidnap the Windsors.

Perhaps it was fitting that their residence outside Lisbon along the Estremadura Peninsula at Cascais was called *o boca do inferno*—"the mouth of hell." Once there, Edward was all too conscious he was being spied upon. On July 2 he was handed a cable from Churchill: "YOUR ROYAL HIGHNESS HAS TAKEN ACTIVE MILITARY RANK AND REFUSAL TO OBEY DIRECT ORDERS OF COMPETENT MILITARY AUTHORITY WOULD CREATE A SERIOUS SITUATION." In other words, return to England or face a court-martial. Recognizing that Churchill meant to carry out his threat, Edward relented at last and agreed to return to England without further delay or preconditions. He, nonetheless, wrote that he abhorred Churchill's "gangster methods," which the duchess had him change to "dictator methods" in his reply.[8]

But before arrangements could be made, Edward received word that his brother George VI would be pleased if he would take up the duties of the governor of the Bahamas as soon as possible. Edward petulantly accepted, threatening to "reconsider his position" if the travel arrangements *he* wanted were not agreed upon and told his Spanish "friends" who were also Nazi agents. He intended to go via New York, and no one would stop him. Edward made tentative arrangements to travel on a small ship of the American Export Line, sailing on August 1. Of course, he was unmindful that President Roosevelt had just been renominated as the Democratic candidate for his controversial third term and that welcoming the ex-king would have been manna to FDR's Republican opponent, Wendell Willkie. In no circumstances was it convenient for the Windsors to come. So when Churchill's request to Roosevelt that the vessel, the *Excalibur,* divert to Bermuda before docking at New York, the president agreed.[9] From Bermuda, the Windsors would board another ship for Nassau.

As THE DAYS turned into weeks, Edward's hemming and hawing over what he might do became increasingly problematic. In fact, on July 11, Berlin was advised of the duke's appointment as governor of the Bahamas by the German ambassador to Lisbon, Oswald von Hoyningen-Huene. He wrote that it is "intended to keep him far away from England, since his return would bring with it very strong encouragement to English friends of peace," the official record shows. It says categorically that the duke's "arrest at the instance of his opponents would certainly have to be expected." Indeed, message no. 661 from Lisbon on July 11 to Berlin goes on to state that Edward would delay his departure for the Bahamas as long as possible "in hope of a turn of events favorable to him. He is convinced that if he had remained on the throne war would have been avoided." Huene concludes with the treasonous statement from Edward, "The Duke definitely believes that continued severe bombings would make England ready for peace."[10]

Edward was aware that there were MI6 operatives among the staff, and that the Portuguese, too, were keeping a vigilant eye on his every word and deed, yet he still confided in his friend and Nazi agent Tiger Bermejillo y Schmidtlein. On reading the telegram Ribbentrop became fixated on kidnapping the Windsors. He had discussed it with Hitler, who was quite pleased with the plan. Ribbentrop "had a special gift for getting hold of some political idea of Hitler's and then . . . bringing his own ideas into line with it," Weizsäcker noted, "and then outbidding him in the same direction."

When the invasion of Britain came, Edward would be placed back on the throne as the Nazis' puppet. The lamebrained plot—code-named Operation Willi—had gained traction quickly and became part of the Nazi "sacred mythology." Such had been the desire to kidnap the Windsors that Stohrer received a cable on July 12, ordering him to comply with Ribbentrop and whomever he sent to handle the actual kidnapping. A second Spaniard, Don Miguel Primo de Rivera (the civil governor of Madrid), became the next emissary of the Germans while Tiger handled getting the duchess's maid in and out of Paris safely. Don Miguel had known Edward during his visit to Spain in 1927 and had lavishly entertained the Windsors during their nine days in Madrid.

Ribbentrop's elaborate scheme would be executed by Walter Schellenberg, the protégé of Reinhard Heydrich, Himmler's nefarious offsider and one of the main architects of the Holocaust. Schellenberg had been compiling Hitler's "Black Book," outlining what to thieve and who should live or die after the successful invasion of Britain, when he was informed of his new task. He was ordered to fly to Lisbon at once and offer the Windsors safe passage and accommodation as well as fifty million Swiss francs. All the duke had to do in exchange was work for Germany, and Schellenberg would remove him from the clutches of the British. In the meantime, to facilitate Schellenberg's task, the Windsors were repeatedly told by local German agents that they would be murdered by the British if they left Portugal.

Naturally, Churchill did not trust Edward to go to the Bahamas willingly and sent Walter Monckton (who had supported Edward during the abdication) to Portugal to persuade the couple they were in no danger from the British. By the time Schellenberg arrived in Lisbon, Edward had sent a one-line telegram to Churchill confirming their departure on the *Excalibur*. Schellenberg wrote in his diary, *"Willi will nicht"*—meaning Willi, the code name for the duke, would not go.[11]

Herding Cats

O, what a tangled web we weave when first we practice to deceive.
—Sir Walter Scott, *Marmion: A Tale of Flodden Field*

The trade winds blew gently over the Bahamian archipelago that August when the Windsors disembarked at Nassau, New Providence Island. Their "keen disappointment" at their posting was known to the local administrators, since Edward had referred to it in writing as "wretched" and looked upon "the prospect of an indefinite period of exile on those Islands with profound gloom and despondency." To Winston Churchill, he wrote that his appointment as governor was a "banishment" and "as good a war time expedience for a hopeless and insoluble situation as could be found."

As they descended the gangplank, they were greeted by the Governor's Executive Council, the highest decision-making body in the Bahamas. Despite the 85 percent black and mixed-race majority, no black individual sat on the Governor's Executive Council or served in any official capacity. Nonetheless, the Black community turned out in the thousands to welcome the new governor and his wife.[1]

From the outset, the Windsors did little to make themselves amenable to anyone. Complaints about the climate were freely aired. It was mid-August, and the humidity and heat meant they constantly perspired. Wallis dubbed it the "Nassau drip." Government House, their residence, was deemed shabby (which it was), but also structurally unsound (which it may or may not have been) when a chunk of ceiling collapsed during their first week. The council was obliged to agree to an additional expenditure of five thousand pounds to the previous budget of two thousand pounds for the renovation. Edward asked London if he might not be able to take a three-month leave of absence while the works were carried out. London replied: it would be inappropriate. Sir Harry Oakes offered his Cable Beach mansion for the duration of the renovations, which Wallis had the poor grace to call "a shack by the sea." It hadn't been the best of beginnings for a high-unemployment, backward-looking colony or its millionaire inhabitants.[2]*

The economy, so Edward was told, depended heavily on tourism—particularly from the United States. The colony was underdeveloped and had high unemployment, while its white traders, like Harold Christie, his good friend Sir Harry Oakes (who owned the fabulous gold mine next to the Mitfords' dud in Canada), and the Swedish Electrolux millionaire Axel Wenner-Gren thrived.

Of course, Wenner-Gren was known to Edward. Charles Bedaux had introduced him as the man prepared to back Edward's "peace campaign." Wenner-Gren, who owned nearby Hog Island (later rechristened Paradise Island), which he also developed, may not have realized that he had been labeled a Nazi propagandist. He was also noted in MI6's and the FBI's files as a friend of Göring's and as one of the Reichsmarschall's financiers through his bank in Mexico. Wenner-Gren owned the Bank of Bahamas and Andros Bahamas Development Company, too.[3] His relationships also stretched to business and political leaders in Mexico, Argentina, and Peru. His business interests had been watched with some alarm in America, particularly by J. Edgar Hoover at the FBI.

IN THE ABSENCE of any international-intelligence-gathering organization, J. Edgar Hoover's G-men were ordered to work in tandem with Canadian-born William Stephenson, the senior representative of British Security Coordination (BSC), since the British had a good international

---

* What hadn't been accounted for in the renovation costs was an entirely new three-story west wing with four guest suites to accommodate the Windsors' personal staff as well as individual air-conditioning units set in the windows of all the major rooms. The duchess also had to hire a professional interior designer from New York and purchase period French furniture (source: Turnquest, *What Manner of Man Is This?*, 56).

network for undercover work.* Independently, and thanks to William Sebold in his separate operation, the FBI were following the movements of Ritter's most successful spy ring.

Rather surprisingly, the actions of I.G. Farben and its New York subsidiary, Chemnyco, were still under the radar. Back in July 1939, due to an antitrust investigation into nitrogen fertilizers, the Department of Justice sought further information from Chemnyco. In response, Rudolf Ilgner ordered several "minor employees" to "work late the night" before investigators arrived, according to a secret government report, "and cleaned out the files of the company using a pulverizing machine to destroy documents." Caught red-handed without any documents to show, Ilgner "pleaded guilty to the charge of obstructing justice and paid the $1,000 fine." He remained, however, a leading figure in the German-American Chamber of Commerce. As late as July 1941, Ilgner was invited to a conference of American manufacturers, conferring on "the latest methods and practices in employment relations, with particular emphasis on the impact of National Defense."[4]

Vast numbers of expert I.G. Farben employees had been coming to the United States since 1933 "under the auspices of Chemnyco," creating a "veritable bonanza of industrial intelligence." Chemnyco requested visits for them at hundreds of key American industrial plants throughout the country. As an example, Dr. W. Ziegler and Dr. E. de Ridder, heads of the light metals and light metals research division, were received at the West Coast aircraft manufacturers Douglas, Vultee, Consolidated, and Lockheed. The visits, "as part of an inspection tour of aircraft plants from coast to coast, were made with the permission of the United States Department of War, obtained by Chemnyco." Ilgner also personally arranged for German spies to operate at key locations, like Captain E. C. Becker, who worked at the Brooklyn Navy Yard.[5]

I.G. Farben had taken a controlling stake in most of the local chemical firms in Latin America, too, blocking DuPont and other American multinationals from making headway there. Alfredo Moll, an Argentinian

---

* The BSC was informally referred to as the "Baker Street Club." The OSS, the precursor of the CIA, was founded in 1941, with General William "Wild Bill" Donovan as its chief. "Little Bill," as Stephenson was called, worked frequently with Wild Bill.

national and the son of Carl Moll, one of the original I.G. founders, was I.G.'s Latin American powerhouse. Dietrich August Schmitz, the brother of Hermann Schmitz, arranged for these same Latin American companies (controlled by I.G.) to sell their products into the United States. Outlets for sales in Mexico, Brazil, Chile, Peru, Colombia, and Argentina had been in operation since 1925, with the I.G.-owned Swiss bank, Greufert and Cie, listed as their ultimate owner. In addition, monies earned in Latin America were channeled back through Chemnyco, which also collected most I.G. royalties in the Western Hemisphere.

Moll disbursed funds from the "S-Kasse" in Argentina. "S" stood for "special expenses," ranging from off-book/off-balance-sheet transactions for "palm oil" (meaning greasing "palms" for bribes), pensions and "additional salaries" to employees and managers in Latin America (not subject to taxation), payments between Germany and countries where bank clearing was not permitted, contributions to German institutions from schools and consulates to the AO to pay its spies, or any other special purpose as ordered by I.G. Frankfurt or Leverkusen central finance office. The "S-Kassen" throughout Latin America were physically topped up by diplomatic couriers to German embassies and consulates.

In fact, Moll's lieutenants were strategically placed as Bayer employees throughout Central America. Who would question an aspirin workforce, especially if it was not known they were really working for the explosives division? Bayer's Otto Reinebeck in Guatemala handled countries north of the Panama Canal Zone, and Erwin Grosser, the local Bayer manager in San José, Costa Rica, handled the areas to the south. Panama had its own German consul, while Hermann Schmitz personally oversaw how the Panamanian government could take a progressively pro-Axis stance, in the hope of blocking the canal to American shipping. With an imposing organization in Colombia under the direction of Dietrich Schmitz and Walter H. Duisberg (son of another I.G. founder), and over seven billion dollars annually received from Axis companies in the United States, the I.G. threat to America was hydra-headed and palpable.[6*]

---

* The Colombian operations comprised Anilinas Alemanas, Quimica Bayer, and Agfa.

. . .

FRITZ WIEDEMANN WAS reportedly Rudolf Ilgner's man on the West
Coast, specializing in the entry of I.G. agents heading to the United
States and Latin America through the port of San Francisco. It was Princess Stephanie's job to act on I.G.'s orders, too. During 1940, she made
several trips to Central America, particularly to Panama and Mexico,
some with Wiedemann.[7]

In early July 1940, in a little-known incident, Dr. Herbert H. Hoehne
and Dr. Emil Wolff, two chemists (explosives experts, to be precise) who
were employed by I.G., were dispatched to Panama. So, too, was Princess Stephanie—although her presence there would not become part
of the public record until exactly eleven months later. Dr. Hoehne had
entered the United States aboard the Japanese vessel *Amara Maru* at San
Francisco and was met aboard ship by a representative of the German
consulate. Hoehne was rapidly cleared through customs and brought
directly to Fritz Wiedemann, where Hoehne was briefed that the Pacific
Fleet had been moved from San Diego to Pearl Harbor in Hawaii the
previous May. Wiedemann then gave Hoehne documents, maps, and
money to transmit to Ernst Neumann, the German consul in Panama.
Then, Dr. Hoehne, age twenty-nine, set out for Los Angeles and his on-
ward journey to Mexico, Panama, and eventually Argentina.

Simultaneously, the chemist Dr. Emil Wolff landed in Panama, presumably to meet with Consul Neumann and Princess Stephanie. Hoehne
was arrested at Los Angeles Airport by Hoover's G-men just as Wolff was
waylaid in Panama. On July 9, the Hearst newspaper *San Francisco Ex-
aminer* headlined the Hoehne incident as "NAZI CONSUL IN S.F. ADMITS
GIVING AIDE SECRET CODE PAPERS." *The New York Times* connected the
two incidents through Wiedemann, reporting that Wolff had entered the
United States at San Francisco and was acting as a courier, bringing documents to Valparaiso, Chile, as an agent for Fritz Wiedemann.

On July 8, Hoehne, described as "blonde" and "urchin-faced," told
the FBI that he was acting as a courier for Wiedemann despite not being employed by the embassy or consulate. This made Hoehne an agent
of a foreign government under the Foreign Agents Registration Act of
1938. Wiedemann responded from San Francisco that, surely, it was all

a terrible misunderstanding. He was unaware "that transmitting a letter makes a person a foreign agent required to register with the Federal Government!" The question for prosecutors, however, was whether Wiedemann was guilty of a conspiracy to suborn the act. Despite calls for Wiedemann to be expelled, it was doubtful that he would personally face charges, although Dr. Hoehne was bound over to appear before a grand jury.[8]

Wolff, who had been arrested within the Canal Zone, also fell under American jurisdiction. A mysterious powder was found in his possession and was chemically tested as a possible narcotic, but not as an explosive. Wolff's bail was fixed at twelve thousand dollars for each of the charges he faced. The first accusation was for acting as a courier between the German consulates of San Francisco and Valparaiso, Chile. If found guilty, he would face ten years in prison *and* a fine of five thousand dollars. The second charge was violation of the Foreign Agents Registration Act, which carried with it a two-year prison term and fine of ten thousand dollars.[9]

Then, suddenly, all reference to their activities disappeared from public view. Were they carrying microdots (already in use by Germany) with plans detailing where to place explosives in the Panama Canal? Who analyzed the paperwork these two explosive experts were carrying? The FBI? William Stephenson of the BSC? And what was Princess Stephanie's role? The record on the precise plot in the Panama Canal is still sealed in the National Archives in the United States and United Kingdom.

What we know about Stephanie in Panama was that she was introduced to the American consul there by the German consul Neumann. She presented a letter to the hapless American, ostensibly written by Secretary of the Interior Harold Ickes, and asked for a "small" loan—three hundred dollars, to be precise. The loan was granted. Ickes only found out about it eleven months later, when Roosevelt was harping on at him about Stephanie overstaying her welcome and being "deportable" but "undeportable" at the same time because no country other than Hungary would take her. "She went to Panama where she showed a letter as his [Icke's] representative," Roosevelt said, "whereupon the consul loaned her $300" against a check that she presented. The check, of course, "bounced back." Ickes was dumbfounded. Of course, he hadn't written such a letter and could only think that she had somehow got hold of his letterhead and forged his name.[10]

By November, both Wiedemann and Stephanie knew that their stays in the United States were coming to an end. The FBI had followed up on numerous plots involving other German consulates, and even Ilgner and Schmitz at Chemnyco were preparing for the time when they could no longer serve the Third Reich.

At this point, Sir William Wiseman entered the picture. He had held the same position as William Stephenson during the Great War in America. He was a trusted friend of President Woodrow Wilson and Lord Halifax, but not of MI6.* At the end of the 1914–1918 war, Wiseman remained in New York, where he had joined the investment bank Kuhn, Loeb & Company, but always maintained his British nationality and ties to British intelligence. Was it Halifax who suggested Wiseman contact the familiar combination of Wiedemann and Princess Stephanie? Could they possibly broker "another peace," as Halifax believed them capable? Halifax certainly had a hand in making sure Wiseman knew about their previous activities.

On November 27, William Wiseman met with Princess Stephanie and Fritz Wiedemann at his hotel suite, number 1024, at the Mark Hopkins Hotel in San Francisco. Their conversation lasted from 7:30 P.M. until the early hours of November 28, on behalf of Halifax and "a group of Englishmen who believed a satisfactory peace arrangement could still be concluded between Britain and Germany." Wiseman had sounded out the pair about potential peace negotiations, as Britain was being pummeled in the Blitz. If this were true, Halifax was acting entirely without his government's knowledge or approval. By the end of the first session, Stephanie claimed she could get any peace plan before Hitler, and that he would be "delighted to see his 'dear princess' again." Seemingly, it hadn't occurred to Stephanie (though perhaps it did to

---

* Halifax was suddenly parachuted into the job as British ambassador to Washington after the sudden death of Lord Lothian.

Wiedemann) that Hitler had no incentive to stop the war, despite failing to destroy the Royal Air Force in the Battle of Britain. Stephanie was adamant she could persuade Hitler that the United States was poised to enter the war at the slightest provocation—meaning a German failure—just as it had done against the kaiser in 1917.[11]

But the fifty-seventh attorney general, Robert H. Jackson, did not like or trust Wiseman. Neither did Brigadier General Sherman Miles, chief of military intelligence.* Miles alerted J. Edgar Hoover that Wiseman was among a group of Englishmen in America who allegedly had attempted some extragovernmental negotiations with the Nazis in the past. It was Wiseman they had followed to the hotel, and it was Wiseman's conversations they were recording. After the initial meeting between the three conspirators, however, the FBI began tailing them all. Nothing came of their meeting, or the subsequent encounter between Wiedemann and Wiseman only.

PRINCESS STEPHANIE'S VISA to the United States ran out on December 23, 1940. She had been advised initially on December 17 that she would have to leave the country, but that was later amended to "on three weeks' notice." So Stephanie arranged to disappear. Robert H. Jackson had sight of J. Edgar Hoover's report to President Roosevelt on Stephanie, in which FDR issued a presidential decree to get "that Hohenlohe woman" out of the country.[12†]

Soon enough, Stephanie was found. On January 11, feigning a nervous breakdown, she was taken into court on a stretcher by ambulance, in circumstances that the judge found to be wholly unacceptable. He ordered that they adjourn the court to her hotel room instead. She won a temporary postponement, giving her a maximum of twenty days to sail. Never one to give in, Stephanie wrote to the president, "Please spare me the humiliation of having to leave this country under such oppressive

---

* Miles's military career ended with the attack on Pearl Harbor. He had singly failed to recognize the significance of the "Magic" decrypts prior to the attack.

† Stephanie had been "last reported in Mexico," according to the MI6 files (source: KV2–1697–2).

circumstances as though I were a criminal," she wrote. The president never replied.[13]

But the government's mood that February was bleak. Hoover gave the order to review some five million alien-registration histories of immigrants lodged with the Department of Justice. Newspapers called it a "new witch hunt." Then, Wiedemann's former secretary, Mrs. Alice Crockett, an ex-actress, sued Wiedemann for "$8,000 to cover expenses and a salary of $500 a month for six months." Her claim stated that Wiedemann had verbally agreed to pay for her expenses to go to Germany to ask Hitler if he was happy with her boss's performance in July 1939. While there, Crockett met with Hitler, Goebbels, Göring, and others, who mutually assured her that Wiedemann "was properly carrying out his duties as Consul General in San Francisco, and as chief of the German espionage service of the Government of Germany in the United States."[14] Wiedemann called the claim "all bunk," and Mrs. Crockett lost her case.

When Mrs. Crockett sued Wiedemann again, alleging that he had paid over five million dollars for "espionage" since his arrival in the United States on March 5, and that it was Princess Stephanie and other individuals who acted as couriers to pay the German spies, Wiedemann must have felt threatened. Crockett also revealed in her suit that Wiedemann "had obtained information to determine by what method the Panama Canal could be made useless." Wiedemann then knew that, irrespective of the outcome, he would be asked to leave the country.

It was in this atmosphere that Princess Stephanie used every means at her disposal to remain, including claiming that she was too ill to travel, as was her mother, Baroness Szepessy.* Having failed to leave the country within her twenty-day extension, Stephanie was arrested on the orders of Major Lemuel Schofield, head of the U.S. Immigration and Naturalization Service and special assistant to Attorney General Jackson. Intrigued by her dossier, Schofield made the mistake of visiting the

---

* To avoid Stephanie's deportation, her lawyer wrote to over forty consulates, asking if they would accept her, including the Hungarian, Austrian, and British consulates. They all declined. It was noted in HO 382/250 that "to say, for the information of Mr. Winston Churchill, that this woman is prohibited from landing in this country under Article 1(3) (g) of the Aliens Order, 1920" (source: HO 382/250).

princess a few days later at her San Francisco detention center. Obese, balding, and with a face like a disgruntled, overstuffed owl curling its upper lip, Schofield immediately fell for Stephanie's practiced charms. He was a married man with four children, but from the moment he saw her, it was love. She had been the victim of an injustice, she claimed. If they sent her back to Hungary, she would be executed for her anti-Nazi sentiments. She had met Hitler, she knew everyone at the top, and could give him—the U.S. government—highly useful information.

To save her skin, Stephanie may well have betrayed Wiedemann, too. The previous December, she left the Wiedemann family home to go into hiding in a Palo Alto apartment owned by her new best friend, Vilma "Mimi" Owler-Smith. To avoid deportation for overstaying her visa, her lawyer presented an affidavit to the Immigration and Naturalization Service in Washington that she was "not and never have been in sympathy with Germany or the Axis Powers in their present state of war, and that all my sympathies lie with the kingdom of Great Britain and its people." The affidavit continued, "I was perhaps unwise enough to have accepted the invitation of the German government's representative in San Francisco to be his house-guest. As soon as I recognized this fact, I left the residence of the person in question." Both she and Mimi Owler-Smith attempted to extort money through blackmail from Wiedemann, too, before Stephanie was finally interned.

Wiedemann was deeply wounded. On April 7, he wrote to Stephanie, claiming a total of $3,003 she owed him. "I don't know whether we will ever get a chance to discuss the bitterness of the last few days, like sensible human beings. . . . I do know that you no longer wish an approach on my part and that you will do everything to avoid it," Wiedemann continued. "Even so, I cannot simply draw a line under the years which, thanks to you, were among the richest and most wonderful of my life."[15]

Naturally, Schofield knew nothing of the princess's romantic involvement with Wiedemann or of the real role she had been playing on behalf of the Third Reich for the past decade. He did not consider her case in any detail. Instead, on the promise of future "cooperation with the government," Schofield's boss, Robert Jackson, agreed that her deportation order could be halted. The United States needed to understand the Nazi spy network in the Americas, and Stephanie seemed their best chance to break it open. At a stroke, her dubious past was wiped clean. The press was told Princess Stephanie had provided "information of interest" and promised to cooperate in future.*

On May 19, she was released on $25,000 bail (which Mimi Owler-Smith paid). The conditions of her release and continued ability to remain at liberty were that the State Department knew where Stephanie was at all times; that she did not contact any foreign government representatives, make any public statements, or give lectures; and that she live in a small town without an airport. It would be a day or so before Stephanie raised herself from her sickbed in the detention center hospital and walked free. By July 1, 1941, Princess Stephanie and her mother had moved to the Raleigh Hotel in Washington, D.C., where Schofield was also residing, breaking the terms of the agreement. "It was obvious that Princess Hohenlohe had spent the whole night with Major Schofield," the FBI report noted, "as she was found in his room at 8:30 or 9:00 A.M."[16]

UNKNOWN TO PRINCESS Stephanie, the American freighter *Robin Moor,* en route from New York to Cape Town, was stopped off the coast of Brazil by a German U-boat on May 21. The first mate was ordered to present the vessel's papers and to not use his radio. He obeyed. Ten minutes later, the order to abandon ship came through, and twenty minutes after that, the U-boat commander gave the order to sink her—firing midships. The survivors in the lifeboats were told that some food had been given to the captain of the *Robin Moor* by the U-boat commander, and then the Germans left them on the open seas. The inhumane treatment meted out to neutrals was just the excuse the president needed to rid himself of Germans in the United States without fully tipping his hand.[17]

On June 14, the U.S. government placed an embargo on all property of Reich citizens in the United States, freezing their assets. Two days later, the Senate Judiciary Committee approved the bill passed in the House of Representatives permitting "the President to prescribe rules and regulations governing entry into and departure from the United States of

---

* See appendix III.

all persons—citizens and aliens alike—if he deems it in the public inter-est." President Roosevelt immediately ordered the closure of all German consulates and ancillary agencies, including Ulrich von Gienanth's Ger-man Library of Information, the German railway and tourist agencies, and Trans-Ocean News Service (the German newswire, as Transozean was called in the United States). Only the German embassy remained open. All German nationals would have to leave the country no later than July 10. That same day, the aviatrix Laura Houghtaling Ingalls met with Wiedemann to confirm her intention to preach "the truth" about Nazism to Americans.[18]*

Although, according to the State Department, no specific charges were made against individuals, "the offices and individuals involved had engaged in activities 'of an improper and unwarranted character' and that their continued presence here would be 'inimical to the welfare of this country.'" The Associated Press article reflected on the fact that, in comparison to Germany, relations with Japan appeared "less black."[19]

Six days later, on June 22, Hitler launched Operation Barbarossa against the Soviet Union. Time had run out for Hitler's propagandists and spies.

---

* Ingalls was already under surveillance by Leon Lewis's anti-Nazi spy ring in Los Angeles, California. She never went to Germany for training since she was convicted of failing to register as the agent of a foreign government in accordance with the For-eign Agents Registration Act of 1938. She served twenty months in prison and was released on October 23, 1943. In July 1944, she attempted to enter Mexico, but was prevented from doing so.

Pearl Harbor

The principle has been to accept a risk, whether we win the horse
or lose the saddle.
                        —Admiral Matome Ugaki's diary, December 8, 1941

It is difficult to imagine that a close friendship between two students at
Freiburg University might have prevented the attack on Pearl Harbor.
Although it is far-fetched, it is true. Dusan "Dusko" Popov, an easygo-
ing, fun-loving Yugoslav who was fluent in Serbo-Croat, French, German, Italian, and English, loved women and fast cars. His friend Johann
"Johnny" Jebsen from Hamburg did, too. Both were aristocratic, wealthy,
playboy types with a distinct dislike for authority. In September 1937,
shortly after his doctoral thesis was completed, Popov was awakened by
the Gestapo hammering at his door at 6 A.M. He was arrested, "relentlessly questioned," and detained for eight days. When he didn't confess
to being a communist or a "Jew lover," he was told he would be assigned
to a concentration camp. Popov had been denounced for speaking
against Hitler and organizing anti-Nazi speeches at the student black-
tie debating dinner known as the *Herrenessen*, run by Johnny Jebsen.

But when Popov was next summoned to the prison warden's office,
he was shocked to hear that he would be released immediately, as long
as he left Germany within twenty-four hours.[1] The warden mumbled
something about how lucky he was that he had friends in high places.
When he stepped off the train at Basel, Switzerland, Jebsen was waiting
for him. Jebsen, heir to the Hamburg shipping company of the same
name, had pulled strings and revealed all to his friend. Popov was

overwhelmed and swore to do anything Jebsen asked of him in the future.[2]

JEBSEN RECONTACTED POPOV in February 1940, demanding an urgent meeting at Hotel Serbian King in Belgrade. Popov was shocked to see how much his savior had changed. Johnny's self-confidence had evaporated. He was drinking heavily, tossing back whisky after whisky, and chain-smoking. His teeth, fingers, and moustache were nicotine-stained.

Apparently, five German merchant ships had been blockaded in Trieste harbor in nearby Italy by the Allies. Only one of the ships belonged to Jebsen's company, but he had managed to get authorization to sell them all to a neutral country as long as they did not trade with the Allies. Since Yugoslavia still managed to retain its neutrality, could Popov use his contacts to set up the deal before the Nazis understood that any undertaking not to trade with England or France was worthless once the ships passed into neutral ownership? Jebsen boasted it was his way of making a fortune, while "doing his bit" in denying the ships to Germany. Of course, Popov agreed—and succeeded within weeks.

Soon after, Jebsen came to Belgrade and told Popov that, despite his anti-Nazi views, he had volunteered to join the Abwehr as a *Forscher* ("researcher") and would be allowed to carry on his business—as long as he submitted intelligence on his business contacts. He thought it was a safer bet than being called up to serve on the front lines.

Jebsen asked Popov if he would be willing to help him identify French politicians who would be most likely to cooperate with Germany after the fall of France. The invasion of Denmark and Norway hadn't taken place yet, much less the attack on Belgium, Luxembourg, the Netherlands, and France. Surely, Popov had to agree that France was doomed, Jebsen said. Both men were flattered that their opinions mattered, but agreed that if the information requested was of interest to the Abwehr, surely it would also be important to the British legation in Belgrade. It was the beginning of a beautiful double-agent relationship.[3]

By the time France fell that June, Popov was introduced to Jebsen's

German legation contacts, who were impressed by his friendship with the Banac family—big investors in Britain. Surely, Popov wouldn't mind working for the Germans, they suggested, all smiles. Seemingly, his detention three years earlier by the Gestapo was forgotten and the nervous Jebsen had put forward Popov's name to become an Abwehr agent.

The next morning, Popov went to the office of a Mr. Dew at the British embassy in Belgrade, telling him the whole story and that he would only accept the Abwehr offer if the British were willing to take the same intelligence that he gave the Germans. Dew warned him that it may cost him his life. Popov merely shrugged. He was then introduced to the MI6 agent working at passport control. A few days later he was told "London wants you to accept" the Abwehr offer. The Germans gave him the code name Ivan. The British called him Scoot.

When the German army, supported by the Hungarians and Bulgarians, invaded Yugoslavia in April 1941, Jebsen promised Popov that he would look after his family, and he was as good as his word. Over the next nine months, Popov proved to be an incredible source for MI6. The agency's "C" referred to Popov as a "one in a million virtuoso" who moved from role to role without anyone seeing through his masks and deception—even sharing a mission with Ian Fleming of naval intelligence that involved betting thousands of pounds at the casino in Portugal. Traveling repeatedly between Britain and Portugal on his undercover missions for the Germans, Popov's local handler became a tall, aristocratic-looking man who said his name was Major Ludovico von Karsthoff.* He lived in a large Moorish-style villa on the Estoril just beyond the hotel and casino with his blond secretary/mistress, two yapping dachshunds, and a pet monkey.

Soon enough, Karsthoff sent Popov to spy against the British. Popov's cover in England was as a Yugoslav businessman with contacts into the government in exile in London. One of his earliest coups—allegedly for the Germans—was Plan Midas, the arrangement of payments to German agents in Britain. The Germans were thankful, since it worked

---

* His real name was Kremer von Auenrode.

where other endeavors had failed, never realizing that the British were facilitating the payments to unmask the German spies.[4]*

THAT SPRING, POPOV met with a man known only as Colonel Mauer at Karsthoff's Estoril home. Mauer was the head of Abwehr I in the West. He told Popov the Yugoslav government in exile would probably follow the lead of the Abyssinians, Poles, and Dutch and create a token army under the auspices of the British. Popov was ordered to request a job in the ministry, given his international contacts.

Why? Popov asked. Mauer smiled. "Do you think you could swing a job or a mission in the United States? We have more important plans for you" there. Then Mauer cursed the "goddamned bund" who "J. Edgar Hoover . . . picks up by the dozens like whores on the Reeperbahn." Mauer was referring to Nikolaus von Ritter's Duquesne spy ring, which had been blown. Incredibly, the Germans wanted to send Popov to the island of Oahu in Hawaii and to set up a completely new Abwehr spy ring in the United States. Popov was bug-eyed with delight.[5]

POPOV WAS DULY briefed by the Germans. He was told Admiral Isoroku Yamamoto, commander of Japan's Combined Fleet, had begun preparations for an audacious naval attack against the United States. Yamamoto decided in January 1941 that Pearl Harbor would be his target and that the offensive must take place during the moon's gibbous phase, when moonlight was at its brightest—the night of December 8 in Tokyo, December 7 in Hawaii. Yamamoto was universally regarded as "smart and dangerous," not to mention "exceptionally able, forceful, and quick thinking."[6]

---

* Each KV2 (spy) file contains numerous references to all German agents complaining of not being paid. Various ruses from dead-letter drops that failed to meetings that never took place were frequently reported. One of the more comical incidents occurred when double agent Hans Hansen, code name Tate, was told to follow a Japanese man with *The Times* carried in his left hand onto a number 11 bus at Victoria. The plan failed because the number 11 bus did not stop there (source: TNA, KV2/847).

Popov stalled for time until he could speak to Jebsen a week later. They met at a secluded observation point at the Boca do Inferno cliffs—near the last residence of the Windsors in Europe. As the breakers thundered beneath their feet, Jebsen gave Popov chapter and verse about his most recent mission to Taranto, Italy. Back in March 1941, Jebsen said, the Japanese foreign minister, Yosuke Matsuoka, had visited Hitler in Berlin with a huge delegation of the naval top brass to work out the military implications of the Tripartite Pact. Jebsen said the Japanese admiralty was anxious to get all the information it could obtain about the British attack at the port of Taranto the previous November. Ribbentrop, he said, raised himself up on his "toothpick legs and started screaming at Canaris to do something." Jebsen was nominated for the job because of his naval connections.

The Taranto bombing was a "surprise attack" by the British. The heavily fortified port had been decimated. Admiral Cunningham had placed his *Illustrious* aircraft carrier within seventy miles of port and in two sorties of twenty-one bombers in total, the British pummeled the Italian fleet, annihilating it. The Japanese not only wanted all details—they wanted them yesterday. The planned Japanese attack on Pearl Harbor would mimic the British strategy at Taranto. Jebsen also estimated the Japanese attack on Pearl Harbor would take place before year's end, when the Japanese national oil reserves would be reduced to about a year.

Armed with this intelligence, Popov headed to London. As incredulous as he was, the British were alarmed. Could they trust the Americans with this intel? Could they send their best agent to the United States, where they would lose control of him to Hoover's FBI? Again, they probed and prodded Popov for his allegiance to the Allies in a covert way. He was vetted again by Lieutenant Commander Ewen Montagu and Flight Lieutenant Charles Cholmondeley, both of whom later created Operation Mincemeat (best known for its depiction in the 1956 film *The Man Who Never Was*). After vetting, Popov was given the all-clear and the necessary arrangements were made.[7]

ON AUGUST 10, Popov boarded the Pan American flying boat in the Tagus estuary for New York. He carried forty thousand dollars from

Karsthoff to pay his new spies as well as twelve thousand dollars of his own money and another eight thousand from the Bailoni Bank in Belgrade to purchase goods that could no longer be delivered to occupied Yugoslavia. He had a "flying nursemaid" from British intelligence to keep him company, too. The British had wangled an appointment for Popov as the delegate from the Yugoslavian Ministry of Information. On landing at the Port Washington seaplane base, he was passed over to his FBI handler, Charles Lehman.

Although the British had made the significance of Popov's mission abundantly clear and sent ahead a report on the questions the Germans wanted Popov to answer in Hawaii,* nothing had been forwarded to Hoover in Washington. Popov was slack-jawed. His opinion of the Americans did not improve when his interrogator had missed the significance of the documents he carried. The dotted "i's" and "periods" contained microdots. Popov had to fully demonstrate the technology before he was—at last—believed. The American clandestine community seemed to him to be inefficient when he was told he'd have to wait until his FBI contact, Percy Foxworth, received his instructions. The FBI seemed arrogant, perhaps anti-Yugoslav, and certainly looked down its nose at him and his joie de vivre.

But Popov's instructions never came. While he waited, he told the FBI he was planning a weeklong vacation in Florida with a beautiful English girl named Terry Brown who was currently working as a fashion model. The FBI gave him the go-ahead. Then, suddenly, the FBI demanded an urgent meeting with Popov on his way south to Philadelphia. Without any preamble, Popov was told, "The trip to Hawaii is off."

Popov was irate. The FBI was blowing his cover. The British would be angry; Popov would tell British intelligence how the FBI refused to work with him to plant false information with a new set of informants and that, no matter what, he wasn't going to let the FBI stop his mission. The FBI agent then pulled out his trump card. He threatened Popov with the Mann Act—which made it a federal offense to cross a state line with a girl for immoral purposes, irrespective of her age. He was

---

* See appendix II.

ordered to ditch the girl and wait to meet Hoover in New York or face deportation.

An angry and sullen Popov drove back to New York. He was summoned to meet Hoover at Rockefeller Center a few days later. Hoover judged MI6's ace double agent, tried him, and was about to perform his execution. "Sit down, Popov," he said without expression. "You come here from nowhere and within six weeks install yourself in a Park Avenue penthouse, chase film stars, break a serious law, and try to corrupt my officers. I'm telling you right now," he screamed, pounding the desk with his fist, "I won't stand for it." Popov tried to placate him and apologized if he had offended him in any way but remained firm. He had a job to do. "I brought a serious warning indicating exactly where, when, how, and by whom your country is going to be attacked. I brought to you on a silver salver the newest and most dangerous intelligence weapon designed by the enemy."

No one talked to J. Edgar Hoover like that. "I can catch spies without your or anybody else's help," Hoover fulminated. Then he lambasted Popov for inaction, and again Popov stood his ground. He told Hoover that the Germans were paying him to establish a new spy network to replace the consular, Bund, and other information organizations. Popov realized Hoover was riding high because the FBI had just rounded up Ritter's Duquesne spy ring. He argued that his job at Pearl Harbor could not only save American lives but also feed the Germans false information. But Hoover would not be swayed. As Popov got up to leave, Hoover shouted after him, "good riddance."

IN FAIRNESS TO the FBI, there had been little or no organization between it and the naval and military intelligence agencies. There had been talk of creating a new international agency, but in September 1941, it was only talk.* Also, as Hoover understood things, these military

---

* The FBI files do not contain any information whatsoever on Popov or the meeting with Hoover. It also does not acknowledge its first sight of microdots in August 1941, courtesy of Popov. That said, Hoover wrote to Brigadier General Edwin M. Watson, presidential secretary, on September 3, 1941, explaining the microdot system but not

intelligence networks would have to give some information to Popov so that his cover would remain intact. When Hoover heard that one of Popov's letters to Lisbon had been destroyed by the British censor in Bermuda (accidentally), he mistakenly thought the British "may actually distrust Popov," too.

Popov reported his failure with Hoover to his British contact in New York, Colonel Ellis. They agreed there was no way they could get this information to U.S. naval and army intelligence without interference from Hoover. Even having William Stephenson directly approach President Roosevelt would be risky. It was time to turn their attention to inserting Popov safely back into Lisbon with some tale to the Germans to save his skin.[8]

ON DECEMBER 7 at 6:35 A.M., Second Lieutenant Milton Bliss set off back to base at Pearl Harbor. It had been a wild party, and he was still hungover. He was used to being called the "Yonkers Jew boy" by his fellow junior officers, despite—or maybe because of—his charm and movie star good looks. Bliss had been brought up in poverty, held a deep belief in his Jewish faith, and had never given credence to superstition. He was still young enough at twenty-three to be trusting but wise enough to know when he was lied to. That made him a great asset at the provost marshal's office when interviewing suspected malfeasants. Even so, it was years before he knew his mother lied to him each Thanksgiving about the puny turkey served. It was only a kosher chicken.

As he rounded the corner of the mountain, a wizened old woman wearing a red muumuu and accompanied by a little white dog walked toward him. If he offered to help her, and she wanted to continue up the mountain, he'd be late back to base for his 8:00 A.M. shift. If he didn't, he would go against his every belief. Just as he opened his mouth to greet her, the woman opened hers. He would swear he saw fire on her breath and thought he must be more hungover than he realized. "Run!" she cried, her tongue deep red, like molten lava. "The Night Marchers come.

enclosing the questionnaire contained on the microdots. A copy of Hoover's letter to Watson can be found in the FDR Presidential Library, OF10B, box 28.

Huaka'i po!" Then, unbelievably, she seemed to walk through him and carried on her way. His heart raced. Bug-eyed, he looked behind him, but she was gone. Was this the legendary volcano goddess Pele he had heard about?* Bliss was so spooked that he ran, stumbling, looking over his shoulder constantly to see if she followed, and promised himself he'd never drink that much again—ever.[9]

Bliss was unaware that shortly before 4:00 A.M. a navy minesweeper reported a periscope off the entrance to the harbor. The *Ward* had been sent to investigate. Its new captain, Lieutenant Billy Outerbridge, had been awakened to inspect, found nothing, and ordered that the ship should resume her ritual assessment of the harbor mouth.[10]

AFTER METICULOUS PLANNING and much opposition, Yamamoto's plan to attack Pearl Harbor was underway. It was an audacious strategy requiring the intricate refueling by oil tankers of warships on the high seas and the mobilization of thousands of sailors and pilots, not to mention reconfiguration of their ordnance, submarines, and, especially, their torpedoes. That said, the twelve-day, 3,500-mile journey from Hitokappu Bay in Tokyo through the North Pacific had been kind to them. The seas were calm; the skies, free from enemy patrols. As they approached the Hawaiian Islands, Yamamoto's final words were sent to the Combined Fleet: "The fate of our Empire depends on this expedition. Each of you will do your duty, wearing yourself to the bone."

As they approached their target, Commander Minoru Genda aboard the flagship *Akagi* learned that the *Enterprise*, with its 90 aircraft and 2,217 men, and the *Lexington*, with 78 aircraft and 2,791 men, were not in port. On the positive side, they could pick up Oahu's radio stations "as clearly as if we were there." The airwaves swayed with Hawaiian music.

---

* According to Hawaiian legend Huaka'i po (Hawaiian for "Night Watchers") come at the full moon as warriors to protect the islands from invasion. The Hawaiian goddess of volcanos and fire is Pele, who often takes human form as a wizened old woman warning of imminent danger. Bliss spoke for the first time of his experience in June 2004 on his deathbed, age eighty-five.

• • •

AT 6:37 A.M.—THE sun had risen for some ten minutes—Outerbridge was awakened again: "Captain, come on the bridge!" When he got there, wrapped in his kimono, the helmsman and other sailors were staring at a black thing poking out of the water several hundred yards ahead. The navy cargo ship, the *Antares*, was towing a barge and heading into the harbor. The black object seemed to be trying to sneak in between the *Antares* and its tow.

He may have been new at his job, but Outerbridge recognized the object as a conning tower. More important, he knew it was not built like an American one. The helmsman, H. E. Raenbig, said later that Outerbridge had only to give one look before calling General Quarters. The *Ward* sprang into action—each crew member had been drilled to race to their mounts and seal doors and hatches. Ratcheting up to twenty-five knots, the *Ward* set on a collision course for the black object. Once they were close enough, Outerbridge could see that the midget submarine was only eighty feet long, rusted, oval-shaped, blanketed in barnacles, and seemingly unconcerned by the appearance of the destroyer. Outerbridge ordered his men to open fire. "The submarine waded directly into our first charge," enlisted man W. C. Maskzawilz later said. The minisub was hit midships, but kept moving forward, albeit more slowly. Then the order came to roll off four depth charges from the *Ward*'s stern. Oil seeped to the surface. Outerbridge radioed to Pearl: "We have dropped depth charges upon subs operating in defensive sea area." Then, thinking he needed to be more precise, a second message was sent at 6:54 A.M.: "We have attacked, fired upon and dropped depth charges on a submarine operating in defensive sea area."[11]

The first American shots of World War II had been fired. The days of Hitler's aristocrats influencing and manipulating people in power had ended.

Epilogue

The Pearl Harbor controversy rages on until this day. Had Roosevelt placed the Pacific Fleet at Pearl Harbor to inflame Japanese hard-liners, as some believe, or was Pearl Harbor midway between America's weakest links of the Philippines and the Panama Canal, allowing him to hedge his bets against a German attack across the vast Pacific Ocean? The work of Dusan Popov adds to the controversy, particularly since the MI5 and MI6 files make it abundantly clear that the Japanese and Germans were united in a plot to blow up Pearl Harbor in a stealth attack.

Despite J. Edgar Hoover's nearly blowing Popov's cover, on his return to his handler in Spain, he finessed his way out of the life-threatening situation through bluff and bluster. Popov continued to work as a double agent for the British and went on to participate in Operation Fortitude, the grand deception campaign to mislead the Germans about the Allied landings in France. He kept his wartime secrets until the publication of his book *Spy/Counterspy* in 1974, surprising his wife and children. Always a heavy smoker and drinker, Popov died, age sixty-nine, in 1981 after a long illness. His friend Johnny Jebsen was less lucky. He was arrested by the Gestapo in Lisbon in 1944, interrogated, tortured, and murdered. It had a lifelong, profound effect on Popov.

AFTER THE FAILURE of the July 1944 plot to assassinate Hitler, some five thousand military officers, diplomats, civil servants, and other opponents of Nazism were executed. Among them was the former ambassador to Italy Ulrich von Hassell. The highly praised general Erwin Rommel, nicknamed the "Desert Fox," was forced to commit suicide for his role in the plot or to see his wife and children perish at Hitler's hands. Under suspicion since before the July 1944 plot, Admiral Wilhelm Canaris, head of the Abwehr, was put under house arrest before being tried and sent to Flossenbürg concentration camp. In February 1945, he heard his organization was disbanded and divided between the Gestapo and the RHSA under the direction of Walter Schellenberg.* He was humiliated and sent naked to the gallows at Flossenbürg on April 9, 1945, just twenty-nine days before the end of the war.

MOST GERMANS WHO resisted met gruesome ends, while many of those who aided and abetted the criminal and maniacal Nazi regime escaped harsher punishment by swift deaths, infinitesimal jail sentences, or not guilty verdicts at Nuremberg. Hitler married his mistress, Eva Braun, before poisoning her and then shooting himself in his Berlin bunker on April 30, 1945. Goebbels and his wife, Magda, killed their six children and then themselves, leaving Magda's son from her first marriage, Harald Quandt, as her sole heir. Göring committed suicide in his cell after his guilty verdict. Himmler committed suicide while in custody before facing trial. Hjalmar Schacht was acquitted of crimes against humanity. Of the top German Nazis, only Hermann Göring, Joachim von Ribbentrop, and Rudolf Hess were found guilty at Nuremberg. Ribbentrop was executed, and Hess would spend the rest of his life in prison.

Ernst "Putzi" Sedgwick von Hanfstaengl wangled his way into a cozy internment in Virginia for a while, thanks to his friend and presidential adviser, John Franklin Carter. Hanfstaengl had promised to deliver an important psychological profile on all the top Nazis, particularly Hitler, but always found excuses to avoid betraying his old friends. He held

---

* RHSA stands for Reichssicherheitshauptamt or the Reich Security Main Office, under the jurisdiction of Heinrich Himmler in his dual capacity as head of the police and the SS.

out a bit too long, trying American patience, and was sent back to an internment camp in Canada for the rest of the war. Putzi remained an ardent anti-Semite until the end. After the war, he returned to Munich, where he died in 1975.

Leni Riefenstahl always denied that she was a propagandist for Hitler. She was an "artiste," a director, and held no political views. The fact that she filmed the first known atrocity of the war in Poland has been lost from history. What is remembered is that she tried to market her film *Olympia* in the United States and that Walt Disney was the only major producer who agreed to meet with her.

Christoph von Hessen, the brother-in-law of Prince Philip, Duke of Edinburgh, died one month after Italy surrendered to the Allies, when his plane crashed into the Apennine Mountains in northern Italy. His brother Philipp survived the war, despite being interned in Flossenbürg and Dachau concentration camps by the Germans, and later by the Allies. Philipp's wife, Princess Mafalda, was killed in an Allied bombing raid on Buchenwald concentration camp, where she was held captive. Carl Edouard, of all the German aristocrats, was singled out as a leading Nazi. As the head of the German Red Cross, he knew about the murders of over one hundred thousand disabled people and was tried for war crimes but found not guilty. Yet the American authorities insisted he undergo a denazification process. In April 1946 his daughter Sibylla gave birth to the future and current King Carl XVI Gustaf of Sweden.

Of the industrialists, Gustav Krupp von Bohlen und Halbach descended into senility during the war, and although he was theoretically tried at Nuremberg with his son Alfried, he was never punished. He died at his home in 1950. Alfried and ten other Krupp directors were tried at Nuremberg for crimes against humanity: enslavement, imprisonment without trial, torture, murder, extermination, deportation, and use of slave labor. All were found guilty. Inmates of 138 concentration camps were slave laborers for Krupp, and Krupp moved them from camp to camp as suited the company's needs. Over 520 Jewish girls, many of whom were young children, worked as slaves at the heart of the Krupp works in Essen. Six other directors were also found guilty of economic spoliation. The trial lasted until July 1948, and Alfried received a twelve-year prison sentence. He was pardoned in 1951. Within six years after the end of the war, Alfried Krupp was back in the saddle and in control of his fortune. Twenty years after the end of the war, Adolf Hitler's greatest industrialist protégé was the richest man in Europe and the most powerful industrialist in the Common Market.[1]

Fritz Thyssen had taken refuge in France after his flight from Germany. After the fall of France in 1940, the Vichy government arrested him and his wife and sent them home. Initially, the Thyssens were sent to Sachsenhausen concentration camp, then Dachau. As the Allies closed in, they were among the 139 prominent concentration camp inmates moved to the Tyrol. Thyssen agreed in court to the harm he had done to Jewish employees until 1938 and agreed readily to pay a fine of 15 percent of his assets as reparations. In 1950 he and his wife moved to Buenos Aires, where he died the following year.

The I.G. Farben trial of Carl Krauch and twenty-two other directors held the most damning of indictments for "Crimes against Peace, War Crimes, and Crimes against Humanity." Accused of the "planning, preparation, initiation of wars of aggression and invasions of other countries" and deportation and enforced slave labor of the civilian populations of the countries invaded, the litany went on to include charges of enslavement, terrorization, murder, plunder, spoliation of public and private property, production and supply of poison gas for experimental and daily use in concentration camps on its prisoners (Zyklon-B), and the use of Farben drugs on inmates for human experimentation. None of the accused were charged with acting as a quasi-government arm of the Third Reich abroad who engaged in espionage.[2]

All were found not guilty of crimes against peace and participation in the conspiracy to invade other countries. I.G.'s chairman of the supervisory board, Carl Krauch, who served as a loyal servant to Hermann Göring on the Four-Year Plan, was sentenced to six years, including time served. Hermann Schmitz received a sentence of four and a half years, including time served. Georg von Schnitzler was sentenced to two and a half years, including time served. Fritz ter Meer, who was in charge of the chemical plant near Auschwitz, served seven years. Max Ilgner, as head of I.G.'s intelligence and propaganda, received a prison sentence of three years and was released immediately after the verdict, since he had spent longer than three years awaiting trial.

· · ·

THE INDUSTRIALIST AND time-and-motion expert Charles Bedaux went on to become deeply involved in the politics of Nazi Germany and Vichy France. His scheme to build a trans–North African railway for the Germans was his undoing. On January 24, 1943, Bedaux was delivered into the custody of the American authorities and then shipped to the United States for trial where he was charged with treason as an American citizen. While in custody in Miami, he committed suicide and died on February 18.[3]

CHARLEY LONDONDERRY NEVER again held a government post. His reputation has remained blackened the longest, save for Sir Oswald Mosley and his wife, Diana. The Mosleys were arrested in May 1940 under Defence Regulation 18(b) but were never tried. The British Union of Fascists was banned. In 1943 the Mosleys were released from prison, staying initially with Diana's sister Pamela. Since Mosley was unable to resume his political career, they immigrated first to Ireland, then to Paris. Despite several attempts to reenter politics back home, Mosley never again held public sway. He died of Parkinson's disease in 1980. Diana died in Paris in 2003. Mosley's early fascist friend, William Joyce, who became known in Britain as the voice of Lord Haw-Haw, was captured in May 1945 and returned to Britain for trial for treason. He was found guilty and hung.*

The diarist and socialite MP Chips Channon was bisexual and had several affairs with men (possibly with the Duke of Kent and Prince Paul of Yugoslavia) while married to Lady Honor. He never achieved the status he desired in cabinet, although he was knighted a year before his death in 1957. His diaries, recently republished, are his enduring legacy. Harold Nicolson's diaries are important reading and serve as a critical counterpoint.

---

* Bizarrely, William Joyce had lied when he said he was born in Ireland (while still part of the United Kingdom) and therefore British. He had acquired his British passport illegally, but since he masqueraded as British and promoted German propaganda in Britain while using his British passport, he was nonetheless convicted.

As for the Duke and Duchess of Windsor, in April 1945 over four hundred tons of the German foreign ministry archives were discovered at Marburg Castle. Found among the papers were the documents surrounding the Operation Willi affair and other papers regarding Edward. Churchill (serving again as prime minister) wrote to President Eisenhower in June 1953, "to exert your power to prevent . . . publication" of "a Nazi-German intrigue to entangle and compromise a Royal Prince."[4] He was too late. Historian John Wheeler-Bennett (editor of *Documents on German Foreign Policy*) learned of the suppression of the documents and militated with the powers that be—with the help of Tommy Lascelles—until they were finally released. In fact, Lascelles had said to Harold Nicolson at a private lunch on December 14, 1937, that the duke "was like a child in a fairy story, and was given everything in the world, but they forgot to give him a soul."[5]

The first black governor general of the Bahamas, Sir Orville Turnquest, concluded that "the few accomplishments and many failures of the Duke of Windsor's tenure in the office of Governor of The Bahamas" do not make pretty reading. Edward did nothing to mitigate the hard life of the majority Black population or to eliminate the racist culture or improve education. He was weak and preoccupied with the "restoration of his own status" and viewed by the population as prejudiced and racist since he did nothing to raise or eliminate the "color bar" or correct the disenfranchisement of Bahamian women. He lined his own pockets and those of his wealthy friends and was deeply implicated in mismanagement and interference during the investigation of the murder of Sir Harry Oakes in July 1943. As for Wallis, from the start, she viewed her husband's appointment to the Bahamas "with derision." They could not wait to escape in early May 1945 and head back to civilization in France.[6] They would never again live in Britain.

NONE OF THE American bankers who facilitated Mussolini's rise to power, like Thomas W. Lamont, were held to account. Nor was Prescott Bush, who invested money on behalf of the Third Reich until the funds were sequestered in 1942. General Motors and Ford, which had Aryanized its German divisions, still owned and had a controlling stake in their German companies, which both companies denied. Two weeks after the invasion of Poland, James Mooney met with Hitler in Berlin and was personally involved in the conversion of the General Motors plant at Rüsselsheim "to the production of engines and other parts for the Junker 'Wunderbomber.'" In an FBI report of July 23, 1941, Mooney is quoted as saying he would not do anything to "make Hitler mad." After the declaration of war by Hitler on the United States, Ford and General Motors were forbidden further contact with their German companies, with each receiving war damages from the U.S. government for Hitler's sequestering their German factories.[7]

Ambassador William Dodd was forced to resign in 1937 due to his conflict with the State Department about his anti-Nazi stance. On his return to Washington, D.C., he took a teaching position at American University and campaigned to warn Americans of the dangers that Nazi Germany represented. He died in 1940, but his diaries were used in evidence against Hjalmar Schacht at Nuremberg.

Whether Dodd ever knew that his daughter, Martha, was a KGB spy is doubtful, particularly since she had married the New York millionaire Alfred K. Stern Jr. in 1938. She provided little information of value to the Soviets on American wartime activities. That said, the FBI began to look at Martha and Alfred as people of interest in 1948. While the Soviets had discounted their value, in 1955 the couple fled the United States as a result of the FBI investigation into their past Soviet dealings. Escaping first to Mexico, then Prague, they became Soviet citizens and spent their remaining years in the Democratic Socialist Republic of Czechoslovakia.[8]*

The more active Soviet agent in the United States, however, was none other than Congressman Samuel Dickstein, code-named Crook for his avaricious ways. According to a memo from the NKVD station chief, Dickstein handed over the Dies Committee transcripts and lists of American Nazis in June 1939, as well as the budget for 1940, "records of conferences of the budget sub-commission, reports of the war minister, chief of staff and etc." Eventually, he was asked to generally give the Soviets "information about all the important political questions regarding

---

* They were unable to adjust to life in the Soviet Union.

your country and its relations with other countries . . . that could be of use to us." He ran successfully for the New York State Supreme Court in 1945 and served until his death on April 22, 1954. Today, Dickstein has a street named after him in Manhattan.[9]

DESPITE HIS BEING the main spokesman for the America First Committee, Charles Lindbergh stepped aside the moment the attack on Pearl Harbor took place. Not trusted because of his outspoken stance, however, Lindbergh found it difficult to find an appropriate position to match his talents. All meetings with top government authorities, and even Pan American airlines, which he helped to put on the map, came to nothing. Only later did he learn that President Roosevelt himself had said, "I'll clip that young man's wings." Everyone had turned their backs on him except Henry Ford. So Lindbergh went to work on the manufacture of the four-engine high-wing monoplane B-24 Liberator bomber near Dearborn. He remained bemused and stunned by the end of the public's love affair with him, relying heavily on his wife, Anne, for moral support.[10]

The other great naysayer to war, Joseph P. Kennedy, had already reached the pinnacle of his powers as U.S. ambassador to the Court of St. James's in London. Until Pearl Harbor, Kennedy, like his friend Lindbergh, preached isolationism and flirted unknowingly with those who were in Wiedemann's West Coast spy network.* Kennedy never again held a government appointment. Joe Jr. was killed in action in 1943, shortly after his younger brother Jack was gravely injured in the Pacific. Yet Kennedy persevered in his dream that one of his sons would become the first Catholic president. In the words of Jack as President John F. Kennedy, his father "made it all possible" to create the famed American political dynasty.

---

* Kennedy met with a man identified only as Mr. Meier, who allegedly had over three hundred thousand dollars at his disposal for the purpose of promoting isolationism in the United States through Wiedemann. The records are unclear if Kennedy accepted any of this money or contributed to the fund (sources: UCN, NRS Box 103; TNA, KV2–1696–1; HIA Box 3).

. . .

AND WHAT OF Fritz Wiedemann and his princess? Fritz was detained after the war and interrogated. His cover as a "peace maker" was believed by the Americans, and eventually he was released to go home to his farm in Germany. He wrote a book to exonerate himself from his deeds, which is hardly a work of nonfiction.

As for Princess Stephanie, she was arrested shortly after Pearl Harbor and spent the war in a camp for suspect aliens in Sago, Texas. On her release in 1945, Lemuel Schofield was there to greet her and took her to his estate in New Jersey for a few years to recover. But Stephanie could not resist the limelight for long. In 1953, she took part in the New York Easter fashion parade and was featured on the New York Dress Institute's list of "best-dressed women." A year later, Schofield suffered a fatal heart attack.

It turned out that Schofield had been evading taxes for the past six years (so he could pay Stephanie's bills?), and the IRS decided to try to recover back taxes amounting to $250,000 from Stephanie. They were unsuccessful. Then, in 1955, age sixty-four, Stephanie was given a job as a special correspondent for the *Washington Diplomat,* an international society magazine. Soon enough, she was hobnobbing with Lady and Sir Sidney Lawford, the parents of actor Peter, who had married into the Kennedy clan. She was a shoo-in as a member of the Women's Press Club of New York.

Stephanie introduced herself to Drew Pearson sometime in 1962, after she became a journalist consultant to *Quick* magazine of West Germany. Although her official residence with her son, Franzi, was in Geneva in a small apartment on Rue du Bourg-de-Four, she traveled frequently back to the United States. Introducing herself to Pearson as a dear old friend of his former wife's father, Count Gizycki, Pearson was quick to seize on her international contacts, particularly through the Kennedy clan and President Kennedy's former press secretary, Pierre Salinger. She became the prime mover behind the Pearson interviews with presidents Kennedy and Johnson.

Stephanie had become stateless under the communist regime in

Hungary and traveled on an American document issued for that purpose. She had also been granted a green card. That said, Stephanie was
not allowed leave to enter the United Kingdom until 1967, despite her
concerted efforts and those of her son. To this day, several hundred
pages in the British National Archives pertaining to Stephanie remain
closed until 2076.* In 1972, age eighty, she died in Geneva, where no
one ever brought up her Nazi past.

Denazification of former top German officials was not a success,
in part because the first chancellor of West Germany, Conrad Ade-
nauer, insisted that the past should be forgiven, if not forgotten. The
"old enemy"—the Soviets—were at the gates. They had grabbed much
of Eastern Europe and created East Germany from the lands the Soviet
Union had reconquered "for the Allies." The Cold War had begun before the Second World War had ended, leaving the bitter Nazi legacy of
genocide and spoliation. Three generations on, we are still suffering the
aftereffects.

---

* See appendix III.

APPENDIX I

(Undated letter from Captain Fritz Wiedemann to Lord Rothermere, probably written early January 1939)

STRICTLY PERSONAL & CONFIDENTIAL

Dear L. R.

H.S.H. the Princess Stephanie zu Hohenlohe-Waldenburg handed me a short statement about her case against you with all the correspondence between you and the F and all others annexed. The Princess asked me that I shall have them translated and place these papers before the F and request him in her name the permission to use them in her case against you as evidence.

You know my Lord that the F. greatly appreciates the work the Princess did to straighten the relations between our countries. The work was made—and this the Princess never ceased to state and repeat—on your behalf and on your instructions—but though it was done by her with great ability assiduity and tact.

You surely know too that the Princess last May—without your assistance—started the negotiations with Lord Halifax and it was her groundwork which made the "Munich no more war agreement" possible. Furthermore it was the Princess who introduced you to the F a fact he also greatly appreciates.

Under such circumstances and considering the chivalresque character and magnanimity of the F. besides the real friendship he has for the Princess, leave in my mind no doubt that he will grant her any help in her fight to re-establish her personal honour and financial situation. He will grant her the permission to use the above-mentioned correspondence as evidence, as he will feel it will be a great help for a woman in a fight against a powerful man but no doubt it will be very unpleasant for him and he will have a strong aversion against the fact that such case should be argued in open court.

As I know the F. ideas, his idealistic conception on matters of honor and friendship I know he might easily misunderstand or misjudge such a situation. I therefore decided to write you this letter on my own initiative without the F. instruction and without the Princess knowledge. Because I believe it is the best I can do not only to serve my masters personal interests but also the interest of all persons concerned, to tell you that the case pending in Court between the Princess and yourself should be settled a l'amiable and without any publicity and for this reason I offer you should you not find other ways and means to arrange this matter, my personal help as mediator.

Should you accept my offer and instruct me then I will request also the Princess to grant me the same powers and knowing her devotion to the F I have no doubt that she will agree.

I should appreciate your early reply as the Princess requested to get the F. permit as soon as possible as she is waiting in London to give instructions accordingly.

Yours faithfully,

Note: L. R. stands for Lord Rothermere; and F, for Führer.

Reproduced with the permission of the Hoover Institution and Archive, Stanford California.

TRANSLATION OF DUSAN POPOV'S (AKA "TRICYCLE") GERMAN "AMERICAN QUESTIONNAIRE" BY MI5*

(This information was contained on two microdots and given to the FBI in August 1941 before the Japanese attack on Pearl Harbor.)

NAVAL INFORMATION-

Reports on enemy shipments (material foodstuffs—combination of convoys, if possible with names of ships and speeds).

Assembly of troops for overseas transport in USA and Canada. Strength-number of ships-ports of assembly-reports on ship building (naval and merchant ships-wharves (dockyards)-state and privately worked wharves-new works-list of ships being built or resp. having been ordered-times of building.

Reports regarding USA strong points of all descriptions especially in Florida-organisation of strong points for fast boats (E-boats) and their depot ships-costal defence-organisation districts.

HAWAII

Ammunition dumps and mine depots.

1. Details about naval ammunition and mine depot on the Isle of Kushua (Pearl Harbor). If possible sketch.

---

* The British version of the questionnaire can be found in J. C. Masterman's *The Double-Cross System*, 196–98.

2. Naval ammunition depot Lualuelei. Exact position? Is there a railway line (junction)?

3. The total ammunition reserve of the army is supposed to be in the rock of the Crater Aliamanu. Position?

4. Is the Crater Punchbowl (Honolulu) being used as an ammunition dump? If not, are there other military works?

AERODROMES

1. Aerodrome Lukefield-Details (sketch if possible) regarding situation of the hangars (number?), workshops, bomb depots, and petrol depots. Are there underground petrol installations?-Exact position of the seaplane station? Occupation?

2. Naval air arm strong point Kaneche [actually, Kaneohe].-Exact report regarding position, number of hangars, depots and workshops (sketch). Occupation?

3. Army aerodromes Wicham [actually, Hickam] Field and Wheeler Field-Exact position? Reports regarding number of hangars, depots and work-shops, Underground installations? (Sketch). Occupation?

4. Rodger's Airport-In case of war, will this place be taken over by the army or the navy? What preparations have been made? Number of hangars? Are there landing possibilities for seaplanes?

5. Airport of the Panamerican Airways.-Exact position (if possible sketch). Is this airport possibly identical with Rodger's Airport or part thereof? (A wireless station of the Panamerican Airways is on the Peninsula Mohapuu.)

NAVAL STRONG POINTS PEARL HARBOR

1. Exact details and sketch about the situation of the state wharf, of the pier installations, workshops, petrol installations, situations of dry dock No. 1 and of the new navy dry dock which is being built.

2. Details about the submarine station (plan situation). What land installations are in existence?

3. Where is the station for mine search formations? How far has the dredger work progressed at the entrance and in the east and southeast lock? Depths of water?

4. Number of anchorages?

5. Is there a floating dock in Pearl Harbor or is the transfer of such a dock to this place intended?

SPECIAL TASKS

Reports about torpedo protection nets newly introduced in the British and USA navy. How far are they already in existence in the merchant and naval fleet? Use during voyage? Average speed reduction when in use. Details of construction and others.

1. Urgently required are exact details of the armoured strengths of American armoured cars, especially of the types which have lately been delivered from the USA to the Middle East. Also all other reports on armoured cars and the composition of armoured (tank) formations are of greatest interest.

2. Required are the Tables of Organisation (TO) of the American infantry division and their individual units (infantry regiments, artillery 'Abteilung' and so forth). These TO are lists showing strength, which are published by the American War Department and are of a confidential nature.

3. How is the new light armoured car (tank)? Which type is going to be finally introduced? Weight? Armament? Armour?

GENERAL FINANCING

1. Position of British participation and credits in USA in June 1940. What are England's payment obligations from orders since coming into force of the Lend Lease Bill? What payments has England made to USA since the outbreak of war for goods supplied, for establishment of works, for the production of war material, and for the building of new or for the enlargement of existing wharves?

2. Amount of State Expenditure in the budget years 1939/40, 1940/41, 1941/42, 1942/3 altogether and in particular for the army and the rearmament.

3. Financing of the armament programme of the USA through taxes, loans and tax credit coupons. Participation of the Refico and the companies founded by it (Metal Reserve Corp., Rubber Reserve Corp., Defence Plant Corp., Defence Supplies Corp., Defence Housing Corp.) in the financing of the remarmament.

4. Increase of the state debt and possibilities to cover this debt.

All reports on American air rearmament are of greatest importance. The answers to the following questions are of special urgency:

I. <u>How large is:</u>

    (a) the total monthly production of aeroplanes?

    (b) the monthly production of bombers?

    (c) the monthly production of fighter planes?

    (d) <u>the monthly production of training planes?</u>

    (e) the monthly production of civil aeroplanes?

II. <u>How many and which of these aeroplanes were supplied to the British Empire, that is to say:</u>

    (a) to Great Britain?

    (b) to Canada?

    (c) to Africa

    (d) to the Near East?

    (e) to the Far East and Australia?

III. <u>How many USA pilots finish their training monthly?</u>

IV. <u>How many USA pilots are entering the RAF?</u>

REPORTS ON CANADIAN AIR FORCE ARE OF GREAT VALUE.

All information about number and type (pattern) of front aeroplanes. Quantity, numbers and position of the echelons are of great interest. Of special importance is to get details about the current air training plan in Canada, that is to say: place and capacity of individual schools and if possible also their numbers. According to reports received every type of school (beginners', advanced, and observer school) is numbered, beginning with 1.

APPENDIX III

HO 382/250: PRINCESS STEPHANIE'S HOME OFFICE FILE ASSESSED

In September 2020, I made a FOIA request for HO 382/250, Princess Stephanie's closed Home Office file, due to be opened in 2076. In April 2022, just as my manuscript was going into production, three hundred and fifteen pages of the closed file landed on my computer. As I went through these, it became quite evident that HO 382/250 had been heavily redacted under a section 23 exemption. This exemption refers to documents that relate to security bodies, their operations, and defense of the realm, which also includes the government and the Palace.

No mention is made of the telephone wiretaps that were undoubtedly ordered—only the warrant issued to search her mail. Much of the file is dedicated to Stephanie's entries and exits from the United Kingdom in the years 1932–36, but, again, contains little information about how it was determined that she was a danger to national security, other than to state repeatedly that Stephanie had a "shocking record," that she was a "dangerous and undesirable woman," that "she moved in influential circles" and often attracted "adverse publicity" in France, Great Britain, and the United States. Most important, it is remarked that Stephanie's "connections in high places are a little few too many for my liking" and that she had been excluded "for political reasons." After her departure for New York, Stephanie was placed on the Home Office Suspects Index (of foreign agents) on December 21, 1939. Probably the most damning evidence came from Georg von und zu Franckenstein, the former Austrian ambassador to the Court of St. James's. In his November 6, 1939, letter, he states that Stephanie negotiated with the German government on behalf of the Rothermere press for the "give Danzig Back to the Reich Campaign," which was "detrimental to British public opinion." Franckenstein states that she encouraged Hitler to march on Austria by misinforming Hitler about Britain's attitude and that she caused her own and Wiedemann's disgrace. He was even prepared to testify against her in the Rothermere lawsuit. Guy Liddell, head of counterespionage at MI5, agreed with Franckenstein that the "pretense" about her and Wiedemann being "out of favour" because Ribbentrop does not like them was a "façade" to "divert suspicion" from the next phase of their work.

There is much repetition of the Rothermere lawsuit and Stephanie's blaming Esmond Harmsworth (2nd Lord Rothermere) for her remaining gated from the United Kingdom. Interestingly, on March 6, 1941, Stephanie's case was referred to a Mr. McCombe at the Trading with the Enemy Section of MI6, "who may find something of interest." Although the file refers to Captain (really, Lieutenant) Donald Malcolm and his British American Securities firm on Lombard Street in some detail, including a City of London police file on Malcolm, Stephanie, and Wiedemann, a full page of the police report is redacted. An October 13, 1939, telegram from Malcolm, who had left the United Kingdom permanently in July 1938, demands that Stephanie bring "all account records" pertaining to the Giraud Trust (Philadelphia) "suit" urgently. Given my corporate finance background, it is reasonably safe to assume that the trio were engaged in illicit "safeguarding" of valuables belonging to those wishing to flee the Nazi onslaught. Who would have remarked on millions in jewels—the most transportable form of wealth—traveling with Princess Stephanie? Both Malcolm and Stephanie held safe deposit boxes in London. Certainly later, after Stephanie was granted leave to enter England in 1967, she also had a safe deposit box in Geneva.

It is also safe to assume that her connections with the Prince of Wales / Edward VIII / Duke of Windsor and Wallis Simpson are somewhere in the redacted files. When or if that comes to light in 2076, I hope someone else will pick up the threads of this history and publish it in the public interest.

ABBREVIATIONS AND GLOSSARY

ADL Anti-Defamation League

Alleinschulde sole responsibility for causing the war of 1914–1918

Aufsichtsrat a corporate supervisory board

Auslands Organization also known as the "AO" Foreign Organization of the Nazi Party

Aussenpolitische Amt **(APA)** Alfred Rosenberg's foreign office within the Nazi Party

BUF British Union of Fascists

BSC British Security Coordination *or colloquially* Baker Street Club

Contessen soirées countesses' evening parties where virginal women learned the fine art of aristocratic gossip

Deutsches Nachrichtenbüro German News Agency from 1933, known as DNB for short

Edel elder

Comme il faut just so, in the right way

Duce Italian for "leader," title assumed by Mussolini once he became prime minister

Freikorps paramilitary groups noted for their violence and formed from the former German Imperial Army

Freiherr baron

Führer German for "leader," title assumed by Hitler

Graf count

Gau regional areas, provinces in Germany and later conquered territories

Gauleiter the regional leader in Germany and later conquered territories

Hitlergruss the Nazi salute

Landesgruppenleiter local leader of the NSDAP overseas, who often organized foreign intelligence in his locale

Liebe Prinzessin dear princess

MP Member of Parliament

Sicherheitsdienst the intelligence agency of the SS and the Nazi Party

USSR Union of Soviet Socialist Republics (today the Russian Federation)

Volk people

Wehrfreiheit military freedom

Weltanschauung "world view" or "philosophy of life," one of Hitler's favorite expressions

ACKNOWLEDGMENTS

Although writing is a solitary business, especially in repeated "lock-downs," I felt the full support of my husband, fellow writer and historian Dr. D. A. B. Ronald; my editorial team at St. Martin's Press, Charles Spicer and Sarah Grill; and my agent, Alexander C. Hoyt. So many fellow writers and historians gave freely of their time and expertise in their specific areas of interest, and I would like to thank them for their kindness and attention (in alphabetical order): Philip Astor, Elizabeth Buccleuch, Hugh van Dusen, Agostino von Hassell, Alexander Merrow, Professor Jonathan Petropoulos, Justine Picardie, Dr. Helen Rappaport, Andrew Rose, Dr. Laura B. Rosenzweig, Anne Sebba, Adrian Tinniswood, the late Christopher Warwick, Wendy Weiner, and Paul Willetts.

To Kathy Munro and the Johannesburg Heritage Foundation, I would like to give my special thanks. Without you it would have been impossible to trace the real background of Princess Stephanie and how her family came by its position in society. The assistance of the staff at the London Library; the British Library; the National Archives at Kew; Hoover Institution Library and Archives in Stanford, California; University of California at Northridge; and the Bundesarchiv in Berlin enabled me to complete this book to the best of my ability. I thank you all.

NOTES

ABBREVIATIONS

AA Astor Archive
BNA British Newspaper Archive
BOD Bodleian Library, University of Oxford
DBFP *Documents on British Foreign Policy,* Second Series, London, HMSO, 1984
DGFP *Documents on German Foreign Policy*, London, HMSO, 1983
FBI Federal Bureau of Investigation archive, vault.fbi.gov
FDRPL Franklin D. Roosevelt Presidential Library
FOLD3 Online documents from the National Archives, College Park, Maryland
FRUS Foreign Relations of the United States (e-book editions)
HANSARD The official record of the House of Commons and the House of Lords
HIA Hoover Institution Library and Archives, Stanford University, Reference 77020, papers of Princess Stephanie zu Hohenlohe-Waldenburg-Schillingsfürst
JSTOR International scholarly academic publications website
NARA The National Archives (College Park, Maryland)
NCP Neville Chamberlain Papers, University of Birmingham, England
NYT *The New York Times*
ODNB Oxford Dictionary of National Biography (online at www.oxforddnb .com)
RA Royal Archive, Windsor Castle
TBJG *Die Tagebücher von Joseph Goebbels: Sämliche Fragmente*, ed. Ralf Georg Reuth, part 1, *1923–41* (Munich: K. G. Saur, 1987). Translations are my own.
UCN University of California, Northridge, *News Research Service*, CRC Papers, also referred to as the NRS, the abbreviation for *News Research Service*

PROLOGUE

1. Fritz Hesse, *Hitler and the English,* trans. F. A. Voigt (London: Allan Wingate, 1954), 26; Michael Bloch, *Ribbentrop* (London: Abacus, 2003), 131, 133.
2. Bloch, *Ribbentrop,* 132–33; DGFP, Series C, vol. VI, 158–59.
3. UCN: NRS, CRC2–103–1, 8.
4. HIA, 77020, Box 3, Folder 3, 137–38.
5. *The Times,* Court Circular, May 14, 1937.
6. HIA, 77020, Box 3, Folder 3.
7. Ibid.

CHAPTER 1: CHAOS

1. Peter Kurth, *American Cassandra: The Life of Dorothy Thompson* (London: Little, Brown, 1990), 54.
2. Ibid., 62, 65.
3. Ibid., 62, 63.
4. Stefan Zweig, *The World of Yesterday,* trans. Benjamin W. Huebsch and Helmut Ripperger (Plunkett Lake Press e-book by arrangement with Viking, Lexington, MA, 2011), 285–86.
5. Kurth, *American Cassandra,* 67.
6. William J. Chase, "Microhistory and Mass Repression: Politics, Personalities, and Revenge in the Fall of Béla Kun," *Russian Review* 67, no. 3 (July 2008), 459, JSTOR.
7. Kurth, *American Cassandra,* 68.
8. Jim Wilson, *Nazi Princess: Hitler, Lord Rothermere and Princess Stephanie von Hohenlohe* (Stroud, England: History Press, 2011), 28.
9. Ibid. According to the author, Stephanie's half-sister, author Gina Kraus, provided him with incontrovertible evidence that Stephanie was Gina's father's (Max Wiener's) illegitimate daughter. See also: Rudolf Stoiber and Boris Celovsky, *Stephanie von Hohenlohe: Sie Liebte die Mächtigen der Welt* (Munich: F. A. Herbig Verlagsbuchhandlung, 1988), 51.
10. I am indebted to the Johannesburg Heritage Trust and, in particular, Kathy Munro for marshaling their resources to help me to sketch Robert Kuranda's brief biography. It should be noted that Kuranda, too, was prone to flights of fancy in giving his family history. He claimed that his father was an Austrian member of parliament. Sources: numerous email exchanges with the Johannesburg Heritage Trust; *Men of the Times* (1905); *South African Who's Who Social and Business, 1931–1932.*
11. ODNB.
12. Martha Schad, *Hitler's Spy Princess: The Extraordinary Life of Stephanie von Hohenlohe,* trans. Angus McGeoch (Stroud, England: Sutton Publishing, 2004), 7. According to Stephanie's numerous memoir versions (see HIA, Box 3 and Box

5), Stephanie was quite put out that Friedrich Franz had declared that he had no intention of remarrying, and yet he did so quickly afterward.

CHAPTER 2: THE "BIG LIE"

1. Michael Kellogg, *The Russian Roots of Nazism: White Émigrés and the Making of National Socialism, 1917–1945* (New York: Cambridge University Press, 2006), 7, 225.
2. James M. Diehl, *Paramilitary Politics in Weimar Germany* (Bloomington: Indiana University Press, 1977), 78.
3. Ibid., 83.
4. Susan Ronald, *Hitler's Art Thief: Hildebrand Gurlitt, the Nazis, and the Looting of Europe's Treasures* (New York: St. Martin's Press, 2015), 77–80. See also: Robert G. L. Waite, *Vanguard of Nazism: The Free Corps Movement in Postwar Germany, 1918–1923* (New York: W. W. Norton, 1969), 62, 62n.
5. Jonathan Petropoulos, *Royals and the Reich: The Princes von Hessen in Nazi Germany* (New York: Oxford University Press, 2015), 50–51.
6. https://encyclopedia.1914–1918-online.net/article/war_losses_germany.
7. Adolf Hitler, *Mein Kampf,* trans. James Murphy (London: Pimlico, 1939), 159. This has been republished as a Project Gutenberg of Australia e-book, September 2002.
8. William Manchester, *The Arms of Krupp, 1587–1968* (London: Michael Joseph, 1969), 384–85.
9. Ibid., 384.
10. Ibid., 388.
11. Ibid., 389–95.
12. Fritz Thyssen, *I Paid Hitler* (London: Hodder and Stoughton, 1941), 109–11.
13. Kellogg, *Russian Roots*, 194.
14. Ibid., 140; Thyssen, *I Paid Hitler*, 111–14.
15. Peter Conradi, *Hitler's Piano Player: The Rise and Fall of Ernst Hanfstaengl, Confidant of Hitler, Ally of FDR* (London: Duckworth Publishing, 2005), 5.
16. Ibid., 5–6.
17. Ibid., 6–7.
18. Ibid., 10.

CHAPTER 3: THE ALCHEMISTS

1. Diarmuid Jeffreys, *Hell's Cartel: IG Farben and the Making of Hitler's War Machine* (London: Bloomsbury, 2009), 9–13.
2. Ibid., 14–15.
3. John Cornwell, *Hitler's Scientists: Science, War, and the Devil's Pact* (New York: Viking, 2003), 61–63.

4. Susan Ronald, *A Dangerous Woman: American Beauty, Noted Philanthropist, Nazi Collaborator: The Life of Florence Gould* (New York: St. Martin's Press, 2018), 22–23.

5. Cornwell, *Hitler's Scientists*, 59.

6. Jeffreys, *Hell's Cartel*, 81.

7. Ibid., 114–15.

8. Ibid., 104.

CHAPTER 4: "BRIDESHEAD"

1. Henry Hemming, *M—Maxwell Knight, MI5's Greatest Spymaster* (London: Arrow Books, 2017), 23–24.

2. Richard Griffiths, *Fellow Travellers of the Right: British Enthusiasts for Nazi Germany 1933–1939* (London: Faber Finds, 2010), 13; A. J. P. Taylor, *English History, 1914–1945* (London: Penguin, 1981), 317.

3. Griffiths, *Fellow Travellers*, 13–14.

4. Ibid., 113.

5. Ibid., 29–31.

6. Martin Pugh, *"Hurrah for the Blackshirts!": Fascists and Fascism in Britain Between the Wars* (London: Pimlico, 2006), 81.

7. I thank Helen Rappaport for her insight into just how "German" young Victoria's court was.

8. Petropoulos, *Royals and the Reich*, 1.

9. Albert Speer, *Inside the Third Reich* (New York: Phoenix, 1995), 419.

10. Evelyn Waugh, *Brideshead Revisited* (London: Penguin Books, 2000), 4.

11. Philip Ziegler, *King Edward VIII: The Official Biography* (London: Collins, 1990), 106. See also: Edward Windsor, *A King's Story: The Memoirs of HRH the Duke of Windsor* (London: Cassell, 1951), 132.

12. Ziegler, *King Edward*, 6–8.

13. Ibid., 16.

14. Ibid., 68–69.

15. Ibid., 119–47. For the full facts about the prince and Maggie, read Andrew Rose's compelling book, *The Woman Before Wallis: Prince Edward, the Parisian Courtesan, and the Perfect Murder*.

16. Ibid., 193.

CHAPTER 5: DUPLICITOUS ÉMIGRÉS

1. Neil Baldwin, *Henry Ford and the Jews: The Mass Production of Hate* (New York: Public Affairs, 2001), 206–07.

2. Nuernberg Interrogation Records, Ernst Wilhelm Bohle, M 1270, NARA Catalog 647749, RG 238, Roll 0002, 6.

3. TNA, KV2/15, 97, interrogation of Vera Erickson.

4. FOLD3, www.fold3.com/image/304770696, RG 226, Microfilm Roll 0012, 283.

5. Jeffreys, *Hell's Cartel*, 116.

6. FOLD3, www.fold3.com/image/304770696, RG 226, Microfilm Roll 0012, 286.

7. FOLD3, www.fold3.com/image/304770696, RG 226, Microfilm Roll 0012, 287.

CHAPTER 6: AMERICA AND THE FINANCE WIZARDS

1. Ron Chernow, *House of Morgan: An American Banking Dynasty and the Rise of Modern Finance* (New York: Grove Press, 2001), 247, 276.

2. Winston S. Churchill, *Great Contemporaries*, ed. James W. Muller, Paul H. Courtenay, and Erica L. Chenoweth (Wilmington, DE: ISI Books, 2019), 279.

3. Adolf Hitler, *Mein Kampf*, trans. Ralph Manheim (London: Pimlico, 1997), 136.

4. Chernow, *House of Morgan*, 196, 199–200. See also: Stephen Birmingham, *"Our Crowd": The Great Jewish Families of New York* (New York: Harper and Row, 1947), 344, 363.

5. Sir Nevile Henderson, *Failure of a Mission: Berlin, 1937–1939* (London: Hodder and Stoughton, 1940), 229.

6. Arthur M. Schlesinger Jr., *The Age of Roosevelt: The Coming of the New Deal* (London: Heinemann, 1960), 420–22.

7. www.investor.gov/introduction-investing/investing-basics/role-sec/laws-govern-securities-industry#secact1933.

8. Chernow, *House of Morgan*, 354–55.

CHAPTER 7: THE GAMBLER AND PROPAGANDIST

1. Ronald, *Dangerous Woman*, 108–09.

2. Wilson, *Nazi Princess*, 36; HIA, 77020, Box 3, folder 3.

3. Kenneth Young, ed., *The Diaries of Sir Robert Bruce Lockhart*, vol. 1, *1915–1938* (London: Macmillan, 1973), 239.

4. HIA, 77020, Box 3, folder 3.

5. Ibid., 48.

6. Ibid., 49.

7. Ibid., 50–51.

8. *Daily Mail*, June 27, 1927.

9. HIA, Box 3, folder 3, 53.

10. S. J. Taylor, *The Great Outsiders: Northcliffe, Rothermere and the Daily Mail* (London: Weidenfeld and Nicolson, 1996), 260.

CHAPTER 8: HOPE AND RENEWAL

1. Petropoulos, *Royals and the Reich*, 96; Ernst Hanfstaengl, *Unheard Witness* (Philadelphia: J. B. Lippencott, 1957), 165–66.

2. In their biography of Göring, Roger Manvell and Heinrich Fraenkel maintain

that Göring met Philipp in 1924 in Rome and that Philipp introduced him to Mussolini. I thank Dr. Jonathan Petropoulos for his take on the state that Göring was in at the time, and have omitted this inference here.

3. Nicholas H. Dimsdale, Nicholas Horsewood, and Arthur van Riel, "Unemployment in Inter-War Germany: An Analysis of the Labour Market 1927–36," *Journal of Economic History*, 66, no. 3 (September 2006), 779–80; Manchester, *Arms of Krupp*, 385.

4. Ibid.

5. Conradi, *Hitler's Piano Player*, 80.

6. Ibid., 81.

7. William L. Shirer, *The Rise and Fall of the Third Reich* (London: Mandarin Paperbacks, 1991), 121–22.

8. Conradi, *Hitler's Piano Player*, 84.

9. Kurth, *American Cassandra*, 159.

10. Ibid. (Italics in the original, but as author, I shortened the quotation.)

11. Conradi, *Hitler's Piano Player*, 84–85, 86–87.

12. Kurth, *American Cassandra*, 160.

13. *TBJG*, March 31, 1924.

14. *TBJG*, April 10, 1924.

15. Toby Thacker, *Joseph Goebbels: Life and Death* (London: Palgrave Macmillan, 2009), 48; HIA, 77020, Box 3, folder 3.

16. Peter Longerich, *Goebbels*, trans. Alan Bance, Jeremy Noakes, and Lesley Sharpe (London: Vintage, 2016), 163–64.

17. Gerhard L. Weinberg, ed., *Hitler's Second Book: The Unpublished Sequel to "Mein Kampf" by Adolf Hitler*, trans. Krista Smith (New York: Enigma Books, 2003), xx.

18. Ibid., xxiv.

19. Shirer, *Rise and Fall*, 120.

20. Ernest W. D. Tennant, *True Account* (London: Max Parrish, 1957), 136.

21. Alan Bullock, *Hitler: A Study in Tyranny* (London: Book Club Associates, 1964), 152. These figures are from the International Labour Organization and are printed in the League of Nations Year Books for the years.

22. Conradi, *Hitler's Piano Player*, 80.

23. http://ghdi.ghi-dc.org/sub_document.cfm?document_id=3918, Adolf Hitler's speech to the Industry Club in Düsseldorf, January 27, 1932.

24. Manchester, *Arms of Krupp*, 400–02.

25. http://ghdi.ghi-dc.org/sub_document.cfm?document_id=3918, Adolf Hitler's speech to the Industry Club in Düsseldorf, January 27, 1932.

26. Tennant, *True Account*, 148.

27. Kenneth Young, *Stanley Baldwin* (London: Weidenfeld and Nicolson, 1976), 84–85; Winston S. Churchill, *The Second World War: The Gathering Storm*, vol. 1 (London: Reprint Society, 1956), 49.

CHAPTER 9: WINDS OF CHANGE

1. *TBJG*, March 11, 1932.
2. *NYT*, TimesMachine, March 12, 1932.
3. BNA, *Truth*, March 9, 1932.
4. BNA, *Nottingham Journal*, March 15, 1932.
5. Taylor, *The Great Outsiders*, 292.
6. Pugh, *"Hurrah for the Blackshirts!,"* 126.
7. BNA, *Yorkshire Evening Post*, March 17, 1932.
8. Longerich, *Goebbels*, 173.
9. Manchester, *Arms of Krupp*, 402.
10. *NYT*, TimesMachine, April 2, 1932.
11. Shirer, *Rise and Fall*, 145.
12. Ibid., 160–61.
13. *TBJG*, May 8, 1932.
14. André François-Poncet, *The Fateful Years: Memoirs of a French Ambassador in Berlin, 1931–1938*, trans. Jacques LeClercq (London: Victor Gollancz, 1949), 20.
15. Ibid., 24.
16. Shirer, *Rise and Fall*, 165.
17. *TBJG*, December 8, 1932.
18. Manchester, *Arms of Krupp*, 403–04.
19. Ibid., 405.

CHAPTER 10: CHARADE

1. HIA, Box 3, folder 3, 177.
2. HIA, Box 3, folder 3, 177; gallica.bnf.fr: January 9, 1933, *La revue hebdomadaire*; May 3, 1933, *Femme de France*; May 3, 1933, *Dernière heure*; September 12, 1933, *La liberté*.
3. HIA, Box 2, folder 3, 16.
4. HIA, Box 3, folder 3, 146.
5. HIA, Box 3, folder 3, 115–16.
6. Martha Schad, *Hitler's Spy Princess—The Extraordinary Life of Stephanie von Hohenlohe*, trans. Angus McGeoch (Stroud: Sutton Publishing, 2004), 23.
7. TNA: HO 382/250. In a letter contained in the file, Rothermere reassures Gömbös that Stephanie has not been paid by the Hungarian government. This is likely due to the fact that pro-Nazi Admiral Horthy, the regent, had kept this information from Gömbös and that Stephanie had kept Rothermere equally in the dark.
8. HIA, Box 3, folder 3, 177.
9. TNA: HO 382/250. According to MI5, Prince von Lichtenstein had also been promised a further £600,000 if Hitler took the Polish corridor and Danzig

without bloodshed within thirty months of the first article appearing in the *Daily Mail*.

10. TNA: KV2–1692–2, 37, 44, 62.

11. Michel Trebitsch, "L'intellectuel dans l'action: Lettres de Georges Canguilhem à Jean-Richard Bloch (1927–1946)," *Vingtième siècle revue d'histoire* 50 (April-June 1996), 50, 116.

12. Ronald, *Dangerous Woman*, 178–9; Peter Jackson, "French Intelligence and Hitler's Rise to Power," *History Journal* 41, no. 3 (September 1998), 801, JSTOR.

13. Jeffreys, *Hell's Cartel*, 117–18.

14. Ibid., 135.

15. Ibid., 140–41; Manchester, *Arms of Krupp*, 406.

16. Manchester, *Arms of Krupp*, 406–07.

17. Ibid., 407.

18. François-Poncet, *Fateful Years*, 50–51.

19. Ibid., 52.

20. Longerich, *Goebbels*, 209.

21. Shirer, *Rise and Fall*, 192; François-Poncet, *Fateful Years*, 52.

22. Longerich, *Goebbels*, 209.

23. Shirer, *Rise and Fall*, 193.

24. Ibid., 195–96.

25. Ibid., 200.

26. Thomas Ferguson and Hans-Joachim Voth, "Betting on Hitler: The Value of Political Connections in Nazi Germany," *Oxford Quarterly Journal of Economics* 123, no. 1 (February 2008), 113.

27. www.ushmm.org/learn/timeline-of-events/1933–1938/anti-jewish-boycott.

28. www.ushmm.org/learn/timeline-of-events/1933–1938.

29. François-Poncet, *Fateful Years*, 56.

CHAPTER 11: THE WOUNDED GIANT

1. Robert O. Paxton, *The Anatomy of Fascism* (London: Penguin Books, 2005), 49.

2. Rory McVeigh, Daniel J. Myers, and Edward Sikkink, "Corn, Klansmen, and Coolidge: Structure and Framing in Social Movements," *Social Forces* 83, no. 2 (2004), 653–90, JSTOR.

3. www.bridgemi.com/michigan-government/henry-ford-and-jews-story-dearborn-didnt-want-told.

4. encyclopedia.ushmm.org/content/en/article/charles-e-coughlin.

5. Chernow, *House of Morgan*, 346–48.

6. Susan Ronald, *The Ambassador: Joseph P. Kennedy at the Court of St. James's, 1938–1940* (New York: St. Martin's Press, 2021), 13; Michael R. Beschloss, *Kennedy and Roosevelt: The Uneasy Alliance* (New York: W. W. Norton, 1980), 70–73. See also: Irwin F. Gellman, *Secret Affairs: Franklin Roosevelt, Cordell Hull, and Sumner Welles* (Baltimore: Johns Hopkins University Press, 1995), 11.

7. Ronald, *Ambassador*, 11.
8. www.newspapers.com/image/414671036/?terms=%22Hitler%22&match=1; www.newspapers.com/image/414668701/?terms=%22Hitler%22&match=1.
9. www.newspapers.com/image/276580156/?terms=%22Hitler%22&match=1; www.newspapers.com/image/577184751/?terms=%22Hitler%22&match=1.
10. The%20Avalon%20Project%20:%20First%20Inaugural%20Address%20of%20 Franklin%20D.%20Roosevelt.webarchive.
11. https://millercenter.org/the-presidency/presidential-speeches/march-12– 1933-fireside-chat-1-banking-crisis.
12. Gellman, *Secret Affairs*, 17.
13. Ibid., 15.
14. www.newspapers.com/image/355102416/?terms=%22Hitler%22&match=1.
15. William E. Dodd Jr. and Martha Dodd, eds., *Ambassador Dodd's Diary, 1933– 1938* (London: Victor Gollancz, 1941), 17.

CHAPTER 12: SALUTING HITLER

1. Dodd and Dodd, *Ambassador Dodd's Diary*, 22.
2. Schlesinger, *Age of Roosevelt*, 420–21.
3. Dodd and Dodd, *Ambassador Dodd's Diary*, 8, 12–13.
4. Manchester, *Arms of Krupp*, 410–11, 432.
5. Dodd and Dodd, *Ambassador Dodd's Diary*, 30–31; www.ushmm.org/learn /timeline-of-events/1933–1938.
6. Cornwell, *Hitler's Scientists*, 138.
7. Ibid., 139.
8. Jeffreys, *Hell's Cartel*, 145.
9. Martha Dodd, *My Years in Germany* (London: Victor Gollancz, 1939), 38.
10. Ibid., 28–29.
11. Dodd, *My Years in Germany*, 43; Conradi, *Hitler's Piano Player*, 121.

CHAPTER 13: "HIS LORDSHIP'S AMBASSADRESS"

1. Taylor, *Great Outsiders*, 291–92; HIA, Box 3, folder 3, 223.
2. HIA, 77020, Box 3, folder 3, 4.
3. *NYT*, TimesMachine, March 22, 1933.
4. HIA, 77020, Box 3, folder 3, 4.
5. Petropoulos, *Royals and the Reich*, 166.
6. Ibid., 167–68.
7. Bloch, *Ribbentrop*, 27.
8. HIA, 77020, Box 3, folder 3, 2. The box holding Stephanie's memoirs has been heavily culled, presumably by her son, to omit any references to Stephanie's own pro-Nazi sentiments. Only a small portion of intimate details remain of that evening and many other eventful moments in Stephanie's life. Some of

Stephanie's biographers have this meeting occurring later in the year, but given Stephanie's own account, I must rely on her dates in April.

9. HIA, 77020, Box 3, folder 3, 2.

10. Thyssen, *I Paid Hitler*, 144.

11. Larry Eugene Jones, "Franz von Papen, the German Center Party, and the Failure of Catholic Conservatism in the Weimar Republic," *Central European History* 28, no. 2 (2005), 191, JSTOR.

12. HIA, 77020, Box 3, folder 3, 2. These remarks are handwritten in the margin of the page, but it does not look like Stephanie's handwriting.

13. Ibid., 3, 8. Again, others state that this "first" meeting was arranged by Prince Auwi. According to Stephanie, it was arranged by Wilhelm.

14. Ibid., 28–32.

15. Ibid.

CHAPTER 14: "HURRAH FOR THE BLACKSHIRTS!"

1. Young, *Stanley Baldwin*, 59.

2. ODNB entry, Stanley Baldwin.

3. Taylor, *Great Outsiders*, 272; Young, *Stanley Baldwin*, 59.

4. Tennant, *True Account*, 165.

5. Taylor, *Great Outsiders*, 272–73.

6. Churchill, *Second World War*, 73.

7. Ibid., 70.

8. BNA, *The Times*, August 6, 1933.

9. BBC *Newswatch*, November 17, 2016; John Simpson, *Unreliable Sources: How the Twentieth Century Was Reported* (London: PanMacmillan, 2010), e-book, 302–03.

10. Taylor, *Great Outsiders*, 290.

11. Ibid., 292; Simpson, *Unreliable Sources*, 308.

12. Ian Kershaw, *Making Friends with Hitler: Lord Londonderry and Britain's Road to War* (London: Penguin Books, 2005), 77.

13. Kershaw, *Making Friends*, 16–18; Nick Smart, ed., *The Diaries and Letters of Robert Bernays, 1932–1939: An Insider's Account of the House of Commons* (London: Studies in British History, 1996), 18.

14. Kershaw, *Making Friends*, 80. For further reading on British pacifism, read *Pacificism in Britain, 1914–1945: The Defining of a Faith*, by Martin Ceadel (Oxford: Clarendon Press, 1980).

15. Kershaw, *Making Friends*, 77.

16. Ibid., 78–79.

17. Ibid., 79.

18. Pugh, *"Hurrah for the Blackshirts!,"* 127.

19. Olson, *Harold Nicolson Diaries*, 37.

20. Anne de Courcy, *The Viceroy's Daughters: The Lives of the Curzon Sisters* (London: Phoenix, 2000), 181; Olson, *Harold Nicolson*, 41.

21. Nicholas Mosley, *Beyond the Pale: Sir Oswald Mosley and Family, 1933–1980* (London: Seeker and Warburg, 1983), 10; www.nationalarchives.gov.uk/cabinetpapers /alevelstudies/1930-depression.htm; Courcy, *Viceroy's Daughters*, 170–71.

22. Kershaw, *Making Friends*, 127.

23. Taylor, *Great Outsiders*, 280.

24. Nigel Nicolson, *Harold Nicolson: Diaries and Letters*, vol. 1, *1930–1939* (London: Faber Finds, 2009), 107.

25. Pugh, *"Hurrah for the Blackshirts!,"* 131; Mosley, *Beyond the Pale*, 30.

26. Pugh, *"Hurrah for the Blackshirts!,"* 132–33, 218.

27. *Daily Mail*, January 21, 1934.

28. Mosley, *Beyond the Pale*, 71.

CHAPTER 15: CORRALLING THE MALCONTENTS

1. Peter Duffy, *Double Agent: The First Hero of World War II and How the FBI Outwitted and Destroyed a Nazi Spy Ring* (New York: Scribner, 2014), 52.

2. Bradley W. Hart, *Hitler's American Friends: The Third Reich's Supporters in the United States* (New York: Thomas Dunne Books, 2018), 239; Ronald, *Ambassador*, 36.

3. Allen Weinstein and Alexander Vassiliev, *The Haunted Wood: Soviet Espionage in America—The Stalin Era* (New York: Modern Library, 1999), 4.

4. Schlesinger, *Age of Roosevelt*, 20–21.

5. HIA, 77020, Box 3, folder 3, 177.

6. Hart, *Hitler's American Friends*, 9.

7. Anne Sebba, *That Woman: The Life of Wallis Simpson, Duchess of Windsor* (London: Weidenfeld and Nicolson, 2011), 93; Paul Willetts, *Rendezvous at the Russian Tea Rooms: The Spy Hunter, the Fashion Designer and the Man from Moscow* (London: Constable, 2016), 10, 29; Courcy, *Viceroy's Daughters*, 220.

8. Taylor, *Great Outsiders*, 282.

9. Laura Thompson, *The Six: The Lives of the Mitford Sisters* (New York: Picador, 2017), 129, 146; Anne de Courcy, *Diana Mosley: Mitford Beauty, British Fascist, Hitler's Angel* (New York: William Morrow, 2003), 129–30.

10. Taylor, *Great Outsiders*, 283.

11. Ibid.; Courcy, *Diana Mosley*, 130–31.

12. Tennant, *True Account*, 175.

13. Bloch, *Ribbentrop*, 64.

14. Churchill, *Second World War*, 96.

15. Peter Longrich, *Heinrich Himmler*, trans. Jeremy Noakes and Lesley Sharpe (Oxford: Oxford University Press, 2012), 173–74.

16. www.newspapers.com/image/99486621/?terms=Hanfstaengl&match=1.

CHAPTER 16: MEN ON WHITE HORSES

1. *NYT*, TimesMachine, December 21, 1934.
2. Frederick Rudolph, "The American Liberty League, 1934–1940," *American Historical Review*, 56, no. 1 (October 1, 1950), 19–20.
3. BBC Radio, "The White House Coup," www.youtube.com/watch?v=UXGUg FXoRu4&list=PL2A96F711C461483A.
4. *NYT*, TimesMachine, November 21, 1934.
5. James Morris, *America's Armed Forces* (Upper Saddle River, NJ: Prentice Hall, 1996), 204.
6. *NYT*, TimesMachine, November 21, 1934.
7. Investigation of Nazi Propaganda Activities and Investigation of Certain Other Propaganda Activities by the McCormack-Dickstein House Committee on Un-American Activities (Washington, D.C.: Government Printing Office, 1934), 10–15, 15–20.
8. Ibid., 20–21.
9. BBC Radio, "White House Coup"; Schlesinger, *Age of Roosevelt*, 470; Rudolph, "American Liberty League," 24–25.
10. Weinstein and Vassiliev, *Haunted Wood*, 140–49.
11. Schlesinger, *Age of Roosevelt*, 470.

CHAPTER 17: HITLER'S "LISTENING POSTS"

1. Arthur L. Smith Jr., "Kurt Lüdecke: The Man Who Knew Hitler," *German Studies Review* 26, no. 3 (October 2003), 601–02.
2. Wilson, *Nazi Princess*, 47.
3. Thomas Jones, *A Diary with Letters, 1931–1950* (London: Oxford University Press, 1954), 137; Churchill, *Second World War*, 98–99.
4. Churchill, *Second World War*, 99.
5. Tennant, *True Account*, 177.
6. Griffiths, *Fellow Travellers*, 113–16; Lockhart, *Diaries of Sir Robert Bruce Lockhart*, 254.
7. Bloch, *Ribbentrop*, 67.
8. Bloch, *Ribbentrop*, 67–68; HIA, No. XX031, Louis P. Lochner Collection, letter to Hitler, dated August 25, 1934.
9. ODNB entry, William Maxwell Aitken, 1st Baron Beaverbrook.
10. Richard Griffiths, *Patriotism Perverted: Captain Ramsay, The Right Club and British Anti-Semitism, 1939–1940* (London: Constable, 1998), 70; Benny Morris, *The Roots of Appeasement: The British Weekly Press and Nazi Germany During the 1930s* (London: Frank Cass, 1991), 44.
11. James J. Barnes and Patience P. Barnes, *Nazis in Pre-War London, 1930–1939: The Fate and Role of German Party Members and British Sympathizers*

(Brighton, England: Sussex Academic Press, 2005), 75–77; Peter Ustinov, *Dear Me* (London: Arrow Books, 2000), 80.

12. Robert Rhodes James, ed., *Chips: The Diaries of Sir Henry Channon* (London: Weidenfeld and Nicolson, 1967), 19; Simon Heffer, ed., *Henry 'Chips' Channon: The Diaries, 1918–38* (London: Hutchinson, 2021), 365.

13. Courcy, *Viceroy's Daughters*, 212–14.

14. Ibid., 210–12; Siân Evans, *Queen Bees: Six Brilliant and Extraordinary Society Hostesses Between the Wars* (London: Two Roads, 2016), 205.

15. Adrian Fort, *Nancy: The Story of Lady Astor* (London: Vintage, 2013), 220.

16. Ibid., 238.

17. Evans, *Queen Bees*, 205.

18. Ibid., 206–07.

19. James, *Chips*, 35–36.

20. Philip Ziegler, *Edward VIII: The Official Biography* (London: Collins, 1990), 223.

21. James, *Chips*, 23; Heffer, *Henry 'Chips' Channon*, 381.

22. Ziegler, *Edward VIII*, 250–51.

23. Sebba, *That Woman*, 103.

24. "Prince George—The Queen's Lost Uncle," www.youtube.com/watch?v=pSmQP Zi1P00. I also thank the wonderful historian Christopher Warwick, who has sadly recently died.

25. Sebba, *That Woman*, 101; Bloch, *Ribbentrop*, 68; Willetts, *Rendezvous*, 194.

CHAPTER 18: MAN OF PEACE

1. Tennant, *True Account*, 184.

2. Ibid., 185.

3. Ibid., 186–87; G. Ward Price, *I Know These Dictators* (London: George G. Harrap, 1937), 29–31; Taylor, *Great Outsiders*, 294.

4. William L. Shirer, *Berlin Diary: The Journal of a Foreign Correspondent, 1934–1941* (New York: Ishi Press International, 2010), 26.

5. Bloch, *Ribbentrop*, 73.

6. Shirer, *Berlin Diary*, 26.

7. Dodd and Dodd, *Ambassador Dodd's Diary*, 220–22.

8. Ibid., 223–24.

9. Weinstein and Vassiliev, *Haunted Wood*, 51; KGB Archives, Moscow, File 14449, vol. 1, 25.

10. Kellogg, *Russian Roots*, 1–17.

11. Dodd, *My Years in Germany*, 174–75.

12. Weinstein and Vassiliev, *Haunted Wood*, 56; KGB Archives, Moscow, File 14449, vol. 1, 38–44; Shirer, *Berlin Diary*, 40–42.

13. Shirer, *Berlin Diary*, 41; Ziegler, *Edward VIII*, 206.

14. Ziegler, *Edward VIII*, 206.

15. Shirer, *Berlin Diary*, 27.

16. Ibid., 27–28; Kershaw, *Making Friends*, 100–01.

17. Kershaw, *Making Friends*, 102–04; Manchester, *Arms of Krupp*, 422.

18. Kershaw, *Making Friends*, 104.

19. Manchester, *Arms of Krupp*, 423.

20. Kershaw, *Making Friends*, 104–08.

21. Schad, *Hitler's Spy Princess*, 201–03.

22. Kershaw, *Making Friends*, 65.

23. Ibid., 60–61; Thomas Jones, *A Diary with Letters, 1931–1950* (London: Oxford University Press, 1954), 514–15.

24. Shirer, *Berlin Diary*, 37.

25. Ibid., 37–39; Dodd and Dodd, *Ambassador Dodd's Diary*, 253–54.

CHAPTER 19: PARTY DAY PROPAGANDA

1. FRUS, British Commonwealth, Europe 1935, vol. II, 862.404/144, No. 2281, Dodd to Hull, September 6, 1935; Longrich, *Heinrich Himmler*, 276–78; Victor Klemperer, *I Will Bear Witness, 1933–1941: A Diary of the Nazi Years* (New York: Modern Library, 1999), 129. (Italics are in the original.)

2. Longrich, *Heinrich Himmler*, 140.

3. Stephen Bach, *Leni: The Life and Work of Leni Riefenstahl* (London: Little Brown, 2007), 49–50, 9.

4. Bach, *Leni*, 110; *London Observer*, December 3, 1933.

5. Longrich, *Heinrich Himmler*, 224–26.

6. Bach, *Leni*, 112–13.

7. Ibid., 134–35.

8. Conradi, *Hitler's Piano Player*, 134.

9. Griffiths, *Fellow Travellers*, 110–11.

10. Ibid., 111–12.

11. Bloch, *Ribbentrop*, 84–85; Tennant, *True Account*, 193–94.

12. David Pryce-Jones, *Unity Mitford: A Quest* (London: Weidenfeld and Nicolson, 1976), 17.

13. Thompson, *The Six*, 44–45.

14. "Hitler's British Girl" documentary, Channel 4 (UK), 2007. https://pro.imdb .com/title/tt3563444/?ref_=instant_tt_1&q=Hitler%27s%20British%20.

15. Thompson, *The Six*, 154.

16. HIA, Box 3, folder 3, 135; Pryce-Jones, *Unity Mitford*, 83–84.

17. Ziegler, *Edward VIII*, 207.

18. Ibid., 208. The Bingham to FDR letter dates from December 24, 1935.

19. James, *Chips*, 29–30; Young, *Diaries*, 319–20.

20. Young, *Diaries*, 322–23.

21. Ziegler, *Edward VIII*, 209; Griffiths, *Fellow Travellers*, 129–30.

22. Griffiths, *Fellow Travellers*, 130–31.

23. DGFP, Series C, vol. IV, HMSO 1962, 23.

24. Moshe Gottlieb, "The American Controversy Over the Olympic Games," *American Jewish Historical Quarterly*, 61, no. 3 (March 1972), 184. JSTOR.

25. Alan Bullock, *Hitler: A Study in Tyranny* (London: Book Club Associates, 1973), 335–36; Jeffreys, *Hell's Cartel*, 154–55, 173–75.

26. Wilson, *Nazi Princess*, 69–71; HIA, 77020, Box 1, folder 10, 52.

CHAPTER 20: INEVITABILITY OF WAR

1. Anne Morrow Lindbergh, *Locked Rooms and Open Doors: Diaries and Letters of Anne Morrow Lindbergh, 1933–1935* (New York: Harcourt Brace Jovanovich, 1974), 331, 333, 336.

2. FRUS, https://history.state.gov/historicaldocuments/frus1936v02/d129.

3. Edgar B. Nixon, *Franklin D. Roosevelt and Foreign Affairs*, vol. 3, *September 1935–January 1937* (Cambridge: The Belknap Press of Harvard University Press, 1969), 154.

4. Ibid., 154, 156.

5. Ibid., 179–80.

6. Ziegler, *Edward VIII*, 240.

7. Susan Ronald, *Condé Nast: A Biography* (New York: St. Martin's Press, 2019), 305–06.

8. James, *Chips*, 54.

9. Courcy, *Viceroy's Daughters*, 243; Sebba, *That Woman*, 121.

10. DGFP, Series C (1933–1937), vol. IV, 1024–25.

11. John Julius Norwich, ed., *The Duff Cooper Diaries, 1915–1951* (London: Weidenfeld and Nicolson, 2005), 228.

12. James, *Chips*, 57; *Hitler's Favourite Royal* (ITV, Timeline Production), www.youtube.com/watch?v=FgnrCBlaaTI.

13. Courcy, *Viceroy's Daughters*, 243; Nicolson, *Harold Nicolson*, 241; Adrian Tinniswood, *The Long Weekend: Life in the English Country House Between the Wars* (London: Vintage, 2018), 18.

14. Kershaw, *Making Friends*, 119, 134–35.

15. Ibid., 136–37.

16. Nicolson, *Harold Nicolson*, 245; Kershaw, *Making Friends*, 137.

17. Kershaw, *Making Friends*, 138–39.

18. Ibid., 139.

19. Kershaw, *Making Friends*, 140; James, *Chips*, 58–59; Heffer, *Henry 'Chips' Channon*, 496.

20. Kershaw, *Making Friends*, 142–44; BNA, *Manchester Guardian*, February 24, 1936.

21. François-Poncet, *Fateful Years*, 191–93.
22. https://hansard.parliament.uk/Commons/1936–03–26/debates/83f6b52d
    -e792–4bef-abba-1f9a80da4493/EuropeanSituation?highlight=churchill
    #contribution-02d6ead8-aa45–4d70-b3ac-1dae70b4ddc0.
23. Hesse, *Hitler and the English*, 22; Ziegler, *King Edward VIII*, 270.

CHAPTER 21: UPPING THE ANTE

1. Courcy, *Diana Mosley* and *Viceroy's Daughters*, 239 and 177 respectively; Pugh, *"Hurrah for the Blackshirts!,"* 222–23.
2. Courcy, *Viceroy's Daughters*, 239; Nicolson, *Harold Nicolson*, 254; Pugh, *"Hurrah for the Blackshirts!,"* 213, 226–27.
3. Nicolson, *Harold Nicolson*, 240–41.
4. Sebba, *That Woman*, 124–25.
5. Ibid., 120–122.
6. Andrew Morton, *17 Carnations: The Royals, the Nazis, and the Biggest Cover-Up in History* (New York: Grand Central Publishing, 2015), 49–50.
7. Sebba, *That Woman*, 123; Duff Hart-Davis, ed., *King's Counsellor: Abdication and War: The Diaries of Sir Alan 'Tommy' Lascelles* (London: Weidenfeld and Nicolson, 2020), 5.
8. Sebba, *That Woman*, 125.
9. TNA, KV2–2869–1, Princess Mira Dimitri.
10. Wolfgang zu Putlitz, *The Putlitz Dossier* (London: Allan Wingate, 1957), 110; DGFP, Series C, vol. V, (1936–1937), 253, 287.
11. Zu Putlitz, *The Putlitz Dossier*, 111–2.
12. Bloch, *Ribbentrop*, 99–100.
13. James, *Chips*, 62; Kershaw, *Making Friends*, 160.
14. Kershaw, *Making Friends*, 154–56; Bloch, *Ribbentrop*, 103.
15. Kershaw, *Making Friends*, 162–63; BNA, *The Star*, June 2, 1936.
16. Kershaw, *Making Friends*, 164–65.
17. Ibid., 165; Bloch, *Ribbentrop*, 103; DBFP XX, No. 379.
18. ODNB; Nicolson, *Harold Nicolson*, 263–64.
19. Nicolson, *Harold Nicolson*, 262; Chernow, *House of Morgan*, 436–47; AA, letter to Nancy Astor, June 4, 1937.
20. Manchester, *Arms of Krupp*, 425; Anne van Wynen Thomas and A. J. Thomas Jr., "Non-Intervention and the Spanish Civil War," *Proceedings of the American Society of International Law at Its Annual Meeting (1921–1969)*, April 27–29, 1967, vol. 61, 2.
21. Hart, *Hitler's American Friends*, 167. See also: Truman Smith Papers (Yale University), Box 1, Lindbergh to Smith, June 5, 1936.
22. *NYT*, TimesMachine, July 26, 1936.

CHAPTER 22: OLYMPIANS AND TITANS

1. Hart, *Hitler's American Friends*, 169. See also: Truman Smith Papers (Yale University), Box 1, Lindbergh to Smith, August 6, 1936.
2. Manchester, *Arms of Krupp*, 425; Ronald, *Hitler's Art Thief*, 172–73.
3. Ronald, *Dangerous Woman*, 214–15.
4. George Eisen, "The Voices of Sanity: American Diplomatic Reports from the 1936 Berlin Olympiad," *Journal of Sports History* 11, no. 3 (Winter 1984), 59–60, JSTOR.
5. FOLD3, NARA Catalog 647749, RG 238, Roll 0002, 8; Dodd and Dodd, *Ambassador Dodd's Diary*, 349.
6. Longerich, *Goebbels*, 321; Dodd and Dodd, *Ambassador Dodd's Diary*, 349.
7. Leonard Mosley, *The Reich Marshal: A Biography of Hermann Goering* (New York: Dell, 1974), 258–59; Robert Rhodes James, *Chips* (Weidenfeld and Nicolson, 1967), 110–111; HIA, 77020, Box 1, folder 11; Heffer, *Henry 'Chips' Channon*, 557.
8. Mosley, *The Reich Marshal*, 258.
9. Bloch, *Ribbentrop*, 106–08; James, *Chips*, 109–10; Lord R. G. V. Vansittart, *The Mist Procession: The Autobiography of Lord Vansittart* (London: Hutchinson of London, 1958), 524.
10. Heffer, *Henry 'Chips' Channon*, 564.
11. Mosley, *The Reich Marshal*, 258; www.ushmm.org/exhibition/olympics/?content =aa_responses&lang=en interview with Ralph Metcalfe.
12. James, *Chips*, 113; Nicolson, *Harold Nicolson*, 272–73.
13. Ziegler, *King Edward VIII*, 282.
14. Ibid., 282–84; Sebba, *That Woman*, 135; "She Is as Hard as Nails and She Doesn't Love Him," *Times* [London], February 4, 2003, p. 4[S1]+, *The Times Digital Archive*.
15. Ziegler, *King Edward VIII*, 292.

CHAPTER 23: FIFTH COLUMNISTS

1. Peter Duffy, *Double Agent* (New York: Scribner, 2014), 13, 85; TNA, KV2–86–1, Ritter/Dr. Rantzau, 58, 60.
2. FOLD3, Chemnyco, OSS Washington Secret Intelligence/Special Funds Records, 1942–1946, RG 226, Roll 0012, 283.
3. FOLD3, Chemnyco, OSS Washington Secret Intelligence/Special Funds Records, 1942–1946, RG 226, Roll 0012, 284.
4. Ronald, *Ambassador*, 34; Ronald, *Dangerous Woman*, 249–50.
5. www.theguardian.com/world/2004/sep/25/usa.secondworldwar; John A. Kouwenhoven, *Partners in Banking: An Historical Portrait of a Great Private Bank Brown Brothers Harriman & Co., 1818–1968*. Privately published by Brown Brothers Harriman & Co., Garden City, New York, 1969.

6. Ronald, *Ambassador*, 34–35; Norman J. W. Goda, "Banking on Hitler: Chase National Bank and the Rückwanderer Mark Scheme, 1936–1941," *U.S. Intelligence and the Nazis* (New York: Cambridge University Press, 2009), 183.

7. W. A. Swanberg, *Citizen Hearst* (New York: Galahad Books, 1996), 468–69, 476.

8. Ibid., 470, 471.

9. Ralph G. Martin, *Cissy: The Extraordinary Life of Eleanor Medill Patterson* (New York: Simon and Schuster, 1979), 349.

10. Hitler, *Mein Kampf*, trans. Manheim (1997), 164–65.

11. Taylor, *Great Outsiders*, 318.

12. Ibid., 305, 308, 309, 313.

13. Jeffreys, *Hell's Cartel*, 178–79.

14. Stoiber and Celovsky, *Stephanie von Hohenlohe*, 121–23.

15. Ibid., 135; Pryce-Jones, *Unity Mitford*, 228; Courcy, *Diana Mosley*, 174–75; Pugh, *"Hurrah for the Blackshirts!,"* 227.

CHAPTER 24: DASHED DREAMS

1. Bloch, *Ribbentrop*, 131–32.

2. Morton, *17 Carnations*, 50.

3. Norwich, *Duff Cooper Diaries*, 233–34; K. Young, *Stanley Baldwin*, 133–34.

4. BNA, *Evening Telegraph*, December 3, 1936; *Belfast Telegraph*, December 3, 1936.

5. HIA, 77020, Box 1, folder 10, 7–9.

6. Taylor, *Great Outsiders*, 298; Schad, *Hitler's Spy Princess*, 39–40; Norman Ohler, *Blitzed: Drugs in Nazi Germany* (London: Penguin Books, 2016), 32; *TBJG*, January 5–9, 1937.

CHAPTER 25: THE BOILING CAULDRON

1. FDRPL, PSFA 0497, Bingham to Roosevelt, September 4, 1936; www.theguardian.com/books/booksblog/2010/oct/25/poem-of-the-week-john-cornford.

2. Gabriel Gorodetsky, ed., *The Maisky Diaries,* trans. Tatiana Sorokina and Oliver Ready (London: Yale University Press, 2016), 72–73.

3. FDRPL, PSFA 0497, Bingham to Roosevelt, September 4, 1936.

4. www.theguardian.com/books/2013/jun/06/china-war-japan-rana-mitter-review.

5. Tim Bouverie, *Appeasing Hitler: Chamberlain, Churchill and the Road to War* (London: Vintage, 2020), 120.

6. Duffy, *Double Agent*, 9; Louis De Jong, *The German Fifth Column in the Second World War,* trans. C. M. Geyl (London: Routledge and Kegan Paul, 1956), 3–5.

7. *The Times*, April 28, 1937, 17.

8. Duffy, *Double Agent*, 10–11; Anthony Beevor, *The Battle for Spain: The Spanish Civil War, 1936–1939* (London: Penguin Books, 2006), 173.

9. *The Times*, April 28, 1937; *NYT*, TimesMachine, April 28, 1937; Duffy, *Double Agent*, 15–16.

10. https://history.state.gov/milestones/1921–1936/neutrality-acts.

11. Bouverie, *Appeasing Hitler*, 130; NCP, NC 18/1/815.

12. Churchill, *Great Contemporaries*, 251–52.

13. Bloch, *Ribbentrop*, 135–38; DGFP C/VI, No. 201; DBFP, 2/XVII, No. 167.

14. Bloch, *Ribbentrop*, 139; *TBJG*, March 3, 1937.

15. Speer, *Inside the Third Reich*, 165.

16. Reinhard Spitzy, *How We Squandered the Reich*, trans. G. T. Waddington (London: Michael Russell, 1997), 67–68; Heffer, *Henry 'Chips' Channon*, 683.

17. Jim Christy, *The Price of Power: A Biography of Charles Eugène Bedaux* (New York: Doubleday, 1984), 157–58; Ziegler, *King Edward VIII*, 267.

18. Christy, *Price of Power*, 143–46; TNA, KV2/4412.

19. HIA, Box 1, folder 12, 4.

20. Heffer, *Henry 'Chips' Channon*, 682–83; *TBJG*, May 17, 1937; Bloch, *Ribbentrop*, 139–40.

21. DGFP, 783–1075.

22. Bouverie, *Appeasing Hitler*, 120.

23. Ibid., 126–27; Ronald, *Ambassador*, 84.

24. Bouverie, *Appeasing Hitler*, 127–29, 132–33; Ronald, *Ambassador*, 84–85.

CHAPTER 26: APPEASEMENT

1. https://hansard.parliament.uk/Commons/1936–03–26/debates/83f6b52d -e792–4bef-abba-1f9a80da4493/EuropeanSituation?highlight=debate #contribution-94da757d-1c4c-4c5e-8ba5–7232117e19a3.

2. Keith Feiling, *The Life of Neville Chamberlain* (Hamden, CT: Archon Books, 1970), 323–24.

3. Pugh, "Hurrah for the Blackshirts!," 228–29.

4. Griffiths, *Patriotism Perverted*, 39, 43, 45–46; Pugh, "Hurrah for the Blackshirts!," 232.

5. Pugh, "Hurrah for the Blackshirts!," 229, 233.

6. Richard Cockett, *Twilight of Truth: Chamberlain, Appeasement and the Manipulation of the Press* (London: Weidenfeld and Nicolson, 1989), 4–5.

7. Ibid., 8–9.

8. ODNB; BOD, MS Eng. c. 6654, 6656.

9. Cockett, *Twilight of Truth*, 22–23.

10. Stoiber and Celovsky, *Stephanie von Hohenlohe*, 125, 143; Christy, *Price of Power*, 160.

11. Christy, *Price of Power*, 158–59; FDRPL, PSFA 0497, Bingham to Roosevelt, October 19, 1937.

12. Ziegler, *King Edward VIII*, 371; Christy, *Price of Power*, 148–49.

13. Ziegler, *King Edward VIII*, 386; FOLD3: www.fold3.com/image/287204657?terms =wenner,axel,gren; www.fold3.com/image/304726890?terms=wenner,axel,gren.

14. BNA, BL_0000273_193_71018_297_0010, Monday, October 18, 1937; BL_ 00000_38_193_71019_183_0007, Tuesday, October 19, 1937.

15. BL_0001898_19371_012_023_0001, Saturday, October 23, 1937; *NYT*, Times-Machine, October 23, 1937; Stoiber and Celovsky, *Stephanie von Hohenlohe*, 143.

16. Ronald, *Ambassador*, 66.

17. NCP, NC/1/17/1–26, letter dated December 16, 1937; William C. Mills, "Sir Joseph Ball, Adrian Dingli, and Neville Chamberlain's 'Secret Channel' to Italy," *International History Review*, 24, no. 2 (June 2002), 282, JSTOR.

18. https://millercenter.org/the-presidency/presidential-speeches/october-5– 1937-quarantine-speech; Bouverie, *Appeasing Hitler*, 214.

CHAPTER 27: ESPIONAGE

1. Pryce-Jones, *Unity Mitford*, 90–91, 153–55; Conradi, *Hitler's Piano Player*, 204.

2. Dodd, *My Years in Germany*, 224.

3. Conradi, *Hitler's Piano Player*, 195–96.

4. Ibid., 197–209.

5. *NYT*, TimesMachine, November 26, 1937.

6. Stoiber and Celovsky, *Stephanie von Hohenlohe*, 144.

7. Ibid., 145. See also: Princess Stephanie FBI file dated May 21, 1940.

8. FOLD3: OCCPAC Interrogation Transcripts, Ulrich von Gienanth, NARA M1270, Roll 0005, 80, 28; OSS Secret Intelligence Records, NARA M1934, RG 226, Roll 0001, 88–89.

9. FOLD3: OCCPAC Interrogation Record prepared for War Crime Proceedings at Nuremberg 194547, Fritz Wiedemann; NARA M1270, RG 238, Roll 0022, 184–85.

10. FOLD3: www.fold3.com/image304730200, "Sequel to the Apocalypse," 60.

11. FOLD3: OSS Secret Intelligence Reports, Chemnyco, M1934, RG 226, Roll 0012, 285, 289, 290, 292, 293.

12. FOLD3: OSS Secret Intelligence Reports, M1934, RG 226, Roll 0009, 117, 120, 122; Nuernberg Interrogation Records, Ernst Bohle, M1270, RG 238, Roll 0002, 12, 13, 33.

13. FOLD3: OCCPAC Interrogation Transcripts, Ulrich von Gienanth, NARA M1270, Roll 0005, 12, 13, 16, 22, 24–25.

14. Steven J. Ross, *Hitler in Los Angeles: How Jews Foiled Nazi Plots Against Hollywood and America* (New York: Bloomsbury USA, 2017), 134–38.

15. Ibid., 214–25.

16. Duffy, *Double Agent*, 17, 21–23.

17. Ibid., 24–25.

18. Ibid., 27–28.

CHAPTER 28: SECRET MANEUVERS

1. Galeazzo Ciano, *Ciano's Hidden Diary, 1937–1938*, trans. Andreas Mayor (New York: E. P. Dutton, 1953), 16.

2. Ibid., 27.

3. Ronald, *Ambassador*, 102; Ciano, *Ciano's Hidden Diary*, 35.

4. https://avalon.law.yale.edu/imt/hossbach.asp; HIA, Box 1, folder 13, 2; Anthony Cave Brown, *Bodyguard of Lies* (London: Star Books, 1975), 159–62; HIA, Box 1, folder 13, 6.

5. Ronald, *Ambassador*, 75–76.

6. HIA, Box 1, folder 13, 6.

7. Bouverie, *Appeasing Hitler*, 166–69; Heffer, *Henry 'Chips' Channon*, 822–23.

8. Ronald, *Ambassador*, 78, 83–86.

9. Ibid., 91; NCP, NC 18/1/1045, Chamberlain to Hilda, March 13, 1938.

10. DBFP, telegrams no. 70 and 71, Halifax to Henderson, 5–6.

11. Amanda Smith, ed., *Hostage to Fortune: The Letters of Joseph P. Kennedy* (New York: Viking, 2001), 240–43.

12. Ronald, *Ambassador*, 96–97; Brown, *Bodyguard of Lies*, 163.

13. Brown, *Bodyguard of Lies*, 164–65.

14. https://hansard.parliament.uk/Lords/1938–03–16/debates/2afae47d-9879–412a -8fe7–341bb9338c4c/SituationInEurope?highlight=astor#contribution -92db49d0-bdcc-4ae7-b046–797bff65c6ef; Kershaw, *Making Friends*, 215; Griffiths, *Fellow Travellers*, 296.

15. https://hansard.parliament.uk/Lords/1938–03–16/debates/2afae47d-9879–412a -8fe7–341bb9338c4c/SituationInEurope?highlight=astor#contribution -92db49d0-bdcc-4ae7-b046–797bff65c6ef.

16. *The Times*, March 12, 1938.

17. Heffer, *Henry 'Chips' Channon*, 836.

18. A. Scott Berg, *Lindbergh* (New York: G. P. Putnam and Sons, 1998), 365–66.

19. Ibid., 367–68.

20. Nicolson, *Harold Nicolson*, 332–33. Italics are mine.

21. Ibid., 343; Anne Morrow Lindbergh, *The Flower and the Nettle: Diaries and Letters, 1936–1939* (New York: Harcourt Brace Jovanovich, 1976), 271–72.

22. Griffiths, *Fellow Travellers*, 292–96; Mount Temple letter to *The Times*, February 16, 1938; Taylor, *Great Outsiders*, 328; Wilson, *Nazi Princess*, 118–19; HIA, Box 1, folder 3, telegrams throughout; Jeffreys, *Hell's Cartel*, 205.

23. Taylor, *Great Outsiders*, 319; Wilson, *Nazi Princess*, 118–19; HIA, Box 3, folder 3, references to 1938 throughout.

CHAPTER 29: SWAPPING HORSES MIDSTREAM

1. HIA, Box 1, folder 13, 2, February 2, 1938.
2. TNA, KV-2-1697-2, 44. According to MI5, Stephanie and Donald C. Malcolm worked together in this endeavor.
3. HIA, Box 1, folder 14, 43. *NYT,* TimesMachine, May 6, 1938.
4. HIA, Box 1, folder 18, 7–8, February 4, 1941.
5. Ibid., folder 14, 24, May 4, 1938.
6. BNA: BL_0000957_19380702_036_0004.
7. HIA, Box 3, folder 3, 126, no date; Ronald, *Ambassador*, 131–32; TNA: KV2-1696-1_1938_1939, 23.
8. HIA, Box 3, folder 3, 228; Ronald, *Ambassador*, 83–85.
9. Ronald, *Ambassador*, 140.
10. Ibid.; DGFP, Series D (1937–1945), vol. 9 (London: HMSO, 1956), 716.
11. HIA, Box 3, folder 3, 231–42.
12. Schad, *Hitler's Spy Princess*, 47–49.
13. NCP, NC18/01/1059, Chamberlain to Hilda, July 9, 1938.
14. Ronald, *Ambassador*, 136, 139.
15. Ibid., 150–52; DGFP, Series D (1937–1945), vol. 9 (London: HMSO, 1956), 721–72.
16. Brown, *Bodyguard of Lies*, 167–68.
17. Ibid., 168.
18. Schad, *Hitler's Spy Princess*, 89.
19. ODNB.
20. Kershaw, *Making Friends*, 240.
21. HIA, Box 3, folder 3, 118. Previous biographers have claimed that there was an article in *The Times* of London that Stephanie had been at the talks. Having gone through *The Times* digital archive, I could find no such reference.
22. "Herr Hitler's Speech of September 12, 1938," *Bulletin of International News* 15, no. 9 (September 24, 1938), 8–11, JSTOR.

CHAPTER 30: FALL FROM GRACE

1. Ziegler, *King Edward VIII*, 398–99.
2. Shirer, *Berlin Diary*, 144.
3. Ibid., 137.
4. Harold Deutsch, *The Conspiracy Against Hitler in the Twilight War* (Minneapolis: University of Minnesota Press, 1968), 82–83; Ulrich von Hassell, *The Ulrich von Hassell Diaries, 1938–44,* trans. Geoffrey Brooks (London: Frontline Books, 2011), 5–6.
5. https://api.parliament.uk/historic-hansard/commons/1938/oct/03/personal -explanation.

6. Ronald, *Ambassador*, 169–70.

7. Ibid., 185.

8. Max Domarus, *Hitler's Speeches and Proclamations, 1932–1938*, vol. 2 (London: I. B. Taurus, 1992), 955; Hassell, *Ulrich von Hassell Diaries*, 7.

9. Stoiber and Celovsky, *Stephanie von Hohenlohe*, 188.

10. Baldwin, *Henry Ford and the Jews*, 283, 284–85.

11. A. Lindbergh, *Flower and the Nettle*, 437; Baldwin, *Henry Ford and the Jews*, 284–89; James Newton, *Uncommon Friends: Life with Thomas Edison, Henry Ford, Harvey Firestone, Alexis Carrel, and Charles Lindbergh* (New York: Harcourt Brace Jovanovich, 1987), 221–22; 237–48; Berg, *Lindbergh*, 376, 377–78.

12. Ronald, *Hitler's Art Thief*, 184; Baldwin, *Henry Ford and the Jews*, 290.

13. Ronald, *Hitler's Art Thief*, 184.

14. *NYT*, TimesMachine, November 12, 1938.

15. Bouverie, *Appeasing Hitler*, 308; BNA: *News Chronicle*, November 11, 1938; *The Times*, November 11, 1938.

16. Hassell, *Ulrich von Hassell Diaries*, 9–10.

17. https://encyclopedia.ushmm.org/content/en/article/immigration-to-the-united-states-1933-41.

18. Fritz Wiedemann, *Der Feldherr Werden Wollte* (Wuppertal-Barmen: Blick and Bild Verlag für Politische Bildung, 1964), 234–35; Bloch, *Ribbentrop*, 248.

19. *NYT*, TimesMachine, March 5, 1939.

20. *NYT*, TimesMachine, January 21, 1939.

21. UCN: NRS, CRC2–103–1, *NYT*, January 22, 1939.

22. FOLD3: WASH-SPDF-INT-1: Documents 3971–3981, M1934, RG 226, Roll 0012; OSS Secret Intelligence Reports, M1934, RG 226, Roll 0024; Richard Polenberg, "Franklin Roosevelt and Civil Liberties: The Case of the Dies Committee," *Historian* 30, no. 2 (February 1968), 165–78, JSTOR; Albert Alexander, "The President and the Investigator: Roosevelt and Dies," *Antioch Review* 15, no. 1 (Spring 1955), 106–17.

23. *NYT*, TimesMachine, March 5, 1939.

24. UCN: NRS, CRC2–103–1, 15 (Anti-Defamation League Letter, dated March 22, 1939).

CHAPTER 31: LAST THROW OF THE DICE

1. Kershaw, *Making Friends*, 254; William C. Mills, "Sir Joseph Ball, Adrian Dingli, and Neville Chamberlain's 'Secret Channel' to Italy 1937–1940," *International History Review* 24, no. 2 (June 2002), 310–11, JSTOR.

2. Kershaw, *Making Friends*, 279–80.

3. Ibid., 280–81; Ronald, *Ambassador*, 305–07.

4. Hart-Davis, *King's Counsellor*, 53.

5. Kershaw, *Making Friends*, 282, 284, 286.

6. Ronald, *Ambassador*, 231–32; David Blaazer, "Finance and the End of Appease-ment: The Bank of England, the National Government and the Czech Gold," *Journal of Contemporary History* 40, no. 1 (2005), 25–39; Courcy, *Diana Mosley*, 201.

7. Kershaw, *Making Friends*, 285–86; Courcy, *Diana Mosley*, 197–202.

8. Young, *Diaries*, 403; Ziegler, *Edward VIII*, 398.

9. Ziegler, *Edward VIII*, 398–99.

10. James, *Chips*, 211–26.

11. TNA, KV2-1696-1, 35.

CHAPTER 32: THE EXILES

1. Courcy, *Diana Mosley*, 190; Bach, *Leni*, 185; Shirer, *Berlin Diary*, 180.

2. Gorodetsky, *Maisky Diaries*, 218; Nicolson, *Harold Nicolson*, 411–13.

3. Ronald, *Ambassador*, 250–51.

4. Bach, *Leni*, 185; Ziegler, *Edward VIII*, 400–01.

5. Ziegler, *Edward VIII*, 400–01; Ronald, *Ambassador*, 247; FDRPL: PSFA 0322, Great Britain.

6. Ronald, *Ambassador*, 250–51.

7. Ronald, *Ambassador*, 253; Gorodetsky, *Maisky Diaries*, 222.

8. Ziegler, *Edward VIII*, 402–04.

9. Kurth, *American Cassandra*, 308–10.

10. Bach, *Leni*, 185, 186–88.

11. Kurth, *American Cassandra*, 310–12; "Col. Charles A. Lindbergh's Radio Address, September 15, 1939," *World Affairs* 102, no. 3 (September 1939), 164–65, JSTOR.

12. Shirer, *Berlin Diary*, 200.

13. Pryce-Jones, *Unity Mitford*, 234–42.

14. TNA: KV-2-469-1, 59–60; Conradi, *Hitler's Piano Player*, 236–27.

15. Thyssen, *I Paid Hitler*, 33–41.

16. TNA: KV-2-469-1, 13.

17. HIA: Box 3, folder 3, 125–6.

18. TNA: KV-2-1696_1938_1939, 24–25; Nigel West, ed., *The Guy Liddell Diaries*, vol. 1. *1939–1942* (London: Routledge, 2005), 34.

19. *The Times*, Law Report Section, 16 November 1939, BNA, *Daily Herald*, November 14, 1939.

20. Taylor, *Great Outsiders*, 322.

21. https://hansard.parliament.uk/Commons/1939-12-07/debates /6755495c-ce50-4941-9ad8-909ab879c04b/PrincessHohenlohe ?highlight=%22hohenlohe%22#contribution-40113ef7-ec9d-4296-bc53 -a19cc29305a3.

CHAPTER 33: THE AMERICAN DIMENSION

1. https://search.ancestry.com/cgi-bin/sse.dll?dbid=50018&h=3129884&indiv=try;
https://search.ancestry.com/cgi-bin/sse.dll?indiv=1&dbid=60579&h=4106977
&tid=&pid=&queryId=48eabb57434a76873b1a08ea09e5c4d4&usePUB
=true&_phsrc=skE26&_phstart=successSource.

2. Taylor, *Great Outsiders*, 326.

3. HO 382/250. Passport Control at Southampton reported to MI5 that they had searched her baggage and nothing significant had been found.

4. Schad, *Hitler's Spy Princess*, 122; HIA, Box 1, folder 16, 9.

5. UCN: CRC2–066–22, 2.

6. HIA, Box 1, folder 14, 37; Box 1, folder 17, 27–28.

7. www.googlebooks.com//LIFE%20-%20Google%20Books%20Wiedemann
.webarchive.

8. *NYT*, TimesMachine, June 25, 1937; Laura B. Rosenzweig, *Hollywood's Spies: Undercover Surveillance of the Nazis in Los Angeles* (New York: New York University Press, 2017), 178–79; University of Michigan, *Germany in America*, mdp.39015008405519-175-1589014114Hathai-Trust. See also: University of California Northridge: *News Research Service* files: *Summary Report*, September 1938, part 2, CRC Papers, 2.26.6–7, 2.28.12–16.

9. www.newspapers.com/image/704017172/?terms=%22Wiedemann%22
&match=1.

10. Kurth, *American Cassandra*, 311.

11. Duffy, *Double Agent*, 90–92, 130–32; Hart, *Hitler's American Friends*, 47–48.

12. www.googlebooks.com//LIFE%20-%20Google%20Books%20Wiedemann
.webarchive.

13. American Dictionary of National Biography: www-anb-org.lonlib.idm.oclc
.org/view/10.1093/anb/9780198606697.001.0001/anb-9780198606697-e
-0700076?rskey=vCeJWW&result=1.

14. Polenberg, "Franklin Roosevelt and Civil Liberties"; Alexander, "The President and the Investigator."

15. FDRPL, PSFC000049; Kenneth O'Reilly, "A New Deal for the FBI: The Roosevelt Administration, Crime Control, and National Security," *Journal of American History* 69, no. 3 (1982), 652, JSTOR.

16. Hart, *Hitler's American Friends*, 194–95; West, *Guy Liddell Diaries; MI5's Director of Counter-Espionage in World War II* (Abingdon: Routledge, 2005), 140; www.googlebooks.com//LIFE%20-%20Google%20Books%20Wiedemann
.webarchive.

17. history.state.gov/milestones/1921–1936/neutrality-acts; Chernow, *House of Morgan*, 442–43.

18. Ronald, *Ambassador*, 173–74; Berg, *Lindbergh*, 374–77, 382–83.

19. Chernow, *House of Morgan*, 443–45; A. Lindbergh, *Flower and the Nettle*, 573–55.

CHAPTER 34: MYSTERIES WITHIN AN ENIGMA

1. UCN: CRC2-066-22, 16-19.
2. Chernow, *House of Morgan*, 445-46; www.youtube.com/watch?v=ie6Lkec0tIw.
3. Ibid., 446-47; Berg, *Lindbergh*, 406.
4. FDRPL: PSF 000412, Vincent Astor Letter to Missy LeHand May 15, 1940; Duffy, *Double Agent*,163.
5. David Kahn, *Hitler's Spies: German Military Intelligence in World War II* (London: Hodder and Stoughton, 1978), 330-31; Duffy, *Double Agent*, 204-12.
6. Kahn, *Hitler's Spies*, 332-33; *NYT*, TimesMachine, April 6, 1936, advertisement to Theodor Koerner.
7. www.fbi.gov/history/famous-cases/duquesne-spy-ring.
8. West, *Guy Liddell Diaries*, 19, 25, 39, 40, 76.
9. Ibid., 19.
10. Ibid., 80; email correspondence with Paul Willetts, author of *Rendezvous at the Russian Tea Rooms*; FDRPL, Small Collections, OF10-6, Memorandum December 13, 1940, Tyler Kent; TNA: KV-2-543, Tyler Kent.
11. Charles A. Lindbergh, *The Wartime Journals of Charles A. Lindbergh* (New York: Harcourt Brace Jovanovich, 1970), 306-48; TNA: FO371/24248, FO371/24249.
12. Ronald, *Ambassador*, 304-07; TNA: KV2/1698 Del Monte, KV2/543 Kent.
13. West, *Guy Liddell Diaries*, 81-82.
14. Courcy, *Diana Mosley*, 210-11, 295-96.
15. TNA: KV/2-2869_1 Princess Mira Dimitri.
16. Conradi, *Hitler's Piano Player*, 249.
17. Michael Bloch, *Operation Willi: The Plot to Kidnap the Duke of Windsor, July 1940* (London: Weidenfeld and Nicolson, 1984), 21-23, 112.
18. Ibid., 23.

CHAPTER 35: "WILLI"

1. Ibid., 46-47. See also: FO 800/326, f. 185.
2. Bloch, *Operation Willi*, 48; see Templewood Papers (XIII/16/29), Hoare to Churchill, June 27, 1940.
3. Bloch, *Operation Willi*, 49-55.
4. Ibid., 56-57.
5. Ibid., 58, 60-61, 111.
6. Morton, *17 Carnations*, 154-58; Bloch, *Operation Willi*, 62.
7. Bloch, *Operation Willi*, 64-65; Sebba, *That Woman*, 232.
8. Bloch, *Operation Willi*, 74.
9. Sebba, *That Woman*, 233; Bloch, *Operation Willi*, 118.
10. DGFP, No. 152, July 11, 1940.
11. Morton, *17 Carnations*, 184-90.

CHAPTER 36: HERDING CATS

1. Sir Orville Turnquest, *What Manner of Man Is This? The Duke of Windsor's Years in the Bahamas* (Nassau: Grant's Town Press, 2016), 47–49; Sebba, *That Woman*, 235.
2. Turnquest, *What Manner of Man Is This?*, 54; Sebba, *That Woman*, 236.
3. FOLD3: www.fold3.com/image/312772230, 137; www.wennergren.org/sites/default/files/AWG.FINAL%20Version.%20May%202021.pdf.
4. FOLD3: WASH-SPDF-INT-1, 3971–3981, NA Identifier: 411934, RG 226, Roll 0012, 300–1, 303.
5. Ibid., 302.
6. FOLD3: "Secret Intelligence Reports I. G. Farben," M1934, RG 226, Roll 0024, 11–17, 21–3; www.fold3.com/image/312772230, 59–60, 66; Schad, *Hitler's Spy Princess*, 133.
7. FOLD3: www.fold3.com/image/312772230, 60.
8. www.newspapers.com/image/457834334; *NYT*, TimesMachine, July 10, 1940.
9. Ibid.
10. Harold L. Ickes, *The Secret Diary of Harold L. Ickes, vol. 3, The Lowering Clouds, 1939–1941* (London: Weidenfeld and Nicolson, 1955), 534–35.
11. Wilson, *Nazi Princess*, 158; Schad, *Hitler's Spy Princess*, 135.
12. Ickes, *Secret Diary*, 395; FDRPL: PSFA0031 (FBI Report on Princess Stephanie); www.newspapers.com/image/419865126/?terms=%22Princess%2BHohenlohe%22.
13. Ickes, *Secret Diary*, 454; Schad, *Hitler's Spy Princess*, 143–45.
14. *NYT*, TimesMachine, February 20, 1941.
15. www.newspapers.com/image/171126370/?terms=%22Lemuel%20Schofield%22&match=1; Schad, *Hitler's Spy Princess*, 141–43.
16. *NYT*, TimesMachine, May 20, 1941; Schad, *Hitler's Spy Princess*, 143–46; www.newspapers.com/image/171126370/?terms=%22Lemuel%20Schofield%22&match=1; www.newspapers.com/image/592459375/?terms=%22Lemuel%20Schofield%22&match=1.
17. *NYT*, TimesMachine, June 13, 1941.
18. UCN: NRS, CRC2-071-20, 6–7.
19. www.newspapers.com/image/147650476/.

CHAPTER 37: PEARL HARBOR

1. Russell Miller, *Codename Tricycle: The True Story of the Second World War's Most Extraordinary Double Agent* (London: Pimlico, 2005), 16–17.
2. Ibid., 18–19.
3. Ibid., 21.
4. TNA: KV-2/487; Dusko Popov, *Spy/Counterspy* (London: Weidenfeld and Nicolson, 1974), 124–27.

5. Popov, *Spy/Counterspy*, 108–15.
6. Ibid., 117–18; www.facebook.com/186822448054743/posts/pearl-harbor-and-the-moontoday-december-7th-is-a-date-which-will-live-in-infamy-/277571515626579/; KV-2/487.
7. Popov, *Spy/Counterspy*, 118–26; KV-2/487.
8. Ibid., 129–43; KV-2/487; Miller, *Codename Tricycle*, 96–103; https://vault.fbi.gov/sir-william-stephenson/sir-william-stephenson/view.
9. Milton Bliss, interview with the author, June 6, 2004.
10. Steve Twomey, *Countdown to Pearl Harbor: The Twelve Days to the Attack* (New York: Simon and Schuster Paperbacks, 2016), 272.
11. Ibid., 272–74.

EPILOGUE

1. Manchester, *Arms of Krupp*, 22–25.
2. www.loc.gov/rr/frd/Military_Law/pdf/Law-Reports_Vol-10.pdf.
3. Christy, *Price of Power*, 281–87.
4. Bloch, *Operation Willi*, 231.
5. BOD, Balliol College, unpublished papers of Harold Nicolson.
6. Turnquest, *What Manner of Man Is This?*, 124–26, 133–35, 142–45.
7. "Ford and GM Scrutinized for Alleged Nazi Collaboration," *Washington Post*, December 12, 1998; "Ford and the Führer," *Nation*, January 24, 2000, 11–16.
8. Weinstein and Vassiliev, *Haunted Wood*, 69–71.
9. Ibid., 140–49.
10. Berg, *Lindbergh*, 433–43.

SELECT BIBLIOGRAPHY

ARCHIVAL SOURCES

Neville Chamberlain Papers, University of Birmingham

FDRPL, PSFA 0497, 0322, PSFC000049, PSF 000412, PSFA 0031

NARA: RG 226, RG 238, OCCPAC Interrogation Transcripts, OSS Secret Intelligence Reports, "Secret Intelligence Reports I. G. Farben," Nuernberg Interrogation Records

HIA 77020, Boxes 1–5

University of California Northridge: CRC2–103–1; CRC2–066–22; CRC2–26; CRC2–28, CRC2–071–20

TNA: KV2–1692/1–2, TNA, KV2/4412, KV2/469–2, KV2/1698, KV2/543, KV-2/487, FO371/24248, FO371/24249, KV/2–2869_1

ARTICLES

Alexander, Albert. "The President and the Investigator: Roosevelt and Dies." *Antioch Review* 15, no. 1 (Spring 1955).

Blaazer, David. "Finance and the End of Appeasement: The Bank of England, the National Government and the Czech Gold." *Journal of Contemporary History* 40, no. 1 (2005).

Chase, William J. "Microhistory and Mass Repression: Politics, Personalities, and Revenge in the Fall of Béla Kun." *Russian Review* 67, no. 3 (July 2008).

Dayer, Roberta A. "Strange Bedfellows: J.P. Morgan & Co., Whitehall and the Wilson Administration during World War I." *Business History* 18, no. 2 (1976).

Dimsdale, Nicholas H., Nicholas Horsewood, and Arthur van Riel. "Unemployment in Inter-War Germany: An Analysis of the Labour Market 1927–36." *Journal of Economic History* 66, no. 3 (September 2006).

Eisen, George. "The Voices of Sanity: American Diplomatic Reports from the 1936 Berlin Olympiad." *Journal of Sports History* 11, no. 3 (Winter 1984).

Ferguson, Thomas, and Hans-Joachim Voth. "Betting on Hitler: The Value of Political Connections in Nazi Germany." *Oxford Quarterly Journal of Economics* 123, no. 1 (February 2008).

Jackson, Peter. "French Intelligence and Hitler's Rise to Power." *History Journal* 41, no. 3 (September 1998).

McVeigh, Rory, Daniel J. Myers, and Edward Sikkink. "Corn, Klansmen, and Coolidge: Structure and Framing in Social Movements." *Social Forces* 83, no. 2 (2004).

Mills, William C. "Sir Joseph Ball, Adrian Dingli, and Neville Chamberlain's 'Secret Channel' to Italy." *International History Review* 24, no. 2 (June 2002).

O'Reilly, Kenneth. "A New Deal for the FBI: The Roosevelt Administration, Crime Control, and National Security." *Journal of American History* 69, no. 3 (June 2002).

Polenberg, Richard. "Franklin Roosevelt and Civil Liberties: The Case of the Dies Committee." *Historian* 30 (February 1968).

Trebitsch, Michel. "L'intellectuel dans l'action: Lettres de Georges Canguilhem à Jean-Richard Bloch (1927–1946)." *Vingtième siècle revue d'histoire* 50 (April–June 1996).

BOOKS

Bach, Steven. *Leni: The Life and Work of Leni Riefenstahl*. London: Little Brown, 2007.

Baldwin, Neil. *Henry Ford and the Jews: The Mass Production of Hate*. New York: Public Affairs, 2001.

Barnes, James J., and Patience P. Barnes. *Nazis in Pre-War London, 1930–1939: The Fate and Role of German Party Members and British Sympathizers*. Brighton, England: Sussex Academic Press, 2010.

Berg, A. Scott. *Lindbergh*. New York: G. P. Putnam's Sons, 1998.

Bloch, Michael. *Operation Willi: The Plot to Kidnap the Duke of Windsor July 1940*. London: Weidenfeld and Nicolson, 1984.

———. *Ribbentrop*. London: Abacus, 2003.

———. *The Secret File of the Duke of Windsor*. London: Corgi Books, 1988.

Bouverie, Tim. *Appeasing Hitler: Chamberlain, Churchill and the Road to War*. London: Vintage, 2020.

Breitman, Richard, and Norman J. W. Goda, *U.S. Intelligence and the Nazis*. New York: Cambridge University Press, 2005.

Brown, Anthony Cave, *Bodyguard of Lies*. London: Star Books, 1977.

Bullock, Alan. *Hitler: A Study in Tyranny*. London: Book Club Associates, 1973.

Cartland, Barbara. *The Isthmus Years*. London: Hutchinson, 1943.

Chadwin, Mark Lincoln. *The Hawks of World War II*. Chapel Hill: University of North Carolina Press, 1968.

Christy, Jim. *The Price of Power: A Biography of Charles Eugène Bedaux*. Toronto: Doubleday Canada, 1984.

Churchill, Winston S. *Great Contemporaries*. Edited by James W. Muller, Paul H. Courtenay, and Erica L. Chenoweth. Wilmington, DE: ISI Books, 2019.

———. *The Second World War*. Vol. 1, *The Gathering Storm*. London: Reprint Society, 1956.

Ciano, Galeazzo. *The Ciano Diaries, 1939–1943*. New York: Doubleday, 1945.

———. *Ciano's Hidden Diary 1937–1938*. Translated by Andreas Mayor. New York: E. P. Dutton, 1953.

Conradi, Peter. *Hitler's Piano Player: The Rise and Fall of Ernst Hanfstaengl, Confidant of Hitler, Ally of FDR*. London: Gerald Duckworth, 2005.

Crowson, N. J., ed. *Fleet Street, Press Barons and Politics: The Journals of Collin Brooks, 1932–1940*. Camden Fifth Series, vol. 2. London: Royal Historical Society, 1998.

De Courcy, Anne. *Diana Mosley: Mitford Beauty, British Fascist, Hitler's Angel*. New York: HarperCollins, 2003.

———. *1939: The Last Season*. London: Phoenix, 2005.

———. *Society's Queen: The Life of Edith, Marchioness of Londonderry*. London: Phoenix, 1992.

———. *The Viceroy's Daughters: The Lives of the Curzon Sisters*. London: Phoenix, 2001.

De Jong, Louis. *The German Fifth Column in the Second World War*. London: Routledge and Kegan Paul, 1956.

Documents on German Foreign Policy, 1918–1945. Series C, vol. 5, The Third Reich: First Phase, March 5, 1936–October 31, 1936. London: HMSO, 1966.

Documents on German Foreign Policy, 1918–1945. Series C, vol. 6, The Third Reich: First Phase, November 1, 1936–November 14, 1937. London: HMSO, 1983.

Documents on German Foreign Policy, 1918—1945. Series D, vol. 4, The Aftermath of Munich, October 1938–March 1939. London: HMSO, 1951.

Dodd, Martha. *My Years in Germany*. London: Victor Gollancz, 1939.

Dodd, William E., Jr., and Martha Dodd, eds. *Ambassador Dodd's Diary, 1933–1938*. London: Victor Gollancz, 1941.

Evans, Siân. *Queen Bees: Six Brilliant and Extraordinary Society Hostesses between the Wars*. London: Two Roads, 2016.

François-Poncet, André. *Au Palais Farnèse: Souvenirs d'une ambassade à Rome, 1938–1940*. Paris: Librairie Arthème Fayard, 1961.

———. *The Fateful Years: Memoirs of a French Ambassador in Berlin, 1931–1938*. London: Victor Gollancz, 1949.

Fromm, Bella. *Blood and Banquets*. Secaucus, NJ: Carol Publishing Group, 1990.

Fry, Helen. *Inside Nuremberg Prison*. London: CreateSpace, 2011.

Gellman, Irwin F. *Secret Affairs: Franklin Roosevelt, Cordell Hull, and Sumner Welles*. Baltimore: Johns Hopkins University Press, 1995.

Gorodetsky, Gabriel, ed. *The Maisky Diaries: The Wartime Revelations of Stalin's Ambassador in London*. Translated by Tatiana Sorokina and Oliver Ready. New Haven: Yale University Press, 2016.

Griffiths, Richard. *Fellow Travellers of the Right: British Enthusiasts for Nazi Germany, 1933–1939*. London: Faber Finds, 2010.

———. *Patriotism Perverted: Captain Ramsay, The Right Club and British Anti-Semitism, 1939–1940*. London: Constable, 1998.

Hart, Bradley W. *Hitler's American Friends: The Third Reich's Supporters in the United States*. New York: Thomas Dunne Books, 2018.

Hart-Davis, Duff, ed. *King's Counsellor: The Diaries of Sir Alan 'Tommy' Lascelles*. London: Weidenfeld and Nicolson, 2020.

Hassell, Ulrich von. *The Ulrich von Hassell Diaries: The Story of the Forces Against Hitler Inside Germany*. London: Frontline Books, 2011.

Heffer, Simon, ed. *Henry 'Chips' Channon: The Diaries, 1918–38*. London: Hutchinson, 2021.

Hemming, Henry. *Maxwell Knight: MI5's Greatest Spymaster*. London: Arrow Books, 2017.

Hesse, Fritz. *Hitler and the English*. London: Allan Wingate, 1954.

Hitler, Adolf. *Mein Kampf*. Translated by Ralph Manheim. London: Pimlico, 1997.

Hobsbawm, Eric. *Age of Extremes: The Short Twentieth Century, 1914–1991*. London: Abacus, 1999.

Hohenlohe, Prince Franz. *Steph: The Fabulous Princess*. London: New English Library, 1976.

Hyde, H. Montgomery. *The Quiet Canadian: The Secret Service Story of Sir William Stephenson*. London: Hamish Hamilton, 1962.

Ickes, Harold. *The Secret Diary of Harold Ickes*. Vol. 2, *The Inside Struggle*. London: Weidenfeld and Nicolson, 1955.

———. *The Secret Diary of Harold Ickes*. Vol. 3, *The Lowering Clouds, 1939–1941*. London: Weidenfeld and Nicolson, 1955.

Johnson, Gaynor, ed. *Our Man in Berlin: The Diary of Sir Eric Phipps, 1933–1937*. London: Palgrave Macmillan, 2008.

Jones, Thomas. *A Diary with Letters, 1931–1950*. London: Oxford University Press, 1954.

Kahn, David. *Hitler's Spies: German Military Intelligence in World War II*. London: Hodder and Stoughton, 1978.

Kellogg, Michael. *The Russian Roots of Nazism: White Émigrés and the Making of National Socialism, 1917–1945*. New York: Cambridge University Press, 2005.

Kershaw, Ian. *Making Friends with Hitler: Lord Londonderry and Britain's Road to War*. London: Penguin Books, 2005.

Klemperer, Victor. *I Will Bear Witness, 1933–1941: A Diary of the Nazi Years*. New York: The Modern Library, 1999.

Kurth, Peter. *American Cassandra: The Life of Dorothy Thompson*. Boston: Little, Brown, 1990.

Lindbergh, Anne Morrow. *The Flower and the Nettle: Diaries and Letters, 1936–1939*. New York: Harcourt Brace Jovanovich, 1976.

————. *Locked Rooms and Open Doors: Diaries and Letters of Anne Morrow Lindbergh, 1933–1935*. New York: Harcourt Brace Jovanovich, 1974.

Lindbergh, Charles A. *The Wartime Journals of Charles A. Lindbergh*. New York: Harcourt Brace Jovanovich, 1970.

Lippman, Walter. *The Good Society*. London: George Allen and Unwin, 1937.

Lochner, Louis P. *The Goebbels Diaries*. London: Hamish Hamilton, 1948.

Longerich, Peter. *Goebbels: A Biography*. London: Vintage, 2016.

Lovell, Mary S. *The Riviera Set: 1920–1960—The Golden Years of Glamour and Excess*. London: Abacus, 2016.

Masterman, J. C. *The Double-Cross System: The Classic Account of World War II Spymasters*. London: Vintage Books, 2013.

Morton, Andrew. *17 Carnations: The Royals, the Nazis, and the Biggest Cover-Up in History*. New York: Grand Central Publishing, 2015.

Mosley, Nicholas. *Beyond the Pale: Sir Oswald Mosley and Family, 1933–1980*. London: Secker and Warburg, 1983.

Nicolson, Nigel, ed. *Harold Nicolson: Diaries and Letters*. Vol. 1, *1930–1939*. London: Faber Finds, 2009.

————. *Harold Nicolson: Diaries and Letters*. Vol. 2, *1939–1945*. London: Collins, 1967.

Paehler, Katrin. *The Third Reich's Intelligence Services: The Career of Walter Schellenberg*. Cambridge: Cambridge University Press, 2017.

Petropoulos, Jonathan. *Royals and the Reich: The Princes von Hessen in Nazi Germany*. New York: Oxford University Press, 2009.

Popov, Dusko. *Spy/Counterspy*. London: Weidenfeld and Nicolson, 1974.

Price, G. Ward. *I Know These Dictators*. London: George G. Harrap, 1937.

Rhodes James, Robert, ed. *Chips: The Diaries of Sir Henry Channon*. London: Weidenfeld and Nicolson, 1967.

Ribbentrop, Joachim von. *The Ribbentrop Memoirs*. London: Weidenfeld and Nicolson, 1954.

Roberts, Andrew. *"The Holy Fox": A Biography of Lord Halifax*. London: Weidenfeld and Nicolson, 1991.

Roosevelt, Elliott, ed. *The Roosevelt Letters: Being the Personal Correspondence of Franklin Delano Roosevelt*. Vol. 3, *1928–1945*. London: George G. Harrap, 1952.

Rose, Andrew. *The Prince, The Princess and the Perfect Murder: The First Great Love of Edward VIII's Life, the Sensational Consequences, and the Establishment Cover Up*. London: Hodder and Stoughton, 2013.

Schad, Martha. *Hitler's Spy Princess: The Extraordinary Life of Stephanie von Hohenlohe*. Stroud: Sutton Publishing, 2004.

Schlesinger, Arthur M., Jr. *The Age of Roosevelt: The Coming of the New Deal*. London: Heinemann, 1960.

———. *The Age of Roosevelt: The Politics of Upheaval*. London: Heinemann, 1961.

Shirer, William L. *Berlin Diary: The Journal of a Foreign Correspondent, 1934–1941*. New York: Ishi Press International, 2010.

Sherwood, Robert E. *Roosevelt and Hopkins: An Intimate History*. New York: Harper and Brothers, 1948.

Smith, Amanda, ed. *Hostage to Fortune: The Letters of Joseph P. Kennedy*. New York: Viking, 2001.

Spitzy, Reinhard. *How We Squandered the Reich*. Norwich, England: Michael Russell, 1997.

Stafford, David. *Roosevelt and Churchill: Men of Secrets*. London: Little Brown, 1999.

Stoiber, Rudolf, and Boris Celovsky. *Stephanie von Hohenlohe: Sie Liebte die Mächtigen der Welt*. Munich: F.A. Herbig Verlagsbuchhandlung, 1988.

Summers, Anthony. *The Secret Life of J. Edgar Hoover*. London: Ebury Press, 2011.

Swanberg, W. A. *Citizen Hearst*. New York: Galahad Books, 1996.

Tate, Tim. *Hitler's British Traitors: The Secret History of Spies, Saboteurs and Fifth Columnists*. London: Icon Books, 2018.

Taylor, Fred, ed. *The Goebbels Diaries, 1939–1941*. London: Hamish Hamilton, 1982.

Taylor, S. J. *The Great Outsiders: Northcliffe, Rothermere and The Daily Mail*. London: Weidenfeld and Nicolson, 1996.

Tennant, Ernest W. D. *True Account*. London: Max Parrish, 1957.

Thompson, Laura. *The Six: The Lives of the Mitford Sisters*. New York: Picador, 2015.

Tinniswood, Adrian. *The Long Weekend: Life in the English Country House Between the Wars*. London: Vintage, 2018.

Thyssen, Fritz. *I Paid Hitler*. London: Hodder and Stoughton, 1941.

Turnquest, Sir Orville. *What Manner of Man Is This? The Duke of Windsor's Years in the Bahamas*. Nassau: Grant's Town Press, 2016.

Urbach, Karina. *Go-Betweens for Hitler*. London: Oxford University Press, 2015.

Vassiltchikov, Marie. *The Berlin Diaries, 1940–1945*. London: Pimlico, 1999.

Vickers, Hugo. *Alice: Princess Andrew of Greece*. London: Hamish Hamilton, 2000.

Weinberg, Gerhard L. *The Foreign Policy of Hitler's Germany: Diplomatic Revolution in Europe, 1933–1936*. Chicago: University of Chicago Press, 1970.

———, ed. *Hitler's Second Book: The Unpublished Sequel to "Mein Kampf" by Adolf Hitler*. Translated by Krista Smith. New York: Enigma Books, 2003.

Weinstein, Allen, and Alexander Vassiliev. *The Haunted Wood: Soviet Espionage in America—The Stalin Era*. New York: Modern Library, 2000.

West, Nigel, ed. *The Guy Liddell Diaries*. Vol. 1, *1939–1942*. Abingdon: Routledge, 2005.

Wiedemann, Fritz. *Der Mann, der Feldherr werden wollte*. Wuppertal-Barmen, Germany: Blick und Bild Verlag für Politische Bildung, 1964.

Willetts, Paul. *Rendezvous at the Russian Tea Rooms: The Spy Hunter, the Fashion Designer and the Man from Moscow*. London: Constable, 2015.

Wilson, Jim. *Nazi Princess: Hitler, Lord Rothermere and Princess Stephanie von Hohenlohe*. Stroud: History Press, 2011.

Wyman, David S. *Paper Walls: America and the Refugee Crisis, 1938–1941*. Boston: University of Massachusetts Press, 1968.

Young, Kenneth. *Stanley Baldwin*. London: Weidenfeld and Nicolson, 1976.

———, ed. *The Diaries of Sir Robert Bruce Lockhart*. Vol. 1, *1915–1938*. London: Macmillan, 1973.

INDEX